SOUTHERN
PRESBYTERIAN
LEADERS
1683 – 1911

SOUTHERN PRESBYTERIAN LEADERS
1683 – 1911

Henry Alexander White

THE BANNER OF TRUTH TRUST

THE BANNER OF TRUTH TRUST
3 Murrayfield Road, Edinburgh EH12 6EL, UK
P.O. Box 621, Carlisle, Pennsylvania 17013, USA

★

Previously published by the Neale Publishing
Company, New York, 1911

★

First Banner of Truth edition 2000
ISBN 0 85151 795 1

★

Printed and bound in Great Britain by
The Bath Press

THIS VOLUME IS DEDICATED TO MY
WIFE'S FATHER, JUDGE BEVERLEY
RANDOLPH WELLFORD, JR., AND TO HER
UNCLE, CHARLES EDWARD WELLFORD,
ESQ., THE ONE A RULING ELDER AND THE
OTHER A DEACON OF THE FIRST PRESBY-
TERIAN CHURCH, RICHMOND, VIRGINIA,
WORTHY TYPES OF THAT EFFICIENCY IN
SERVICE, THAT NOBILITY OF CHARACTER
AND THAT PURITY IN THOUGHT AND PUR-
POSE THAT FROM THE BEGINNING HAVE
MARKED THE OFFICE-BEARERS IN OUR
SOUTHERN PRESBYTERIAN CHURCH.

CONTENTS

2   *Contents*

PART II

PART III

Contents 3

PART IV

SOUTHERN PRESBYTERIAN LEADERS SINCE 1861

4 *Contents*

PORTRAITS

PREFACE

This series of biographical sketches is based upon original sources as far as these are now available. Among such sources are included the minutes and other records of presbyteries, synods and assemblies, autobiographical statements and personal letters incorporated in some of the formal biographies. A number of family records in addition to those mentioned in the bibliography have been of material advantage in the writing of this volume.

Among the secondary sources, there are many excellent biographies and memoirs, named in the list given on pages 463-469. These have been of much service in the preparation of Southern Presbyterian Leaders.

I desire to make special acknowledgment of indebtedness to the *Sketches of North Carolina* and the *Sketches of Virginia* by Dr. William Henry Foote, and the *History of the Presbyterian Church in South Carolina* by Dr. George Howe.

It will be understood, of course, that the outlines of personal history contained in this volume are presented as sketches, and not as biographies in the full sense of that term. It is the hope of the writer, however, that taken together they will constitute in some measure a continuous narrative dealing with the work and the character of the Presbyterian people of our Southern Commonwealths.

HENRY ALEXANDER WHITE.

COLUMBIA, S. C.
April 15, 1911

SOUTHERN PRESBYTERIAN LEADERS

Part I.—Presbyterian Leaders of the Colonial
Period. 1683-1774.

CHAPTER I.

FRANCIS MAKEMIE ORGANIZES THE FIRST AMERICAN PRESBYTERY.

Francis Makemie was a Scot, born about the year
1658, near the town of Rathmelton, or Ramelton,
province of Ulster, north Ireland. Ramelton stands on
the western shore of a long inlet, or lake, called Lough
Swilly, whose waters are driven by the fierce winds of
the North Atlantic in a winding course among the
hills of Donegal. The records of the town tell us that
in the early years of the seventeenth century a company
of farmers and craftsmen from the lowlands of Scotland made their way across the narrow sea and built
homes in this part of Ireland. Among these settlers,
most probably, came the father and mother of Makemie.
The traveller today finds no trace left of the house in
which the child Francis was born. One may stand,
however, on the site of the old mill around which, as a
boy, tradition says, he played games with his comrades.
The old ferry-boat still moves back and forth across
the waters from which young Francis no doubt often
caught the salmon. The church was there with the
Scotch form of worship; likewise the rude schoolhouse
with naught but the earth as a floor. We may suppose
that Francis came in the early morning to this place of
study, bearing under one arm the peats for the fire,

9

and under the other a Bible, a Virgil and a Homer. When the Bible verses had been repeated, and the lines of the Latin and Greek bards had been turned into good English words, then the boy ran to the top of a swelling knoll to watch the great waves on Lough Swilly or to look eastward across its waters toward the blue, dreamy hills that stand on guard around Londonderry.

Makemie's schoolmaster was a minister who persuaded his pupil to become both student and Christian. A few years later Makemie told the presbytery about "a work of grace and conversion wrought in my heart at fifteen years of age, by and from the pains of a godly schoolmaster, who used no small diligence in gaining tender souls to God's service and fear."

Makemie's father must have been a man of substance and of wisdom for he gave the son a complete education. In his later years, the son spoke of his mother as kneeling in prayer for her child. Beyond these meagre details we know nothing about the early days of Makemie at Ramelton.

In February, 1676, this young man went across the channel to Scotland and began a course of study as a member of the third class in the University of Glasgow. Today, one may see his name written in the old record-book of the University in the Latin form as follows: "Franciscus Makemius............Scoto-Hibernus."

This means Francis Makemie, a Scot of Ireland. In our day, we write the two Latin words Scoto-Hibernus in English form thus, Scotch-Irishman. Through his father, Francis belonged in every respect to the people of Scotland, but his dwelling place was Ireland.

Three years, perhaps, were spent by the young Scot at the University of Glasgow. He must have studied Hebrew there, as well as Latin and Greek. In May, 1680, he was again in Ireland, engaged in the study of "divinity" under the control of the Presbytery of

Laggan. This body held jurisdiction over the entire region of Londonderry, Donegal and Tyrone. Less than two years before, the Presbyterians of Scotland had made their brave fight against the royalist forces at Bothwell Bridge (1679) and now the men of Ulster were ready for the struggle in Ireland. The Presbytery of Laggan was made up of the men who stood in the breach and saved their country at Enniskillen and at Londonderry, in 1689. Even while Makemie was "giving in his pieces of trial," some of the ministers of the Presbytery were lying in prison because they would not take the oath acknowledging the king's supremacy in matters of faith and worship. Among these was Thomas Drummond, Makemie's pastor at Ramelton, and John Traill, the Hebrew scholar; also Adam White and William White. Time and again the Presbytery of Laggan called before them the young graduate of Glasgow and tested his knowledge. On April 20, 1681, Makemie delivered a "homily" upon I. Tim. 1 : 5, and was approved; May 25, 1681, he delivered his "private homily" on Matt. xi. : 28; this also, was approved. Afterwards the presbytery passed upon his exegesis of Scripture passages in Hebrew and Greek and in the autumn of 1681 he was licensed to preach the gospel.

At that critical hour, when five other ministers of the Presbytery were sent to join those already in prison, letters asking help came from the island of Barbadoes in the West Indies and from Colonel William Stevens, of Maryland. The latter poured out the prayers of the Presbyterians in Maryland and Virginia for help in the preaching of the gospel. After his release from imprisonment, William Traill, moderator of the presbytery, crossed the seas, in 1682, and spent a number of years in Maryland. In 1683, the presbytery ordained Makemie; that is, by the laying on of hands and with prayer, they set him apart as an evangelist and bade him go to the aid of his brethren beyond the Atlantic. He

was thus the first minister of the Presbyterian faith who
was appointed in regular form as a preacher for the people of the American colonies.

The colony on the James River, in Virginia, was
established in 1607, by the Virginia Company of London. This company was to a great extent under the
control of English Puritans who remained within the
Established Church and were seeking to reform it from
within. Some of the colonists sent to Virginia by the
company were Puritans. Among these was the Rev.
Alexander Whitaker, the "Apostle of Virginia," son
of Dr. William Whitaker, Puritan Professor of Divinity at Cambridge, and cousin of Dr. William Gouge,
member of the Westminster Assembly of divines.
Whitaker organized a congregational presbytery in
the colony as may be seen from a letter written by him
in June, 1614: "Every Sabbath day we preach in the
forenoon, and catechize in the afternoon. Every Saturday, at night, I exercise in Sir Thomas Dale's house.
Our church affairs be consulted on by the minister and
four of the most religious men. Once every month
we have communion, and once a year a solemn fast."

In 1617 Whitaker was drowned in James River and
was succeeded by George Keith, who was also a Puritan. Afterwards, so many Puritans came that in 1638
there were as many as one thousand of them in the colony
of Virginia, about seven per cent. of the entire population. Their chief settlements were south of James River,
in the counties known as Isle of Wight and Nansemond.
Governor Berkeley insisted, however, that they must
worship in accordance with the forms of the Established
Church. In 1649, therefore, about 1,000 Puritans removed from Virginia into Maryland and made their
homes thenceforth near the mouth of the Severn River,
not far from the present city of Annapolis.

Several years before this migration of Puritans from
Virginia into Maryland, the Dutch had established con-

gregations of the Reformed type in the province now
known as New York. These Dutch Reformed churches
were in every essential respect Presbyterian. Many
of the Puritan congregations of New England were then
maintaining the Presbyterian form of church government. Some of these drifted southward to Long Island,
under the leadership of Richard Denton, and in 1644
founded a Presbyterian church at a point on that island
called Hempstead. Afterwards, however, this church,
sometimes called the oldest Presbyterian church in
America, passed under the control of its Congregational members. Another Presbyterian church founded
at Jamaica, Long Island, in 1656, lived apart to itself
as an Independent congregation until after the organization of Makemie's presbytery.

Francis Doughty, of Gloucester, England, came first
to Massachusetts and then became the first Presbyterian minister in New York City (1643-1648). He
came thence to Maryland where he preached to the
Puritans until his death. Doughty's work in Maryland was carried forward by Matthew Hill, a Presbyterian minister from York, England, but neither one
of these evangelists organized a church. Soon after
the year 1670 a large number of Scots and Scotch-
Irish came to Barbadoes, Maryland and Virginia. In
response to the appeal made by these people, his countrymen, Makemie set forth from Ireland in 1683. His
journey across the ocean was broken by a visit to Barbadoes. The Scots who dwelt there and also some of
the English settlers were Presbyterians, and to them
Makemie first delivered his message.

He then came to the eastern shore of Maryland and
was there received as minister by the people of Snow
Hill, a town located in the present county of Worcester,
Maryland. Makemie organized a church at Snow Hill
in that same year, 1683-84, or not long afterwards.
Congregations were brought together also at Salisbury,

Rehoboth and other places in Maryland. About the same time Makemie's eager spirit led him across the Virginia line. He organized churches at Pocomoke and at Onancock, in the county of Accomac, and on the Elizabeth River near the present city of Norfolk, in Virginia. These congregations in Maryland and Virginia were the mother churches of the Presbyterian body in America.

Francis Makemie was united in marriage with Naomi, eldest daughter of William Anderson, a merchant of Accomac County, Virginia. Makemie then made his home near Onancock, the county seat of Accomac, and became himself a merchant. Most probably he preached every Sunday and supported his family by selling merchandise during the week. Some of his customers did not pay for what they bought. In 1690 Makemie entered suit in the county court of Accomac to force a customer to pay for molasses that had been sold to him. Many other suits were entered in like manner by Makemie to force customers to pay their debts.

During all of these years, Makemie's chief work was the preaching of the gospel. He went on board a little vessel and tried to sail to South Carolina in order that he might preach to the people of that province. Strong winds drove the vessel back to Virginia, however, and our evangelist spent most of his years of labor in that colony. A part of his work there was the writing of a catechism for the instruction of the members of his churches.

In 1698, William Anderson died and left by will to Makemie and his wife, Naomi, one thousand acres of land near Onancock, three town lots in Onancock, nine hundred and fifty acres at Pocomoke, four negro slaves and a small boat called a sloop.

How did Makemie use the property thus acquired? The sloop, we may be sure, carried him along the seashore and up the rivers to the places where he was in the habit of preaching. On October 15, 1699, the year after William Anderson's death, Makemie presented himself in the county court of Accomac and asked the judges of the court to set apart his dwelling-house at Onancock and his house at Pocomoke as places where he might lawfully call the people together and preach the gospel to them.

This was done in accordance with the law that prevailed in Virginia at that time. In that colony and in some of the other colonies, the Episcopal Church, with its ministers, was then supported by a tax called the tithe. The colonists were required by law to attend the services of this church every Sunday. If any one refused to attend, he was punished. A special law called the Toleration Act provided, however, that those Christians, who were called dissenters, because they were not willing to worship according to the forms used in the Episcopal Church, might worship God in their own way. Under this Toleration Act, Makemie declared in the court room of the county of Accomac that he was a loyal subject of the king and queen of England and that he accepted certain specified articles of religious belief set forth by the Church of England. The clerk of the court then made an entry in his record-book, stating that Makemie's two dwelling-houses were registered as regular houses of public worship, and that Makemie himself had authority to preach there.

In the year 1704 Makemie sailed back across the Atlantic to tell his brethren in Ireland and Scotland about his work and to ask for help. He went to London, also, and told the Presbyterians of that city about the churches in Maryland and Virginia. When he returned to the colonies, two ministers came with him. One of these was John Hampton, of Ulster, a member of Makemie's own presbytery of Laggan. The other was George McNish, a Scot. The Presbyterians of London furnished money to pay the expenses of these two preachers for two years. They began at once to labor among the churches founded by Makemie in Maryland.

One day, early in the year 1706, seven Presbyterian ministers met in the city of Philadelphia. The leading man among them was Francis Makemie, who represented the churches which he had founded in Virginia. John Hampton, George McNish and Nathaniel Taylor represented the Presbyterian churches established in Maryland. Samuel Davis and John Wilson were then preaching in Delaware and Jedediah Andrews was pastor in Philadelphia. Wilson and Taylor were Scots from Scotland and Davis was a Scot from Ireland. Andrews was a native of Massachusetts. He received his education at Harvard College and began to preach at Philadelphia in 1698. The record-book, in which was written an account of the meeting of these seven men of God, has been handed down to us. The first leaf of this book, however, has been torn off and lost. We do not know, therefore, the exact day and the hour when they came together. We may believe that the Word of God was opened and read, and that prayer was made. Then the seven solemnly constituted themselves as a presbytery, the first classical presbytery organized in America. The establishment of this presbytery was almost entirely the work of Francis Makemie.

In January, 1707, Francis Makemie and John Hampton sailed northward from Virginia along the Atlantic Coast to preach the gospel in New England. When he reached New York some of the people of that town asked the governor to allow him to conduct religious worship in the Dutch Church. The governor refused to give permission, and Makemie preached, therefore, to a small congregation in a private dwelling-house. The same day Hampton preached in a church on Long Island.

Lord Cornbury, royal governor of New York, called

Makemie and Hampton before him and said, "How dare you to take it upon you to preach in my government without my license?"

Makemie replied, "We have liberty from an act of Parliament made in the first year of the reign of King William and Queen Mary [1689], which gave us liberty, with which law we have complied." Makemie then produced certificates written out by the courts in Barbadoes, Virginia and Maryland, showing that he had obeyed all the requirements of the English law.

"These certificates do not extend to New York," said Cornbury.

"I have complied with the English law," replied Makemie, "and that same law extends to all of the dominions of the English sovereign." At the same time, Makemie and Hampton told the governor that they were ready to appear before the New York judges and take out certificates there if it was considered necessary.

"You shall not spread your pernicious doctrines here," commanded the governor.

"As to our doctrines, my Lord, we have our Confession of Faith, which is known to the Christian world, and I challenge all the clergy of [New] York to show us any false or pernicious doctrines therein."

"You must give bond and security for your good behavior, and also bond and security to preach no more in my government," threatened Cornbury.

"Endeavoring always so to live as to 'keep a conscience void of offence towards God and man,' yet if your lordship requires it, we would give security for our behavior; but to give bond and security to preach no more in your exellency's government, if invited and desired by any people, we neither can nor dare do." These were Makemie's bold words in reply.

"Then you must go to jail," said the governor.

"We are neither ashamed nor afraid of what we

have done, and we have complied and are ready still to comply with the Act of Parliament which we hope will protect us at last."

For six weeks and four days Makemie and Hampton were kept in prison. Then the charge against Hampton was dropped and his comrade was allowed to go forth for a time on bail. He returned to Virginia and Cornbury supposed that the minister would not dare to go again to New York to face a trial. Makemie went, however, and on June 6, 1707, he stood up before a jury in the courtroom in New York to be tried for the crime of preaching a sermon in that town in the previous January!

Witnesses were brought in to prove the fact that he had preached. He waved these men aside with the declaration, "I own the matter of fact as to preaching. * * * I have done nothing therein of which I am ashamed or afraid." Three friends spoke for Makemie and then he stood up to plead his own case before the jury. He showed that he had full and clear knowledge of every law of England and every law adopted in any of the colonies, in so far as they were concerned with his case. The lawyers and the judges were filled with astonishment that Makemie had such intimate acquaintance with the laws and that he made so strong a plea for justice to himself and other ministers. The jury at once brought in their verdict that the preacher had not broken any law and that he should be set free. The governor and the judges were so unjust, however, that they made him pay about four hundred dollars to meet the expense of the trial.

Makemie then entered the Huguenot Church in New York and preached. His sermon was printed and scattered broadcast. Cornbury again sought to lay hands on the bold minister, but the latter escaped and wrote back to the governor that he was under solemn obligations "both to God and the souls of men to embrace

all opportunities for exercising those ministerial gifts
vouchsafed from heaven." Cornbury said of Makemie
that he was a "jack-at-all-trades, a preacher, a doctor
of physic, a mechanic, an attorney, a counsellor-at-law,
and, which is worst of all, a disturber of governments."
Cornbury himself was soon afterwards removed from his
office in New York because of his injustice and corrup-
tion.

Makemie's work on earth came to an end in 1708,
the year after the trial for the crime of preaching. He
died most probably in Accomac County, Virginia, for
his last will was placed on record there on August 4,
1708.. A long sickness marked the end of his days,
for Doctor Charles Barrett brought a charge of five
pounds against the estate for visits made in his
last illness. Moreover, William Coman presented a
charge of twelve pounds for the funeral expenses, and
for his "trouble" in looking after Makemie's house during the time of his sickness.

In his will he gave to the Presbyterian congregation
in Rehoboth, Maryland, the lot in that town "on which
the meeting-house" was built. All of his law books were
left to his friend Andrew Hamilton. His wife and two
daughters each received "forty volumes of English
books" from this library. Moreover, he charged "all
persons concerned, in the presence of Almighty and
Omniscient God, to give and allow my said children a
sober, virtuous education." "My black camlet cloak,
and my new cane, bought and fixed at Boston," according to the will, were given to Jedediah Andrews.
This same cloak was afterwards appraised at the value
of two pounds. The remaining part of Makemie's
library was also bequeathed to Andrews and, after him,
to his successors in the office of minister of the church at
Philadelphia. "My will is," wrote Makemie, "that as
soon as said books are remitted to Philadelphia, the
number and names of said library may be put upon

record, to be preserved there, as a constant library for
the use of foresaid minister or ministers successively
forever."

Within a period of less than one year after the minister's death, his wife, Naomi, was married to Mr. James
Kemp. Makemie's property was appraised and a
complete list was entered upon the record-book of the
county of Accomac. More than one thousand pounds
in Virginia currency was the value assigned to his
personal property. His store was well filled with
the merchandise needed in a rural community. His
house was amply supplied with good furniture. There
was a great herd of about seventy cows and young
cattle, with other farm animals in large numbers. More
than twenty negro slaves were left to his heirs and
creditors. Two of these were valued by the appraisers
at thirty-five pounds each; the others were assessed
at varying rates down to one crippled negro who was
"valued at nothing." There was one white servant
girl bound over to render ten months of service and
one white boy under bond to serve for seven years.

A total of "896 books in Latin, Greek, English and
Hebrew" was placed on the property list. Moreover, in
the "hall chamber" in his house were found "King William and Queen Mary's pictures." A value of one
pound, ten shillings, was assigned to these emblems of
Makemie's attachment to the Protestant sovereigns of
England.

The presbytery organized by Makemie at Philadelphia, in 1705, consisted as we have seen, of one minister from Virginia, three from Maryland, two from
Delaware and one from Pennsylvania. Soon afterwards, two groups of Congregationalist churches asked
permission to come in, with their ministers, as members
of the presbytery. One of these groups was located in
the eastern part of New Jersey and the other was on
Long Island, in the colony of New York. These Con-

gregationalist churches had been established chiefly by
Puritan-Presbyterian settlers from New England. Additional preachers came across the sea from Scotland
and Ireland, and, in 1716, the number of ministers in
the presbytery was seventeen. A division of this body
into four presbyteries was, therefore, made as follows:
Presbytery of Philadelphia, six ministers; Presbytery
of New Castle, Delaware, six ministers; Presbytery of
Snow Hill, Maryland and Virginia, three ministers;
Presbytery of Long Island, New York, two ministers.
The representatives of these presbyteries formed the
first American Presbyterian Synod at Philadelphia in
1717.

A number of Congregationalist churches in New Jersey and New York were then added to the Synod. Many
Scots came to New Jersey to strengthen the Presbyterians of that region. After 1720 a multitude of Scots
came from Ireland to make their homes in Delaware
and Pennsylvania and that section, for a brief period,
became the center of American Presbyterianism.

In 1729 the ministers who had come from Scotland
and from Ireland persuaded the Synod of Philadelphia
to accept the Adopting Act. This meant that all
preachers who were then members of the Synod and
those who should afterward become members must subscribe to the Westminster Confession and Catechisms
as "good forms of sound words and systems of Christian
doctrine," and must adopt them as the confession of
their own faith.

CHAPTER II.

IN 1683, the year in which Makemie was ordained and sent to the American colonies, a shipload of Scots sailed out of the Clyde River, in Scotland, and started westward across the Atlantic Ocean. Their leader was Lord Cardross. They had not been allowed in Scotland to worship God according to the Presbyterian mode. Charles the Second, King of England, Scotland and Ireland was at that time putting hundreds of Scots to death because they were not willing to worship in the manner that was followed by the members of the Episcopal Church. The king also sent many of the Scots to prison and he drove multitudes of them out of their country. Cardross gathered a number of Presbyterian families into a ship and sailed to South Carolina. He landed on the shore of the beautiful harbor of Port Royal and built homes there for his people. One of the members of the colony established by Cardross was William Dunlop, a Presbyterian minister.

For three years as preacher and as shepherd of the flock, Dunlop did his work well at Port Royal. More than this, he played his part boldly as a soldier. Dunlop was given the title of major of the militia organized for the protection of the settlement against Spaniards and Indians. In 1786 the Spaniards came up from Florida in warships and destroyed the homes of the Scots at Port Royal. Many of the settlers were slain and some of them returned to Scotland. Among the latter was

22

William Dunlop who became (1690) principal of the University of Glasgow. A Scotch writer, Robert Wodrow, said of this early Carolina preacher that he could never name him "without the greatest regard to his memory."

In 1685, King Louis the Fourteenth began to drive away from France those people who would not worship according to the Roman Catholic method. Before that time thousands of the French had become Protestants. They believed in the Presbyterian mode of ruling and teaching a church congregation. The King's soldiers went through the land, tearing down and burning the churches of the French Protestants, who were called Huguenots.

On April 15, 1686, some of the King's men went to the town of Pons in Southern France and began to batter down the Huguenot Church in that place. The people there were threatened with imprisonment and death if they did not leave the country. Elias Prioleau pastor of the Presbyterians at Pons, called his flock together and told them to follow him. Many of them sailed with the minister across the sea to Charles Town in South Carolina. They found a number of Huguenot families already established there. In that same year, 1686, Prioleau organized a congregation of Huguenots in Charles Town. In the following year, 1687, a church was built upon the same plot of ground upon which the present Huguenot church stands.

Soon afterwards other Huguenots came to South Carolina and congregations were organized on Goose Creek, on the eastern branch of the Cooper River, and on the Santee River. The Huguenots continued for many years to speak and write French, the language which they had used in their native land. Their ministers preached in the same tongue. They were quiet, temperate, hardworking people. Elias Prioleau continued to preach as "minister of the holy Gospel in the

French Church of Charles Town" until his death in
1699. All of the other Huguenot congregations entered, one by one, into the fold of the Episcopal Church.
Prioleau's flock, however, remained steadfast, and today
it is the only distinctive Huguenot Church in America.
The present house of worship is on the original site,
and the people of the congregation still use the old
French Presbyterian form of worship as in the days
when the French King's soldiers battered down Protestant sanctuaries.

On the night of December 14, 1695, two small vessels
sailed southward from the harbor of Boston, Massachusetts. They had on board an entire Puritan congregation from the town of Dorchester, Massachusetts.
The leader of the congregation was Joseph Lord who
had just been ordained to the gospel ministry. They
made their way through fierce storms to the harbor of
Charles Town, South Carolina. They then sailed up
the Ashley River and founded a town which they named
Dorchester. It stood near the present town of Summer-
ville, South Carolina. On February 2, 1696, Joseph
Lord called all of his people together at Dorchester and
made them sit down under the spreading branches of a
great oak tree. After preaching the Word he gave them
bread and wine in the solemn observance of the Lord's
Supper. As a Congregationalist minister Joseph Lord
served this people until 1720, when he returned to Massachusetts. Nearly all of the members of the Dorchester
congregation afterwards went to Liberty County, Georgia, and established there the famous church known as
Midway.

One day in July, 1698, a company of 1,200 Scots
sailed out of the port of Leith, Scotland. They expected to establish a colony on the isthmus of Darien,
or Panama, near the place where the Panama Canal
is now located. About one year later another company
of about 1,500 Scots followed them to the same region.

Presbyterian ministers went along as members of the colony. These ministers organized at Panama the separate Presbytery of Caledonia.

Lack of food drove the settlers away from Panama and the colony was never established. One of these ships, on the return journey to Scotland, in the year 1700, cast anchor outside of the harbor of Charles Town. Archibald Stobo, a Presbyterian preacher, with some of his friends, went ashore. While he was in the city a great wind came rushing along the coast and destroyed the vessel in which Stobo had sailed to Charles Town.

About ten years before that time, that is, about 1690, the dissenters of Charles Town had organized a congregation which was at first called the Presbyterian Church. Their house of worship was known as "the White Meeting House" on account of its color; now it is called "the Circular Church" by reason of its shape. The Congregationalists worshipped there with the Presbyterians. Nearly all of the early ministers, however, were Congregationalists. From 1700 until 1707, Archibald Stobo was the pastor of this church. We are told that he was in the habit of preaching long sermons. Sometimes he boldly reproved his people on account of their failings. About 1710, or soon afterwards, Stobo organized the church at Wilton Bluff and led his people in building a house of worship there among the oak trees on the eastern bank of the Edisto about four miles from the present sanctuary. About the same time churches were organized at Cainhoy, on the Wando River, and on James Island, Edisto Island and John's Island. Bethel Church (Walterboro) was organized by Stobo in 1728. The bell that summoned the people to worship in this house of God is still in the possession of the congregation. About the year 1723 a Presbytery was organized on James Island, known as the old Presbytery of South Carolina.

Stobo and John Witherspoon and most of the other
ministers in this presbytery were from Scotland. The
Presbytery remained in close connection, therefore,
with the Church of Scotland, and was never associated
with any other church body in America. About the
time of the Revolution it was dissolved.

Among these churches on the coast of South Carolina,
Stobo labored until his death in 1741. Just ten years
before that date, that is, in 1731, the Presbyterians
withdrew themselves from the White Meeting House
and organized the First Church of Charles Town. As
most of these Presbyterians had come from Scotland
their house of worship is known to this day as the
Scotch Church of Charleston. Their first minister was
Hugh Stewart, a Scot. Their first house of worship
was built of wood and stood near the spot where the
present Scotch Church is located.

I shall now tell you, in a word, about another company
of early Protestant exiles from France. In 1688 a number of Huguenots sailed from Holland with the army
of William of Orange and aided him in obtaining the
crown as King of England. William the Third gave
to these Huguenot soldiers some land in Virginia. In
1699 a body of three hundred Huguenots, men, women
and children, came to Virginia and built houses at Man-
akin Town on the James River, about twenty miles
above Richmond. Two hundred more came the following year. Others followed still later until about eight
hundred of these worthy people were established on the
James River and in the Piedmont region of Virginia.
Among them were the Dupuys, Flournoys, Fontaines,
Lacys, Mortons, Sampsons, Venables, Watkinses and
other well-known Presbyterian families.

The minister who came with the Huguenots to
Virginia was Claude Philippe de Richebourg. He
was given special permission by the Virginia lawmakers to conduct religious worship according to the

Presbyterian mode. He preached to his people in their own French form of speech. About 1710, Richebourg and most of the French settlers left Virginia and moved further southward to the Trent River in North Carolina. Then, in 1712, Richebourg went farther still and made his home among the Huguenots who lived on the Santee River in South Carolina. When their pastor, Pierre Robert, became weak through age, Richebourg took up the work of chief shepherd among the Santee flock. His manner was quiet and his life was marked by deep, earnest piety. About the year 1719, Richebourg entered into the peace which God giveth to His beloved.

CHAPTER III.

I MUST now tell you of the coming of a great multitude of God-fearing people across the Atlantic to the American colonies. They were Scots, but the land from which most of them set forth upon the ocean voyage was Ulster, North Ireland.

And how did it happen that Scots took ship from Ireland to sail to America? The answer is, that for a hundred years and more, Ireland was the dwelling-place of many of these Scots. James the First, King of England, gave lands in Ulster to a large number of settlers from the lowlands of Scotland. In 1610 they began to cross the narrow water-strait from Scotland to Ireland and to build homes in Ulster. Some English settlers came, also, to dwell among the Scots. The Scots and English of Ulster were honest people; they worshipped God and worked hard to make the soil of Ulster bear corn and fruits and flowers. They refused to worship in the way in which the members of the Episcopal Church conducted religious services. The people of Ulster became Presbyterians and built churches and schoolhouses in all of their towns and villages.

When Charles the Second came to the English throne, in 1660, he said that he would force the Presbyterians of Scotland to become Episcopalians. The King sent cruel soldiers under Claverhouse, Carstairs, Sharp, Dalzell and Drummond, to drive the Presbyterians out of their churches and their homes. The brave Scots met together

28

on the wild moorlands and in the valleys and there under the shadow of trees and great rocks they offered worship to God in the simple form taught them by their Presbyterian fathers. The soldiers of King Charles the Second spurred their horses among these quiet worshippers and cut them down with the sword or shot them as they fled across the hills. This "killing time," as it was called, went on for years, but the Scots did not give up their religion. They vowed again and again that they would keep the "Solemn League and Covenant" which their fathers and grandfathers swore that they would keep as the basis of their Presbyterian faith. As a memorial of this vow, the Scots unfurled a blue flag on which was a white cross with the words written in golden letters, "For Christ's Crown and Covenant."

Many of the "Covenanters," as they called themselves, remained at home in Scotland to meet the cruel soldiers and to die. A great multitude of them, however, fled to Ireland, and there for a time found refuge among their kinsmen and friends in Ulster. In 1689, when the Roman Catholics of Ireland tried to take possession of the entire island in the name of King James the Second, the Presbyterians of Ulster assembled in the town of Londonderry and from behind its walls defied the King. The supply of food failed but the men of 'Derry fought on with nothing to eat, sometimes, except leather and old shoes. The defenders of the town grew weak and sick from hunger and some of them died but they never gave up. Aid came at last from William of Orange, who had been made King of England. The Presbyterians thus saved Ireland from Roman Catholic rule.

After the death of William of Orange, known as King William the Third, the rulers of England took away from the Presbyterians of Ireland many of their liberties. English laws were passed to keep Presbyte-

rian ministers from joining men and women together in
marriage, to prevent Presbyterian schoolmasters from
teaching in schools and to take away the profit made by
the people of Ulster in the raising of wool. The Scots
of Ulster, therefore, sought new homes in America.
After the year 1714, their ships began to cross the sea
from Ulster in a long unbroken line. For more than sixty
years they continued to come. It was the most extensive
movement ever made from Europe to America before
the modern days of steamships. Often as many as
12,000 came in a single year. In one week, in 1727, six
ship-loads were landed at Philadelphia. In the two
years, 1773 and 1774, more than 30,000 came. A body
of about 600,000 Scots was thus brought from Ulster
and from Scotland to the American colonies, making
about one-fourth of our population at the time of the
Revolution.

A few of these people of Ulster, led by Thomas Craig-
head, came to Boston, Massachusetts. Craighead was
entered on the records of the University of Glasgow as
Scoto-Hibernus, a Scot from Ireland. In 1718 some
Ulstermen planted the town of Londonderry, New
Hampshire; others established Worcester, Massachu-
setts, and still others went to Casco Bay in the present
State of Maine.

The great body of settlers from Ulster, however,
sailed up the Delaware River and went ashore at Chester and at Philadelphia. They sought homes at first
in western Pennsylvania. They found their way into
the Cumberland Valley of Pennsylvania and Maryland.
Afterwards, many of them turned their faces southward.
Across the Potomac they came in a great stream into
Virginia. They passed along both sides of the Blue
Ridge, and built homes on the banks of the beautiful
streams and under the shadows of the lofty mountains.
Some of them made their way into Tennessee and Kentucky. Others kept on their journey southward and

found homes in North Carolina, South Carolina and Georgia.

From the Highlands of Scotland a great number of Presbyterians came to the Cape Fear region of North Carolina and to the upper Pee Dee country of South Carolina. Just before the Revolution another stream of Scots, chiefly from Ireland, began to enter Charles Town harbor, South Carolina. They pressed into the highland regions of that fair country and settled there. Afterwards they filled up the great Mississippi Valley and moved thence westward; many of them went into Florida and Alabama and built their homes near the waters of the Gulf of Mexico.

Thus came the Presbyterians from Ireland and, also, directly from Scotland to the western borders of the American colonies. They knew how to use the axe and the rifle. They carried with them the Bible, the Westminster Confession of Faith and the Catechisms. Just before the American Revolution, houses and churches and schoolhouses were built in what was then the western part of our country among the mountains of Virginia and among the hills near the mountains in the Carolinas and Georgia.

CHAPTER IV.

WE must return, now, to the northern borders of Virginia and watch the advance of the Presbyterian Scots southward from Pennsylvania across the Potomac River. As early as 1719, a group of families living at a place called Potomac, in Virginia, was eager to find a minister who would furnish them the gospel. The next year, 1720, Daniel McGill organized a Presbyterian congregation at Potomac, probably the same place which now bears the name of Shepherdstown, on the upper Potomac River, in West Virginia. Some Germans, of the German Reformed Church, were members with the Scots of this congregation at Shepherdstown which was the first church organized in the western part of Virginia.

In the summer of 1732, John Lewis, a Scot from Donegal County, province of Ulster, made his way up the beautiful Shenandoah Valley, usually called the Valley of Virginia. His sons were with him, and friends followed in the paths which they made through the forests. Lewis built a house in the valley near the present town of Staunton. Two years later (1734) the stream of settlers flowed through a gap in the Blue Ridge into the present Albemarle County.

About the year 1735, William Hoge, a Scot, came with his family to the lower valley and established a home on Opecquon Creek near the present Kernstown. From this immigrant sprang that long line of worthy men whose lives have given strength to the Presbyterian

Church. William Hoge gave land near his dwelling-house as the site for a place of worship. There in the same year (1735), Samuel Gelston preached to the people of the settlement. A church called the. Opecquon Church was organized about 1738, and during the following summer, John Craig was their minister. Then, in 1740, Craig moved farther up the valley and entered upon a long term of service as shepherd of the flock that had followed John Lewis into the tract of land known as Beverley's Manor, in Augusta County, around and near the present Staunton in the Valley of Virginia.

John Craig was a native of Antrim, North Ireland, and received his education at the University of Edinburgh. The people of his congregation dwelt near the streams known as the Triple Forks of the Shenandoah River, within a region that was about thirty miles in length by twenty miles in breadth. Four other Presbyterian ministers had made brief visits to that Augusta region before Craig came. The latter made his home among the people and remained there as the first permanent pastor in the western part of Virginia.

Every Sunday morning John Craig walked five miles to the place of worship. In one hand he carried a Bible. In the other hand or upon his shoulder he usually carried a rifle, to be used against Indians if they should make an attack. All the men of his congregation likewise brought rifles. A powder horn was hung from each man's shoulder by a long strap. At ten o'clock in the morning the people were seated in their accustomed places upon rude benches made of logs and the service began. The minister continued to preach his sermon until noonday. Then for an hour the men, women and children of the congregation sat down in family groups beneath the shade of the great trees and ate their simple midday meal. At one o'clock, the minister resumed the same sermon and continued until after sunset. It was sometimes so late when the sermon was brought to a close that the leader of the congregational singing could scarcely see how to read the last psalm. One of John Craig's sermons has been handed down in the written form. We may understand how it occupied the attention of the congregation for an entire day, when we learn that it is arranged under fifty-five heads, or divisions.

Two houses of worship were established within the limits of John Craig's congregation. Men, women and children labored together with their own hands to put up these buildings. One was built of stone and was completed in 1748. It is said that the women brought on horseback to the church the sand that was used in cementing the stones together. This stone church, known as the Augusta Church, which still stands upon a ridge in the midst of a grove of oak trees, was made into a fortress in 1755 and used as a place of refuge from the assaults of the Indians. The other church building was made of logs and was built about 1745. Some members of the congregation wished to erect it near a small fountain of water called the Tinkling Spring. Other members, led by the pastor, advocated another location. Those in favor of building the house of worship near the spring had their way, but John Craig was not always like a lamb in his disposition, for he cried out: "Well, I am resolved that none of that water shall ever tinkle down my throat." He kept his word. And yet, although the look of severity sometimes came over the face of this minister, his heart was always full of tenderness. Multitudes were brought into the kingdom of God through his labors.

The Ten Commandments were made a part of the law of the land by the people of John Craig's congregation. The records of the law courts, held at Staunton for Augusta County, show us that at that time men were punished in a public manner for swearing profane oaths, for becoming drunken, for speaking lies and for breaking the Sabbath day by making long journeys and by singing profane songs.

When General Braddock's army was defeated by the French and Indians, in western Pennsylvania, in 1755, there was great fear that the red men would advance into the Valley of Virginia. Some of the settlers there said that all of the white people ought to flee away from the Valley and seek safety elsewhere. "I opposed that scheme," wrote Mr. Craig in a small record book which he kept; "I opposed that scheme as a scandal to our nation, falling below our brave ancestors, making ourselves a reproach among Virginians, a dishonor to our friends at home, an evidence of cowardice, want of faith and noble Christian dependence on God as able to save and deliver from the heathen; and, withal, a lasting blot forever on all our posterity." He urged his people to build forts. The chief fortress used was their stone church building. "My own flock," said the brave minister, "required me to go before them in the work, which I did cheerfully, though it cost me one-third of my estate; but the people followed, and my congregation, in less than two months, was well fortified."

This patriotic man of God lived until the year 1774. Then, just as the war of the Revolution was about to begin, he passed away.

CHAPTER V.

THE terms Old Side and New Side Presbyterians were used in connection with a movement known as the Great Awakening. This movement was a religious revival that swept through the country during the period 1730-'40. It began with the earnest, spiritual preaching of Jacob Frelinghuysen, a minister of the Dutch Reformed Church in New Jersey. His sermons touched the heart of Gilbert Tennent, Presbyterian minister at New Brunswick, son of William Tennent who founded the "Log College" at Neshaminy, Pennsylvania. In the year 1728 Gilbert Tennent's gospel message began to show that he was "a son of thunder, whose preaching must either convert or enrage hypocrites." In 1734 Jonathan Edwards, of Northampton, Massachusetts, added strength to the religious awakening already started by the preaching of Tennent. In 1739, George Whitefield, the Methodist missionary, came from England to extend the great spiritual movement throughout the colonies from Massachusetts to Georgia. Many of the ministers of the Synod of Philadelphia, however, were opposed to religious revivals. They claimed that these revivals were attended with too much excitement and disorder. Those who favored revivals claimed that the latter were signs of the power and grace of God among men. They declared that Whitefield was the model preacher of the word of God. Two parties in the church were formed at once. The Old Side party opposed the practice of holding religious revivals. The New Side party favored such a practice. The strife between the two parties led to a division of the Synod in 1741.

The division among the churches in 1741 led to the formation of a New Side Synod. All of those Presbyterian ministers who had taken part as *revivalists* in the heated discussions of that period organized the Presbytery of New York (1745). It was composed of three Presbyteries: (1) New York Presbytery, (2) New Brunswick Presbytery, (3) New Castle Presbytery, with twenty-two ministers in all. The Synod of Philadelphia, as the Old Side Synod, retained the other twenty-four ministers. During the period when the Old Side and the New Side were thus parted asunder, the New Side Synod (New York) organized the Hanover Presbytery in Virginia (1755).

In 1758 the two synods drew together again and became one under the title of the Synod of New York and Philadelphia. The American Presbyterian churches remained under this form of organization until the establishment of the Presbyterian General Assembly in the year 1789.

CHAPTER VI.

JOHN BLAIR AND JOHN BROWN IN THE SOUTHERN PART
OF THE VALLEY OF VIRGINIA.

In the fall of the year 1737 a Scot, who was well
advanced in years, passed across the Blue Ridge at
Wood's Gap and entered the Valley of Virginia. His
name was Ephraim McDowell, and from him sprang
the well-known McDowell clan of Virginia and Kentucky. With Ephraim came his wife, two sons and
a daughter and the daughter's husband. The little
company of settlers met Benjamin Burden and were
persuaded by him to build cabins on Timber Ridge in
the present Rockbridge County, near the headwaters of
the North Fork of the James River. A tract of 100,-
000 acres in that region had been granted to Burden
by the governor of Virginia. The building of the
McDowell cabins on Burden's grant was the beginning
of the settlement of all that part of the Valley of Virginia that looks towards the southwest, now embracing
the counties of Rockbridge, Botetourt, Roanoke, Montgomery, Wythe and Washington.

The advance of the Scots from Ulster into this region
of rolling hills was so rapid that, nine years afterwards,
three separate church congregations were formed among
the people. John Blair, a Scot from Ireland, was then
dwelling in Pennsylvania. He was in connection with
the New Side Synod of New York. In 1746 he came to
Rockbridge County and organized the congregations of Timber Ridge, New Providence and New Monmouth. Archibald Alexander, grandfather of Dr. Archibald Alexander, of Princeton, was a member of the

first session organized in the Timber Ridge congregation. In the same year, Blair organized the North Mountain congregation in Augusta County. From the latter sprang the two churches of Hebron and Bethel, near Staunton. Blair was afterwards for a time a teacher in Princeton College. His son, John D. Blair, was the first Presbyterian minister in the city of Richmond, Virginia.

In 1753, John Brown, a graduate of Princeton, began his work as pastor over the flocks at Timber Ridge and New Providence. This John Brown was a Scot from North Ireland. He became the head of a family that afterwards bore his name with honor in Kentucky and Louisiana. In 1756 the people of the Timber Ridge congregation, men and women working together, completed the stone house of God, which is standing unto this day upon the hill-top, with the great oak tree beside it. We are told that the women of the congregation carried on horseback a distance of six miles the sand used in making the stone walls. About the same time the New Providence congregation, in like manner, erected a stone church in the place of the two log meeting-houses which had previously served as places of worship. Soon after the year 1760, John Brown withdrew from the pastorate of the Timber Ridge Church and gave himself entirely to the work at New Providence. In addition to the care of the church at that place he also took upon himself the task of superintending a church school, the first of its kind established by the Presbyterians of Virginia.

In 1749, Robert Alexander, a Scot, and also a graduate of Dublin University, Ireland, organized a classical school within the bounds of the present Bethel Church. A few years later, this same school passed under the control of the minister, John Brown. By him it was conducted for the special purpose of training some of the young men of his congregatior as ministers of

the gospel. We learn this fact from a letter written by
Samuel Houston, who was born about 1758 within the
limits of John Brown's congregation. Houston says that
just before the Revolution, "Some men whose sons were
growing up felt a desire for having them, or part of
them, educated liberally, chiefly with a view to the ministry of the gospel. Accordingly, a small grammar
school was formed in the neighborhood of Old Providence, composed of Samuel Doak, John Montgomery,
Archibald Alexander, James Houston, William Tate,
Samuel Greenlee, William Wilson and others, which
greatly increased and drew youths from distant neigh-
borhoods. This grammar school was moved to the place
near Fairfield, called Mount Pleasant (near New Providence Church) ; it was, in 1776, established at Timber
Ridge meeting house and named Liberty Hall."

Five of the seven students here named—Doak, Montgomery, Alexander, Houston and Wilson—became ministers ; Archibald Alexander, however, did not attend
the school until after the Revolution.

When the school was removed to a place near Brown's
dwelling-house at Fairfield, within the limits of the New
Providence congregation, Brown was assisted in teaching by Ebenezer Smith, brother of Samuel Stanhope
Smith, first president of Hampden Sidney College. Ebenezer afterwards became a Presbyterian minister. In
1776, John Brown's School was established under the
shadow of the Timber Ridge Church and named Liberty
Hall Academy, most probably in honor of Liberty Hall,
the place of Brown's birth and childhood in North Ireland. When John Brown laid down his work because of
his advancing years, he sought a place of rest among his
children in Kentucky. In that fair land he spent the
remainder of his days.

CHAPTER VII.

WILLIAM ROBINSON AND JOHN ROAN IN THE PIEDMONT
SECTION OF VIRGINIA.

THE line of travel followed by some of the Ulster
Scots when they moved southward from Pennsylvania
across the Potomac, led them along the eastern base of
the Blue Ridge into the Piedmont section of Virginia.
About the year 1738 Presbyterian congregations were
organized at Cub Creek in Charlotte County and on Buffalo Creek in Prince Edward County. One of the members of one of these congregations in Charlotte was John
Caldwell, a ruling elder from Chestnut Level, Pennsylvania, and great-grandfather of John Caldwell Calhoun,
of South Carolina.

When the Ulstermen entered Virginia they found that
the laws of that colony required all persons to worship
after the Episcopal method. In the year 1738, John
Caldwell sent a petition to the Synod of Philadelphia
asking that body to secure from Governor Gooch, of
Virginia, the permission to worship God in the Presbyterian way. The Synod sent Caldwell's petition to Governor Gooch, who was himself a native of Scotland.
The Synod, therefore, informed him that the new colonists who were seeking homes in Virginia were of the
same religious faith as the Church of Scotland. Gooch
wished to see the Ulstermen established along the western boundary of the colony as a wall of defence against
the Indians. He, therefore, replied that these Scots
from Ulster might worship in their own way, if they
would have the name and location of each of their religious meeting-houses entered in the register of the
county court. Under this authority the Caldwells

came from Pennsylvania and established the Caldwell
Settlement in two divisions, in Charlotte and Prince
Edward counties, Virginia. Three members of the
Caldwell family were ruling elders in the church built
at Cub Creek.

About the year 1740, when Gooch was still governor
of the colony of Virginia, a number of persons began
to withdraw themselves from the Virginia Episcopal
Church. They dwelt in the county of Hanover, near
Richmond. This withdrawal from the Episcopal fold
was caused by the reading of a volume of the sermons
of George Whitefield, the Methodist missionary, and of
the Westminster Confession of Faith. A small group
of persons built a house on the lands of Samuel Morris,
in Hanover, and there met together for reading and for
prayer. A request which they sent brought a Presbyterian minister to Hanover in the year 1743.

William Robinson, a native of England, was ordained,
in 1741, in New Jersey, as a minister of the Presbyterian
Church. He made a journey through Virginia into
North Carolina and preached the gospel in both colonies. On Sunday, July 6, 1743, and on the three days
ensuing, Robinson preached in Samuel Morris' Reading-
House in Hanover. "Such of us as had been hungering
for the word before," says Mr. Morris, "were lost in
agreeable surprise and astonishment, and some could not
refrain from publicly declaring their transports. We
were overwhelmed with the thoughts of all the unexpected
goodness of God in allowing us to hear the gospel preached in a manner that surpassed our hopes. Many that
came through curiosity were pricked to their heart;
and but few of the numerous assembly on these four
days remained unaffected. They returned alarmed
with apprehensions of their former entire ignorance of
religion and anxiously inquiring what they should do to
be saved." A church was organized by Robinson among
these eager inquirers. Many gave him money which he

refused to keep for himself. It was used in educating a minister for the Church of Hanover, and that minister was Samuel Davies, the founder of the Hanover Presbytery. Davies said of Robinson, who died in 1746: "He did much in a little time; and who would not choose such an expeditious pilgrimage through this world?"

William Robinson's work in Hanover was continued by John Roan, the principal of an academy near Philadelphia. He came to Virginia in 1744. His spirit seemed to be touched with the fire of the apostles. His words seemed to melt the hearts of sinners. Converts were multiplied. Opposition was stirred up against Roan, however, and the charge was made to Governor Gooch that Roan was turning the world upside down. In spite of this charge one community after another invited this fiery preacher to declare to them the gospel. In 1745 the governor and council of Virginia gave their attention to this matter and John Roan, the preacher, with a number of citizens, was placed under an indictment for showing opposition to the Episcopal Church of the colony. When the case was brought to trial, the charge against Roan was not sustained by the evidence and he was dismissed as without blame.

CHAPTER VIII.

SAMUEL DAVIES FOUNDS THE HANOVER PRESBYTERY.

Samuel Davies was born in Delaware in the year 1723.
His parents were of Welsh descent. From his mother
he inherited a strong mind. With reference to his
mother, Davies afterwards said: "I am a son of prayer,
like my namesake, Samuel the prophet, and my mother
called me Samuel, because, she said, 'I have asked him
of the Lord.' This early dedication to God has always
been a strong inducement to me to devote myself to Him
as a personal act, and the most important blessings of
my life I have looked upon as immediate answers to the
prayers of a pious mother."

Until he reached the age of ten years Davies remained
at home under the instruction of his mother. She taught
him at the same time how to read and to write and to
pray. At fifteen he publicly announced his faith in
Christ and entered the church. A classical and theological course at Samuel Blair's log-college, Fagg's
Manor, Pennsylvania, completed the training of this
modern prophet and he was ordained as evangelist by
New Castle Presbytery, in February, 1747.

On April 14, 1747, a tall, slender young man, pale
and wasted from sickness, dignified and courteous in
manner, stood before Governor Gooch and his council
at Williamsburg, Virginia. The young man was Samuel
Davies, who asked the governor to allow him to preach
at four meeting-houses in Hanover County. This right
was granted by the governor and council and for several
months Davies gave the word to the people of that
section. Then the wife of Davies was suddenly taken
from the earth and serious illness, also, came upon him.

44

In spite of grief and sickness he continued to preach. Dr. Gibbons, a friend of Davies, says of him at this time:

"Finding himself upon the border of the grave and without any hopes of a recovery, he determined to spend the little remains of an almost exhausted life, as he apprehended it, in endeavoring to advance his Master's glory in the good of souls; and, as he told me, he preached in the day and had his hectic [fever] by night, and to such a degree as to be sometimes delirious and to stand in need of persons to sit up with him."

In the spring of 1748 the strength of his disease abated. Then a messenger came to him from Hanover County bearing a petition signed by about one hundred and fifty heads of families. They urged him to become their pastor. His heart was greatly moved. "I put my life in my hand," he said, "and determined to accept their call, hoping I might live to prepare the way for some more useful successor and willing to expire under the fatigue of duty rather than in voluntary negligence."

Davies took with him to Hanover another minister, his friend John Rodgers. The council, however, said that the dissenters of Hanover and the adjacent counties should have only one preacher. They refused to issue a license to Rodgers and he returned, therefore, to Pennsylvania.

Davies established himself at a point in Hanover County about twelve miles from Richmond. God's favor was bestowed in large measure upon his preaching there. During the first months of his pastorate, that is in the summer of 1748, the people began to make long journeys to hear his teachings. Some of them rode through the forests twenty miles, some forty and some even sixty miles, to attend upon his ministry. The second wife of Davies was Jane Holt, of Hanover, who aided him with counsel and sympathy in all the toilsome work of his ministry.

In the autumn of 1748 Davies presented himself again before the governor and council in Williamsburg. He asked permission to preach at three additional meeting-houses. The attorney-general of the colony of Virginia, Peyton Randolph, spoke against the granting of this request. He asserted that a dissenting minister ought to have but a small number of places for preaching; that the four meeting houses, already granted to Davies, were enough for him.

Davies stood up before the council and spoke for himself and for his people. He said that he had not persuaded the people of Hanover to leave the Episcopal Church. They had gone out, as everybody knew, of their own free will. They wished preachers of their own choosing. According to the Act of Toleration, which had been adopted as a Virginia law, they had a right as citizens to secure license for as many preaching places as would suit their own convenience.

Davies showed such clear knowledge of the law and he spoke with so much reason and justice that a smile went around among the members of the council. "Mr. Attorney-General has met his match today," they said one to another. The request of Davies was granted and seven places of preaching were assigned to him November 1, 1748. Three of these were in Hanover County, one in Henrico, one in Goochland, one in Louisa and one in Caroline. The charge was made that Davies was thrusting himself among the people who were already members of the established Episcopal Church. Davies replied to this charge by writing a long letter to the Bishop of London in which he declared that he had come into the territory occupied by the Episcopal Church only because of the urgent invitation given him by those who had become dissenters and who refused to attend Episcopal services. He told the bishop that the cause of this dissent within the Episcopal fold was the unworthy character of some of the Episcopal ministers who had been sent to Virginia from England. These men, he said, entertained their hearers "with languid harangues on morality" and left out almost entirely "the glorious doctrines of the gospel." Davies wrote to the bishop as he had declared to the governor's council that, under the Toleration Act, the dissenters ought to be permitted to worship in their own way wherever it pleased them to assemble.

For eleven years Davies preached in the Hanover country, making journeys meanwhile to other parts of the colony, and thus he helped to lay the foundations of the Synod of Virginia.

"He seems as an ambassador of some mighty king," said one who was watching Davies. The latter went about his work, however, in a quiet and humble manner. Each year he rode upon a long preaching tour. He usually took with him some young man who rode on before as a pioneer to find a place of lodging. As Davies belonged to the New Side party, he was called a "New Light" preacher. For that reason some of the people would not receive him into their houses. During one of these journeys, his companion was young John Morton. When they came to the home of one of John's relatives, known as Little Joe Morton, the latter was at work in a field. A messenger went out to the field to ask if the man of God might lodge in his house. He gave consent and Davies entered the home. "And with him," we are told, "Christ and salvation came to that house." The two heads of the family heard Mr. Davies and became Christians. A church was organized there and Little Joe Morton became the first elder. When they were without a pastor, he called the people together every Sunday and read them a sermon and then questioned the children from the Shorter Catechism. All of Morton's children became members of that church and many of his descendants became ministers of the gospel. The name of the church thus founded by

Davies was the *Briery Congregation* in what is now Prince Edward County.

In June, 1755, Robert Henry was established as pastor of the Briery Church and of Cub Creek Church in the present Charlotte County. Henry was a man of deep piety and had a great fund of humor. A friend said of him that "he required grace enough for two common men to keep him in order, and he had it." When Henry began his ministry he thought that he ought to write his sermons and read them from the pulpit. One Sunday morning, therefore, he began to read from a written paper laid on the open Bible. A puff of wind came and blew the paper away. Henry watched it as it sailed and fell at the feet of an old elder. The latter put his foot upon the paper. Henry waited for him to bring it back, but the old man looked up as if nothing had happened, and the minister finished his sermon as well as he was able to do so without notes. He never afterwards took a manuscript into the pulpit. We are told that he often spoke in a very loud tone of voice. He preached, however, with great spiritual power and his churches increased rapidly in strength. Davies rode many a time through the forest to speak to Henry's congregations at Cub Creek and Briery.

From November, 1753, until February, 1755, Davies was absent from his field in Virginia. As the most gifted preacher in the American Presbyterian Church at that time, he was asked to visit the towns of England to ask for money to support Princeton College in New Jersey. In company with Gilbert Tennent, another minister, he made the journey and collected a large sum of money for the college.

In making this journey across the ocean, Davies was moved also with the desire to seek relief in London for the Presbyterians of Virginia. During his sojourn in England he wrote the following words in his journal: "I find, by conversation with Dr. Stennet, there is a prospect of obtaining licenses in the Bishop of London's Court for meeting houses in Virginia."

The renown of Davies as a preacher drew together large congregations in England and Scotland to hear him. According to tradition, the King of England, George the Second, attended one of his public services and expressed in loud tones to those near his royal person his satisfaction at hearing and seeing the dissenting minister. Dr. Davies interpreted this conduct as irreverence in the Lord's house. He, therefore, paused and looking at the King, said: "When the lion roars the beasts of the forest all tremble; when King Jesus speaks, the princes of the earth should keep silence." The King kept quiet, it is said, his respect and admiration for the minister being largely increased by the boldness of Davies. Friends in England gave Davies a gold ring and a gold-headed cane. We are told that he carried these with him during his later journeys among the hills and mountains of Virginia.

When Davies came again to Virginia, the red cloud of war was hanging over the western frontier. Colonel George Washington as the leader of the Virginia riflemen was defending the settlers against the attacks made by the French and the Indians. Early in July, 1755, an English army, led by General Braddock, sent to help the colonists, was defeated near the present city of Pittsburg. The western borders of Virginia were thus left open to the attacks of the red men. Some of the settlers left their homes in the mountains and sought safety in other places. In this time of great fear, Davies called upon his people to stand their ground. In his church in Hanover on the 25th of July, 1755, he spoke as follows:—

"Let me earnestly recommend to you to furnish yourselves with arms and put yourselves into a position of defence. What is that religion good for that leaves men cowards on the appearance of danger? And permit me to say that I am particularly solicitous that you, my brethren of the dissenters, should act with honor and spirit in this juncture, as it becomes loyal subjects, lovers of your country, and courageous Christians. * * * * * * * * If I consulted either my safety or my temporal interests, I should soon remove my family to Great Britain or the northern colonies, where I have received very inviting offers. * * * * * * and yet I must declare that after the most calm and impartial deliberation, I am determined not to leave my country while there is any prospect of defending it. Certainly he does not deserve a place in any country who is ready to run from it upon every appearance of danger. The event of the war is yet uncertain; but let us determine that if the cause should require it, we will courageously leave house and home and take the field."

A voluntary company of riflemen was at once raised in Hanover by Captain Overton. To this company, on the 17th of August, Davies preached a stirring sermon from the text, "Be of good courage and let us play the men for our people." On that occasion Davies said: "I may point out to the public that heroic youth, Colonel Washington, whom I cannot but hope Providence has hitherto preserved in so signal a manner for some important service."

About three years later (May 8, 1758), a general muster of the men of Hanover was held for the purpose of raising a company for Captain Meredith. The French and Indian war was still raging and soldiers were needed in the field. Davies preached another great war sermon.

"May I not reasonably insist upon it," he said, "that the company be made up this very day before we leave this place. Methinks your king, your country, nay your own interest command me: and, therefore, I insist upon it. Oh! for the all pervading force of Demosthenes'

oratory—but I recall my wish that I may correct it—
Oh! for the influence of the Lord of armies, the God
of battles, the author of true courage and every heroic
virtue, to fire you into patriotic and true soldiers this
moment, ye young and hardy men, whose very faces
seem to speak that God and nature formed you for
soldiers." He closed his discourse with these words:
"Ye that love your country enlist; for honor will follow
you in life or death in such a cause. Ye that love your
religion, enlist; for your religion is in danger. Can
Protestant Christianity expect quarter from heathen
savages and French Papists? Sure in such an alliance,
the powers of hell make a third party. Ye that love
your friends and relations, enlist; lest ye see them en-
slaved and butchered before your eyes."

When Davies had finished the address, Captain Meredith's company was made up within a few minutes. Soon
afterwards the war against the French came to an end
with Washington's seizure of a fort that stood on the
site of the present city of Pittsburg and with the capture of Quebec. During the progress of the struggle,
the war sermons of Davies had persuaded more men to
enter the field as soldiers than any other agency used.
This settled once for all the question as to whether the
Presbyterians should be allowed to worship as they
pleased. Since they were standing with rifles in their
hands to defend the entire western frontier of the colony
of Virginia against savage foes, their ministers were allowed to preach the gospel whenever they could call together a group of the settlers. The Toleration Act was
from that time interpreted in the most liberal manner
with reference to public worship offered by the Presbyterians, and they established churches wherever they
pleased without asking permission from the county
courts.

On December 3, 1755, a group of ministers
and elders met in the church of Davies in Hanover

County, Virginia. They were the following: Samuel
Davies, of Hanover Church; Robert Henry, pastor of
Cub Creek Church in the present Charlotte County and
of Briery Church in the present Prince Edward; John
Brown, of Timber Ridge and New Providence churches
in the present Rockbridge County; and John Todd, assistant to Mr. Davies and pastor in Louisa County.
With these ministers sat the following elders: Samuel
Morris, Alexander Joice, John Molley. Prayer was
offered constituting these as the Presbytery of Hanover, in connection with the New Side Synod of New
York. By the previous appointment of the Synod, Samuel Davies was moderator. The latter, being sick, asked
John Todd to preach for him. Todd, therefore, began
the formal work of the Presbytery with a sermon. Two
ministers appointed by the Synod as original members
of the Presbytery were not present at this, the first
meeting. These were Alexander Craighead, pastor of
Windy Cove Church in Augusta County, and John
Wright, pastor of the church in Cumberland County,
near the present town of Farmville. The first act of
the Presbytery was to appoint the first day of January,
1756, as a day of prayer and fasting. This was done
in obedience to a recommendation made by the Synod.
The last act of Presbytery before adjournment was to
appoint another day of prayer and fasting during the
following month of June. The reasons given for these
appointments were the danger of the people from savage
warfare and a desire for God's blessing upon the preaching of his word.

The members of this Presbytery represented the
Presbyterian population of the western parts of the
present States of Virginia, North Carolina, and South
Carolina, and the States of Kentucky and Tennessee.
Nearly all of the people who dwelt in that vast region
were Scots from Ireland. They worshipped according to
the manner of their Scotch fathers. The formation

of this Presbytery was in itself the putting forward of
the claim that civil government and church government
are entirely separate and distinct. In offering worship
to God, men must be left free to use any method that
suits them. This was the position taken by Davies and
his associates. Religious freedom was, by them, made
the basis of freedom in civil government. Since these
men were at the same time fighting the battles of their
country they were allowed to enjoy in peace the full
right to worship as they pleased.

In 1758 the New Side and Old Side Presbyterians
agreed to lay aside their differences and to come together
as brethren. The Synod of New York and the Synod of
Philadelphia were united under the name of the Synod
of New York and Philadelphia. In that same year,
1758, President Burr of Princeton College passed away,
and the trustees asked Samuel Davies to become president. Davies said that he must remain in his Virginia
field and declined the election. A second and a third
time they offered him the presidency, but still he refused.
When the trustees for the fourth time selected him,
Davies yielded and in July, 1759, he entered upon his
new work at Princeton. Within less than two years
afterwards, that is on February 4, 1761, a fever carried away this man of God. He was only in his 38th
year when he died. His aged mother came to look
upon him as he lay in the casket. "There is the son of
prayers and my hopes," she said, "my only son, my
only earthly supporter. But there is the will of God,
and I am satisfied."

Samuel Davies, a prince among early American
preachers, was trained for his work, in part, by a life
in the wilderness. Like an ancient Hebrew prophet he
rode from house to house among the settlers in the
Virginia forests. "This has been a busy summer with
me," he wrote once to a friend. "In about two months
I rode about five hundred miles and preached about

forty sermons." In July, 1756, Davies wrote these words:—"About a month ago, I took a journey to Mr. Henry's congregation * * * *, about 120 miles hence, to assist him in administering the sacrament, and in thirteen days I preached 11 or 12 sermons, with encouraging appearance of success. I think Mr. Henry and Mr. Wright's labors continue to be blessed in those parts. At the sacrament in that wilderness, there were about 2000 hearers and about 200 communicants, and a general seriousness and attention appeared among them."

Davies prepared each sermon beforehand with great care. He studied the character of the people to whom he preached and he had in his mind in the clearest outline the purpose for which he preached. "Every sermon I think worthy of the name cost me four days' hard study in the preparation," he said. The sermons were all carefully written and carried to the pulpit. Sometimes he read them to the people; sometimes he preached without reading. The strength of his sympathy was great. He convinced men concerning the truth of his message and thus by reason of the fire enkindled in his own great heart he moved his hearers to believe and act with him.

Davies gave a large share of his attention to the negro slaves who lived in the homes of the people of his congregation. About three hundred of them regularly attended his preaching, he tells us. About one hundred of these he baptized, after having instructed them. "My ministry of late has been most successful among them," he wrote in March, 1756. "Two Sundays ago I had the pleasure of seeing forty of their black faces around the table of the Lord, who all made credible profession of Christianity, and sundry of them with unusual evidence of sincerity." Friends in England sent Bibles and Watts' Hymns to Davies, and he gave them to those negroes that could read them. Many of the Africans spent their leisure hours in learning how to read in order that they might secure the books from Mr. Davies. In the church at Cub Creek, of which Mr. Henry was pastor, there were about one hundred negro members.

Of great importance in the work of Samuel Davies was the bringing of other ministers into the southern colonies. Among these were John Wright, Henry Pattillo, John Martin, William Richardson, James Waddell, and James Hunt. We shall hear again concerning these preachers.

Davies also helped to build up church schools in his congregations and elsewhere. John Todd, his assistant, was for many years the head of a classical school in Louisa County, Virginia. James Hunt had charge of an academy near Rockville, in Maryland.

We must not forget, however, that the churches of Davies were themselves great schools. The instruction of the people was the chief work which this minister laid upon himself. Wherever he spent the night during his many long journeys among the people, in that house he either preached a sermon or explained some portion of the word of God for the benefit of the family. All of the members of his churches were trained to recite the Shorter Catechism. Dr. John H. Rice tells us that during the week the people of Samuel Davies gave much time to study in preparation for the following Sunday. "A mother might often be seen rocking her infant in a cradle, sewing some garment for her husband, and learning her catechism at the same time. A girl employed in spinning would place her book of questions at the head of the wheel, and catching a glance at it as she ran up her yarn on the spindle, would thus prepare for public catechising; and the boys, who were accustomed to follow the plow, were often to be seen, while their horses were feeding at mid-day, reclining under an old oak in the yard, learning the weekly

task. Young and old were willing to be taught by their
preacher." Then on the Lord's day, in the church, as
a part of the public religious services, the minister asked
questions from the catechism. The elders of the church
and heads of families were always questioned first;
then the younger members and the servants. This
exercise was never brief, but always thorough. Then
Mr. Davies from the pulpit pleaded with his people to
give their hearts to their Saviour and to dwell together
in all godliness and honesty. In almost every family,
moreover, a number of helpful books were read and
studied under the pastor's care. Among these books
were Luther's commentary on Galatians, Boston's
Fourfold State, and the works of Baxter, Flavel and
Watson. Strong and worthy men and women were
thus trained in the Virginia churches under the instruction of Samuel Davies. The harvest gave full evidence
to the wisdom of the planting. These people and their
children have continued, even unto this day, to do much
for their church, for their country, and for their God.

During the eleven years of the ministry of Davies in
Hanover, Patrick Henry was growing up from youth
to manhood in that county. Henry often attended the
Hanover Church and heard Mr. Davies preach, for his
mother was a member of the latter's congregation. He
afterwards said that Davies was the greatest orator
that he ever heard. From this minister Henry learned
how to speak in public. He learned, also, from Davies,
those great principles of church government and civil
government which he afterwards set forth in burning
words. The call to arms spoken by Davies during the
French and Indian War, was repeated again and again
by Patrick Henry in the opening years of the American Revolution.

"I am laboring to do a little to save my country, and,
which is of much more consequence, to save souls from
death, from that tremendous kind of death which a soul

can die." Thus wrote Samuel Davies on one occasion to a friend. With reference to the possible close of his own activities here on earth, he said:

"Formerly I have wished to live longer that I might be better prepared for heaven; but * * * * * after long trial I found this world a place so unfriendly to the growth of everything divine and heavenly, that I was afraid if I should live any longer, I should be no better fitted for heaven than I am. * * * * * * Oh! my good Master, if I may dare call thee so, I am afraid I shall never serve thee much better on this side the regions of perfection. The thought grieves me; it breaks my heart, but I can hardly hope better. But if I have the least spark of true piety in my heart, I shall not always labor under this complaint. No, my Lord, I shall yet serve thee; serve thee through an immortal duration, with the activity, the fervor, the perfection of the rapt seraph that adores and burns."

CHAPTER IX.

AFTER the death of Samuel Davies, one of his pupils,
David Rice, undertood the work in the Hanover field.
Rice was born in Hanover County, Virginia, of Welsh
parentage, and he became a Christian under the influence of the preaching of Davies. At the age of twenty
he entered the Latin and Greek school in Louisa County,
whose principal was John Todd, pastor of the church.
James Waddell assisted in the work of teaching in this
school. Rice completed his course of study at Princeton College about the time when Davies died (1761).
His theological training for the work of preaching was
received under the instruction of John Todd. In the
latter part of the year 1763 Rice was ordained and established as pastor of the Hanover Church.

Many of the people who were then living in Hanover
County began, soon after the coming of Rice, to seek
homes in the frontier regions of Virginia and North Carolina. Churches were built up and made strong in the
places last named, through the arrival of multitudes of
men, women and children who had received their Christian training under Davies. The church in Hanover,
however, grew weak through the departure of its members. In 1767 Rice himself became pastor of a congregation in Bedford County, Virginia. There he continued
to labor in all faithfulness throughout the period of the
Revolution. His field of work lay near the foot of the two
great mountains known as the Peaks of Otter. After
the Revolution (1783) we shall find him riding through

the forests into the western country, there to become known as "Father Rice" and as the "Patriarch of the Kentucky Presbyterian Church." When Rice left Hanover, the principal preachers that were left among the Presbyterians east of the Blue Ridge were John Todd and Robert Henry.

James Waddell, the young assistant in John Todd's school in Louisa County, was born at Newry, North Ireland, in 1739. His early years were spent with his Scotch parents in the colony of Pennsylvania. A severe injury to one of his hands caused the hand to wither and thus rendered him incapable of working in the field. His parents, therefore, sent him to Samuel Finley's classical school at Nottingham, Maryland. Young Waddell made such progress in the study of Greek and Latin that he was made assistant in Finley's school.

As a young lad, after the withering of his hand, we are told that Waddell often had a great desire to see Christ again on earth, in order that he might ask the Master to heal his hand. The hand was not healed, but the Spirit of the Master touched Waddell's heart and led him to form the purpose of preaching His gospel.

One day, not long before the close of the ministry of Samuel Davies in Virginia, a tall, graceful young man of about nineteen years, appeared at his home in Hanover. The young man was seeking for a position to teach school in order to support himself through a further course of study with a view to the university. When Davies looked upon the fair, open countenance of the youth, James Waddell, his heart went out to him. He took Waddell to Louisa County and established him there as John Todd's assistant in the Greek and Latin class-room. At the same time Todd began to guide Waddell along the pathway of preparation leading to the sacred ministry. In that academy in the forest, John Todd trained him in the Latin, Greek and Hebrew languages, and in "the sciences of rhetoric, logic, ontology, moral and natural philosophy and astronomy." On these subjects he was examined by the Hanover Presbytery and "on sundry branches of learning" in addition. His examination embraced "divinity," or theology, also. He wrote a thesis in Latin and an exegesis of a portion of the Greek text of one of Paul's epistles; he delivered a popular lecture, preached a sermon and was authorized by the presbytery to try his gifts in the churches. This was done at the Tinkling Spring Church in 1761. In the autumn of the following year, Waddell was established as pastor of the churches in the counties of Lancaster and Northumberland, which constitute the lower part of the region known as the Northern Neck of Virginia.

In that land between the lower Potomac and Rappahannock rivers, Waddell found the Episcopal Church firmly established. Some Scots, however, had recently come to that country and with the assistance of certain citizens who left the Episcopal Church, they organized a Presbyterian congregation. Among these Scots were Colonel James Gordon and his brother John. For a number of years Colonel Gordon kept a journal in which we find a picture given of the life in the homes of the dissenters. The Episcopal preachers spent much of their time in the pulpit in casting scorn and ridicule upon dissenters. This course angered Gordon and his friends and they often remained at home on Sunday and taught their children the Westminster Catechisms. "May the Lord be praised," writes Gordon on a certain Sunday in April, 1762, "I at last have had the comfort of going with my wife and family to meeting where Mr. Waddell performed to admiration." One Sunday, a year later, Waddell administered the sacrament to ninety white persons and twenty-three colored people. The next day, Monday, all of the people were assembled at church and the boys and girls recited the catechism. One young girl in the congregation "said all the Larger

Catechism and all the Shorter." When Dr. Waddell
stood in the pulpit, he was very graphic in his description
tion of Biblical scenes. An old gentleman of Lancaster
County who as a youth was a member of Waddell's congregation, used to speak of the wonderful impression
made upon his heart by the minister's sermons. "The
brazen serpent raised in the wilderness as an emblem of
Christ, won his heart; it seemed to him that like a
wounded Israelite he saw the serpent—and as a sinner
he saw Christ crucified for sin."

One day when a number of sailors were present in the
church, Dr. Waddell preached from the words, "Simon,
son of Jonah, lovest thou me?" Some of the sailors
were moved to tears by the appeals of the preacher.
At one point in his discourse, Dr. Waddell repeated the
question, 'And what does Peter say?' Then an old
sailor, whose name was Peter, arose from his seat in the
congregation and with tears streaming down his cheeks,
made the answer, "Lord, thou knowest all things; thou
knowest that I love thee."

James Waddell married Mary, the daughter of Colonel Gordon. After many years of pleasant toil in the
Northern Neck, Waddell took his family to the Valley
of Virginia, where he became pastor of the Tinkling
Spring Church in Augusta (1778). There we shall see
him during the Revolution preaching a sermon to the
Valley men as they were on their way to the battlefield
of Guilford Court House in North Carolina. Afterwards, a part of his time as pastor was given to the
church in Staunton.

We are told that, at that time, Dr. Waddell was tall
and spare; that he "had a long visage, his forehead
being high, his nose and chin long, his face thin, his
eyes a light blue and his complexion fair. He wore long
white top boots, small clothes buckled at the knee, a
long, loose, strait-bodied coat and a white wig. He was
seldom vehement in delivery; often excited, never bois-

terous; often deeply pathetic in tone and manner,—
very courtly in his manners—and used much gesture
with both hands."

An old man who had a strong love for money was
in the habit of listening to Dr. Waddell's sermons at
Tinkling Spring. The old miser, in speaking about a
certain one of his discourses, the theme of which was the
love of God, said this: "The snow flakes had been falling pretty freely around the house, but had anyone told
me that guineas lay as thick as the snow flakes, I could
not have gone out to gather any till he was done."

In 1785 Waddell removed his family again to the
eastern side of the Blue Ridge and established his home
in Louisa County near Gordonsville. He preached to
the people of that region, in three or four churches, or
chapels, and kept up a classical school in his own
house, which was called Belle Grove. Blindness gradually came upon Dr. Waddell, but his children read the
Bible to him and he continued to preach until his death
in 1805.

One Sunday, William Wirt, a Virginia lawyer who
became afterwards attorney-general of the United
States, heard Dr. Waddell preach in an old wooden
church in the forest not far from Waddell's home near
Gordonsville. "In entering," says Wirt, "I was struck
with his preternatural appearance; he was a tall and
very spare old man; his head, which was covered with a
white linen cap, his shriveled hands, and his voice, were
all shaking under the influence of a palsy; and a few
moments ascertained to me that he was perfectly blind.

"The first emotions which touched my breast were
those of mingled pity and veneration. But ah! how soon
were all my feelings changed! The lips of Plato were
never more worthy of a prognostic swarm of bees than
were the lips of this holy man. It was a day of the administration of the sacrament; and his subject, of course,
was the passion of our Saviour. I had heard the sub-

ject handled a thousand times—I had thought it exhausted long ago. Little did I suppose that in the wild woods of America I was to meet with a man whose eloquence would give to this topic a new and more sublime pathos than I had ever before witnessed.

"As he descended from the pulpit to distribute the mystic symbols, there was a peculiar, a more than human solemnity in his air and manner which made my blood run cold and my whole frame shiver.

"He then drew a picture of the sufferings of our Saviour; his trial before Pilate; his ascent up Calvary; his crucifixion, and his death. I knew the whole history; but never, till then, had I heard the circumstances so selected, so arranged, so colored. It was all new, and I seemed to have heard it for the first time in my life. His enumeration was so deliberate that his voice trembled on every syllable; every heart in the assembly trembled in unison. His peculiar phrases had that force of description that the original scene appeared to be, at that moment, acting before our eyes. We saw the very faces of the Jews; the staring, frightful distortions of malice and rage. We saw the buffeting; my soul kindled with a flame of indignation, and my hands were involuntarily and convulsively clenched.

"But when he came to touch on the patience, the forgiving meekness of our Saviour; when he drew to the life his blessed eyes streaming in tears to heaven, his voice breathing to God a soft and gentle prayer of pardon on his enemies, 'Father, forgive them, for they know not what they do,'—the voice of the preacher, which had all along faltered, grew fainter and fainter, until his utterance being entirely obstructed by the force of his feelings, he raised his handkerchief to his eyes and burst into a loud and impressive flood of grief. The effect is inconceivable. The whole house resounded with the mingled groans and sobs and shrieks of the congregation.

"It was some time before the tumult had subsided so far as to permit him to proceed. Indeed, judging by the usual but fallacious standard of my own weakness, I began to be very uneasy for the situation of the preacher. For I could not conceive how he would be able to let his audience down from the height to which he had wound them, without impairing the solemnity and dignity of his subject, or perhaps shocking them by the abruptness of the fall. But—no; the descent was as beautiful and sublime as the elevation had been rapid and enthusiastic.

"The first sentence with which he broke the awful silence was a quotation from Rousseau,—'Socrates died like a philosopher, but Jesus Christ like a God.'

"I despair of giving you any idea of the effect produced by this short sentence, unless you could perfectly conceive the whole manner of the man as well as the peculiar crisis in the discourse. * * * * * If he had been indeed and in truth an angel of light, the effect could hardly have been more divine. * * * * I have never seen in any orator such a union of simplicity and majesty. He has not a gesture, an attitude or an accent to which he does not seem forced by the sentiment which he is expressing. His mind is too serious, too earnest, too solicitous and, at the same time, too dignified to stoop to artifice. Although as far removed from ostentation as a man can be, yet it is clear from the train, the style and substance of his thoughts that he is not only a very polite scholar, but a man of extensive and very profound erudition. * * * * *"

CHAPTER X.

On Monday, June 16, 1755, a young minister rode on horseback across the upper Potomac River and entered Virginia. His name was Hugh McAden. His father and mother were Scots from Ireland, but Hugh was born in Pennsylvania, and received his education at Nassau Hall, afterwards known as Princeton College. In 1755 he was licensed to preach the gospel and was at once sent by New Castle Presbytery as an evangelist into the country south of the Potomac. Let us follow him as he rode from house to house and from church to church among the Presbyterian people of Virgina and the Carolinas. The journal in which McAden wrote the story of each day's travel and work will be our chief guide.

On Tuesday, June 17, McAden mounted his horse about 12 o'clock and rode up the Valley of Virginia. At the end of a journey of forty miles he reached a small group of houses known as the town of Winchester. The next morning McAden rode three miles to the meeting-house at Opecquon and was kindly received by Robert Wilson, whose house stood near the church. The day was spent there in company with John Hoge, who had come the year before (1754) to be first pastor of the Opecquon congregation. John was the grandson of William Hoge, the early settler who gave the land on which the Opecquon church was built. He remained here as shepherd of this flock and of the neighboring church at Cedar Creek until 1772. We are told that he "was always highly esteemed as a minister and had an unquestioned character for piety."

The Opecquon Church was the mother church of all the congregations of worshippers that live in and around Winchester. It was the largest and most important congregation in the Valley of Virginia at the time when McAden and Hoge were talking about its welfare at Elder Wilson's house. The first, and even the second house of worship that stood here was of wood. At a later time a stone building was erected. A great multitude of people came on foot and horseback for miles and miles through the forests every Sunday to sit in the church in the midst of the grove of oak trees to listen to the gospel from Hoge's lips. A year or two after McAden's visit, George Washington took command of the Virginia soldiers in the country near Winchester. He often rode to Opecquon Church to take part in the worship offered by Hoge's congregation.

On Thursday, June 19, McAden left Wilson's house and continued his journey up the Valley. He was "alone in the wilderness," he tells us; "sometimes a house in ten miles and sometimes not that." About forty miles each day was made by his good horse through the forests. He passed through Staunton and on the fourth Sunday in June (22d) preached at North Mountain near the present Bethel Church. His horse became sick or lame, and he remained to preach there the following Sunday. The sickness of the horse continued another week and, for that reason, McAden preached in "the new court-house" at Staunton on the first Sunday in July. McAden was a member of the New Side party in the church. This was, probably, the reason why John Craig, of the Old Side, did not ask McAden to preach to his congregation. McAden rode on to the house of John Brown, of the New Side, pastor of New Providence and Timber Ridge. "Here," says our traveller, "I was vehemently desired by Mr. Brown to preach in one of his places, having set apart a day of fasting and prayer, on account of the wars and many murders committed by the savage Indians on the back [frontier] inhabitants."

On the Friday following he preached at Timber Ridge to "a pretty large congregation." McAden tells us that he "felt some life and earnestness in alarming the people of their dangers on account of sin, the procuring cause of all evils that befell us in this life or that which is to come; encouraging them to turn to the Lord with all their hearts, to wait upon him for deliverance from all their enemies, the only sure refuge in every time of difficulty; and exciting them to put themselves in the best posture of defence they could, and endeavor, by all possible means in their power, to defend themselves from such barbarous and inhuman enemies." By these last words he meant, of course, that they must have their good, old flint-lock rifles loaded and ready for battle with the Indians. "Great attention and solemnity," he tells us, "appeared throughout the whole assembly; nay, so engaged were they that, though there came up a pretty smart gust, they seemed to mind it no more than if the sun had been shining on them. But in a little time the Lord turned it so about that we were little more disturbed than if we had been in a house."

A few days later, as McAden was pressing southward, he heard of the defeat of General Braddock's army by the French and Indians, which took place on the 9th of July, 1755. "This, together with the frequent accounts of fresh atrocities being daily committed upon the frontiers, struck terror to every heart. A cold shuddering possessed every breast, and paleness covered almost every face." Men, women and children met together in companies, he tells us, and began to build forts for protection against the Indians.

McAden was disturbed about his own duty in this time of fear; whether to go back or to go on. "I re-

solved to prosecute my journey, come what will," he
writes, "with some degree of dependence on the Lord
for his divine protection and support, that I might be
enabled to glorify him in all things, whether in life or in
death." This sense of dependence on the Lord, he
frankly tells us, was not as strong and clear in his own
heart as he desired it to be.

Under the protection of some friendly riflemen who
went with him as a guard, McAden crossed the Blue
Ridge Mountains and passed through Bedford County
to the home of Robert Henry. He found that the crops
were parched by a long and wasting drought. "I was
much refreshed," says McAden, "by a relation of Mr.
Henry's success among his people, who told me of several hopefully brought in by his ministry, and frequent appearance of new awakenings amongst them,
scarcely a Sabbath passing without some life and appearance of the power of God. So, likewise, in Mr.
Wright's congregation, I hear, there is a considerable
appearance of the power of God."

Still onward he pressed, preaching at every place
where the people could be brought together. On Tuesday, July 29, he crossed the Dan River into North Carolina and preached at Mr. Brandon's. The same evening, after riding twelve miles, he came to Solomon Debow's, on Hico River. There he remained and preached
on the first Sunday in August (August 3, 1755). Mc-
Aden determined then not to be so anxious about getting
along in his journey, but to "take some more time to
labor among the people, if so be the Lord might bless
it to the advantage of any."

On Tuesday, the 5th of August, he preached again at
Debow's. He rode ten miles on Wednesday and
preached at the chapel on South Hico. The people there
"seemed exceedingly pleased and returned abundance of
thanks for my sermon, and earnestly entreated me by
all means to call upon them as I came back." His

course was now towards the southeast, and his message was delivered at almost every house where he spent the night. At Eno he found "a set of pretty regular Presbyterians" who appeared in "a cold state of religious feeling." The people at Grassy Creek "seemed very inquisitive about the way to Zion." While he was preaching to large crowds on Fishing Creek, a branch of Tar River, "the power of God appeared something conspicuous and the word seemed to fall with power." Nearly all of the settlers in this region, he tells us, were Scots who had passed into North Carolina through Virginia.

Congregations were gathered everywhere for him. The people were solemn and attentive. His course was now again towards the southwest. A large company of Presbyterians heard him preach at Hawfields. The people of the Buffalo Settlement seemed "solemn and very attentive, but no appearance of the life of religion." Early in September McAden came to Yadkin Ford and preached there in the regular meeting-house. A week later he crossed the Yadkin River and preached at another meeting-house built by Presbyterians. There he met John Andrew, "a serious, good man, I hope, with whom my soul was much refreshed, by his warm conversation about the things of God. How sweet to meet one in the wilderness who can speak the language of Canaan."

On the way southward he passed a large company of men, women and children who had fled from the mountains of Virginia to escape the Indians. The earth was still so dry from lack of rain that he did not see "so much as one patch of wheat or rye in the ground."

On Sunday, October 12, McAden preached at the home of Justice Alexander, on Rocky River, in North Carolina. The following Wednesday he rode three miles and preached at Major Harris's. About six miles on

Friday brought him to David Caldwell's, where he preached again. On Sunday, the 19th, he rode twelve miles to James Alexander's on Sugar Creek, in Mecklenburg County. The congregation that listened to his sermon there was made up of "serious, judicious people." After the sermon McAden rode home with Henry Neely and on Monday, October 20, he turned his horse's head toward the Broad River in South Carolina, sixty miles away.

Two young men who had come from the Broad River country to meet him, rode in front to show the way. The first day's journey carried them beyond the Catawba River. The Catawba Indians gave some trouble, but they soon passed on to the Tyger River and other headwaters of the Broad River, near the present cities of Spartanburg and Greenville, in upper South Carolina. McAden was probably the first minister who visited that region. Presbyterian settlers were rapidly pressing into it and they gave the preacher a warm welcome.

On the 14th of November, 1755, McAden set forth on a northeast course towards the Waxhaws, a district in the present Lancaster County, South Carolina. On Sunday, November 16, he preached in the house of James Patton, to "a pretty large congregation of Presbyterian people." Another sermon was delivered Wednesday at the same place. Then he crossed the Catawba and, five miles beyond that river, preached at the Waxhaws meeting-house on Sunday, November 23, 1755. After the sermon he went home with a friend whose name he wrote as Justice Dickens. It must be, however, that he intended to give the name as Pickens, father of General Andrew Pickens of the Revolution. Justice Pickens was a member of the first bench of magistrates appointed for Augusta County, Virginia, in (1745). He afterwards moved to South Carolina.

McAden now turned northward again towards the

Yadkin. He visited every home in North Carolina at which he had stopped in his southwest journey. On the 28th of November he preached to a large congregatian at Cathey's meeting-house, now called Thyatira Church. The people wanted him to remain as their pastor, but he would not accept the call. He led the worship of a congregation at Captain Hampton's on Second Creek and then rode to the northern bank of the Yadkin.

The 13th day of January, 1756, found McAden riding toward the Cape Fear River. Of course he delivered the gospel message as he went. Among those who heard him were many settlers from the Highlands of Scotland. In the forenoon of Sunday, February 15, 1756, he preached in Wilmington, North Carolina, to a "large and splendid audience." He was much surprised, however, when he went to the place of worship in the afternoon "to see about a dozen met to hear me." Two days later he rode from Wilmington up the northeast branch of the Cape Fear River. He found many people whose affection and entreaties moved him to stay longer. One community made out a call for him and others wished him to become their shepherd. Slowly he made his way across the Neuse and Tar rivers and thence again to the Dan, which he crossed again on his northward journey, May 6, 1756.

The affection of the people whom McAden met just north of Wilmington drew him back again. In 1759 he became the pastor of the Presbyterians in Duplin and New Hanover counties. He labored there about ten years. Then he came as pastor to the Hico River in Caswell County, among the people whom he met when he first crossed the Dan River into North Carolina. His dwelling-house was near the Red House Church. Half a day's ride brought him to a church in Pittsylvania County, Virginia. There in the valley of the Dan River, riding back and forth across that stream, Mc-

Aden spent the rest of his life until its close in 1781.

McAden's son tells us that his father "always spent one or two days every week in private study, and if he walked into the fields he always carried his Bible with him. He visited with his elders, once a year, all the families within the bounds of his congregations and he would exhort and pray with them during his stay. He would collect all of his congregations once a year at his churches, and hold an examination of those present. He administered the sacrament at each of his churches twice every year. He spent his life in attempting to convince all of their sins, and in rendering happy those who were members of his congregations."

CHAPTER XI

ALEXANDER CRAIGHEAD was a Scot, born in North Ireland. He crossed the Atlantic to the colony of Pennsylvania and was there ordained as a minister by the Presbytery of Donegal, of the Synod of Philadelphia, about the close of the year 1735. Craighead's heart was filled with love for his fellowmen. With warm, eager appeals he sought to persuade them to become Christians. He heard Whitefield preach and was filled with admiration for the man and his ways. Craighead possessed in a large measure the same power to move men's hearts that marked Whitefield. Of course he became a member of the New Side party and tried to promote revivals of religion among his people. Craighead had strong, clear views about the right of the individual man to do as he pleased in the matter of religious worship, and about the rights of the individual man in the government of the community. A pamphlet concerning civil government was circulated in the colony of Pennsylvania. This pamphlet gave great offense to the governor of the colony. He thought that the writer of it claimed too much freedom for each citizen of the province. When the governor was told that Alexander Craighead was the writer of the paper, he laid the pamphlet before the Synod of Philadelphia of which Craighead was a member. The synod expressed its disapproval of the views set forth in the pamphlet. It said, also, that Craighead had not been given the authority to speak for the synod with reference to matters of civil government. It was charged

that Craighead was "tinged with an uncharitable and
party spirit." Probably for the reason that he found
himself in advance of his brethren in Pennsylvania
concerning freedom in church and in state, Craighead
left that colony and came to the mountains of
Virginia.

In 1749 Craighead made his home on the Cow Pasture River, in Augusta County, Virginia, within the
borders of the present Windy Cove congregation. In
1755 he was one of the original members of the Hanover
Presbytery. Then came the days of terror that followed
the defeat of Braddock in July, 1755. Craighead's
people lived in a place of danger on the western border of the Virginia settlements. Many of them, therefore, gathered up their household goods and moved
eastward across the Blue Ridge. Then they turned
their faces southward, crossed the Dan and Yadkin
rivers, and found homes in the beautiful country
between the Yadkin and the Catawba, in North and
South Carolina. Craighead went with his people.
Another reason led him away from the Virginia frontier, in addition to the danger from the Indians. That
reason was the injustice shown at that time to dissenting ministers by the colonial government in Virginia.
These ministers were not allowed to perform the rite
of marriage for their own people. Craighead loved
liberty and he wished for himself and brethren privileges as great as those enjoyed by Episcopal ministers.
Since these were not granted in Virginia, he sought
North Carolina as a place of freedom.

About ten years before Craighead entered North
Carolina, that is, about 1746, a stream of Scots began
to move across the Yadkin from the northward. These
early settlers built homes in that fair region between
the Catawba and Yadkin which is sometimes called
Mesopotamia. Many of the family names of these

early settlers in North Carolina, and also of the colonists in the upper part of South Carolina, were the names borne by John Hoge's people on the Opecquon and by John Craig's congregation, in the Valley of Virginia. The same homes in the north of Ireland, no doubt, sent forth all of these God-fearing men and women to build homes and churches and schoolhouses in Virginia and the Carolinas. Similar names were given to mountains and streams in the frontier regions of these three colonies. Bethel, Bethesda and Providence, as the names of churches, have been left, moreover, all along the pathway of the Scots as they journeyed from Pennsylvania to Georgia. The place of worship was for them the house of God (Bethel), the house of mercy (Bethesda), and the symbol of Jehovah's protecting care (Providence).

In the year 1758, Alexander Craighead became pastor of the Presbyterian congregation on Rocky River, in North Carolina. He was installed in this office by William Richardson, who was appointed by the Hanover Presbytery to perform this service. Rocky River was, therefore, the name of the oldest church in the western Carolina country. Until the time of his death, in 1766, Craighead was the only pastor in the land between the rivers Yadkin and Catawba.

Within the bounds of the Rocky River congregation there ran a little creek with the Indian name of Sugaw. It is now called Sugar Creek. On the bank of that little stream a log church was built and Craighead preached there regularly to a part of his congregation. For a distance of fifteen or twenty miles on every side, Craighead's people walked or rode to the Sugar Creek Church. As this place of worship stood near the center of the land occupied by the Scots between the Yadkin and Catawba, it soon became the largest of Craighead's congregations.

In the year 1762, the county of Mecklenburg was laid off in this region and named after the wife of King George the Third of England, Queen Charlotte, who was a princess of the German house of Mecklenburg. A town was established within the bounds of Sugar Creek congregation, about three miles from the church, as the county seat of Mecklenburg County. This town was called Charlotte, likewise in honor of the queen.

About 1765 two ministers, Spencer and McWhorter, came to North Carolina, bearing the authority given to them by the Synod of New York and Philadelphia. In accordance with Craighead's desire, these two evangelists divided the territory of Mecklenburg County into a number of separate church congregations. In the usual solemn manner elders were chosen and ordained by the laying on of hands in the following churches: Steel Creek, Providence, Hopewell, Centre, and Poplar Tent.

These congregations, with the Rocky River congregation, formed a circle around the Sugar Creek Church. Craighead was chief shepherd, while he lived, of the entire group of seven churches. These congregations were spread over the territory of the present Mecklenburg and Cabarras counties and a part of the present Iredell County, North Carolina.*

The lives of the people who lived in this region were moulded in large measure by Alexander Craighead. The religious beliefs in which he carefully instructed them were drawn from the Bible in accordance with the Westminster Confession of Faith. He taught them that God must be worshipped every day in the home and every Lord's Day in the church in a solemn and devout manner. The standard of conduct which he set before them by precept and example was that type of simple piety in

---

*The church of Thyatira in Rowan county was probably organized at the same time by Spencer and McWhorter.

which the warm heart and the generous hand unite together to give expression to the Christian's faith in God.

Craighead taught his people also those principles of individual liberty in the home, in church government and in state government, that now form the basis of our lives as Christians and as citizens of a common country. He came from Virginia to North Carolina to assert his rights and privileges as a minister in the Church of Christ. He continued to claim that the British colonial government had no right nor authority to take away his privileges as an ordained officer in the church. He taught his people that they, as home-builders and as defenders of the Western Carolina country, had the right to manage their home affairs—a right which the governor of the colony could not take from them.

We shall see how Craighead's teaching bore much good fruit in the land of Mecklenburg, not very long after he was laid to rest (1766) in the old church yard at Sugar Creek. Two small sassafras branches were used to carry his body to the place of burial by the side of the old log church, about half a mile west of the present brick house of worship. The two branches were set in the ground to mark the head and foot of Craighead's grave. They took root and grew up as tall, strong trees. In like manner the words and the example of this man of God took root and grew in the lives of the people of that land.

On the third Friday in May, 1768, Joseph Alexander, a relative of John McKnitt Alexander, became Craighead's successor as the pastor of Sugar Creek Church. All of the ministerial work of Craighead was for the time laid upon him. Alexander established an advanced school, known as a classical school, at the Sugar Creek Church. In this work he was aided by a teacher named Benedict. In 1770 this school was removed to the town of Charlotte and called Queen's Museum, or College. After the Revolution began, the name of the school was changed to Liberty Hall Academy. Alexander himself went to Bullock's Creek in York District, South Carolina, and there for nearly thirty years he was pastor of the church and the principal of a famous Greek and Latin school.

CHAPTER XII

JOHN WITHERSPOON, OF THE LOWER SANTEE RIVER, AND
JAMES CAMPBELL, OF THE UPPER CAPE FEAR RIVER.

In the year 1732, a small company of Scots came from
the North of Ireland to the coast region of South Carolina. They were given a tract of land on Black River,
between the lower Santee and Pee Dee rivers. This
country was called Williamsburg Township, in honor of
William the Third, King of England. In the autumn
of the year 1734, another group of Scots sailed from
Belfast, Ireland. Storms tossed their ship sorely during the voyage across the Atlantic, but just three weeks
before Christmas they landed at Charles Town. After
Christmas they were put in an open boat with food to
last them for a year. Each grown-up man was given,
also, an ax, a broad hoe and a narrow hoe. The boat
shaped its course by way of Georgetown Harbor and
thence up the Black River to Williamsburg Township.
The leader of this company of Scots was John Witherspoon, kinsman of the famous John Witherspoon, Presi-
den of Princeton College, who was one of the signers
of the Declaration of Independence. He brought the
emigrants ashore and they began to build houses not far
from a large white pine tree on the bank of the river.
For the reason that trees of this kind were kept for the
use of the King of England, this beautiful pine, which
threw its shadow over the homes of the Scots, was called
the King's Tree. Such was the beginning of the present
town of Kingstree, in South Carolina.

John Witherspoon was a man of stout heart, for we
are told that he and his sons comforted the people whom

he led into the wilderness. When the emigrants found nothing on the shore of the Black River but a great forest and a few log-cabins built by the Scots who had come two years before, their spirits sank. Then, says Robert Witherspoon, grandson of John, "My father gave us all the comfort he could, by telling us we would get all those trees cut down and in a short time there would be plenty of inhabitants, so that we could see from house to house."

The fire, which the settlers had brought with them, went out, but John Witherspoon's son hastened through the pathless forest to the next group of houses, and brought some live coals. When darkness came on "the wolves began to howl on all sides." John Witherspoon loaded his gun and kept his people in safety. For a long time there was no door to his house and the earth itself formed the only floor. Wild beasts and Indians were driven away and under the leadership of John Witherspoon the axes of the settlers were kept at work in the woods. Corn was planted and in the autumn there was bread in abundance from their own fields.

"Well, we must have a minister," said one of the Witherspoons, whose first name was Gavin. John Willison, of Dundee, Scotland, was the preacher whom he named when asked about his choice. "But the minister must have a muckle sight o' money for his living." "An' that we must gie him," said Witherspoon. "An' how much, Mister Wotherspoon, wull ye gie?" "Ten poonds," was the ready answer. "But, Mister Wotherspoon, whar wull ye get the ten poonds?" "Why, if warst comes to warst," said Witherspoon, "I can e'en sell my cou [cow]." Willison was sent for, but he could not come. Robert Heron came, however from North Ireland, and in August, 1736, he organized a Presbyterian Church among the Scots of Williamsburg. About three years afterwards, however, Heron returned to Ireland and remained there until his death. Soon after the founding of the church near the King's Tree, Presbyterian Churches were organized at Salem, on the Black River, at Indian Town, at Aimwell, on the Pee Dee, at Mount Zion and at Brewington. Most of the people who established these churches bore the family names of Cooper, Gordon, Irwin, James, McCutchen, McDonald, Wilson and Witherspoon.

In 1743 John Rae came to be the preacher at the King's Tree. He continued his labors there until his death in 1761. He was "a man of heavenly spirit," we are told, who went about "reproving the negligent, encouraging the doubtful and desponding, visiting the sick, comforting mourners and relieving the distressed." Under his wise care harmony was preserved in the congregation, "the piety and graces of the parents seemed to have descended upon their offspring, and the young, as they grew to manhood, became with few exceptions, members and ornaments of the church of their fathers." New settlers came and wide fields gave their harvests each year. From Sunday to Sunday, all of these churches of the Santee and Pee Dee country were filled with earnest worshippers. David McKee, a godly man, followed Rae in the work of the ministry at the King's Tree. After three years, McKee went to Salem, on Black River, and Hector Alison became shepherd at the King's Tree.

While these people from the Lowlands of Scotland were growing in numbers and strength near the coast of South Carolina a large body of settlers from the Scotch Highlands was worshipping God in the Presbyterian way, on the upper waters of the Cape Fear River. They began to enter this region about the time when John Witherspoon and his followers were building homes near the King's Tree on the Black River (1734). Soon after the year 1746, the Highlanders came in large numbers and established themselves in the region around Cross Creek, now called Fayetteville, on the Cape Fear.

From that point some of them moved gradually westward across the upper Pee Dee River. Today their descendants hold a large part of the land in the counties
of Cumberland, Bladen, Robeson, Sampson, Moore,
Richmond, and Anson, in North Carolina.

These Scots from the Highlands were Presbyterians.
Some years passed away before they could secure a
preacher. In 1757, however, James Campbell became
their spiritual shepherd and he held that office until his
death in 1781.

James Campbell, a minister of the Church of Scotland, came first to the colony of Pennsylvania (1730)
and preached there to a congregation of Scots. His
mind became clouded with doubt concerning his call to
the ministry, and after a few years he ceased to preach.
Then Whitefield came through that land and Campbell
heard him speak. He sought out Whitefield and told
him of his spiritual unrest. Whitefield gave good counsel and urged Campbell to take up again the work of
the ministry. In 1755, therefore, when Hugh McAden
set forth upon his journey southward, he found Campbell in charge of a congregation in western Pennsylvania.

Two years later, that is, in 1757, James Campbell
came to North Carolina and began to speak the gospel
message to the Highlanders of the Cape Fear country.
His home was on the left bank of that stream, thirteen
miles above Cross Creek. The Scots required him to
become a member of the Presbytery of South Carolina
and this he did at once. On his own plantation, "beneath the shade of his own lofty oaks," he first preached
Christ to his countrymen in their native language. The
news that a Gaelic, or Highland, preacher had settled
among them passed throughout the region occupied by
the Scots "almost with the speed of the fiery cross in
the Highlands, when sent to summon the clansmen to
the fight. Soon multitudes came to hear the Word ex-

pounded and to listen to the accents of his Highland tongue."

Across the river from Campbell's home stood a high bank called the Bluff. At that place lived Hector McNeill, who was known from the place of his residence as Bluff Hector. Just below the Bluff, in a meeting-house near Roger McNeill's, which was called "Roger's meeting-house," Campbell preached for ten or twelve years. Hector McNeill and Alexander McAlister were the elders in this church.

Another place of preaching was the house of John Dobbin on Barbacue. About 1766 a house of worship was built there called the "Barbacue Church." The first elders were Gilbert Clark, Duncan Buie, Archibald Buie and Daniel Cameron, known as Daniel of the Hill. These elders were so honest and worthy in their lives and so faithful in attending to all of their duties in the church that they were called "the little ministers of Barbacue." The congregation was well trained after the old Scotch method. The Bible was read with care in every home. Every member of the community went to church on Sunday, whether the minister was present or not. They all repeated the Catechism as a part of the public worship in the church. This exercise was under the management of the elders when Mr. Campbell was preaching in some other part of his field. When the minister was present and began his sermon, Bibles were opened and every text that he mentioned was sought out at once and read. The people were so well instructed in Biblical doctrines that John McLeod, who came afterwards from Scotland to assist Mr. Campbell, said that "he would rather preach to the most polished and fashionable congregation in Edinburgh than to the little critical carls of Barbacue." The man who stood in their pulpit had to guard his tongue against mistakes or they would set him right when the service came to a close.

A third place where Campbell preached regularly was at MacKay's house. A church was afterwards built there, now known as Longstreet Church. At each place where he preached Campbell gave the people two sermons. One was spoken in English and the other in Gaelic, the tongue of the Highlanders. He rode beyond the borders of the Highlanders' settlement and gave the gospel to the Scotch-Irish of the neighboring regions. The people of Purity Church, near the center of the present Chester county, South Carolina, had James Campbell as their first minister. For more than a year he made the long journey across the country at regular times to serve them.

Campbell's preaching, we are told, was "exegetical and practical—expounding and explaining chapters or portions of the Scriptures. In this he imitated Whitefield, to whom he felt much indebted."

From 1770 until 1773 John McLeod assisted Campbell in preaching to the Highlanders on the Cape Fear. Then McLeod set sail for Scotland and was lost at sea.

Just before the Revolution, the famous Flora McDonald and her husband, Allan McDonald, came from Scotland to North Carolina. They lived at first in the town of Cross Creek (Fayetteville), and afterwards made their home at Cameron's Hill, twenty miles above Cross Creek. There they were regular in their attendance at the Barbacue Church.

During the early years of Flora McDonald, Prince Charles Edward put forward the claim that the crown of England belonged to him. He fought for the crown, but was defeated in the battle of Culloden (1746). The Prince escaped from the battle-field and then the English government offered a great sum of money to any person who would capture him. Flora McDonald's heart was touched with pity for the wandering Prince and she helped him to escape from the Scotch Highlands across the sea to France. Long afterwards, Flora came to

America to dwell for a time among her countrymen on the Cape Fear River. There as a "dignified and handsome woman," she sat in the Barbacue Church and heard the gospel from the lips of James Campbell in her own Highland form of speech. We shall hear more about the McDonalds and the other Scots when the war of the Revolution begins.

CHAPTER XIII

ARCHIBALD SIMPSON, EVANGELIST IN THE REGION
BETWEEN CHARLES TOWN AND SAVANNAH.

ARCHIBALD SIMPSON grew up as a child in his native city of Glasgow, Scotland. In 1748, when he was fourteen years of age, Archibald began to write down in a journal an account of the daily thoughts and events of his life. At first he wrote chiefly about his impressions and experiences as a young Christian. He continued to keep this diary for a period of nearly forty years, until he filled up ten books with the record of his life and work.

While Archibald Simpson was a student at Glasgow University, reading the Bible and engaging in prayer in company with his beloved friend, William Richardson, he made up his mind to become a preacher. In 1753 he came to Georgia and assisted George Whitefield in the management of Bethesda, a home for orphans. In the following year (1754), however, Simpson moved into South Carolina and began to preach at the Wilton Church. The people of this congregation soon became divided in opinion with reference to the location of a new house of worship. Some of the church members became the enemies of Simpson himself. One fine Sunday morning in the spring of 1756 when he went to the house of worship he found it closed against him. Simpson preached, therefore, under the shade of the trees in a grove not far from the meeting-house. Then the people of Indian Land, or Stoney Creek, near Beaufort, asked Mr. Simpson to become their minister. His wife had come from Scotland to join him and together they went to Stoney Creek, an independent or Congregational Church. The year before (1755) the Independent Church in Savannah had been organized.

Simpson's journal gives us many glimpses of the sessions of the Presbytery of South Carolina, of which he was a member. The journal tells us also about Simpson's own work in the pulpit. Just before the celebration of the Lord's Supper on a certain occasion at James Island Church, he tells us that he "preached the preparation sermon from Sam. III., 11; endeavored to put the crown on the Mediator's head." On the following Monday Simpson "preached from John III., 2; had an opportunity to be a witness for the divinity of my glorious Lord, Jesus Christ, against a young man who denied it, and yet sat down yesterday at the Lord's table." The entry for July 23, 1756, is as follows: " This afternoon went over to Port Royal Island, to preach at Beaufort next Sabbath to the remains of a Presbyterian Church. Lord's-day, 25th: Was much pleased with the solid appearance of the congregation, which was pretty numerous, as there was no preaching in the church [Episcopal]."

In 1761 Simpson made a journey into Georgia to preach to some congregations who had invited him to become their pastor. He went by way of Savannah, thence to the Midway congregation in Liberty County and farther still to Darien. He was pleased with the fine plantations and the large, well-built house of worship which the Congregationalists from Dorchester, South Carolina, had established at Midway. He found Scotch Highlanders on the Sapelo and Scots from North Ireland on the Altamaha River. Some of the latter were just moving into that region from Williamsburg Township, South Carolina.

In 1769 he made another journey to the Midway Church to take part with the people there in the celebration of the Sacrament of the Lord's Supper.

Although Midway was a Congregational Church and, therefore, independent in its government, yet we are told that up to the year 1849 this congregation had furnished more Presbyterian ministers than all of the other churches in Georgia.

On one occasion when some of his brethren were speaking harshly about Whitefield "and ministers of his stamp," Simpson thought it his duty, he says, "to speak freely, and stand up for the preaching warmly and zealously the doctrines of grace, the necessity of regeneration, the catholic practice of preaching in all pulpits, employing pious ministers of every denomination, and holding occasional communion with all sound Protestants, with all Christians who held of the glorious Head, and both lay and ministerial communion."

Many times Mr. Simpson went back to visit the people of Wilton. He rejoiced to see the handsome new house of worship which they had built and he entered it and preached. Several times the people tried to make amends for the work of that early day during his ministry, when he was barred out of the old church. They called him to become their pastor again, but he refused to accept the invitation. Not far from his home on Stoney Creek he founded the Saltketcher Church. He travelled much on horseback to carry the story of his Master's sacrifice to the people of the region near the coast. At the same time, also, he was writing in his diary those daily notes that tell us about the upbuilding of God's kingdom in lower South Carolina.

A wasting fever seized Archibald Simpson and his wife and carried them both down to the gates of death. The beloved wife passed through the gates to dwell with the Redeemer. Simpson himself was brought back to health. Afterwards he took his three daughters to Scotland to enter them at school (1772). Then the war of the Revolution came on and he was unable to se-

cure passage back to Charles Town. He preached, therefore, to a congregation near Glasgow, although his
heart was with his people in South Carolina. After
the Revolution, he came again to his former home near
Beaufort. All was desolate because of the ravages of
the British soldiers. His cattle and horses had been
carried away. With a troubled heart he went to look
at the tombs of his wife and four children who had
died. He found "the once beautiful fields" around
his house all in a state of desolation; "no garden, no
enclosure, no mulberry, no fruit trees, nothing but
wild fennel, bushes, underwood, briars, to be seen,—
and a very ruinous habitation. Some young negroes
were at work in the woods. They saw me and ran with
transports of joy, holding me by the knees as I sat on
horseback, and directly ran off to the plantation to
give notice to Mr. Lambert [the overseer]. They asked
me if I was going to leave them after they had stayed
on the plantation when the British wanted them to go
away."

James Gourlay, a Scot, had been the minister in
Archibald Simpson's field during a part of the period
of the latter's absence. Simpson left Gourlay there
and returned to Scotland, where he passed away at an
advanced age.

CHAPTER XIV

WE have seen that in November, 1755, Hugh McAden
preached at the meeting-house in the Waxhaws. The
night afterwards, he went to the house of Justice Pickens, the father of General Andrew Pickens, a soldier of
the Revolution. Waxhaws is the name still given to the
district east of the Catawba River, lying on the border
where Union County, North Carolina, and Lancaster
County, South Carolina, are joined together. This entire region was occupied by Scots from Ireland. For a
few months in 1756 Robert Miller preached to the people of the Waxhaws under the shade of the trees. A
log house for worship was built among the trees and in
1759 William Richardson began his work there as minister.

William Richardson was born in England and was
educated at the University of Glasgow, Scotland. One
of his fellow-students in Glasgow was Archibald Simpson. The latter made the following entry in his journal
with reference to a certain Saturday in the autumn of
the year 1748: "Spent the entire afternoon, with my
friend W. R., in the field, in prayer, praise, and reading
God's Word." The two students parted, and both
afterwards came to America. Richardson found a
home under the roof of Samuel Davies in Hanover,
Virginia, and was there led into the gospel ministry.
In 1759 Simpson was pastor of the church at Stoney
Creek, near the South Carolina coast. On the 16th of

April in that year he wrote in his diary as follows:—
"Dear old comrade W. R. [William Richardson] came
to my house. He was licensed and ordained by a Presbytery in Virginia [Hanover]. Had gone some months
ago a missionary to the Cherokee Indians, but finding
no good could be done among them as they were
inclined to join the French, he has laid down his mission
and accepted an invitation from a people at the Waxhaws, about two hundred miles beyond Charles Town;
is come down to join Presbytery and accept their call,
they being in our bounds." Richardson preached for
his friend Simpson at Pon, Pon and at Beaufort. Then
on the 16th of May Richardson was formally received
as a member of the Presbytery of South Carolina, and
order was taken to install him as chief shepherd at the
Waxhaws.

Far and wide throughout the region near the headwaters of the Catawba and Broad rivers in the upper
part of South Carolina, Richardson made many journeys as a preacher of the gospel. We are told that
messengers who had come from distant settlements,
were often seen riding to his home to ask him to come
to teach them the way of life. Nancy, one of the daughters of Alexander Craighead, of Sugar Creek, in Mecklenburg, became the wife of Richardson and she helped
him much in his great work. Providence, one of Craighead's churches, which stands in the grove of oaks
about twelve miles south of Charlotte, in Mecklenburg,
was for a time one of Richardson's regular places for
preaching. During the early part of his ministry
churches were organized, in part through his labors,
as follows: Catholic and Purity churches in the present
Chester County, Fishing Creek Church, in York County,
Fair Forest Church, on Tyger River, in Union County,
and the Indian Creek and Grassy Spring churches, in
Newberry County, South Carolina. One of the congregations that was established afterwards as the result of

his labors was Union Church in the center of Union
County. In 1764 Richardson rode into the northern
part of the present York County, South Carolina,
preached to the Scots of that region, and then organized them into a church that was named Bethel Church.
About 1769, Bethesda Church in York County was
organized and this was probably also the work of
Richardson. Nazareth Church in Spartanburg County
and many other houses of worship were established
about the same time.

In February, 1756, a number of Scotch families built
homes on Long Cane Creek in the present Abbeville
County, South Carolina. Most of these settlers bore
the name of Calhoun. Among them was Patrick
Calhoun, whose first wife was a daughter of Alexander
Craighead. After her death, Patrick Calhoun married
a daughter of another Scotch settler, John Caldwell,
and she became the mother of John Caldwell Calhoun,
South Carolina's great statesman.

In February, 1760, the Cherokee Indians attacked
the Calhoun settlement at Long Cane and there killed
and captured a large number of people. The rest fled
away, some of them to the Waxhaws. Afterwards they
went back and built again their houses at Long Cane.
In 1764, William Richardson made a visit to this settlement, preached the gospel to the people and baptized many of their children. Within a few years after
this visit, a number of congregations were organized in
Abbeville County, and these churches began at once to
ask for shepherds.

William Richardson adopted as his own son, his
nephew from England, who was named William Richardson Davie. The boy was sent to the Queen's
Museum at Charlotte and then to Princeton College.
When the war of the Revolution came, Davie spent the
estate which the great preacher left him in buying guns
and horses for that famous body of North Carolina

horsemen who fought so well against the King of England.

William Richardson's body was vigorous, but his labors were continuous and heavy. The long rides through the forests and across deep streams wore out his strength. Moreover, he fasted much, praying all the time. Sickness came and with it despondency. One day Mr. Richardson was found dead in his room. A story was spread abroad that he had died by his own hand. On the contrary, the journal of his life-long friend, Archibald Simpson, contains this record:

"His death was something remarkable. He was of a strong and robust make, and in general healthy, but of a heavy, melancholic disposition, subject from his very youth to vapory disorders. His labors for some years were very great. About three or four years ago he began to decline; his vapory disorders increased, his intellect seemed to fail. He turned very deaf and lost much of his spirits and liveliness in preaching, but was still very useful to his own people. About three months ago, he seemed sickly, but his people and family thought he fancied himself worse than he was, as he did not keep his bed, but appeared as usual, and only kept his house. Some time in June [1771], one of his elders was visiting him, and in order to divert him, had entered into some argument with him, in which Mr. R. talked with a good deal of spirit, and afterwards went upstairs to his room, but was to be down to dinner as usual. Accordingly when dinner had waited for some time, they went upstairs and found him dead on his knees, one hand holding the back of a chair and the other lifted up as in prayer. So that he seemed to have expired in the act of devotion, and to all appearance had been dead some time; a most desirable death indeed. O Lord God! let me die the death of the righteous and let my latter end be like his."

Upon the stone that marks the place where William

Richardson's body rests in the old Waxhaws burial
ground, there is this tribute:

> He lived to purpose;
> He preached with fidelity;
> He prayed for his people;
> And being dead he speaks.

A part of his property was left for the use of his
wife and adopted son. A considerable sum was set
apart to buy books for the poor people among the
churches to which he had given his life.

CHAPTER XV

HENRY PATTILLO AND DAVID CALDWELL ORGANIZE THE
PRESBYTERY OF ORANGE IN THE CAROLINAS.

ON the 12th of July, 1758, the Presbytery of Hanover
met at Captain Anderson's house in Cumberland
County, Virginia. Two young men who had been
already licensed to preach, offered themselves for ordination. Their names were Henry Pattillo and William
Richardson. Samuel Davies, moderator of the Presbytery, preached the sermon. Then the two young
men knelt down and the hands of the members of the
Presbytery were laid upon them. Thus were they solemnly appointed unto the ministry. Richardson was
sent out as a missionary to the Cherokees and finally
found his field of work in the Waxhaws and the neighboring regions. Pattillo took some time to settle in
his chief place of labor.

Pattillo was a Scot. In his early years he came
from Scotland to the colony of Virginia. At first he
was a clerk in a store. Then he became a teacher and
while engaged in the work of instructing the children
committed to his care he gave his heart to Christ. At
once Pattillo became a personal worker in behalf of his
Master. He sought individual men and women and
pleaded with them to become Christians. Then he determined to become a minister of the gospel, and in 1751
he went to live in the house of Samuel Davies in Hanover. There he went through a course of study under
the guidance of Davies.

On the 10th of August, 1754, Pattillo began to write
in a journal an account of his daily experiences. His

reasons for writing were chiefly that he might mark his "growth or decay in the divine life," and "accurately observe the workings of my own heart and the methods the Lord may take for my reclamation in my strayings from him."

In 1755, before his course of study was completed, Pattillo married a wife. He began teaching again in order to gain a support for his wife and himself. They went to live in a "house 16 by 12 and an outside chimney, with an 8-foot shed,—a little chimney to it." This was both home and schoolroom. Six small pupils came to him each day to be taught. One day in June, 1757, a stroke of lightning shattered the chimney attached to the shed. No harm was done to the six pupils nor to the members of Pattillo's family. The writing in the journal was brought to a close, however, for that was the last day on which he made an entry in it. For about six years after his ordination Pattillo preached to various congregations in Virginia. In 1765 he was called to Hawfields, Eno and Little River in the northern part of North Carolina. He came at once and during the next thirty-five years gave his life to the churches in Orange and Granville counties. In 1780 he became pastor of Nutbush and Grassy Creek in Granville County. These congregations were at first made up of settlers from Hanover and the adjacent counties of Virginia.

In 1764, a year before his permanent establishment in North Carolina, Pattillo made a brief journey to that colony and founded the church of Alamance, near Greensboro. After his regular pastorate began Pattillo established a classical school among his people and this he kept up for many years.

When the first provincial or colonial Congress of North Carolina met in the town of Hillsboro, Pattillo took his seat in that body as a delegate. Every morning during its sessions he led the Congress in prayer.

On one important occasion he sat in the presiding officer's seat as chairman of the Congress.

In 1801, when Pattillo, then an old man, lay on his deathbed, a friend asked him, "Where is your hope now?" The minister opened his eyes, and with both hands pointed upward as if to indicate "that heaven," says an eye-witness, "which had been the object of his fervent prayers, and to which he had constantly looked forward as the place of his everlasting rest."

The associate of Pattillo in the northern part of North Carolina was David Caldwell. He was of Scotch descent and was born in Pennsylvania. As a young man he became a carpenter and worked at that trade until he was twenty-five years of age. Then he became a Christian and resolved to become a preacher of the gospel. He sought an education with all the eagerness of a strong, earnest man. Night and day he toiled at the courses of study that were set before him. While he was a student at Princeton College, it was his habit in warm weather, he said, to sit with his books before him on a table near an open window. He studied in this manner until a late hour at night. Then he would "cross his arms on the table, lay his head on them, and sleep in that position until morning." In the year 1761, when Caldwell was thirty-six years of age, he completed the courses of study at Princeton and was given a collegiate degree.

In 1765 Caldwell came to North Carolina as an ordained minister to become shepherd of the two congregations of Buffalo and Alamance, near Greensboro. In the following year (1766) he married Rachel, third daughter of Alexander Craighead, of Mecklenburg. Soon afterwards he established in his own house a classical school, which was continued as a fountain of learning and of piety for many years. Five of Caldwell's students became governors of states, several of them were made judges, about fifty became ministers of the gospel, and a large number were lawyers and doctors. His school was academy, college and theological seminary, for the ministers whom he taught received from him their theological education as well as their Latin, Greek and Hebrew.

Many of the young men who had entered Caldwell's school as careless, irreligious boys, became Christians through his influence and then entered the ranks of the ministry. Eli W. Caruthers, who succeeded Caldwell as pastor of the two churches, tells us that he and nine of his schoolmates were drawn into the gospel ministry by their teacher, David Caldwell. The wife of Caldwell, however, had much to do in leading the students into the service of Christ. The treasures of her kindness, her judgment and her intelligence were all bestowed upon the young men who were members of her household. New courage was given to many a faint hearted youth who grew weary in the path of learning. Her sympathy and hopefulness were infused into the hearts of the students. It was said that "Doctor Caldwell makes the scholars and Mrs. Caldwell makes the ministers."

David Caldwell's days were filled with labor. Every morning at four o'clock he arose and began his studies. Five days in the week he gave to the management of his school of fifty or sixty boys. As there was no physician in the neighborhood, he read books on the practice of medicine and then made long journeys to visit the sick. Every member of his two large congregations was questioned in the Catechism twice a year. There were four communions a year and each season of this kind lasted four days. Besides all of these duties, he laid upon himself the work of carrying the gospel message into congregations that were without a minister.

In March, 1770, a petition was sent to the Synod of New York and Philadelphia asking for a presbytery in the Carolinas. In May the petition was granted and Hugh McAden, Henry Pattillo, James Creswell, David Caldwell, Joseph Alexander, Hezekiah Balch and Hezekiah James Balch were set apart as Orange Presbytery. They met at the Hawfields Church and Pattillo opened the work of the presbytery with a sermon.

In 1770 the county of Guilford was marked off from the counties of Orange and Rowan. Caldwell's congregation of Buffalo lay in the center of the new county embracing Guilford Court House, the county seat. In the following year (1771) a number of people in this region, who called themselves Regulators, refused to pay taxes and to submit to the colonial government. A few of the members of Caldwell's churches were among them. Governor Tryon marched against the Regulators with an army and met them at Alamance. Caldwell pleaded with both parties not to fight. While the two lines of battle were only three hundred yards apart, the men standing ready with loaded rifles, Caldwell rode along the line of the Regulators and urged them to go home. The command was given and the firing began. Then Caldwell gave up his efforts to keep the peace and the Regulators were defeated and scattered. A few years later Caldwell heard the crash of the rifles at Guilford, near his home, when the men of the Southern colonies met the army of Cornwallis and forced it to march out of the Carolinas.

CHAPTER XVI.

CHARLES CUMMINGS AND SAMUEL DOAK ON THE HOLSTON RIVER.

In the summer of 1773, a man whose age was about forty years, rode through the forest into the valley of the Holston River in southwest Virginia. He had received a call to become the preacher and pastor of the people of the Holston country. The call bore the signatures of one hundred and twenty heads of families living in that region. Virtually all of these signers were Scots. They were a part of that stream of settlers from the North of Ireland who were then slowly moving through the Valley of Virginia into Tennessee and Kentucky. Among the names attached to the Presbyterian minister's call were those of the families of Blackburn, Vance, Logan, Edmondson, Trimble, Christian, Buchanan, Montgomery and Campbell.

The young prophet thus asked to dwell on the Holston was named Charles Cummings. He was born in North Ireland, but at an early age came to Virginia and found his way to James Waddell's congregation in Lancaster County. There he maintained himself as a teacher. In the course of time he married Milly Carter, daughter of John Carter of that region. No doubt it was the influence of Waddell that led Cummings into the ministry. In April, 1776, he was licensed to preach, by Hanover Presbytery, and at once began to deliver his message at Brown's meeting-house, in Augusta County. Then the call came from the one hundred and twenty leading men of the Ebbing Spring and the Sinking Spring congregations on the Holston, and Cummings went to their aid.   He built a house for his family near the present town of Abingdon.

The first church erected for Cummings at Sinking Spring was a log-cabin of rough logs, about eighty feet long and forty feet wide. The church at Ebbing Spring was of the same shape, but not so large. Every Sunday morning, we are told, it was the habit of Cummings to dress himself neatly, then put on his bullet pouch, mount his horse and, with his rifle in his hand, ride off to one of his churches. Each man in the congregation also brought a rifle to the church and usually held it in his hands during the time of public worship. This was done to guard against any sudden attack that the Indians might make against them. When Cummings went into the pulpit, he was in the habit of setting his rifle in a corner near him. Then he took off his bullet pouch and began the religious service.

Cummings was about five feet ten inches in height, and his figure was well formed. His manner was marked by great firmness and dignity. His articulation was clear and distinct and his voice was so strong that without apparent effort, it was said, "he could speak to be heard by ten thousand people." The mind of Cummings was strong; he had a clear understanding of the system of religion in which he believed, and he set it before the people with solemn earnestness. He insisted, also, that this same solemnity must be shown by all who listened to him. "He could not tolerate any movement among the congregation after preaching commenced. He uniformily spoke like one having authority, and laid down the law and the gospel with great distinctness as he understood them."

Like the other ministers of that time, Mr. Cummings began the service early in the day, and preached two sermons, one in the morning and another in the afternoon to the same congregation. Twice a year the sacramental table was placed before the people in the grove of trees near the church. At Sinking Spring he preached, we are told, "to one of the largest, most respectable and most intelligent congregations ever assembled in western Virginia. His congregation at Ebbing Spring was equally respectable and intelligent, but not so large."

A large plantation called the Royal Oak, on the Holston River, was the home of that branch of the Campbell family of which Colonel Arthur Campbell was a member. General William Campbell, a cousin of Arthur, lived in the same county. The members of both of these households attended the churches of Charles Cummings. On a little hill south of Abingdon, "and on the spot where David Campbell's gate stands," a fort was built to protect the settlers against Indians. To that fort Cummings always took his family in times of danger. In July, 1776, Cummings left his family in the fort, and with three of his neighbors and a servant, started in a wagon toward his farm. Not far from the church a body of Indians attacked them. The driver of the wagon was killed at the first fire and, a little later, the two other neighbors were wounded. Cummings and his servant, whose name was Job, both of them armed with good rifles, kept up the fight and drove the Indians away. Friends ran out from the fort and helped to bring in the men who had been shot down. In October, 1776, Cummings went with Colonel William Christian's expedition against the Cherokee Indians in the Tennessee country. Joseph Rhea, another preacher, also marched with the soldiers. Cummings and Rhea preached to the men at every camping-place along the way, with their rifles always near at hand. This was the first regular preaching of the gospel within the present State of Tennessee.

The first minister who made his home in Tennessee, however, was Samuel Doak. He was born of Scotch-Irish parentage in the year 1749, within the limits of the New Providence congregation, in what is now Rockbridge County, Virginia. At the age of sixteen he became a Christian. His early training was received at the academy which was maintained by John Brown, pastor of New Providence. In 1773, Doak entered Princeton College and remained two years. Then he became an assistant in Hampden-Sidney College, in Prince Edward County, Virginia, and at the same time studied theology under the direction of John Blair Smith, president of the college. In October, 1777, he was licensed to preach by Hanover Presbytery, and soon afterwards established himself as a minister in the Holston settlement in Tennessee, where he founded New Bethel, known as the Fork Church. At a later time he removed to the Little Limestone, in Washington County, Tennessee, where he built a church and a school house on his own land and organized Salem congregation. Doak's school was afterwards known as Washington College. In 1818 he removed to Bethel congregation, in Greene County, and there founded Tusculum College.

We shall learn later how Cummings and Doak took part in the defence of their country, and how they labored to establish freedom in religion, as well as freedom in civil government.

CHAPTER XVII

THE HANOVER PRESBYTERY LEADS THE FIGHT IN BEHALF
OF FREEDOM IN RELIGION

THE right to worship when and where and in what
manner they pleased—this was the freedom claimed by
the members of the Hanover Presbytery at the time of
its organization in 1755. This claim was granted in
part, as we have seen, for the reason that the Presbyterians fought so well against the French and Indians
on the frontier. Another reason why the claim was
more and more allowed was that the Presbyterians won
friends for their cause among the members of the Episcopal Church. A great leader among these friends was
Patrick Henry.

Henry grew up as a lad in Hanover County, Virginia,
near the home of Samuel Davies. Henry's mother was
a member of Samuel Davies's church and attended the
preaching of that fervent speaker. The boy, Patrick,
went with her during the period from his eleventh to
his twenty-second year, and sat in the church to drink
in the teaching and the eloquence of Davies, Todd, Waddell and other members of the presbytery. In later years
Patrick Henry often said that Davies and Waddell
were the greatest orators that he had ever heard. When
Henry grew up he became a lawyer. In his first great
speech in a law court he made himself famous by uttering opinions which, no doubt, he learned directly from
Davies, Waddell and Todd. This speech was made in
1763 in the case known as the Parsons' Cause.

Since the year 1696 there had been a law in Virginia which required that the clergymen of the Established, or Episcopal Church, should receive their salaries in tobacco. Sixteen thousand pounds was the amount of tobacco to be paid each year to each cleryman. When tobacco became scarce this law was repealed, and the Virginia Assembly, in 1758, passed another law, called the Twopenny Act, allowing the people to pay their clergymen at the low rate of two pence for each pound of tobacco promised in the way of salary. The King of England vetoed this act. In many of the counties of Virginia, however, the people gave no heed to the veto, but paid the salaries in money at the reduced rate.

John Camm, Episcopal minister at Williamsburg, wrote a paper in which he said that the new law made by the assembly was unjust. Colonel Richard Bland and Colonel Landon Carter, members of the Episcopal Church, wrote a severe reply to Camm in which they asserted that the Virginia lawmakers were right. Camm wrote again in reply, and this second paper he called "The Colonels Dismounted." The Colonels replied to this, and asserted that they had not been overthrown in the debate. The sympathies of many of the members of the Episcopal Church were enlisted with Bland and Carter against the claims made by Camm. The chief reason for this was the unworthy character of many of the Episcopal ministers, who had come from England to live in the colony of Virginia. With reference to the Episcopal clergy of that time, William Meade, late Bishop of Virginia, has told us that they were men "who could not find promotion and employment at home," that is, in England. As shepherds of the churches in Virginia, Bishop Meade says that they were "insufficient as to numbers and worse as to character."

These facts about the Episcopal ministry were well known, of course, to Samuel Davies. In his letter to the Bishop of London, however, Davies said: "In all the sermons I have preached in Virginia, I have not wasted one minute in exclaiming or reasoning against the peculiarities of the Established [Episcopal] Church, nor so much as assigned the reasons of my own nonconformity. I have not exhausted my zeal in railing against the established clergy, in exposing their imperfections, some of which lie naked to my view; or in depreciating their characters." "The plain truth is," said Davies, further, "a general reformation *must* be promoted in this colony by some means or other, or multitudes are eternally undone; and I see alas! but little ground to hope for it from the generality of the clergy here." To these clergymen themselves Davies once wrote that he had "no ambition to Presbyterianize the colony." He declared that he had only a sincere desire to spread "the catholic religion of Jesus in its life and power," and that he felt "little anxiety about the denomination its genuine members assume." Purity in religion, we thus already see, was that which Davies attempted to uphold in Virginia. This same purity was the starting-point in Patrick Henry's great speech in the court house of Hanover County in 1763.

After the debate between John Camm and the two Colonels, Bland and Carter, an Episcopal minister, whose name was James Maury, brought suit in the County Court of Hanover for the full amount of his salary in tobacco. The old law was in Maury's favor. Since the King had vetoed the new law of 1758, the county magistrates decided that the people of Maury's parish must pay him in accordance with the old law. But how much must they give him as "back pay"? A jury was called to settle this amount. At this point Patrick Henry entered the case to speak for the people of the parish against the clergyman. The words spoken by Henry on that occasion with reference to the Episcopal clergymen then living in Virginia were very severe. He charged them with selfishness, and said that they had greater concern about their salaries than about the souls of the people. Then he spoke of the King of England, who had sent such ministers into the colony, and had vetoed the law about salaries passed by the Virginia Assembly. The King had no right, said Henry, to veto a law made by the Virginia lawmakers for the good of the people. The King's veto of this law showed that the King himself was a tyrant, he declared, and that he had lost all right to the obedience of the people. The jury was in sympathy with Henry's view and gave Mr. Maury only one penny in the way of additional pay: The King's veto was defied. The people were ready to uphold Henry's claim, that the Virginia Legislature had the right to make laws for the colony. Three or four members of the jury that sat in the Parsons' Cause were members of the congregation of Samuel Davies. All of the jurymen lived in Hanover, whose people had learned from Samuel Davies first and now were learning from Patrick Henry the fundamental principles of religious and civil liberty.

In May, 1765, Patrick Henry introduced his famous resolutions in the Virginia Assembly concerning the Stamp Act. These resolutions declared that the Virginia Legislature had the exclusive right to lay taxes upon the Virginians, and that they would not submit to a tax-law passed by the British Parliament. This was the principle upon which the entire American Revolution was based. Henry made an impassioned speech about the tyranny of the British King and Parliament, and then his resolutions were passed by a vote of twenty-one to twenty, and thus the Revolution began, although the fighting did not commence until ten years later. Nearly all of the twenty-one members who voted with Patrick Henry on that memorable day were delegates from the upper counties of Virginia. So said Thomas Jefferson, who was present when the vote was taken. The upper counties of Virginia, located in the Piedmont and the Valley, were then occupied by the congregations of the Hanover Presbytery. The people of these sections formed at that time the majority of the population of the colony. Members and officers of the Presbyterian Church, for the most part, thus formed that party that stood with Henry in 1765 in favor of complete freedom in civil government.

It was after this time that the Baptists took part in the battle. Although they had entered Virginia about 1714, the increase in their numbers was slow. From 1764 onwards there were many of them in the region now known as Guilford County, North Carolina; a few were also in South Carolina and in the northern parts of Virginia. Their ministers travelled from place to place preaching the gospel, but they did not secure licenses from the county courts. For this reason some of them were arrested and put into prison under the charge that they were disturbers of the peace. In 1768 Patrick Henry used his great powers as a lawyer to gain freedom for three Baptist ministers, who had been thrust into prison in Spottsylvania County, Virginia. Then the Baptists began to discuss in their conventions the right of ministers to preach 'wherever the people were willing to listen to them.

In 1772 a bill was presented to the legislature, proposing to grant certain privileges to those Christians who were outside of the Episcopal Church. But these outsiders, or dissenters, as they were called, were not pleased with the proposed law. The Presbytery of Hanover met at the Rockfish meeting-house in Nelson County, Virginia, October 15, 1773, and appointed John Todd, a minister, and John Morton, a ruling elder, as commissioners to attend the next session of the legislature for the purpose of guarding the interests of Presbyterians in connection with the measure concerning worship. On November 11, 1774, the presbytery met at the house of Colonel William Cabell, of Amherst, to draw up a remonstrance against certain parts of the bill then before the legislature. The paper began as follows: "The petition of the Presbytery of Hanover in behalf of themselves and all the Presbyterians in Virginia, in particular, and all Protestant dissenters, in general." The Presbytery called attention, first of all, to the fact that Governor Gooch in 1738 had given in writing "the most ample assurances" that Presbyterians "should enjoy the full and free exercise of their religion and all the other privileges of good subjects." Resting upon this agreement "several thousand families of Presbyterians" had made homes in the frontier parts of the colony of Virginia, and had there formed a barrier against Indian attacks. In view of these facts, the Presbyterians asked to be treated "upon an equal footing" with their fellow citizens of Virginia. They were ready, ran the memorial of the presbytery, to have all their places of worship entered upon a registry book, but at the same time they wished permission for their ministers to preach wherever they found it convenient to do so. "The number of Presbyterians in this province is now very great," they said, "and the number of clergymen but small; therefore, we are obliged frequently to itinerate and preach through various parts of the colony that our people may have an opportunity to worship God and receive the sacraments in the way agreeable to their own consciences."

The bill before the legislature proposed that negro slaves should not be admitted into a dissenting church without the consent of their masters. With reference to this matter the presbytery made the following declaration: "And as to baptizing or receiving servants into our communion, we have always anxiously desired to do it with the permission of their masters; but when a servant appears to be a true penitent or makes profession of his faith in Christ, upon his desire it is our indispensable duty to admit him into our church, and if he has never been baptized, we are to baptize him according to the command of Christ."

"We are petitioning in favor of a church that is neither contemptible nor obscure," said the presbytery. "It prevails in every province to the northward of Maryland, and its advocates in all the more southern provinces are numerous and respectable; the greatest monarch in the north of Europe adorns it [Frederick the Great of Prussia]; it is the established religion of the populous and wealthy states of Holland; it prevails in the wise and happy cantons of Switzerland; and it is the possession of Geneva, a state among the foremost of those which, at the Reformation, emancipated themselves from the slavery of Rome; and some of the first geniuses and writers in every branch of literature were sons of our Church." Thus spake the presbytery with reference to the body of Scotch-Irish Presbyterians, some 600,000 in number, at that time established in the American colonies.

The petition was signed by David Rice as moderator and by Caleb Wallace as clerk of the presbytery. The paper itself was drawn up, most probably, by Wallace. And who was this Caleb Wallace, the writer of this strong public appeal in behalf of religious freedom? Caleb's grandfather, Peter Wallace, was a Scot, a member of the Woods colony established at the western edge of Albemarle County in 1734. Peter's son, Samuel Wallace, went to Charlotte County and became a member of the Caldwell settlement on Cub Creek. In that region Caleb Wallace was born about 1742. He was educated at Princeton and was ordained as shepherd of the flock at Cub Creek in October, 1774, about one month before he wrote the presbytery's petition in behalf of liberty.

In response to this and other appeals made by the Presbyterians and other dissenters, the Virginia Convention declared, on May 15, 1776, that they had been driven to make choice between "abject submission to those overbearing tyrants or a total separation from the crown and government of Great Britain." The convention, therefore, chose separation, and instructed the Virginia delegates in the Continental Congress to propose to that body "to declare these united colonies free and independent states." On June 12, 1776, the convention adopted a Bill of Rights. Then, on June 29, the convention agreed upon a Constitution, elected Patrick Henry as governor, and organized Virginia as an independent, self-governing state. The sixteenth clause of the Bill of Rights ran as follows:—

16. "That religion, or the duty we owe our Creator, and the manner of discharging it, can be directed only by reason and conviction, not by force or violence, and, therefore, all men are equally entitled to the free exercise of religion, according to the dictates of conscience, and that it is the mutual duty of all to practice Christian forbearance, love, and charity toward each other."

Another champion of liberty appeared upon the scene when this clause of the Bill of Rights was under discussion. This champion was James Madison, son of a Virginia planter, a recent graduate of Princeton, where he had imbibed the lofty principles taught by John Witherspoon. The original draft of this sixteenth clause, proposed by Patrick Henry, contained the word "toleration" as indicating the extent of privilege belonging to all men in the matter of religion. Madison, however, a more radical exponent of Presbyterian theories than Henry, although he was not a member of the Presbyterian Church, persuaded the convention to omit the word "toleration," and in its place to substitute the expression, "free exercise of religion according to the dictates of conscience."

Religious freedom, in theory, at least, was thus already won in Virginia in 1776. To the Presbyterians more than to any other body of people this victory was due. For they formed not only the majority in the colony, but they were also foremost in advocating freedom. In fact, however, the Episcopal Church was still in the enjoyment of many advantages and privileges that were withheld from the dissenters. The latter, however, did not pause in their fight. As we shall see in a later chapter, the Presbyterians and the Baptists continued the struggle until complete religious freedom as an actual fact was established in the commonwealth.

CHAPTER XVIII.

ONE morning, early in the month of September, 1774, a tall, strong man stood in the gateway of an old log fort in the mountains of western Virginia. He was more than six feet in height, had uncommon strength and his form was finely moulded. "He had a stern and invincible countenance, and was of a reserved and distant deportment which rendered his presence more awful than engaging." His fringed hunting shirt and his leggings were made of dressed deerskin. His feet were covered with moccasins of the same material. Upon his head rested a bearskin cap. A powder-horn was slung about his neck by a long cord. The rifle upon which he leaned for the moment, had a long black barrel and a heavy black stock, and was of the flintlock pattern. The man thus dressed, ready for battle, was Andrew Lewis, a brigadier general in command of Virginia riflemen. The colonial governor of New York, who had met Lewis not long before the time of which we speak, said of him that "the earth seemed to tremble under him as he walked along."

Andrew Lewis was one of the sons of John Lewis, who came from the north of Ireland to Virginia in 1732. The other sons of John were Thomas, William and Charles. John Lewis made his home near the present city of Staunton, in Augusta County, and was a member of John Craig's Church at Tinkling Spring.

Andrew Lewis was a soldier from his early years. He held the title of major during the French and Indian War and served with George Washington. He established himself on a plantation near the present town of Salem, now in Roanoke, but then located in Botetourt County.

The log fort in whose gate Andrew Lewis was standing on that September morning, in 1774, was then called Fort Union. It was built in the beautiful, little mountain valley upon the spot where the town of Lewisburg is now located. General Lewis was casting a keen glance through the camp of the army of riflemen who had met him at Fort Union for the purpose of marching to meet the Indians of the Ohio Valley. He looked first, no doubt, for the regiment from Augusta County led by his brother, Colonel Charles Lewis. There they were in eight companies, each man armed with a rifle and dressed like the general in command. Every man in a certain company was said to be six feet in height. Most of these Augusta men were from the congregations of John Craig and John Brown. The Botetourt regiment of seven companies was led by Colonel William Fleming. Colonel John Field led the men from Culpeper County, many of whom were to call themselves afterward the "Culpeper minute men." Captain Thomas Buford brought the men of Bedford County, and Captain Evan Shelby brought a company from the Holston River, among whom were Evan's son Isaac, and William Campbell. The news came, also, that Colonel William Christian, founder of the towns of Fincastle, in Botetourt, and Christianburg, in the present Montgomery County, was on the march with the men of Southwest Virginia. Most of these stalwart riflemen in Andrew Lewis's army were members of the congregations of the Hanover Presbytery. They formed a kind of church militant as they set out westward through the wilderness on the 11th of September, 1774. Matthew Arbuckle and John Stuart, of Greenbrier County, were in the army to lead the way to Point Pleasant, on the banks of the Ohio River, just at the place where the Kanawha pours its waters into that stream.

Early on the morning of October 10, 1774, the army under Lewis, which numbered about eleven hundred men, was attacked by a force of about eleven hundred Indians led by the chiefs Cornstalk and Logan. When the redmen came near the camp of the Virginians, General Lewis quietly lit his tobacco pipe and told his brother, Colonel Charles Lewis, and Colonel Fleming to lead their men into the battle. The fight raged all day long. It was the hardest struggle that the white settlers had with the Indians during the whole colonial period. Colonel Field and Colonel Charles Lewis and six of the captains were slain. Colonel Fleming was desperately wounded. About one-fifth of Andrew Lewis' army was disabled, but the stern face of the leader kept his men in line, and they won the fight. When Colonel Christian arrived with his forces at midnight he found that the savages had fled across the Ohio. The victory of the Presbyterian riflemen at Point Pleasant opened the Ohio River as a highway of travel into Kentucky and Tennessee. This made possible the rapid settlement of those commonwealths and the settlement of the region north of the Ohio River.

CHAPTER XIX.

THE MOUNTAIN MEN OF VIRGINIA AND NORTH CAROLINA LEAD THE WAY TO INDEPENDENCE.

DURING the month of September, 1774, the first Continental Congress, made up of delegates from the American colonies, met in Philadelphia. The reason why these delegates came together was that earlier in the same year the British Parliament had passed some laws that were considered to be oppressive by the people of the colonies. One of these laws was the Quebec Act, adding all of the country north of the Ohio River to the province of Quebec, in which Roman Catholicism was the recognized religion. These new British laws of 1774 only made more intense the indignation of the colonists concerning the tax-laws previously passed by the British Parliament. The Continental Congress adopted a Declaration of Rights, sent petitions to the British rulers and British people, and urged the colonists not to buy goods from British merchants. Then the members of the Congress rode away from Philadelphia and went back home.

The people of the colonies were now getting themselves ready for action. In nearly every county a committee of citizens was organized, which began to hold meetings to talk about the situation.

On the 20th of January, 1775, the committee of Fincastle County, Virginia, adopted a paper that sent the blood in a swifter current through the veins of all that read it. Fincastle County at that time embraced the whole of Southwest Virginia. The committee which met near the present Abingdon was made up almost entirely of men who were members of the two congrega-

116

tions of Charles Cummings, as follows: Colonel William Christian, Chairman; Rev. Charles Cummings, Colonel William Preston, Captain Stephen Trigg, Major Arthur Campbell, Major William Ingliss, Captain Walter Crockett, John Montgomery, James McGavock, William Campbell, Thomas Madison, Daniel Smith, William Russell, Evan Shelby and William Edmundson. To the second Continental Congress which was soon to meet, this committee sent an address which contained the following:

" * * * We by no means desire to shake off our duty or allegiance to our lawful sovereign, but on the contrary, shall ever glory in being the loyal subjects of a Protestant prince descended from such illustrious progenitors, so long as we can enjoy the free exercise of our religion as Protestants and our liberties and properties as British subjcts.

"But if no pacific measures shall be proposed or adopted by Great Britain, and our enemies will attempt to dragoon us out of those inestimable privileges which we are entitled to as subjects, and to reduce us to slavery, we declare that we are deliberately and resolutely determined never to surrender them to any power upon earth but at the expense of our lives."

These words of defiance were written, probably, by Charles Cummings himself, and were adopted by the men to whom he spoke from the pulpit every Sunday.

On the 22d of February, 1775, the people of Augusta County held a mass-meeting in Staunton and selected Thomas Lewis, brother of General Andrew Lewis, and Captain Samuel McDowell to represent them in the Virginia Convention to be held at Richmond the following month (March 20, 1775). To these delegates the people gave written instructions containing the following words: " * * * Many of us and our forefathers left our native land, and explored this once savage wilderness to enjoy the free exercise of the rights

of conscience and of human nature. Those rights we
are fully resolved with our lives and fortunes inviolably
to preserve; nor will we surrender such inestimable
blessings, the purchase of toil and danger, to any ministry, to any Parliament, or to any body of men upon
earth by whom we are not represented and in whose decision, therefore, we have no voice."

About the same time, also, the people of Botetourt
County, in Southwest Virginia, adopted the following
sentiments:

" * * * We are too sensible to the inestimable
privileges enjoyed by subjects under the British
Constitution even to wish for a change while the free
enjoyments of those blessings can be secured to us.
* * * But, should a wicked and tyrannical ministry,
under the sanction of a venal and corrupt Parliament,
persist in acts of injustice and violence towards us,
they only must be answerable for the consequences.
Liberty is so strongly impressed on our hearts that
we cannot think of parting with it, but with our lives.
Our duty to God, our country, ourselves and our posterity, all forbid it. We, therefore, stand prepared for
every contingency."

On March 20, 1775, the second Virginia Convention met in St. John's Church, Richmond. The leading figure in that body was Patrick Henry, who was
supported in his views by a majority of the members.
That majority was furnished by the Piedmont and Valley counties of the colony, whose delegates were nearly
all adherents of the Presbyterian faith. The instructions
given by the people of Augusta County to Thomas
Lewis and Samuel McDowell represented the political
opinions of the majority of the delegates. After the convention met, Patrick Henry presented a resolution,
"That this colony be immediately put into a state of defence," and that an army should be at once embodied,
armed and drilled for that purpose.

Many of the counties in the American colonies had armed their militia, but none of the colonies had as yet organized an army for defence. This was the meaning of Henry's resolution, which he supported by an outburst of wonderful eloquence: "Our petitions have been slighted," said Henry; "our remonstrances have produced additional violence and insult; our supplications have been disregarded; and we have been spurned, with contempt, from the foot of the throne. In vain, after these things, may we indulge the fond hope of peace and reconciliation. *There is no longer any room for hope.* If we wish to be free,—if we mean to preserve inviolate those inestimable privileges for which we have been so long contending,—if we mean not basely to abandon the noble struggle in which we have been so long engaged, and which we have pledged ourselves never to abandon until the glorious object of our contest shall be obtained,—we must fight! I repeat it, sir, we must fight! An appeal to arms and to the God of Hosts is all that is left us."

"Sir, we are not weak," he continued, "if we make a proper use of those means which the God of nature hath placed in our power. Three millions of people, armed in the holy cause of liberty and in such a country as that which we possess, are invincible by any force which our enemy can send against us. Besides, sir, we shall not fight our battles alone. There is a just God who presides over the destinies of nations, and who will raise up friends to fight our battles for us. * * * The war is inevitable, and let it come! I repeat it, sir, let it come! It is in vain, sir, to extenuate the matter. Gentlemen may cry peace, peace, but there is no peace. The war is actually begun. The next gale that sweeps from the north will bring to our ears the clash of resounding arms. Our brethren are already in the field. Why stand we here idle? What is it that gentlemen wish?

What would they have? Is life so dear, or peace so sweet, as to be purchased at the price of chains and slavery? Forbid it, Almighty God! I know not what course others may take; but as for me, give me liberty or give me death!"

The Convention adopted Henry's proposal and the army was organized. On May 2, 1775, Patrick Henry led a large body of Virginia volunteers from Hanover County toward the colonial capital, Williamsburg. Supported by this same armed force, Henry compelled the royal governor, Lord Dunmore, to make full payment for a quantity of powder belonging to Virginia which the governor had removed from the public store house.

In May, 1775, the committee representing the people of Mecklenburg County, North Carolina, held a meeting at Charlotte and practically declared their independence of Great Britian by adopting the following resolves:

"I. That all commissions, civil and military, heretofore granted by the crown to be exercised in these colonies, are null and void, and the constitution of each particular colony wholly suspended. II. That the Provincial Congress of each Province, under the direction of the great Continental Congress, is invested with all legislative and executive powers within their respective provinces, and that no other legislative or executive power does or can exist at this time in any of these colonies." The committee then announced that the people of the county of Mecklenburg should organize themselves into military companies and appoint their own officers "independent of the crown of Great Britain." Further than this, the people were to appoint a body of eighteen "select men," to be known as the "Convention" of the county. This Convention was to manage all affairs of government in the county in place of the King's officers "until instructions from the Provincial Congress regulating the jurisprudence of the province shall provide otherwise, or the legislative body of Great Britain resign its unjust and arbitrary pretensions with respect to America."

The members of the Mecklenburg committee belonged to the seven congregations of Mecklenburg County. The chairman of the committee, Abraham Alexander, was an elder of the Sugar Creek Church. John McKnitt Alexander, secretary of the committee, and Hezekiah Alexander were elders of Hopewell. Hezekiah J. Balch, member of the committee, was pastor of Poplar Tent; David Reese, another committeeman was an elder from Poplar Tent. Adam Alexander and Robert Queary were elders from Rocky River and Robert Irwin was an elder from Steele Creek. Most probably some of the other committeemen were also elders.*

*Note.—The names of the members of the Mecklenburg committee were the following:

Abraham Alexander, Chairman.
John McKnitt Alexander, Secretary.

Ephraim Brevard.	Charles Alexander.
Rev. Hezekiah J. Balch.	Zaccheus Wilson, Jun.
John Phifer.	Weightstill Avery.
James Harris.	Benjamin Patton.
William Kennon.	Matthew McClure.
John Ford.	Neill Morrison.
Richard Barry.	Robert Irwin.
Henry Downe.	John Flenniken.
Ezra Alexander.	David Reese.
William Graham.	John Davidson.
John Queary.	Richard Harris, Jun.
Adam Alexander.	Thomas Polk.
Hezekiah Alexander.	

Several years afterwards some of the members of this committee made statements from memory to the following effect: That on the morning of the 20th of May, 1775, the Mecklenburg committee adopted a paper written by Ephraim Brevard. This paper, which was read to the people of the county assembled in front of the courthouse at Charlotte, contained the statement that the citizens of Mecklenburg thereby declared themselves to be "a free and independent people." In the year 1800 Brevard's original paper was burned in the house of John McKnitt Alexander. Copies of it had been made, however, and these copies were declared to be true and exact by surviving members of the committee.

The rest of the counties of North Carolina were in sympathy with Mecklenburg. The result was, that, early in August, 1775, the royal governor, Martin, fled to a British warship in the Cape Fear River and British government came to an end forever in North Carolina. The convention of the people met at once and took charge of the government.

Most of the Highlanders on the upper Cape Fear River had been living only a few years in America. They did not understand the quarrel between the colonies and Great Britain, and determined, therefore, to fight for the king. In February, 1776, Donald McDonald led about one thousand five hundred Highlanders from Cross Creek (Fayetteville) down the Cape Fear toward Wilmington to join the British army and fleet. Colonel Richard Caswell and Colonel Alexander Lillington led a force from the lower Cape Fear, from the Newbern district and from Wake and Duplin counties, and defeated McDonald's army at Moore's Creek Bridge. Ten thousand men in North Carolina then seized their rifles and stood ready to fight. The British army was afraid to go ashore from the warships. They, therefore sailed farther south and on June 28, 1776, both the British fleet and army were defeated by Colonel William Moultrie and William Thomson in front of Charles Town, South Carolina.

In April, 1776, the people of North Carolina met in Convention for the fourth time. The place of meeting was Halifax. The Convention sent a message to the North Carolina delegates in the Congress at Philadelphia giving them authority "to concur with the delegates from the other colonies in declaring independence." This was the first voice heard from a whole colony in favor of complete American freedom.

Early in May, 1776, the people of Virginia met in Convention at Williamsburg. On the 10th of May, Thomas Lewis and Samuel McDowell, delegates from

Augusta County, offered to the Convention a memorial, or petition, sent by the committee of the county of Augusta. This memorial set forth "the present unhappy situation of the country," and "the necessity of making the confederacy of the united colonies the most perfect, independent and lasting, and of framing an equal, free and liberal government that may bear the test of all future ages."

The complete independence of all the colonies, thus so clearly suggested by the people of Augusta, was adopted as the view of the Convention of Virginia. On the 15th of May, five days after the reading of the Augusta memorial, the Convention sent instructions to the Virginia delegates in the Continental Congress, commanding them to propose that the Congress declare the colonies to be free and independent States. The Virginia delegates followed these instructions and on the 4th of July, 1776, Thomas Jefferson's great paper, the Declaration of Independence, was adopted at Philadelphia by the votes of twelve of the States. The movement in behalf of independence originated among the body of 600,000 Scots who occupied the frontiers of the colonies. The leaders in the movement, as we have seen, were the Scotch-Irish of Virginia and North Carolina.

CHAPTER XX

As early as October, 1771, The Hanover Presbytery expressed its sense of "the great expediency of erecting a seminary of learning somewhere within the bounds of this presbytery." In October, 1774, the presbytery resumed "the consideration of a school *for the liberal education of youth,* judged to be of great and immediate importance. We do, therefore, agree to establish and patronize a publick school, which shall be confined to the County of Augusta. At present it shall be managed by Mr. William Graham, a gentleman properly recommended to this Presbytery—and under the inspection of the Rev. Mr. John Brown." William Graham was recommended to the presbytery by the Rev. Samuel Stanhope Smith, of Princeton College. In this manner, the presbytery assumed control of the school which had been hitherto organized as a church school under the control of Rev. John Brown.

At the same meeting, the presbytery appointed the Rev. John Brown, the Rev. David Rice, the Rev. Samuel Cummings, the Rev. William Irwin and the Rev. Caleb Wallace to take subscriptions for the school in the congregations of Providence, North Mountain, Pastures, Botetourt, Fincastle, Tinkling Spring, Stone Church, Brown's Settlement and Fork of James River.

At the same meeting, also, the presbytery recommended it to the congregations of Cumberland, Prince Edward and Briery to take subscriptions for the erection of *a public school for the liberal education of youth*, in the region south of the Blue Ridge. On February 2, 1775, the presbytery decided to establish this school in Prince Edward County. The presbytery appointed trustees for the Prince Edward Academy and chose Samuel Stanhope Smith as rector. With reference to this academy the presbytery, in February, 1775, declared that "every necessary branch of human literature will be taught to good advantage, *on the most catholic plan*, and whereas, some gentlemen who are unacquainted with our sentiments, may encourage this seminary with reluctance because it is to be under the guardianship of this presbytery, we take this opportunity to assure the publick, that *though the strictest regard shall be paid to the morals of the youth, and worship carried on, evening and morning, in the Presbyterian way;* yet on the other hand, all possible care shall be taken that no undue influence be used by any member of this presbytery, the rector, or any assistant, to bias the judgment of any; but that all, of *every denomination, shall fully enjoy his own religious sentiments.*"

Two months later, April 12th, 1775, the presbytery met in the Timber Ridge Church, and made the following statement with reference to Augusta Academy: "The presbytery as guardians and directors, take this opportunity to declare their resolution to do their best endeavor to establish it [Augusta Academy] *on the most catholic plan* that circumstances will permit."

"The most catholic plan" of administration, thus announced, is evidently the same that was set forth by the presbytery two months before with reference to Prince Edward Academy, that "the strictest regard shall be paid to the morals of the youth, and worship carried on, evening and morning, in the Presbyterian way," and, yet, at the same time each member of *any other denomination "shall fully enjoy his own religious sentiments."*

With reference to this declaration of the presbytery, Dr. Henry Ruffner, in his history of Washington College, makes the following statement: "As no seminary above the rank of common school had yet been established in the Valley, the presbytery saw fit on this occasion to declare that they meant not to confine the ben· efits of the Academy to their own denomination of Christianity, but to manage it on such liberal principles that all the country might enjoy the benefits of the institution. They meant, no doubt, as in duty they were bound, to give a religious and moral education to the pupils of this academy; but *not to manage it with the sectarian view of making Presbyterians of all who might resort to it.*" (Historical Papers—I., p. 14.)

At this same meeting, April, 1775, "Presbytery finding that they cannot, of themselves, forward subscriptions in a particular manner, do, for the encouragement of the Academy to be established in Augusta, recommend it to the following gentlemen to take in subscriptions in their behalf, viz., the Rev. Mr. Cummings, Col. Wm. Preston, Col. Wm. Christian [Fincastle], Col. Lewis, Col. Fleming and Mr. Stockheart [Botetourt], Capt. John Bowyer, Capt. Wm. McKee, Capt. Adlai Paul, Capt John Maxwell and Mr. James Trimble [Fork of James River], Mr. Saml. Lyle and Capt. Samuel McDowell [Timber Ridge], Rev. John Brown, James Wilson and Charles Campbell [Providence], Wm. McPheeters, Wm. Ledgerwood, and John Trimble [North Mountain and Brown's Settlement], Moses Stewart and Walter Davis [Tinkling Spring], Sampson Mathews [Staunton], Capt. George Mathews, Capt. George Moffitt and James Allen [Augusta Church]. These men were Presbyterians and were appointed to take subscriptions within the bounds of Presbyterian congregations for the support of Augusta Academy.

It is further recorded concerning the Presbytery at Timber Ridge, April, 1775, that the Presbytery went in a body to pay an official visit to William Graham's Academy at Mt. Pleasant near Fairfield and "attended a specimen of the proficiency of the students, in the Latin and Greek languages, and pronouncing orations, with which they were well pleased."

William Graham was a man of twenty-eight years when he began to teach Greek and Latin at Mount Pleasant on the ridge near Fairfield in the present Rockbridge County, Virginia. He was slightly above medium height, his eyes were dark and he had a slender, delicate frame. Graham was born in Pennsylvania of Scotch-Irish parentage and until he reached the age of twenty-two, worked on his father's farm. He then went to the home of his pastor and gave all of his time to the study of books; for just a year before, at the age of twenty-one years, he had given his heart to Christ. Five years were spent by Graham at Princeton under the guardianship and instruction of the great John Witherspoon, then president of the College. Henry Lee, of Virginia, afterwards known as "Light-Horse Harry" Lee, and father of General Robert E. Lee, was one of Graham's fellow-students at Princeton. The latter completed the course of study there in 1773 and for a year afterwards gave himself to the study of theology. Then he answered the call of Hanover Presbytery, and began his work as teacher in the fall of 1774. At its October meeting, in 1775, the presbytery gave him license to enter the pulpit.

At the close of Graham's first year as teacher in the academy, that is, in the spring of 1775, as we have just seen, the presbytery held one of its daily sessions in the school house and there listened to recitations, by Graham's students, in the Latin and Greek languages. They also heard orations delivered by some of the students.

The method of teaching pursued by Graham has been described for us by Dr. Samuel Campbell who, after Graham's death, was principal of the same school. "I happened at Mount Pleasant during Mr. Graham's superintendence," says Dr. Campbell. "It was near the hour of recitation. Here was seen a large assemblage of fine, cheerful, vigorous looking youth, apparently from ten to twenty years of age. They were mostly engaged in feats of strength, speed, or agility; each emulous to surpass his fellows in those exercises, for which youth of their age generally possess a strong predilection. Presently the sound of a horn summoned all to the business of the afternoon. The sports were dropped as by magic. Now you may see them seated singly or in pairs, or in small groups, with book in hand, conning over their afternoon's lesson. One portion resorted immediately to the hall, and ranging themselves before the preceptor in semi-circular order, handed him a book containing their recitations. He seemed not to look into the book and presently closed it; thinking, I supposed, he knew as well as the book.

"Of the recitation I understood not a syllable, yet it was highly agreeable to the ear, sonorous and musical; and, although more than sixty winters have rolled away since that time, the impressions then made have not been entirely effaced from my memory. I have since discovered that the recitation was a portion of that beautiful Greek verb, *tuptō,* in which the sound of the consonants, pi, tau, mu, theta, predominate. It was observable that during the recitation the preceptor gave no instructions, corrected no errors, made no remarks of any kind. He seemed to sit merely as a silent witness of the performance. The class itself resembled one of those self regulating machines of which I have heard. Each member stood ready, by trapping and turning down, to correct the mishaps and mistakes of his fellows; and as much emulation was discovered here as had been an hour before on the theatre of their sports in their athletic exercises.

"During this recitation an incipient smile of approbation was more than once observed on the countenance of the preceptor, maugre [in spite of] his native gravity and reserve. This happened when small boys, by their superior scholarship, raised themselves above those who were full grown. This class having gone through, several others, in regular order, presented themselves before the teacher and passed the ordeal. The business of the afternoon was closed by a devotional exercise * * * The systematic order of the place struck my attention. A signal called the whole school together; a signal announced the hour of recitation; each class was summoned by a signal. These signals were obeyed without delay—and without noise. The students might pursue their studies in the hall or the open air, as pleased them best. Talking or reading aloud was not permitted in the hall. The dignity of the preceptor and his well known fitness for the station gave him respectability, and he was respected. * * * "

On May 1, 1776, the presbytery met again at Timber Ridge Church. Two days later (May 3), it went in a body to Mt. Pleasant, and again held its session in the academy building and proceeded to examine Graham's school. Again the presbytery listened to recitations in Greek and Latin, heard some orations delivered and gave formal approval to teacher and students. There is, probably, no other case like this on record, wherein a presbytery emphasized its absolute ownership of the school by formally organizing itself in the schoolroom and for a time assuming complete control of the work and exercises of the students.

Mr. Graham reported that in accordance with the order of the presbytery he had purchased books and apparatus for the use of the Academy to the amount of about 160 pounds and that the gentlemen appointed by the presbytery had collected and paid into his hands about 128 pounds, in Virginia money.

On the 6th of May, 1776, Presbytery decided to remove the Augusta Academy from Mt. Pleasant to Timber Ridge Church for the following reasons:—

(1) Timber Ridge Church is a convenient place;

(2) The Timber Ridge Church has secured as pastor, Rev. William Graham, Rector of the Academy;

(3) Capt Alexander Stewart and Mr. Samuel Houston have each offered to give forty acres of land as a site for the school;

(4) The congregation of Timber Ridge Church offers to erect a building for the Academy.

On the same day, May 6th, Presbytery appointed a board of trustees consisting of twenty-four members, five of them Presbyterian ministers, namely William Graham, John Brown, James Waddell, Charles Cummings and William Irwin, with nineteen elders and laymen from the Presbyterian Church. The presbytery reserved to itself, however, "The right of visitation forever, as often as they shall judge it necessary; and of choosing the Rector and his assistant." John Montgomery, afterwards a Presbyterian minister, was at that time Mr. Graham's assistant.

The executive committee of this board was also named by the presbytery. This committee met on May 13, 1776. It consisted of one minister and five elders of the Presbyterian Church, viz: Rev. William Graham and Alexander Stewart, Samuel Lyle, Charles Campbell, John Houston and William McKee. These men gave to the school, in its new location, the name of Liberty Hall Academy, most probably for the reason that Liberty Hall was the name of the country home of the family of Rev. John Brown in county Limerick, Ireland. (See Report of U. S. Bureau of Education, No. 2: p. 306.) The committee also secured the erection of the school building. As it stood ready for William Graham in 1777, The Liberty Hall Academy possessed 80 acres of land, two houses, a library of 300 volumes and some apparatus, all of the value of about 400 pounds, or nearly two thousand dollars.

"This Academy," says Dr. Henry Ruffner (Hist. Papers I., 25), "owed its foundation, first, to the enlightened policy and pious zeal of the *Presbyterian clergy* of the land; secondly, to the contributions of the Presbyterian people of the Valley; thirdly, to the energy and talents of the rector [Rev. Wm. Graham]; and, lastly, to the attention given to its affairs by a few of the neighboring trustees, and the gratuitous aid in land, labor and materials, given by some members of the Timber Ridge congregation."

In 1777 the region in which Liberty Hall Academy was located was laid off as Rockbridge County. A call for soldiers to fight in the Revolutionary army was sent out by the Virginia legislature. When the people of Rockbridge met together to consider this call, they were addressed by William Graham. He urged the men to offer themselves for the battle, but only a few stepped forward. Then Graham walked out from the crowd and offered himself as a soldier. A large number of men followed him; the company of soldiers was made up at once and William Graham was chosen Captain. In a later chapter of this book we shall see him leading his men to meet Tarleton's British horsemen on the Blue Ridge near Charlottesville.

In 1778 the Trustees appointed by the presbytery in 1776 prepared a petition and sent it to the Virginia legislature, asking for the incorporation of the school. Since the Hanover Presbytery was then engaged in the struggle before the legislature to secure complete separation of church and state affairs, the charter of incorporation was not granted. In 1779, the Liberty Hall Academy was removed to Graham's farm near the town of Lexington, the county seat of Rockbridge. On the 24th of October, 1782, the Presbytery of Hanover appointed eight ministers and seven Presbyterian

laymen and elders as additional trustees to fill vacancies in the board of trustees of Liberty Hall
Academy.   Within less time than one month after
the appointment of these members, the Rector, William
Graham, in the name of the board appointed by the
presbytery sent the following petition to the legislature:—

"To the honourable, the Speaker and gentlemen of the
    House of Delegates, the petition of the Trustees
    of Liberty Hall Academy most humbly showeth,
    "That your petitioners, very sensible of the great
utility arising from the regular education of youth,
have for some time been associated for that purpose;
and finding our efforts attended with good success, are
induced, from the experiment made, to believe that a
seminary may here be conducted to very general advantage.   And we are the rather inclined to be more
fully of this opinion, when we consider the extensive
fertile country around the place, the fine air and pure
water with which it is blessed, contributing so power-
fully to health of body; having also procured one
hundred and twenty acres of land in the neighborhood
of Lexington for the use of the Academy, a valuable
library of well chosen books and a considerable mathe-
mathical and philosophical apparatus.   Under these
advantages and many more that might be named, we
doubt not, should we be so happy as to obtain the approbation and patronage of the honourable house, of
being instruments under the smiles of Heaven, of
conveying down to posterity, the most valuable blessing and the purest pledge of true patriotism we are
capable of.
    "We, therefore, pray the honourable Assembly to
take the matter under consideration and grant us an
act of incorporation with such powers and privileges
as will enable us and our successors more effectually

to carry on the laudable design and give all possible encouragement to a polite and solid education.

"We hope also that a patriot Assembly will see the reasonableness of, and grant an exemption from militia draughts, to the professors and masters of the said seminary and to all students thereto belonging, under the age of twenty-one years. And your petitioners as in duty bound shall pray.

"Signed in behalf of the Trustees.

"Wm. GRAHAM, C. B."

"JAMES LYLE, JR., *Clerk*."

In response to this request, the legislature on December 13, 1782, passed a law forming the trustees appointed by the Hanover Presbytery into a body called a corporation.* This body, in 1782, consisted of twenty members; four of these were minister, William Graham, Caleb Wallace, John Montgomery and William Wilson, and sixteen were elders and members of the churches of the presbytery. Seven members of the incorporated board were members of the board of 1776.

It was not the desire nor the purpose of the Presby-

---

*The Journal of the House for November 23, 1782, contains the following: "Mr. Thornton presented from Committee for Religion

" 'A petition of the trustees of Liberty Hall Academy, in the county of Rockbridge; setting forth that they are possessed of land and other property, and conceive it would be a great advantage to the institution to incorporate the same; and praying that an act may pass to that effect.'

"Referred to Committee."

The Journal for November 27, 1782, quotes: "Charles Carter reported from Com.

"That it is the opinion of this Com. that the petition of the trustees of Liberty Hall Academy, praying an act of incorporation to enable them and their successors more effectually to encourage and promote literature, and that the professors, masters and students thereof, under the age of twenty-one years, may be exempted from military drafts, is reasonable."

Journal for December 13, 1782: "Engrossed bill 'for incorporating the rector and trustees of Liberty Hall Academy' was read third time;" then the motion to pass prevailed.

tery in permitting its trustees to secure incorporation, to surrender control of the Academy. The incorporation of the presbytery's trustees was the only way then open under the laws of Virginia whereby the presbytery could own or manage its property. A few months later (May, 1784) in a memorial address to the legislature of Virginia, the presbytery used these words:—"The Episcopal Church is actually incorporated and known in law as a body, so that it can receive and possess property for ecclesiastical purposes without trouble or risk in securing it, *while other Christian communities are obliged to trust to the precarious fidelity of trustees chosen for the purpose.*"

Since the presbytery was thus compelled to resort, in October, 1782, to "*the precarious fidelity of trustees,*" they were careful in the choice of the members of the Board which was to perpetuate itself.

Eleven members of the incorporated Board came together, January 30, 1783, to organize the new administration of the academy. They were the following:

Rev. William Graham, Rector.

John Bowyer, of Botetourt County, member of Presbytery's Board of 1776.

Andrew Moore, of Lexington.

William Alexander, of Timber Ridge Church, father of Dr. Archibald Alexander.

Joseph Walker, of Falling Spring Church.

Alexander Campbell, of Timber Ridge Church.

John Wilson, of Augusta County.

John Trimble, of Rockbridge County.

John Hayes, of Hayes' Creek.

William McKee, Timber Ridge Church, member of the Board of 1776.

Samuel Lyle, Timber Ridge Church, member of the Board of 1776.

These eleven members were all Presbyterians. Four of the eleven were members of the board of 1776. Nine of them were from the churches of Rockbridge County, one was from Botetourt and one from Augusta.

The transfer of the school from the control of the presbytery to that of a self-perpetuating board was thus merely nominal. Every member of the new board was part and parcel of the presbytery itself. There was no purpose on the part of the presbytery to surrender the school which it had established. The self-perpetuating board was placed in charge, to guard the interests of the presbytery, simply because a charter could not be obtained in any other way. In the following year, 1783, Hampden Sidney College secured a charter in exactly the same way, and was likewise placed under the control of a self-perpetuating board.

William Graham, Founder of Liberty Hall Academy, was a great and successful teacher of Greek and Latin literature. He was also an inspiring teacher of the philosophy of the mind. Through the reading of books and through long years of meditation, Graham formulated a system of mental philosophy which was peculiarly his own and of which one of his students, Dr. Archibald Alexander, afterwards said that it was, "in clearness and fulness, superior" to any other system set forth up to that time. After 1789 he was pastor of the New Monmouth and Lexington churches. Dr. Alexander tells us that Graham's manner of delivery was usually "rather feeble and embarrassed, and his dark-colored eyes had rather a dull appearance." Sometimes, however, says Alexander, he became excited, his eyes took on a piercing look and his whole manner was full of expression. On rare occasions he spoke to the people with the same zeal, no doubt, that he showed on a certain occasion, when he made a visit to the Briery congregation in Prince Edward County, Virginia. On that particular Sunday morning John Blair Smith preached the first sermon. The sacrament was then administered and afterwards William Graham preached from Isaiah 40:1, "Comfort ye, comfort ye, my people, saith your God." Strong and tender feeling were shown in his voice and manner and "he poured forth gospel truth like floods of milk and wine," wrote one who heard him; "while the melting eyes and glowing countenances of a large assembly showed that many were eating as friends and drinking abundantly of the consolations provided for them of their God. He brought some of his young people with him [from the Valley of Virginia], hoping that in the midst of the outpouring of the Spirit they might receive the grace of God. His hopes were not in vain. Archibald Alexander was one of that young company."

Graham's sermon at Briery made a deep impression and was remembered for years. A young member of the Briery congregation asked Mr. Graham how long it had taken him to compose the sermon. "About twenty years," replied Graham.

From 1789 onwards for several years, Graham gave regular instruction in the Academy at Lexington to a class of theological students. Seven or eight young men were in regular attendance upon his courses of study in preparation for the ministry.

In 1791, the Synod of Virginia proposed to institute some "plan calculated to educate persons designed for the Gospel Ministry." Synod recommended that there be two general "seminaries" for "religious instruction," under the patronage of that body, one in Rockbridge, Virginia, under Rev. Wm. Graham, the other in Washington County, Pennsylvania, under Rev. John McMillan. In 1792 at Winchester, Synod requested the Board of Liberty Hall Academy to fill vacancies out of the Presbyteries of Hanover and Lexington, that the Academy might become one of the seminaries of the synod.

In 1793, the trustees of the academy agreed to Synod's conditions, and stated that they had contracted for new buildings to the amount of 900 pounds, and asked Synod's aid. Synod enjoined it upon the two presbyteries to raise money for the Academy. This work was done at once by the presbyteries, and on the 1st of January, 1794, the new stone building was occupied by Rector Graham. He now held the twofold position of Professor of Theology under the synod, and Principal of the Academy under the chartered board.

Thus the stone ruins of Liberty Hall Academy, still standing on the hill near Lexington, represent the *Academy building erected, in part, by the two presbyteries as the first Theological Seminary in Virginia.*

Dr. Archibald Alexander, in his address before the alumni of Washington College, 1843, states that prior to this coalition between the Academy and the synod, Rector Graham was a teacher of theology and that "most of those who entered the holy ministry in this Valley" were prepared for the ministerial work by Graham. After the coalition with the synod, "Mr. Graham had a theological class of seven or eight members," says Dr. Alexander, "which was kept up for several years." The seminary was continued until the resignation of the offices of rector and theologian by Mr. Graham in 1796.

Early in the year 1796, the trustees of Liberty Hall Academy heard of the purpose of General George Washington to devote certain shares of canal stock to some school located on the waters of the James River. These shares had been offered to Washington as an expression of esteem by the legislature of Virginia. He refused to accept the money for himself, but announced his readiness to bestow it upon some institution of learning in the mountain region of the state. The trustees of Liberty Hall came together and asked Graham to prepare a statement to be sent to General Washington. In the name of the trustees, Graham wrote, in part, as follows:—

" * * * As early as the year 1776 a seminary

before conducted in these parts under the form of a grammar school received the nominal title of an academy and money was collected to purchase the beginnings of a library and some of the most essential parts of a mathematical and philosophical apparatus.

"The question then was, where should the seminary be fixed? Staunton was proposed by some." Graham spoke of the headwaters of the James River as more convenient within the upper country than Staunton.

"We therefore concluded," he writes, "that some spot in the tract of country now known as Rockbridge would be the proper place. We, therefore, organized the seminary and set it in motion. * * * Through the calamities of a long and dangerous war * * * we were enabled to preserve the Academy in a state of considerable reputation and usefulness until the year 1782, when we were aided by an act of incorporation from the legislature of Virginia, which was the first granted after the Revolution." "There is one fact more," continued Graham, "which we would beg leave to state. In 1793 by voluntary contribution and some sacrifice of private property, we were enabled to erect and finish plain but neat buildings, sufficiently capacious to accommodate between forty and fifty students, and the business of education is now in full train and the seminary is in as high reputation as could be expected without funds. * * * The buildings and other furniture of the Academy could not be estimated at much less than two thousand pounds."

This sum of two thousand pounds, that is about ten thousand dollars, constituted the original endowment of Liberty Hall Academy. For that day and time it was no small amount and was made up from the gifts of the Presbyterian people of Virginia.

Graham wrote to Washington as if speaking for the Hanover Presbytery and as referring to the debates in that body over the location of the school. The board of trustees, in whose behalf he sent the petition, claimed an origin prior to the war of the Revolution. In the minds of the members of this board, they evidently regarded themselves as constituting the same official body that was created by the act of Hanover Presbytery in 1776. As such they asked General Washington for the shares of stock, and to this board as representing and continuing the board of 1776 Washington gave the money. During the darkest period of the Revolution, Washington had said that if he should be driven from every other position he would make a final stand in Augusta County, Virginia. He was now merely turning over some of Virginia's money to the people who had done more than any other Virginians to defend the commonwealth against the British. The trustees recognized his generosity by naming the school Washington Academy. Afterwards it was called Washington College and later still, the Washington and Lee University.

The income received by Graham for his work as teacher and preacher was not large enough to furnish bread to his family. In the latter part of the year 1796, therefore, he gave up his position as Rector of the Academy and moved westward into the Ohio Valley. It was his purpose to establish a Scotch-Irish colony upon a large tract of land near the Ohio River. A journey to Richmond became necessary in order to secure the title to the land. The long horseback ride through the wilderness fatigued him. The chilling effects of the rains that fell upon his slender frame during the journey brought on serious sickness and Mr. Graham suddenly died in Richmond in June, 1788. His body was laid to rest in that city near the south door of St. John's Church. Thus passed away the principal founder of Washington College. We shall look upon his work again, in this volume, in connection with the final battle in behalf of religious freedom.

CHAPTER XXI

SAMUEL STANHOPE SMITH, JOHN BLAIR SMITH AND
HAMPDEN SIDNEY COLLEGE.

JUST before the beginning of the Revolution, two men of God came southward from Pennsylvania to help the causes of education and religion. They were brothers and both had received their early training in the log college of their father, Robert Smith, among the Scotch-Irish at Pequa, Pennsylvania. Both attended Princeton College. Samuel Stanhope Smith, the elder brother, was licensed to preach and came to try his gifts in Prince Edward, Cumberland and Charlotte counties, in Virginia. He told the members of Hanover Presbytery about William Graham and, through Smith's influence, Graham was made principal of John Brown's Academy in the Valley. At the same session of the presbytery at which Graham was appointed, that is, in October, 1774, it was decided to start a subscription in behalf of an academy to be located on the south side of the Blue Ridge, in Prince Edward or in Cumberland, Virginia. It was made a part of the record of Presbytery that Samuel Stanhope Smith would probably take charge of the school. The work of raising money was completed within less than four months. Early in February, 1775, the presbytery held a special meeting to consider the problem of making the best use of the sum of about six thousand five hundred dollars which had been subscribed by the Presbyterians of eastern Virginia. They decided to build an academy in Prince Edward County upon a plot of ground given for the purpose by Peter Johnston. Samuel Stanhope Smith was chosen Rector of the Prince

Edward Academy. A board of trustees was appointed to manage the money affairs of the school. This board consisted of five ministers, namely: Samuel Stanhope Smith, Richard Sankey of Buffalo Church, in Charlotte, John Todd of Louisa, Samuel Leake of Albemarle and Caleb Wallace of Cub Creek Church, with eight elders and Presbyterian laymen. At the same time the presbytery sent out an address in which they assured the people of the commonwealth that although, in the management of the Academy, "the strictest regard shall be paid to the morals of the youth and worship carried on, evening and morning, in the Presbyterian way; yet, on the other hand, all possible care shall be taken that no undue influence be used by any member of this presbytery, the Rector, or any assistant, to bias the judgment of any; but that all [students], of every denomination, shall fully enjoy their own religious sentiments and be at liberty to attend that mode of public worship that either custom or conscience makes most agreeable to them, when and where they may have an opportunity of enjoying it."

This was broad ground upon which the presbytery stood in the matter of managing the two academies that were just then coming under the control of the presbytery. Sectarian the schools certainly were, in the broad meaning of that term, for they were the property of the Presbyterian sect. Sectarian in the narrow and objectionable sense the schools certainly were not. They were not established for the purpose of Presbyterianizing the students who attended them. The fundamental principles of the Christian religion were to be taught and the students were to be called together twice a day for the worship of God. Beyond that, each student was to be left to the freedom of his own choice in the matter of his religious beliefs and worship. It is safe to say that up to that time no school had been placed upon foundations so free and liberal.

In the autumn of 1775 the presbytery added five members to the board of trustees, namely: The Reverend David Rice, Colonel Patrick Henry, Colonel John Tabb, Colonel William Cabell and Colonel James Madison, Jr. Henry and Madison, and perhaps the other two laymen just named were not Presbyterians. In November, 1775, Samuel Stanhope Smith became the regular pastor of the Cumberland and Prince Edward churches. Then in January, 1776, the work of the Prince Edward Academy began. John Blair Smith, as first assistant, and Samuel Doak and David Witherspoon as assistants, were associated with the Rector.

The walls of the academy building were meanwhile rising, log upon log. In May, 1776, these walls were about three feet high. About one hundred and ten students had come by that time to secure the advantages of the academy. Since the homes of the people who dwelt near the place could not hold these young men, they were allowed to build little huts with the shingles that were intended to form the roof of the academy. Eight or ten of these huts were erected and the students were packed within, as one of them said, like the grains of sugar in a sugar loaf. There was only one plank as a seat for three or four boys. At night a candle was placed in each hut, and there, until nine or ten o'clock every night, the young men were busy with their studies.

After July, 1776, all of the students over sixteen years of age, about sixty-five in number, were organized as a military company. John Blair Smith was chosen captain. Each of the young soldiers wore as a uniform a hunting shirt colored with purple dye. The next year (1777) they answered the governor's call and marched to Williamsburg to meet the British.

In October, 1779, Samuel Stanhope Smith gave up his work in Prince Edward and went to New Jersey to become a teacher in Princeton College, and after-

ward president of that school. His brother, John
Blair Smith, was ordained as a minister and was at the
same time made Rector of Prince Edward Academy.
In October, 1782, the Hanover Presbytery appointed
trustees to fill vacancies in the boards of both of its
schools, Liberty Hall and Prince Edward Academy.
The Liberty Hall trustees secured at once an act of
incorporation. In the following year, 1783, the legislature incorporated the Prince Edward Academy
under the title of Hampden-Sidney College. The board
of trustees, appointed by the presbytery and incorporated, consisted of five ministers, namely: John Blair
Smith, Richard Sankey, John Todd, David Rice and
Archibald McRoberts, with twenty-two elders and laymen; two or three of the latter, such as Patrick Henry
and James Madison, were outside of the Presbyterian
fold. The college building was by this time completed,
and every year its rooms were crowded with students.

John Blair Smith, president of the college, was pastor also of the Cumberland and Briery Churches. In
addition to this work, he also spent much of his time
in teaching theology to some young men who were
under preparation as preachers of the gospel. Moreover, he took a leading part in the battle for religious
freedom, as we shall learn later. In the year 1787 President Smith's earnest preaching brought about a revival
of religion which spread from the College throughout
Virginia and the Carolinas. Of this revival we shall
learn more in a later chapter of this book.

In 1789 Smith gave up the presidency of the Col-
lege, and at a later time became pastor of a church in
Philadelphia, and then president of Union College,
New York. He died in 1799 and was laid to rest in
Philadelphia.

CHAPTER XXII.

THE WINNING OF THE BATTLE AT KING'S MOUNTAIN.

ONE bright Sunday morning in the month of June, 1780, a company of men, wearing the red coats of British soldiers, rode up Fishing Creek within the limits of the present Chester County, South Carolina. They were looking for the log building used as a house of worship by one of the Presbyterian congregations of which John Simpson was the pastor. When they came to the church they found the door closed. The congregation was not assembled on that day, for they had heard about the approach of the British. The soldiers then went to the house of Simpson, which was near at hand. Simpson's wife and children fled, and the cruel soldiers set fire to the house and burned it to the ground. They burned, also, a small building which contained all of the minister's books. The house of the widow McClure was destroyed the same day, and then the soldiers rode back to their camp near the mouth of Fishing Creek.

Just a few days before this raid was made, British soldiers had been twice defeated in this same region. Most of the riflemen who won these two victories were members of the Fishing Creek and Bethesda Churches, led by John McClure and William Bratton, who had been aroused to action by the voice of their preacher, John Simpson. After these fights, John McClure, a member of one of these congregations, organized a company of horsemen for regular warfare. Simpson himself took his rifle and his horse and rode away with McClure as a soldier in his company. They marched to join the army of patriots which General Thomas Sumter was then gathering from among the people of the upper parts of South Carolina. On that Sunday morning when the British set fire to Simpson's home, nearly all of the men of his congregation were resting quietly in Sumter's camp.

A brief glance at the events of the American Revolution from 1776 to 1780 will enable us to understand the situation at the time when our present story begins. Within the first half of the year 1776, the chief victories on the American side were won at Moore's Creek Bridge, in North Carolina, and at Charles Town, South Carolina. Even the forcing of the British out of Boston, in March, 1776, was effected through the aid of Southern soldiers. There was only one regiment of these, but they were all skilled riflemen from the congregations of the Valley of Virginia. Their leader, Daniel Morgan, who became an elder in the Presbyterian Church, was in the habit of praying for God's blessing when he went into battle. In 1777, Morgan and his riflemen helped the men of the Middle States to win the victory over Burgoyne's army on the upper Hudson River.

Washington's campaigns in New Jersey and Pennsylvania from 1776 until 1778 were fought by the soldiers of the Middle and Southern States. Six regiments from a colony as far south as North Carolina were with Washington in the battles around Philadelphia. In July, 1779, when Anthony Wayne captured Stony Point, on the Hudson River, soldiers from North Carolina marched in front with fixed bayonets and were the first to rush over the walls of the fortress.

During the same period, from 1776 until 1778, the Southern colonies had to meet the Indians and the British in the West and Southwest. The Indians advanced against the frontiers, but each time they were driven back by the men of the mountains. In July, 1776, the men of the frontier won a victory over the Indians at

Island Flats, on the Holston River, in Tennessee. About the same time Robertson and Sevier successfully held Watauga Fort, in Tennessee, against an attack by red men. Williamson, of South Carolina, and Rutherford, of North Carolina, united their forces and laid waste the villages of the Cherokees. Then in October, 1776, Colonel William Christian led a force of Virginians and North Carolinians into the Tennessee country and defeated the Cherokees. On this expedition, as we have seen, Charles Cummings preached to the soldiers at every camping place. In the winter of 1778-1779, George Rogers Clark led a force of frontier riflemen from Virginia and the Kentucky country into the Northwest beyond the Ohio River, and won all of that vast region from the British. In April, 1779, an army of one thousand North Carolinians under Issac Shelby went down the Tennessee River and subdued the savages who had been aiding the British in the Southwest.

Near the close of the year 1778 the British rulers decided to attempt again to conquer the South. From 1778, therefore, until the close of the war in 1781, the fighting between the Americans and the British was chiefly in Georgia, the Carolinas and Virginia. Savannah was captured, and then in May, 1780, Charles Town fell into the hands of the British. Lord Cornwallis led his forces into the upper parts of Georgia and South Carolina and overran those regions. At the Waxhaws in South Carolina a body of British horsemen under Colonel Tarleton fell upon Buford's regiment of Virginians and put most of them to death with great cruelty. The wounded men among the Virginians were taken to the Presbyterian Church and there tenderly nursed by the good women of that congregation. The news of the work done by "Bloody Tarleton" spread like wildfire among the Presbyterian people who filled this upper country. John Simpson continued to speak out against the cruel British invaders and the men of his two congregations, as has been seen, led by McClure and Bratton, won two victories over British detachments. Then the British soldiers burned Simpson's home and his books and made many threats against his people. This brings us again to the beginning of the story about the struggle in the upper parts of the Carolinas.

General Rutherford now urged the men of western North Carolina to prepare for war. Nine hundred of them met near Charlotte and there Alexander McWhorter, Presbyterian minister and president of Liberty Hall Academy in Charlotte, spoke to the soldiers. He urged every man to stand ready with his rifle to defend his country. When, therefore, a large force of Tories assembled at Ramseur's Mill, near the present town of Lincolnton, Francis Locke of Rowan County led a body of Presbyterian riflemen to the Tory camps and defeated and scattered their force.

Nearly a month afterwards, that is, in July, 1780, Captain Huck led his British cavalry into Bethesda congregation in York County, South Carolina. This, as we know, was one of the churches under the pastoral care of John Simpson. Huck's men tried to frighten the women and children to make them tell where their husbands and fathers were hiding. Mary McClure, a young girl, mounted a horse and rode rapidly across the country to General Sumter's camp. There she told her brothers about the cruelty of Captain Huck. A force of about two hundred and sixty riflemen, most of them from John Simpson's two congregations, led by William Bratton, Edward Lacey, John McClure, Andrew Neil and McConnell, urged their horses through the forests and came upon Huck at Williamson's plantation. At early dawn on the morning of July 12, 1780, the crashing report of their rifles was heard in the British camp. Every bullet went straight to its mark. Huck was slain, his force was defeated and many of his men were captured.

John Thomas was an elder of the Fairforest congregation in the present Spartanburg County, South Carolina. He was commander of the Spartanburg regiment. Colonel Thomas was captured by the British, but his son John became leader of that regiment. On the day after Huck's defeat, young Thomas and his Presbyterian riflemen defeated a force of British cavalry. At once, then, the men of all the Presbyterian congregations in upper South Carolina went out to fight. They knew how to ride well and to shoot straight. With their long black-barrelled rifles in their hands they rode away on horseback under the gallant Sumter to take part in the fight against Cornwallis. At the same time the men of the North Carolina congregations followed William L. Davidson and Joseph Graham and William Richardson Davie into the field. Thomas H. McCaule, pastor of Centre congregation, in Mecklenburg County, spent a part of his time in the campaigns with Davidson. Davie had been brought up in the home of his uncle, William Richardson, preacher at the Waxhaws. He studied at Princeton College and became a lawyer in North Carolina. Davie was not a member of any church, but the Presbyterian horsemen were ready to follow the tall, handsome young soldier into battle. Sumter and Davie, therefore, joining their forces together, struck the head of the British column at Hanging Rock and defeated it. Then Thomas Taylor, afterwards an elder in the First Church of Columbia, South Carolina, led some of Sumter's men to Camden Ferry and seized an entire British wagon train. After receiving such blows as these, Cornwallis knew that he must fight with all his strength to keep his army in the upper country, or that he must retreat to Charles Town.

All at once the fortune of war changed in favor of the British. General Gates led his American force to Camden, and there, because of the poor leadership of Gates, he lost the battle. Then Tarleton made a sudden dash into Sumter's camp and defeated him. John Simpson, the preacher, one of Sumter's men, was mending a bridle when the British soldiers made their attack. He leaped upon the back of his mare without a saddle or bridle, and made her jump fences and ditches until her swift feet saved him. In the same manner most of Sumter's men fled into North Carolina.

Cornwallis, thus encouraged, took up again the line of march northward. When he entered Mecklenburg County the men of the seven churches of Mecklenburg met him. They were led by Davie, Joseph Graham, Locke, Irwin and other gallant commanders. Rutherford had been made a prisoner at Camden. James Hall was then the pastor in charge of three Presbyterian congregations at and near the present Statesville, in Iredell County. When Cornwallis first drew near the upper country, Hall summoned his flocks, and in burning words told them about the wrongs suffered by their countrymen in South Carolina. He called upon his people to take up arms and fight. A cavalry company was the first body of soldiers organized. This was made up at once and then the men told their minister that he must lead them into battle. Hall accepted the command. He was more than six feet in height and possessed great bodily strength. He put on a three-cornered hat, buckled a long sword about him and rode away into the field. Whenever his men went into camp he preached to them the gospel of grace and liberty.

With leaders like these the men who lived between the Yadkin and Catawba made a bold resistance. Cornwallis had to fight for every foot of ground over which he marched. One night Davie made a wide circuit, and in the early morning dashed through a cornfield into the camp of a small body of British soldiers. The latter were defeated and Davie's force galloped away without the loss of a man. Every body of troops sent out by Cornwallis to collect food was assailed and driven back.

About midnight on the 25th of September, 1780,
Davie and Graham rode into Charlotte and posted their
men behind the courthouse and behind dwelling houses
and garden fences.   The next morning the men at the
head of the British column rode into the town from the
southward, but the Carolina riflemen drove them back.
A larger force of British cavalry then dashed forward,
the best men in the army of Cornwallis, but the deadly
rifles again forced them to retreat.   Cornwallis then
brought up his whole army, and Davie and Graham
slowly withdrew northward, fighting as they went.
Cornwallis pitched his camp in Charlotte, but the men
of Mecklenburg kept up so fierce a fight against him
that Cornwallis himself called their country "the hornets' nest."   One morning thirteen of these "hornets,"
led by Captain James Thompson, walked silently
through the woods to McIntyre's house, a point eight
miles from Charlotte.   Among the riflemen was George
Graham, a brother of Joseph.   A body of more than four
hundred British was plundering the house.   The men of
Mecklenburg opened fire with their rifles.   Every ball
went straight to its mark.   The fire was repeated again
and again, and the entire British force fled to the camp
of Cornwallis.   Soon afterwards, Cornwallis wrote, "It
is evident   *   *   *   that the counties of Mecklenburg
and Rowan are more hostile to England than any in
America."

While Cornwallis with his main army was making his
way toward Charlotte, a second British column, consisting of 1,200 men, led by Major Ferguson, was
moving northward through the region near the headwaters of the Broad and Catawba rivers.   The men of
the present counties of Laurens, Union and Spartanburg, in South Carolina, took up arms.   Their chief
leader was James Williams, an elder in the church of
Little River, in Laurens.   Aided by Elijah Clarke, of
Georgia, and Isaac Shelby, of the Watauga River, in the

Tennessee country, Williams won a brilliant victory over a part of Ferguson's force at Musgrove's Mill, on the Enoree River. Ferguson then moved northward, laying the country waste. He established his force near the present Rutherfordton, in western North Carolina, and there made wild threats against the men beyond the mountains.

A messenger swiftly crossed the mountains to warn the settlers on the Watauga and Holston rivers. Four hundred Virginians from the congregations of Charles Cummings on the Holston seized their rifles, mounted their horses and rode away under William Campbell. Four hundred and eighty more from the congregations of Samuel Doak, on the Watauga, and elsewhere in upper East Tennessee, followed Isaac Shelby and John Sevier to the appointed meeting place at Sycamore Shoals, on the Watauga River. At that place, on the morning of the 26th of September, 1780, the very hour when Cornwallis was fighting his way into Charlotte, the horsemen of Campbell, Shelby and Sevier made ready to march. They assembled together and then waited in silence with uncovered heads while Samuel Doak, the minister, offered a prayer for them. Tradition affirms that Doak earnestly besought the Lord of hosts, the God of their fathers, to bless and preserve these defenders of their homes, and to give them victory in the approaching battle. Doak then bade each one of the soldiers to be of good courage and to play the man in the fight. "Go forth, my brave men," said the preacher, "and may the sword of the Lord and of Gideon go with you."

Silently and swiftly these bold men rode eastward through the mountain passes to the headwaters of the Catawba River, in North Carolina. There they were reinforced by four hundred and ten men from western North Carolina under McDowell, Cleveland and Winston. Sixty North Carolinians came also under William

Graham and Frederick Hambright. Then four hundred
South Carolinians, a part of Sumter's brigade, led by
Edward Lacey, James Williams and William Hill, joined
them. William Campbell was chosen to lead the army,
and he marched the men swiftly toward the Broad River
in search of Ferguson. The American leader was six
feet two inches in height, as straight as an arrow, with a
fair complexion and blue eyes. He was quiet and polished
in manner, and a new enthusiasm filled the backwoods-
men when their stalwart commander mounted his horse
and gave the order to move forward.*

Ferguson heard of the approach of the mountain
men, and started eastward to join Cornwallis at Charlotte. Campbell picked out about one thousand of his
best horsemen and pressed forward in hot pursuit. He
found Ferguson encamped on the top of a ridge called
King's Mountain, near the North Carolina line, but
within the limits of Bethel Presbyterian congregation in
York County, South Carolina.

At three o'clock in the afternoon of October 7, 1780,
Campbell's army made ready to attack Ferguson's
camp. The horses were tied in the forest at the foot of
the ridge. The officers told every man to see that his
rifle was well primed with powder, then to go into the
battle and fight until he died. Campbell's riflemen then
surrounded the mountain, climbed the steep sides of the
ridge upon which the British were encamped and began
the attack. Ferguson's men fought with great courage,
but they could not stand against the deadly aim of the
mountain riflemen. Ferguson was slain, and his entire
force was either killed or captured. On the American
side James Williams was among the dead.

*Colonel Campbell afterwards married Elizabeth Henry, sister
of Patrick Henry, the great Virginia orator. The only child of
this marriage was Sarah Buchanan Campbell, who became the
wife of General Francis Preston. The oldest son of the latter
was William Campbell Preston, of South Carolina, the famous
statesman and educator.

It was a glorious victory. When the news came to Cornwallis he had already started northward from Charlotte. He gave orders at once, however, that his army must turn back southward again toward Charles Town. Through rain and mud his forces slowly retreated, some of the men falling at every step. The men of Mecklenburg, armed with their deadly rifles, swarmed about the rear of his army. The men of Lancaster, York, Chester and Fairfield counties, South Carolina, assailed both flanks. They captured the baggage and supplies of the British army and cut off every scouting party. The starving and defeated forces of Cornwallis spent two weeks in moving over the short distance to Winnsboro. The glad news brought new hope to every American patriot. The tide of the war was turned at last in favor of the American cause.

And who were the men who destroyed Ferguson's force and caused the plans of Cornwallis to fail? They were mounted riflemen from the Presbyterian congregations of the Carolinas, Virginia, Tennessee and Georgia.

CHAPTER XXIII.

PRESBYTERIAN RIFLEMEN, LED BY FRANCIS MARION,
ASSAIL THE BRITISH IN THE EASTERN PARTS
OF SOUTH CAROLINA.

THE heavy blows which have just been described were delivered by the men of Sumter, Davie and Campbell against the front and the flanks of the army of Cornwallis as he moved northward into North Carolina. During the same period, heavy blows were directed against the rear of his forces, and his line of communication with Charles Town was often cut. This was the work of a body of horsemen made up of Scots, Huguenots and Welsh from the present counties of Williamsburg and Marion, in South Carolina. Nearly all of these were from the Presbyterian congregations of that region, and their chief leader was Francis Marion, of Huguenot descent.

The leader who first called these fighting men into the field, however, was Major John James, son of William James, whose wife was a daughter of the pioneer, John Witherspoon. John James was a mere infant when his father brought him up the Black River to the King's Tree in Williamsburg Township. He spent most of his early years on horseback chasing cattle over the meadows and through the forests of his father's plantation, twelve miles above Kingstree. He became a bold huntsman, also, and as a mature man was made an elder in the Presbyterian Church at Indiantown. When the war with England began John James led a company of his neighbors to Charles Town to help to defend that city. He was raising a larger body of soldiers at the time when Charles Town fell (1780).

154

Then Major James rode into Georgetown to ask what the British meant to do. Captain Ardesoif, a British officer, told him that the South Carolinians must fight for the King. James replied that his people would never give aid to the British. Ardesoif became angry at this reply, and threatened James with his sword. The latter seized a chair, waved it in the face of Ardesoif and held him back. Then James rushed to his horse, mounted him and galloped away. Six companies of soldiers were formed at once from the Presbyterian congregations of Williamsburg, and Major John James and Major Hugh Giles were chosen to lead them. Other officers bore the Huguenot names of Horry and Mouzon and the Scotch names of McCottry, McCauley, Baxter, Postell, Cooper, Conyers, Ervin and Witherspoon. Then Marion took the chief command and made unceasing attacks against the rear of Cornwallis' army. Cornwallis sent a force of British troops into Williamsburg to lay waste the country. These men burned the church at Indiantown, burned the home of Major James and other leaders, and flung into the fire every copy of the Bible and of the Scotch version of the Psalms that they could find. The British regarded the war in this region as against Presbyterians, and in revenge they destroyed houses of worship and books of devotion. The members of these congregations at once flocked to Marion's standard and his brigade was increased to three regiments, commanded by Colonels Peter Horry, Hugh Horry and John Ervin, who was succeeded by John Baxter. Five of Marion's captains were elders of the Hopewell Presbyterian Church; these were John and Hugh Ervin, and John, Gavin and Robert Witherspoon. Nearly all of the remaining officers under Marion were officers of the Presbyterian churches of Williamsburg Township. The swift riding of the Presbyterian horsemen of this region, and the deadly aim of their rifles, forced the British troops to leave Williamsburg.

The danger from this quarter had much to do, also, with the retreat of Cornwallis after the battle of King's Mountain. When he moved back from Charlotte, Cornwallis sent Tarleton to catch Marion. Tarleton marched for days through the swamps, but could not find Marion's rangers. As soon as Tarleton turned to join the main British army Marion's riflemen began again their deadly work. They rode almost to Charles Town, captured the supplies intended for Cornwallis, and in a dozen battles defeated the bodies of troops that were guarding his rear.

When Cornwallis again moved northward, a large British force was sent toward Williamsburg. They came to a bridge thrown across the Black River near the town of Kingstree. On the opposite side of the river near the other end of the bridge were posted Major James' men. Among the latter were the riflemen led by William McCottry, a member of the Indiantown Church. The homes of John Witherspoon, of John James, of William McCottry and of all the rest of the Scots were in the immediate vicinity. These patriots were standing almost in the sight of their wives and daughters. The British cannon opened fire, and the British infantry started to cross the bridge. At the crack of McCottry's rifle the leading British officer fell. A hail of bullets swept across the river; the men at the cannon were cut down and the whole British force was defeated and driven back. Colonel Watson, their commander, said that he "never saw such shooting" during the whole of his experience as a soldier. A day or two later, Watson saw more of the same kind of shooting. He took up his quarters at the house of John Witherspoon, two miles from the bridge where James defeated him. James followed the British to that place. Then Sergeant McDonald climbed a hickory tree at the end of Witherspoon's lane, and at the distance of 200 yards sent a rifle ball through the knee of a British lieutenant who was standing near the Witherspoon house. Colonel Watson waited no longer, but fled at the top of his speed to Georgetown, on the coast. The news of this repulse in the British rear came to the ears of Cornwallis when he was far advanced upon his second entrance into North Carolina. Let us now trace the steps in that movement.

CHAPTER XXIV.

THE COWPENS AND GUILFORD COURTHOUSE.

In December, 1780, General Nathanael Greene led a force made up of Virginia, Maryland, Delaware and Pennsylvania soldiers into the Carolinas. Daniel Morgan, with a regiment of riflemen from Virginia and Maryland, joined Greene, and was sent into the western part of South Carolina.

In the churches and in the camps of the soldiers the Presbyterian ministers of this region kept up the work of urging the men of their congregations to fight. William Martin, a Scotch-Irish preacher, was put into prison by the British. At Winnsboro this gray-haired old minister was led before Cornwallis. "You are charged," said the British commander, "with preaching rebellion from the pulpit,—you, an old man and a minister of the gospel of peace,—with advocating rebellion against your lawful sovereign, King George III!"

Martin fixed his eyes on Cornwallis and said: "I am happy to appear before you. For many months I have been held in chains for preaching what I believe to be the truth. As to King George, I owe him nothing but good will. I am not unacquainted with his private character. * * * As a king he was bound to protect his subjects in the enjoyment of their rights. Protection and allegiance go together, and when the one fails the other cannot be expected. The declaration of Independence is but a reiteration of what our [Scotch] Covenanting fathers have always maintained."

Meanwhile, after the battle at King's Mountain, the men of the Carolinas led by Sumter and Marion were making the position of Cornwallis unsafe.

Sumter rode within a short distance of the British camp at Winnsboro and defeated a large British detachment at Fishdam Ford. Then at Blackstock, on the Tyger River, in the present Union County, South Carolina, Sumter defeated a part of Tarleton's legion of horsemen. Sumter was wounded in this battle, and then Andrew Pickens rode into the field to fight Cornwallis. Pickens was a Scot who came as a child with his parents from Augusta County, Virginia, to the Waxhaws. He built a home on the west side of the Broad River, in the present Abbeville County, and became an elder in the Long Cane Church. In 1779, he called together five hundred men from the congregations near his home, crossed the Savannah River and defeated a much larger British force at Kettle Creek, in Georgia. Now in 1781, he led his riflemen to join Daniel Morgan on the Pacolet River, in South Carolina. Cornwallis was forced to move, and he decided to march again into North Carolina and thence to Virginia. He, therefore, sent Tarleton with 1,100 picked men to attack Morgan and Pickens. Tarleton rode swiftly into western South Carolina and came up with the American forces at a grazing ground on Broad River called the Cowpens.

Morgan placed his small body of Maryland men at the top of a long slope. At the left end of the line stood a company of riflemen from the Presbyterian congregations of Rockbridge County, Virginia, led by Gilmore, Caruthers and McCorkle. At the right end of the line was a company from Augusta, Virginia, led by Tate and Buchanan. In front of these, on the slope of the hill, three hundred riflemen of upper South Carolina took their places under the direction of Pickens. Among the trees further down the slope were Cunningham's Georgians and McDowell's North Carolinians. William Washington's Virginia cavalry and James McCall's South Carolina cavalry guarded the flanks. It was almost entirely a Presbyterian army. Morgan and Pickens, the Presbyterian elders, went among the men to see that every gun was ready; then with sleepless eyes they prayed to God throughout the night and asked Him to give them the victory. When the day dawned, Pickens was again among his men at the front, telling every third man to fire while two held their loaded guns in reserve.

Just at sunrise on the morning of January 17, 1781, Tarleton's cannon were moved forward to begin the fight. Through the thick cannon smoke the British foot soldiers and horsemen advanced up the slope, led by Tarleton himself. The men of McDowell and Cunningham delivered their fire and fell back. When the enemy came within fifty yards of the line of Pickens, the latter gave the word, and nearly every British officer was shot down. Again the rifles spoke and the front line of British soldiers fell. Another volley and Tarleton's men staggered and paused. The force of Tarleton's attack was broken. The victory was practically won where Pickens fought. But Tarleton would not give up the fight. He urged his men to advance with fixed bayonets. The force under Pickens fell slowly back and the British were met by Morgan's line on the top of the hill. Washington and McCall came sweeping around with their horsemen to the right and rear of the British. Pickens turned his men against Tarleton's left. The British were surrounded and nearly all of them were captured. One-third of the army of Cornwallis was thus snatched from him when he was in the sorest need of soldiers.

Greene and Morgan were not yet strong enough to meet Cornwallis in battle. After the victory at the Cowpens, Morgan joined Greene, and they both moved northward. Cornwallis followed with his army. He burned the Waxhaws Church. Bibles and Psalm-books were destroyed everywhere by his soldiers. Thomas H. McCaule, minister of Centre Church in Mecklenburg County, led all the men of his flock into General Davidson's camp. James Hall called the men of his congregation together under the oaks that still stand by the side of the Presbyterian Church at Statesville. Then, as their captain, Hall mounted his horse and led the men of Iredell to help Davidson. Samuel E. McCorkle, the minister at Thyatira, near Salisbury, urged his congregation to fight. It was Mrs. Steele, mother of McCorkle's wife, who gave to General Greene a bag of gold and silver coin, all the money she had.

The men of North Carolina, led by Davidson and Graham, and the men of Mecklenburg stood across the pathway of the British and attempted to hold Cornwallis in check at the Catawba River, but Davidson was killed in the fight and the British crossed the stream. Andrew Pickens then took command of the riflemen of both Carolinas and fought the British at every step as they marched through North Carolina. Morgan escaped with the prisoners taken at the Cowpens. Greene crossed the Dan into Virginia and Cornwallis established his camp among the people of the two congregations, Alamance and Buffalo, of which David Caldwell was pastor. Some of the British soldiers went to Hugh McAden's church at the Red House, and encamped in the house of worship, and burned all of McAden's books. The main body of the British army encamped for a time on Caldwell's plantation; some of the officers drove out the preacher's family and made their home in his house. Moreover, they burned his Bible and Psalm-books, and with them all the rest of his library and his papers. One or two of Caldwell's sermons escaped the flames. Let us hear a few words from one of these discourses, based on the text, "The slothful shall be under tribute." (Prov. 12:24):

"   *   *   * Our forefathers, or many of them, sacrificed at Londonderry and Enniskillen [in North Ireland] their lives, that they might hand down to us the fair inheritance of liberty and the Protestant religion; and in the whole course of their conduct in the support and defense of their rights, they have set us an example which ought not to be disregarded." The preacher told his people about the attempts of the British King and Parliament to pass unjust laws and to lay heavy burdens on the American colonists, and then said: "If we stand up manfully and unitedly in defense of our rights, appalled by no dangers and shrinking from no toils or privations, we shall do valiantly."

"Our foes are powerful and determined on conquest; but our cause is good, and in the strength of the Lord, who is mightier than all, we shall prevail. If we fail to do our duty in this momentous crisis, bondage and oppression, with all their unnumbered and interminable woes, will be entailed upon us; but if we act our part well as men and as Christians in defense of truth and righteousness, we may with the help of the Lord obtain a complete and final deliverance from the power that has oppressed us."

There is little doubt that Cornwallis had heard of the patriotic preaching of Caldwell, for the story has come down to us that the British commander offered a reward of one thousand dollars for the capture of Caldwell. The minister, however, joined the American army with the men of his two congregations.

Many other churches, near and far, sent riflemen to help Greene in the approaching fight with Cornwallis. William Campbell led some of the King's Mountain men to Greene's aid. Three companies were called out from the congregations of the Valley of Virginia and placed under the command of Samuel McDowell. James Waddell, the blind preacher, delivered a sermon to these soldiers as they stood ready to march. He encouraged the patriots to keep back the invaders. Then, with the minister's prayers and blessings ringing in their ears, they marched to meet Cornwallis. One company of horsemen from Prince Edward and Amelia was already serving with Greene in the legion of "Light Horse Harry" Lee.

Another company was now sent from Prince Edward to fill up the ranks of William Washington's cavalry. William Morton, an elder, a son of Little Joe Morton, raised a company of riflemen from the churches of Charlotte and set forth to join Greene. John Blair Smith, minister and President of Hampden Sidney, started with Morton's company, but soon returned home to preach in behalf of liberty.

On the morning of March 15, 1781, Greene drew up his army on a hill near Guilford Court House to await the attack of Cornwallis. In Greene's front line, posted behind a fence, were the North Carolina riflemen. Some distance in the rear of them were the Virginia riflemen, forming the second line. The third line stood in the rear, on the top of the hill. It was made up of two brigades of regular troops, one from Maryland and another from Virginia. Washington's cavalry guarded the right flank of the American army. Lee's legion and William Campbell's mountain men were on the left flank.

As Cornwallis' army advanced across the open field in front, Captain John Forbes, from one of Caldwell's congregations, fired the first shot. The North Carolinians of Greene's first line took the signal from Forbes and sent in a deadly fire. One-half of the Highland regiment in the British front fell from that fire. The Carolinians fired another volley and retreated. Then Greene's second line, the Virginia marksmen, held Cornwallis in check for a time. Twice they advanced and broke the British line. The British came on, however, led by Colonel Webster. They were met by Greene's last line on the hilltop. The fighting was desperate.

When William Morton, of Charlotte, Virginia, fired his heavy gun, filled with eight buckshot, Colonel Webster fell. Colonel Washington made a daring charge against the flank of Webster's force. In this charge Peter Francisco, of Prince Edward County, Virginia, cut down eleven British soldiers with his own hand. Cornwallis had the larger force, however, and Greene's men could not hold the field. They withdrew a few miles and stood ready to fight again.

Cornwallis was unable to move forward. The strength of his army had been broken by the desperate fighting through which he had passed. He turned about at once and led his men to the seacoast at Wilmington. There his army was fed from the stores on the British ships. Cornwallis then moved northward into Virginia, but he was no longer strong enough to meet an army in the field. He marched to Yorktown, on the Chesapeake Bay, in Virginia, to secure help once more from his warships. At that place General Washington, with the aid of the French fleet, surrounded the British and captured them.

Meanwhile, Andrew Pickens and his riflemen took Augusta, Georgia, from the enemy. Then the men of Sumter, Marion and Pickens swarmed around the British that still remained in South Carolina. They fought Rawdon's British force at Eutaw Springs, and at last drove all of the enemy out of the Carolinas and Georgia. The men who did most of this work of breaking the strength of the army under Cornwallis, thus winning American independence, were the men of the Presbyterian congregations of the Southern States.

CHAPTER XXV.

THE WINNING OF THE FIGHT FOR RELIGIOUS FREEDOM.

"ALL men are equally entitled to the free exercise of religion according to the dictates of conscience." Thus ran, as we have seen, certain words in the Virginia Bill of Rights adopted June 29, 1776, through the influence of James Madison. In theory, therefore, the cause of freedom in religion was made a part of the law of the state. In fact, however, the Episcopal Church was still the established Church of Virginia. The Episcopal clergymen were paid by means of a tax laid on all of the people. Since the great majority of the people of Virginia were Presbyterians and Baptists, they did not wish to pay for the support of worship according to the Episcopal method.

When the first legislature of the new and independent State of Virginia met, October 7, 1776, the Hanover Presbytery sent to that body another memorial, written probably by Caleb Wallace, asking that the state should have no established church at all. The dissenters, they said, "annually pay large taxes to support an establishment from which their consciences and principles oblige them to dissent." "We ask no ecclesiastical establishments for ourselves, neither can we approve of them when granted to others," they urged in conclusion.

Other petitions also were presented to the legislature, from "Sundry Inhabitants of Prince Edward," from Lutherans, from Methodists, from "The County Committee for Augusta County," and from various "Dissenters," some of whom were Baptists. The strongest of these memorials was from Presbyterian sources. This petition from Hanover Presbytery received full consideration on the part of the lawmakers, and the proceedings with reference to it filled an entire page in their Journal.

A bitter debate took place over the issue, and then, in December, 1776, the legislature passed a law setting dissenters free from the tax for the support of the Episcopal Church. During this entire period of legislative debate, from October 5 until December 5, 1776, Caleb Wallace was present in Williamsburg, Virginia's capital, as a deputy sent by the Hanover Presbytery to look after the interests of Presbyterians. A few months later, that is, in April, 1777, Wallace wrote to James Caldwell, of New Jersey, as follows: "An American ought to seek an emancipation from the British King, ministry and parliament at the risk of all his earthly possessions of whatever name. Nor is it the fear of danger that has prevented my preaching this doctrine in the army at headquarters." Wallace considered it his duty to remain among his own people and there to preach and labor in behalf of both religious and civil liberty.

Many members of the state legislature now declared that every denomination of Christians ought to be under the management and control of the state government. In April, 1777, therefore, the Hanover . Presbytery adopted another memorial written by Samuel Stanhope Smith and David Rice. "The Kingdom of Christ and the concerns of religion are beyond the limits of civil control," they declared in the paper addressed to the legislature. The Baptists sent in a paper, also, urging the same view.

In May, 1779, Thomas Jefferson wrote out a bill "establishing religious freedom," which was presented to the legislature for adoption. For six years the battle raged around this measure. The Presbyterians and Baptists supported Jefferson's Bill, for this measure contained all of the principles thus far set forth in the memorials of the Hanover Presbytery. In May, 1784, this Presbytery met at Bethel Church, Augusta County, and adopted a memorial written by John Blair Smith and James Waddell. In the name of "The united clergy of the Presbyterian Church in Virginia" they addressed the legislature, and asked for "an entire and everlasting freedom from every species of ecclesiastical domination." "The Episcopal Church," continued the memorial, "is actually incorporated and known in law as a body, so that it can receive and possess property for ecclesiastical purposes, without trouble or risk in securing it, while other Christian communities are obliged to trust to the precarious fidelity of trustees chosen for the purpose." The Presbytery claimed that their church should have privileges under the state government equal to the privileges enjoyed by any other body of Christians. They had fought for the freedom of the state, they said; "we shun not a comparison with any of our brethren," continued the memorial, "for our efforts in the cause of our country and assisting to establish her liberties, and, therefore, esteem it unreasonable that any of them should reap superior advantages for, at most, but equal merit." They had fought for political and religious liberty, and they desired a full and equal share of both. Such was the claim advanced by the Presbyterians and supported by the Baptists. Patrick Henry was an advocate of the plan to levy a general tax upon the people for the support of all religious denominations. It was now reported throughout the state that the legislature would certainly enact a law to carry out this policy. The Hanover Presbytery, therefore, at its meeting held at Timber Ridge, October 27, 1784, approved a memorial proposed by William Graham and John Blair Smith.

This memorial was sent by the Presbytery to the legislature. At some length they urged again the principle that religion "as a spiritual system and its min-

isters in a professional capacity, ought not to be under
the direction of the State." Understanding, however,
that in spite of their protests the lawmakers had made
up their minds to pass a law imposing some kind of assessment for religious purposes, the Presbytery's memorial declared that the only endurable kind of assessment must be based upon "the most liberal plan," and
that it must not "violate" the happy privilege we now
enjoy of thinking for ourselves in all cases where conscience is concerned."*

Under Patrick Henry's leadership a law was passed
to the effect that every denomination of Christians that
asked for it might be incorporated. The Episcopal
Church, therefore, asked for incorporation, and secured
it in a manner even more definite and binding than ever
before. This was not the "liberal plan" which some of
the Presbyterians had been willing to endorse. To meet
the issue, therefore, the entire body of Presbyterians in
Virginia took action at once. Hanover Presbytery, in
session at Bethel Church, Augusta County, May 19,
1785, declared that they were "unanimously against"
any kind of assessment by the legislature for the support of religion. A general convention of Presbyterians was called to meet a few months later in this same
church. Accordingly, on August 10, 1785, the Presbyterians assembled again at Bethel. In behalf of the
convention, William Graham drew up a memorial and it
was adopted as setting forth the views of "the ministers
and lay representatives of the Presbyterian Church in
Virginia, assembled in convention." They called themselves "citizens of the State" who had "willingly con-
formed to the system of civil policy adopted for our

*This memorial has been widely misinterpreted to the effect
that the Presbytery was inconsistent; because, it is charged, this
paper advocated the assessment plan, looking to a union of
church and state. Such an interpretation does injustice to the
patriots who wrote the paper. Mark the action of the Presbytery at its next meeting, at Bethel Church, May 19, 1785.

government and defended it with the foremost at the risk of everything dear to us." The hope of securing complete liberty, they said, "nerved our arm in the day of battle." Then, in the form and style of Jefferson's great Declaration of Independence, they uttered their vigorous protest, with about twenty special reasons assigned, against the recent course of the legislature. "It would be an unwarrantable stretch of prerogative in the legislature to make laws concerning religion, they said; "and it would be a fatal symptom of abject slavery in us were we to submit to the usurpation."

In October, 1785, this paper was presented to the legislature. At the same time, John Blair Smith, President of Hampden Sidney College, was given permission to speak to the lawmakers. On three successive days he pleaded with them in behalf of complete freedom in matters of religion. James Madison spoke on the same side with Smith. A number of memorials and protests came in from various parts of the state. Madison himself brought in his famous "Memorial and Remonstrance" with a large number of names of citizens attached.

The victory was won. In December, 1785, the legislature, by a vote of sixty-seven to twenty, adopted the bill written six years before by Jefferson, to the effect that "all men shall be free to profess and by argument to maintain their opinion in matters of religion." This was the first complete separation of church affairs from the control of the state government. The other states afterwards followed the example of Virginia. Through the urgent insistence of Patrick Henry, James Madison afterwards accepted the view that this principle should be incorporated in the Federal Constitution. Madison used his influence, therefore, to secure the adoption of the first amendment to that great document, establishing religious freedom in the entire republic.

The great cause was won chiefly by the Presbyterians, supported by the Baptists and by some Episcopalians.

In 1802 the lands in Virginia known as glebe lands, held by the Episcopal Church, which had been paid for by a tax upon all of the people, were made the property of the state. Thus the men who did more than any others to establish freedom in civil government, led the way in securing that liberty which we now enjoy in all of the affairs of religion.

CHAPTER XXVI.

REVIVALS OF RELIGION THAT FOLLOWED THE WAR OF THE REVOLUTION.

WHEN the fighting came to an end, the people of our Southern country found themselves in a weakened condition. Plantations had been laid waste and many churches and homes had been burned. The passing of armies back and forth and the establishing of camps of soldiers had broken up, to some extent, the regular work of the ministers in the churches. Harmful manners and customs had crept into many communities. Against these the preachers set their faces like flint. The faithfulness of these men was the agency used of God to stir up His people in many parts of the land.

During the campaign that ended in North Carolina with the battle at Guilford Court House, General Greene wished to appoint James Hall to the military office of brigadier general. Hall declined to take the position, and fought through the war as captain of a company of horsemen and chaplain of the regiment. When the fighting ceased, he went back to his churches in Iredell County and gave himself entirely to the work of preaching the gospel.

He set himself with all his strength against the tide of evil. His preaching was simple, earnest and tender even unto tears. The strong, sympathetic nature of the pastor won the hearts of the wayward. A great revival of religion took place in his churches and large numbers were brought into the fold. It was the first marked revival in any of the Southern churches after the Revolution. Hall made journeys into the eastern and western parts of North Carolina and into Kentucky, preaching

171

as he passed along. In the year 1800 he went into the lower Mississippi Valley to preach to the Natchez Indians.

This man of deep piety had his periods of spiritual darkness. At one time he ceased to preach for a year and a half because, as he said, "God had hidden his face from him." One Sunday morning while in this state of depression Hall appeared at Bethany Church. The elders urged him to preach, but he refused. Then one of the elders stood up and prayed as follows: "O Lord, cast the deaf and dumb devil out of our pastor; this deaf devil that will not allow him to hear the promises of the gospel, and this dumb devil that will not suffer him to preach as he has heretofore done." At the close of the prayer the pastor entered the pulpit and spoke his message with all his former tenderness and power.

As early as 1778, James Hall founded a school on Snow Creek, in the Bethany Congregation. This school, called Clio's Nursery, was kept up after the Revolution. More than twenty ministers of the gospel, as well as a number of judges and governors, were sent forth within a short period of time by Hall and his assistants. Among these was Moses Waddel, the great Christian teacher of Georgia and South Carolina.

On the 27th of July, 1785, the South Carolina presbytery held its sessions in the open air at a point between Upper Long Cane and Saluda, the present Greenville Church. There Robert Hall, from North Carolina, was solemnly ordained as pastor of the above named churches. General Andrew Pickens was then one of the elders of Upper Long Cane and Hugh Wardlaw was an elder of Saluda (Greenville). Robert Hall was a brother of James Hall, and received his training in Clio's Nursery, in Iredell County, North Carolina. Robert had to some extent the strong and earnest nature of his brother James, and his preaching stirred the people of the upper country of South Carolina.

The work of ordination was done by the new presbytery of South Carolina, which had been cut apart from Orange Presbytery and organized just three months before, in April, 1785. The old presbytery of South Carolina had been dissolved.

Two days after this meeting, that is, on July 29, the same presbytery met in the open air at Davis's Bridge at a point between the congregations of Lower Long Cane and Rocky River, in Abbeville. One of the elders of Lower Long Cane at that time was Patrick Calhoun, father of John C. Calhoun. On the green grass, beneath the shadow of the great oaks, young Robert Mecklin stood up in the presence of the presbytery to answer questions upon his course of study. Then he knelt and the hands of the brethren were laid upon him to ordain him as pastor of the two churches. During a brief pastorate the voice of Mecklin was heard by great crowds. With a small Bible opened in his hand, Mecklin stood before his people and made the Word of God plain to them. Sometimes the whole congregation was melted to tears, it was said, by the appeals of this man of God. Then after three years of labor among the two congregations, Mecklin passed away from the earth.

Soon afterwards, Doctor Thomas Reese came to the upper country. He had been pastor of the Salem Church, Black River, during the Revolution. He took charge of Carmel and Hopewell near the town of Pendleton. General Pickens moved into this region and was one of the elders of Hopewell. In 1802 a stone house of worship was erected at Hopewell which is still known as "The Old Stone Church." It was the center of a pious community.

John Simpson, the fighting preacher of Fishing Creek, came to the Pendleton district after the war, as pastor of Good Hope and Roberts churches. He was as active and zealous in ministerial labors as he had been in the battles against invaders. His temper was mild and his life was blameless. The preaching and the prayers of Simpson won rich blessings for his people. Numbers were added to his churches, and later, in 1802, a wonderful revival of religion took place among his flocks.

In 1785, the year in which the Presbytery of South Carolina was organized, Thomas H. McCaule came from the pastorate of Centre Congregation, North Carolina, to be president of Mount Zion College at Winnsboro, South Carolina. From sixty to eighty young men assembled there to receive instruction from the minister. At daybreak each morning the winding of a horn called upon the students to leave their beds. Another blast of the horn at sunrise called them to prayers and to study. The work continued all day with brief intermissions and then, in the late afternoon, prayers were offered again and the students sent to their rooms.

Many ministers were trained in this log college at Winnsboro. Among the first were two who returned to spend long pastorates in their native land of Mecklenburg County. One of these was Humphrey Hunter who led the flock of Steele Creek Church in the path of peace for nearly a quarter of a century. The other was James Wallis who set forth a pure religion before the people of New Providence Church. He established a school within his congregation and thus continued the work of multiplying the number of ministers. Another preacher who sat under McCaule's guidance at Winnsboro was James White Stephenson, who had taken his first lessons in Latin and Greek at the school near the church in the Waxhaws. He fought bravely as one of Sumter's soldiers. Then after the course of preparation at Winnsboro he became shepherd of the flock at Bethel and Indiantown in Williamsburg County. His wife was a daughter of Major John James. Stephenson prayed without ceasing and taught his people to pray. Through faithfulness in preaching, he aroused the people of his congregations so that a great revival swept over that part of the country. In 1802, a large number of families from these two congregations, accompanied by their pastor, left Williamsburg and made their homes in Maury County, Tennessee. There they built Zion Church near the town of Columbia. Thus was scattered some of the godly seed that first came to our country with Witherspoon and James.

Early in the year 1787, John Blair Smith organized the elders of his two churches, Briery and Cumberland, in Virginia, into separate groups. Each group met regularly to pray for a revival of true religion in the congregations. Numbers of the congregations joined the prayer meetings of the elders and thus large prayer circles were formed. With great fervor and animation Smith preached the gospel to his people. President Smith was slender and of medium height. His hair was black. It was divided on the top and fell on each side of his face. His mouth was large. When aroused, his blue eyes seemed to grow dark and piercing. His speaking was so earnest and impetuous that on one occasion he broke a blood vessel and had to be carried from the pulpit to his home. His preaching was plain and practical and free from ranting. Sometimes he spoke about the punishment of sinners. More often, however, he dwelt upon the love of the Father and the pity and compassion of the Son, Jesus Christ. He was always seeking to find the consciences of his hearers, and his words went home to their hearts. The Spirit of God came down upon the two churches and upon the young men in Hampden Sidney College. Sinners were awakened and lukewarm Christians were aroused.

The first student of Hampden Sidney who gave his heart to Christ during this revival was Cary Allen. His father was an elder in the Cumberland Church. Cary grew up as a lad marked by mirthfulness and humor; his merry spirit would often start his comrades to laughing. President Smith's preaching at the college, however, made him think about his soul, and he fell under deep conviction concerning sin. Then he went to hear a Methodist preacher in a chapel near his father's home. While the minister 'was speaking Cary fell upon the floor in great spiritual agony. Before he arose he declared that he had found peace in believing in the Lord Jesus.

When the lad returned to the college, Dr. Smith questioned him closely about his experience, and gave him books to read. Cary's faith was clear and his whole life was changed.

Allen's neighbor at home in Cumberland, and his friend at college, was young William Hill. President Smith's preaching touched Hill's heart also, and he became troubled. After Allen's conversion, Hill's spiritual anxiety increased and he would fall upon his knees and weep and pray. He often seemed to feel upon his head the hand of his pious mother who had died, and he thought that he could hear her saying to him, "Is this your mother's little preacher for whom she so often prayed?" He had no Bible, but borrowed a copy, and one Saturday went into the woods and read through the Gospel of Matthew. Then he asked William Calhoun, a classmate whose home was near the college, to bring him a book on religion. Calhoun brought from his home *Alleine's Alarm to the Unconverted* and gave it to Hill. Another student, young James Blythe, from North Carolina, entered Hill's room and found this old book. "Are you anxious about your soul?" said Blythe, with much emotion. "Yes, I am," said Hill. "I have neglected it too long, I fear too long. I am resolved to be more earnest hereafter." "What a sinner I am," cried Blythe; "would you believe I came from Carolina a professor of religion? Here I have neglected my Bible and have become hard and cold." Both lads wept and confessed their faith to each other. Clement Reed, a student from Charlotte, who was under religious conviction, joined Allen, Hill and Blythe, and the four went into the woods on Saturday to pray. The next Saturday they held the meeting for prayer in a room in the college. A number of wild, thoughtless lads among the students made a great noise and broke up the prayer meeting. When President Smith learned all the facts, the tears started in his eyes as he said, "Is it possible that some of my students desire to pray? And is it possible that any desire to hinder them?" He invited the four young men to hold their next meeting for prayer in his house. When they came a large company of students came with them and Dr. Smith led the devotions of the assembly. The whole college was shaken and many believed. The four young leaders became preachers along with Nash Legrand, a classmate. Drury Lacy, a teacher in the college, had been already licensed to preach.

From President Smith's churches, as from a fountain, the revival flowed in many directions. James Mitchell, a minister in Bedford, came to see and hear, and through his agency the revival was borne into Bedford and Campbell counties. Henry Pattillo came from beyond the Dan River, bringing a number of young people from his churches. Then they returned and scattered the blessed influences among the people of Granville and Caswell counties, in North Carolina. James McGready also tarried awhile with President Smith and then went to Orange and Guilford, in North Carolina, to extend the movement of grace.

In August, 1789, three horsemen passed slowly eastward through a gap of the Blue Ridge into Prince Edward County, Virginia. These were William Graham, Rector of Liberty Hall Academy, and two of his students, Archibald Alexander and Samuel Wilson. As the three journeyed along the chief subjects of conversation were Justification and Regeneration. They had heard

of the great revival which had been in progress in John
Blair Smith's congregations for nearly two years, and
they were on the way to attend the celebration of the
Lord's Supper at Briery, one of Smith's churches.
When the three horsemen came near the church, they
met a large company of worshippers returning from
Saturday's service. Most of them were young people
on horseback, who were singing hymns as they passed
along the roadway through the forest. Some of these
had come a distance of fifty or sixty miles from Caswell County, North Carolina, to attend the sacrament.
With them came their young preacher, a recent convert, Nash Legrand. Behind the whole company of
singers came John Blair Smith with the elders of his
church. As soon as Smith saw Graham, who was waiting at the roadside, he went to meet him, and the two
ministers greeted each other in the most hearty and
eager manner. These two men, Graham and Smith,
were at that time the foremost intellectual and spiritual
leaders among all the Christians of the commonwealth of
Virginia. Both of them had worn swords as captains in
the war of the Revolution. Now they were the chief
captains in the great war against evil and spiritual
wickedness.

On Saturday evening a meeting was held in the home
of Little Joe Morton, and the place was crowded with
worshippers. One recent convert led in prayer, and
young William Hill made "a warm and pungent address" on the parable of the barren fig tree. When John
Blair Smith arose to speak "his appearance was more
solemn than that of anyone I had ever seen," said Archibald Alexander, "and caused a feeling of awe to come
over me." Smith himself delivered "a powerful and
solemn discourse" to the company.

The next day at Briery a great multitude met together. The services were held under an arbor outside
of the church. Dr. Smith preached the Action Sermon,

as the discourse preceding the sacrament was then called. His text was Psalm 51:17: "The sacrifices of God are a broken spirit." After the sacrament Dr. Graham preached that sermon on Isaiah 40:1, "Comfort ye, comfort ye my people," which was spoken of as long as any people of that period remained alive. "The good people of Briery were entranced," says Alexander. "They had expected a very cold and dry discourse." But Graham's heart had been touched by the Spirit. His message was delivered in burning words that set on fire the spirits of his audience.

When the three horsemen, Graham and Alexander and Wilson, left Charlotte County they returned to the Valley by passing again through Bedford County. In the church near the Peaks of Otter, of which Mitchell was pastor, the sacrament was celebrated. James Turner, who had recently turned from profanity unto a godly life, was preaching also in the congregation. Then the travelers, accompanied by Legrand and a large company of other friends, returned to the Valley of Virginia. There Graham spoke his message with great fervor, accompanied with appeals that moved men and women to tears. Legrand preached also, and a great revival began. Archibald Alexander and a large number of his young associates professed their faith in Christ, and some of them began at once to prepare themselves for the work of preaching the gospel. In many other parts of the South, and also in the North, the Spirit of God moved in like manner upon the hearts of the people, and multitudes of them were added daily to the churches.

One of the immediate effects of the growth of the church was the organization of the General Assembly. In May, 1788, the Presbyterian Churches in the United States divided themselves into four synods, two in the North and two in the South; namely, (1) Synod of New York and New Jersey, consisting of four presbyteries; (2) Synod of Philadelphia, consisting of five presbyteries, one of which, the Presbytery of Baltimore, was located in Maryland; (3) Synod of Virginia, consisting of the four presbyteries of Redstone, Hanover, Lexington and Transylvania, the latter being in the Kentucky country; (4) Synod of the Carolinas, consisting of the three presbyteries of Abingdon, Orange and South Carolina. There were thus eight presbyteries in the South and eight in the North. The Synod of Virginia held its first meeting at New Providence Church, Rockbridge County, on October 22, 1788. On November 5, 1788, the Synod of the Carolinas held its first meeting at Centre Church, in North Carolina, David Caldwell being chosen moderator. Then, on the 21st of May, 1789, delegates from all of the sixteen presbyteries met in Philadelphia to constitute the first General Assembly.

CHAPTER XXVII.

ARCHIBALD ALEXANDER, PRESIDENT OF HAMPDEN SIDNEY
COLLEGE, AND FIRST TEACHER OF THEOLOGY
IN PRINCETON SEMINARY.

ONE morning in the autumn of the year 1789, a young
man, who was then in the eighteenth year of his age, began to climb the long slope of a hill near the little town
of Lexington, in the Valley of Virginia. He carried
a Bible in his hand. With rapid steps he made his way
among the trees that covered the side of the hill until he
came to a large rock within a little valley. At the foot
of the rock he knelt in prayer for his own salvation.
He wished to have the conscious feeling within his own
heart that his soul was redeemed.

Then a passage was read from the Bible and another
prayer was offered. Thus he read the word and
prayed, and read and prayed again and again, until
his strength was gone, for the young man had not tasted
food that day. Weak as he was and in despair, it
seemed to him that God would not hear him. His own
heart seemed to him to become harder and more and
more devoid of every serious emotion. He knelt again
on the ground and uttered one broken cry for help,
"when, in a moment," he tells us, "I had such a view of
a crucified Saviour as is without a parallel in my experience.

"The whole plan of grace appeared as clear as day.
I was persuaded that God was willing to accept me, just
as I was, and convinced that I had never before under-

stood the freeness of salvation, but had always been striving to bring some price in my hand, or to prepare myself for receiving Christ. Now I discovered that I could receive him in all his offices at that very moment, which I was sure at the time I did. I felt truly a joy which was unspeakable and full of glory. How long this delightful frame continued I cannot tell. But when my affections had a little subsided I opened my Bible and alighted on the eighteenth and nineteenth chapters of John. The second page appeared to be illuminated; the truths were new, as if I had never read them before; and I thought it would be always thus. Having often thought of engaging in a written covenant with God, but having never before found a freedom to do so, I now felt no hesitation, and, having writing materials in my pocket, I sat down and penned it exactly from my feelings and solemnly signed it as in the presence of God."

The name signed to the covenant was that of Archibald Alexander. In this paper he solemnly gave himself unto God. The struggle within his own spirit which had been in progress for months had ended in the peace which he found under the shadow of the great rock in the forest. Soon afterwards he stood up among the people of William Graham's congregation and made a public profession of his faith in Christ.

Three brothers who were Scots bearing the names of Archibald, Robert and William Alexander, came from North Ireland to Pennsylvania about the year 1736. A few years afterwards two of the brothers, Archibald and Robert, moved southward into the Valley of Virginia. Robert established there, in 1749, the Augusta Academy, which was afterwards called the Liberty Hall Academy. Archibald built a home on South River, a branch of the James, within the limits of the present Rockbridge County. He was a member of the first body of elders of the Church at Timber Ridge.

The first Archibald Alexander, called "Old Ersbell"

by his neighbors, was below the common height. He
was "thick-set, broad-breasted and strongly built.
His face was broad, his eyes large, black and prominent." He was a man of great kindness of heart. As
captain of riflemen, he led his neighbors in their fights
against the Indians. His life was marked by the
strictest honesty. "No one expects a descendant of
'Old Ersbell' to be greedy, or avaricious, or pinch-
ing, or unkind, or indolent, or ignorant, or very rich,"
says Dr. W. H. Foote. "But the public did expect
them to know their catechism, to be familiar with their
Bible, to keep the Sabbath, to fear God, keep a good
conscience, with industry and economy to be independent
and at last to die Christianly." Archibald Alexander's
eldest son, William, also became an elder. He knew
all of the Larger Catechism and nearly all of Watts's
Psalms and Hymns. William built a log house near his
father's home on South River and there on April 17,
1772, his son Archibald was born.

Archy Alexander, as this boy was called, was
trained to use the rifle, to ride horseback and to swim
in the mountain streams. An Irish servant, John Rear-
don, who lived in his father's home, taught him a little
Latin. The Catechisms were, of course, committed to
memory. Then Archy entered Liberty Hall Academy
and was drilled in Latin and Greek and the philosophy
of the mind by William Graham. He did not think,
however, that he made rapid progress in his studies.
Of his own writing and composition at that time he
says that "nothing could have been more miserable."
"Once I attempted to take part in a debate, but it
was an utter failure." The winter after he completed
his sixteenth year was occupied by young Alexander as a teacher in the family of General John Posey,
who lived near Fredericksburg. Hard work there
laid the foundation for good scholarship in the Latin
language and in history. He became disturbed about

the spiritual state of his own soul and was led to read the works of John Flavel. In later life he believed that he became a Christian during that winter in General Posey's home. He returned to his father's home in 1789, made the journey to Charlotte with Mr. Graham and afterwards passed through a spiritual struggle which ended, as we have seen, in the making of that covenant with his God which was written under the shadow of the great rock near the town of Lexington.

For many months after this time, however, Alexander's spirit was passing back and forth from the sunshine into the shadow. He was often again in despair about himself. A burning fever came and wasted away his frame. Then in the summer of the year 1790 he decided to become a preacher, although he considered himself as entirely unfit for this sacred calling.

When Alexander went to William Graham to begin his studies in preparation for the ministry, he asked the teacher to give him a list of books for reading. Graham smiled and said, "If you mean ever to be a theologian, you must come at it not by reading, but by thinking." He told Alexander that he must learn to think for himself and to form his own opinions from the Bible. "This conversation," says Alexander, "discouraged me more than if he had told me to read half a dozen folios. For as to learning anything by my own thoughts I had no idea of its practicability. But it did me more good than any directions or counsels I ever received. It threw me on my own resources and led me to feel the necessity of disciplining my own thoughts and searching into the principles of things."

Seven or eight young men formed the class in the study of theology that began, in 1789, to sit at Graham's feet. They listened to Graham's lectures on the philosophy of the mind. At the same time the young students read a few standard books by such authors as Edwards, Owen and Boston. They also carried on daily discussions among themselves and debated all of the points in controversy between Calvinists and Arminians. Every Saturday they met Mr. Graham in his study. There was first a recitation upon the lectures delivered by the teacher. Then each student read a paper upon some prescribed subject. The work of the day was concluded with a debate upon a number of subjects previously assigned. Graham gave to the students the benefit of his own views upon these themes, but he was stern and dogmatic in announcing his own opinions. He did not show any respect for an opinion opposed to that which he himself held, and he did not like to be contradicted. In spite of all this, he brought into exercise all the powers of the students. In this manner Graham trained some of the greatest preachers of our country for their work.

In October, 1790, Alexander was taken under the care of Lexington Presbytery. Then Graham took two of his ministerial students, Archibald Alexander and John Lyle, to the house of John McKee, near Lexington, and asked them to make a religious address to the people assembled there. "Lyle appeared to be much animated and elevated," says Alexander. "He told me that he had a remarkable flow of thought, and seemed confident of a prosperous issue; which only discouraged me the more as I was weighed down with a heavy burden. After singing and prayer, Mr. Graham called first upon Lyle, who arose with an awful cloud upon his brow, seized hold of the chair upon which he had been sitting and with many contortions of countenance forced out a few words; but his flow of thought had deserted him. He hummed and groaned, rolled up his pocket handkerchief into a ball, made a few convulsive gestures and sat down. After another prayer and hymn, I was called upon. Although I did not know a single word which I was to utter, I began with a rapid-

ity and fluency equal to any I have enjoyed to this
day. I was astonished at myself, and as I was young
and small, the old people were not less astonished.
From this time I exhorted at one place and another,
several times every week."

In the spring of 1791, Alexander was examined by
the presbytery on the Latin and Greek languages
and the sciences. He read his exegesis and his
homily to the presbytery. Then William Graham
urged that a subject be assigned to Alexander for
a trial sermon to be delivered the next meeting
of presbytery. Alexander wished to postpone this
sermon, pleading his youth and lack of preparation. Graham said, however, that the young student's
acquirements were greater than usual and that he was
ready for active work. On September 20, 1791, Alexander stood before the Lexington Presbytery, according to the custom of that time, and opened the proceedings with a sermon on Jeremiah 1:7: "Say not, I
am a child." He was so small in stature that he seemed
but a little boy. His eye was dark and piercing and
his voice rang out in a silver tone, as clear and as musical as a flute. Every one present was surprised at
the clearness of his reasoning and the ease and rapidity
of his speaking. Graham wept for joy when he saw
the power manifested in the sermon of his pupil. The
members of the presbytery rode at once to Winchester to attend Synod, and there they held a meeting and
licensed Alexander to preach.

The young minister preached next in a house near
Winchester and there the old soldier of the Revolution,
General Daniel Morgan, was among those who listened to
him. Then he went to Charlestown and began to preach
from a written outline which he placed in front of him.
A puff of wind came through the open door and carried
the paper away until it fell among the congregation. "I
then determined," he says, "to take no more paper into

the pulpit." During the winter he preached for Moses Hoge at Shepherdstown, for William Hill at Charlestown and for Nash Legrand at Opecquon. Every where crowds came to hear him speak, for he was full of animation in those early years and gave free swing to his imagination. Dr. Speece said that Alexander, in his youth, was like "a young horse of high blood, let out into a spacious pasture, exercising every muscle and careering in every direction with extravagant delight."

His sermons were not written, but were studied out as he rode from house to house on horseback. In his own mind, by silent thought, he arranged in systematic order the sentences and the very words of his discourses. For all the labors of that winter he received not one cent of pay. He expected nothing, however, for he was only "trying his gifts." He had to buy a pair of trousers and for these he sent back the money after returning to his father's house.

As he rode homeward along the Valley, everybody was eager to hear the preaching of "the boy," Archy Alexander. A great crowd assembled in Staunton to listen and admire. The people of his home town, Lexington, filled the court house and were delighted. Then he went to the Oxford Meeting-house, near Lexington, and another crowd met him. The people were pleased and profited to hear the rapid flow of his words, and the tender appeals contained in his message.

Two faults, he tells us, marked his preaching at that time. One was the extreme rapidity of his utterance, for he ran on until he was out of breath. The other fault was a habit of looking steadily down upon the floor. These faults he afterwards corrected. His modesty, however, remained with him. "I was so conscious of my own defects," he says, "that often after preaching I was ashamed to come down from the pulpit, and wondered that any could speak kindly to me." "I have commonly felt," he wrote again, "that the people who admired my preaching were deceived."

In the summer of 1792, Alexander and his friend, Benjamin Grigsby, were appointed by the Synod of Virginia to travel through the region east of the Blue Ridge and preach the gospel. They journeyed through Prince Edward and Charlotte and all of the adjoining counties. The congregations drank in the words of the evangelists wherever they spoke. On one occasion the people seemed so ready to hear that Alexander continued to preach for nearly two hours. Then he dismissed the assembly, but not one person left the house. Since they held their seats, he arose again and gave them another sermon, three-quarters of an hour in length.

In 1793 Drury Lacy and Archibald Alexander, as colleagues, took charge of the six churches near Hampden Sidney College. Lacy, as Vice-President, was then managing the affairs of the college itself. In the following year Alexander became the regular shepherd of the flocks at Briery and Cub Creek. There he gave himself up to preaching and study. He read every book that he could buy or borrow. He had a burning desire to save the souls of men, and he sought them out in their homes. He made his own home in the family of Major Edmund Read, of Charlotte County. There under the great oaks on the lawn he walked back and forth or sat still while he was drawing out in his mind the thread of a great discourse. Sometimes he wrote these out with great care, after delivery.

Early in 1799 Alexander was made President of Hampden Sidney College. He continued, at the same time, to preach at Briery and at the College Church. His labors here were so incessant that his health was injured. In the summer of 1801, therefore, he made a horseback journey through New England. The young Virginia preacher was invited to preach in all of the

large churches of the East. His sermons were admired
and warmly praised by the ministers of New York,
New Haven, Boston and other centers. At Harvard
College and Dartmouth College, special honors were
shown him.

In April, 1802, Alexander was united in marriage
to Janetta Waddell, daughter of the "blind preacher."
Together they took up the work at the college in May,
1802. Under Alexander's management the school became prosperous. An increasing number of students
came each year. Many of these became ministers and
helped to build up the Presbyterian Church in the
South and Southwest. Archibald Alexander himself
soon became known as the most efficient preacher of his
day in our whole country. As a speaker he was full of
vigor and animation and his delivery was marked by
great charm of manner. His knowledge was widened
with continual study and he became, also, one of the
greatest scholars of his time. His pen soon became busy
in producing the many books and pamphlets which he
left behind him.

In 1807 Dr. Alexander was made pastor of the Pine
Street Church in Philadelphia. Then in 1812 he became the first teacher of theology in Princeton Seminary and held that position until his death in 1851.

Three times during his residence at Princeton, Dr. Alexander came to visit his friends in Virginia. Each
time they poured out their warmest love upon him. His
own strongest affections were lavished, in turn, upon
the friends of his youth.

One Sunday morning in October, 1816, Dr. Alexander stood up to preach in the church at Fredericksburg.
The Synod of Virginia was then holding its sessions in
that place of worship and the members of that body,
with a great company of other persons, were seated
before him. The Lord's Supper was to be celebrated
and the preacher's text was, "Christ our passover is

sacrificed for us" (I. Cor. 5:7). He began his sermon
in a manner so quiet and simple that many were dis-
appointed. One prominent lawyer thought the preaching so poor that he arose from his seat and walked out
of the church. Alexander began to grow warm and his
whole manner was marked by life and action. When he
had described the Jewish passover, he turned the attention of his audience to the sacrifice of Christ by bending forward and looking intently upon the table where
the bread and wine lay covered. "But there is our
lamb," he said. The manner and voice of the preacher
went home to the heart of every member of the congregation. An old Frenchman, seated near the pulpit,
arose to his feet and looked intently at the table, expecting to see the lamb. Alexander's discourse then
moved rapidly forward. As he spoke of the successive
scenes in the suffering of Jesus, tears started from eyes
that were not used to weeping. "When he depicted the
last scene of our Saviour's suffering on the cross, that
power of descriptive painting for which he was remarkable in his pulpit efforts, was displayed in a manner rarely surpassed by the most accomplished orators.
Amidst the unutterable agonies, which Jesus suffered
while hanging on the cross, he introduced Mary, his
mother, among the spectators, beholding the cruel sufferings of her beloved son, and quoted the prediction
of Simeon as there fulfilled: 'Yea, a sword shall pierce
through thine own soul.' Such was his gesture, his
voice, his whole manner, that had Mary actually stood
before the audience, with flowing tears and every token
of deepest sorrow, the impression could hardly have
been increased."

In the summer of 1825, Alexander came again to
Virginia and preached to all of the congregations that
he had once served. The hearts of all of his people
were moved towards him with a great love. During
the remainder of life they dated every event as having

taken place either before or after "Doctor Alexander's visit."

On the 29th of June, 1843, Dr. Alexander, then in his seventy-second year, made an address in the church at Lexington, Virginia. He had come to pay a last visit to the region of his birth and childhood. The commencement exercises of Washington College were in progress, and Alexander was speaking to the alumni of that school. The heat of the summer afternoon was too severe for the speaker. After delivering a part of his discourse he faltered, grew pale, and sank into a seat. He arose and attempted again to speak, but soon gave way and his friends carried him into the open air. These friends urged him to permit another to read the address for him. But this he would not allow. He must perform his own duty, he said. He sat in a chair outside of the church and under its shadow. The graves of his father and mother were within a few yards of him. The stones marking the tombs of those whom he had loved in his youth were all about him. The descendants of those early settlers formed the audience that gathered about his chair and drank in every word as Dr. Alexander spoke of the founder of Washington College, that is, of William Graham, first Rector of Liberty Hall Academy. He gave a sketch of Graham's character and spoke of his great work in behalf of learning and religion. Thus Alexander, in his old age, paid his debt of gratitude to the man who had brought him into the gospel ministry.

Dr. Alexander worked without ceasing until he entered his eightieth year. Then the strength left his body. As the shadows of death gathered about him, his soul was in a state of perfect peace. "He spoke of dying with the same natural cheerfulness with which he would have spoken of going from one room to another." One night, just before the end, he was in a rapture and spoke of the time spent under the shadow of the rock

in the hills near Lexington, where the great joy filled
his youthful heart. As his spirit entered the valley there
seemed to be a light about him. His Saviour was present
to guide and to sustain. "There was nothing excited,
nothing exultant, and yet he seemed to be thoroughly
triumphant," wrote one who witnessed his death; "a
calm, believing, cheerful looking through the gloomy
grave into the glories of the eternal world." Heaven's
door opened and he entered with joy.

CHAPTER XXVIII.

MOSES HOGE, PRESIDENT OF THE COLLEGE AND TEACHER
OF THEOLOGY AT HAMPDEN SIDNEY, IN VIRGINIA.

In October, 1807, a few months after the departure of
President Archibald Alexander, Moses Hoge came to
Hampden Sidney to take up the duties of the presidency of the college. He was then in his fifty-sixth
year, and he spent the remainder of his life upon "The
Hill" in Prince Edward County, training young men
for their work and leading many of them into the gospel
ministry.

Moses Hoge was the son of James Hoge, a man of
"robust intellect and a self-taught theologian," who
dwelt near Winchester, in the beautiful Valley of Virginia. James was a son of William Hoge, one of the
first settlers on Opecquon Creek. James was an elder
in the Opecquon Church where his nephew, John Hoge,
served as minister for many years. When Moses, the
ninth son of James, became a strong-armed lad, he
learned to plow and reap on his father's farm. He was
sent for a short time to a classical school. When he
went back again to the work of planting, he fastened
a book to the plow; at the end of each furrow he ran
his eyes over the printed page and then fixed the contents in his mind while he followed the team across the
field.

"Sanctified learning is the greatest blessing; un-
sanctified learning is the greatest curse." This sentiment, uttered by Samuel Stanhope Smith, sank deep
into the heart of young Moses Hoge. He determined
that he would be a man of learning. At an early age
he gave his heart to Christ and made up his mind to

serve Him in the gospel ministry. He sat under the instruction of William Graham, at Liberty Hall Academy, and in 1781, in the thirtieth year of his age, was licensed to preach. Then in the autumn of 1787 he became pastor of the church at Shepherdstown on the Potomac, and there he remained for twenty years.

Dr. Hoge was a reader of many books and he collected a good library. In 1793 he published a book defending the principles of the Calvinistic system of religion. In 1805 he opened a classical school in his own congregation and trained several young preachers.

In person Dr. Hoge was slender and of medium height; his features were clear-cut and his countenance was grave and dignified. One who knew him well tells us that "his manners, though without much artificial polish, were familiar and agreeable, expressing very strongly the kindness and benignity of his spirit. He possessed a mind of uncommon vigor, capable at once of accurate discrimination and profound research, and withal richly stored with the treasures of scientific knowledge. As a preacher his manner was ungraceful, even uncouth; but there was so much depth and originality of thought, such richness and force of illustration, and such clear and cogent reasoning, that the awkwardness of his manner was very soon quite overlooked or forgotten."

A fellow minister, Joseph Glass, said of Hoge: "It was not that he was unlike other men, but that he was always like himself; not that he was zealously engaged in doing good today, but that in doing good he was zealously engaged every day; not that he performed duty, but that he never tired in performing it; not that he put his hand to the plow, but that he never looked back; not that he knew how to do good, but that he knew not how to do harm; and it was on a foundation composed of these singular materials that he erected the monument of an unspotted life."

During most of Hoge's ministry at Shepherdstown, Nash Legrand was in charge of the two churches at Opecquon and Cedar Creek, where his gentle persuasion and his godly life won many hearts for the Master. In the year 1800 William Hill began his long and successful ministry in the church at Winchester. He was a preacher of surpassing power. Moreover, as the head master of a school for young women, he manifested high qualities of mind and heart.

When Moses Hoge was made president of Hampden Sidney College (1807), he was told that the Hanover Presbytery expected him to become also the chief teacher in a school of theology. In the following year (1808), therefore, be began to give instruction in theology to a group of ministerial candidates. In 1812, however, when Archibald Alexander went to Princeton to establish a seminary, Moses Hoge contiuued with enlarged authority to train preachers at Hampden Sidney; for he was then, in a formal manner, appointed professor of theology by the Synod of Virginia.

Dr. Hoge's preaching grew more impressive as his years advanced. His arms seemed always too long and their movements were awkward, but his words gave expression to the love that filled a great heart. "That man is the best of orators," said John Randolph of Roanoke, who often listened to Hoge's sermons. "He never properly made gestures," writes Dr. Foote, "yet every limb and feature spoke to his hearers. A jerk of his elbow, or a swing of his long arm was the precursor or accompaniment of a sweeping proposition, an unanswerable argument or the assertion of a great truth. The turning and twisting of his handkerchief, with both hands, indicated the evolution of some grand truth, or deep feeling, or pathetic appeal. His old acquaintances understood his motions and felt assured of the richness of his abundant resources of mind and heart. The tremor of his arm would start the expectation of a rich exhibition of truth. The starting tear in his eye would unlock the fountains in their hearts. The hesitation in his speech would make them almost breathless to catch the promised word."

In 1814, during our second war with England, the British landed a force of troops and burned the Capitol at Washington. It was then reported that the same soldiers were marching toward Richmond. This news came to Dr. Hoge one Sunday afternoon just as he was beginning his usual religious service. He stood up at once and spoke to his audience upon the duty of defending home and country. He urged the men present to take their rifles and go to meet the enemy. The next day at noon a company of horsemen was ready and Dr. Hoge again addressed them, urging each soldier to fight even unto death.

Three of the sons of Moses Hoge became ministers; these were James, John Blair and Samuel Davies. The latter left a son, Moses Drury Hoge, of whom we shall hear in a later chapter of this volume. James spent most of his ministerial life in Ohio. John Blair was not strong in body and died at an early eage, but while he lived he was one of the most successful preachers of his time. He first became a lawyer, then studied theology and was minister of the churches of Tuscarora and Falling Waters, near Martinsburg, in the lower Valley of Virginia. His powers of imagination, his command of words and the earnestness of his manner held the attention of all who heard him.

One night in the church at Fredericksburg, John Blair Hoge preached before the Synod of Virginia. It was only a day or two before Archibald Alexander preached his famous sacramental sermon in the same church and in the presence of the same synod. Hoge's text was on the trembling of Felix (Acts 24: 25). His manner, we are told by Dr. Foote, was somewhat awkward and his voice had a slight hoarseness. "He gave a short history of the parties grouped in the text and context, and by his graphic skill we saw them all living and moving before us, the judge, the splendid company and the prisoner, all in our 'mind's eye.' As he went on, his strong features softened and beamed with tenderness and intellect, and any want of gracefulness was lost in his dignified bearing and commanding manner. * * * The attention deepened. All were motionless but the venerable old man [Moses Hoge], whose varying countenance and agitated limbs exhibited the deep emotions of a father listening to a son in the ministry. As the scenes and subject changed from righteousness to temperance, from temperance to judgment to come, we heard his husky voice and saw his strong, ungainly features, with his stretched arm and extended fingers; but they were all lost sight of again, as with a sweep of his strained arm, and half shut hand and laboring chest, he made us see his mental visions, and feel the truth his struggling lungs announced. Felix trembled before us. * * * We heard him say, 'Go thy way for this time.' * * * Suddenly the scene changed, as with the motion of his hand. We ceased to be spectators; we were now actors. He was addressing us like Paul, and we, like Felix, were trembling on the brink of decision. * * * He paused a moment and then bade us cry out to the King of Kings for pardon and for life. Pointing up, with a voice sinking under weariness and emotion, he cried out, 'O, thou recording angel! dip thy pen in the blood of the everlasting covenant and beneath this record of sins and transgressions, write *forgiveness!*' The book of remembrance seemed open in the ceiling and by it stood the angel as about to write, with his pen bloody from the fount of Calvary, on the dark leaves. The silence was awful. Bursting hearts were ready to cry, '*write mine.*' The vision grew dim; we turned to the speaker; he had disappeared. But the deep impression remained. The name of the man was connected with the subject; probably no one that heard that sermon ever forgot either the man or the subject."

Four years after the meeting of the synod at Fredericksburg, Moses Hoge passed away from the earth (1820) leaving behind upon the hearts of those who knew him the impression that he was "the wisest and meekest of men." Then in 1826, John Blair Hoge's brief labors came to an end and he entered into rest.

CHAPTER XXIX.

MOSES WADDEL AND THE WILLINGTON ACADEMY IN
SOUTH CAROLINA.

ONE morning in the late autumn of the year 1794, a Presbyterian preacher left the Georgia side of the Savannah River and crossed over to South Carolina. He was of low stature and had a boyish face, for he was only twenty-four years of age. He rode to a schoolhouse that stood in the Calhoun Settlement, on Long Cane Creek, in Abbeville District, and found assembled there a company of Scotch-Irish people. When he arose to speak, the congregation was surprised to hear a deep-toned, musical voice. The preacher's calm, gray eyes looked straight into their eyes and his earnest, rapid talking caught their attention. When the sermon was ended, Patrick Calhoun, patriarch of the community and elder in the neighboring church, led the minister to his home. While they were seated, that evening, around the wide, old-fashioned fire-place in the Calhoun home, the door was opened and a youthful face looked in, but was at once withdrawn. The face belonged to John Caldwell Calhoun, Patrick Calhoun's son, who afterwards became South Carolina's great statesman. A year later, the young minister, whose name was Moses Waddel, married Catharine Calhoun, sister of John C. Calhoun, and took her to his home beyond the Savannah. There, in Georgia, Waddel was preaching the gospel and teaching Latin and Greek to a group of schoolboys.

Moses Waddel was born (1770) in Iredell County, North Carolina. His parents were Scots from North Ireland. Soon after Moses completed his eighth year

he went to James Hall's school and began to study
Latin. After six years of work, he finished the
courses of study in Greek, Latin and mathematics, as
far as these subjects were taught in the school. Then
he took charge of various schools in North Carolina
and Georgia until the year 1789, when he gave his
heart to Christ. After a long struggle within his own
breast, young Waddel determined to become a preacher.
In the autumn of 1790, therefore, he mounted his horse
and made the long journey from Georgia to Virginia.
In the month of September in that year he began a
course of study at Hampden Sidney College. A little
more than a year later he left the college, and in
May, 1772, was licensed by Hanover Presbytery to
preach the gospel. The year 1794 found him established as pastor of Carmel Church, south of the Savannah. At the same time he organized a school in
Columbia County, Georgia. Near the close of that
year he crossed the Savannah, as we have seen, and
there met Catharine Calhoun, who became his wife
and his helper in the Georgia school. In 1801
Waddel moved his home to Abbeville District, South
Carolina, and there opened his school in the village of
Vienna. A little later, however, he selected a site upon
a ridge near the Calhoun Settlement. There, among
oak and hickory trees, he erected a log house and called
it Willington Academy. Log cabins for the students
were put up near the main building. For a long period
of time, as many as one hundred and eighty students
came each year to receive instruction from this wonderful teacher, Moses Waddel.

The food furnished to the students in Waddel's log
college was plain, for it was usually nothing more than
cornbread and bacon. A blast from a ram's horn
called them all together for morning and evening prayers. When the weather was mild the students sat or
lay beneath the trees to prepare their lessons. The

sound of the horn told the class in Homer when to assemble, and all of the members of it rushed at once to the recitation hall in the main building. Then the horn called up, in regular order, the Cicero, the Horace and the Virgil classes, as well as those engaged in the study of mathematics and English.

Waddel had a clear mind and a strong will. He gave his pupils an admirable training in all of their studies. Moreover, he held them under his own absolute control through strict discipline. The master loved each pupil. He governed them with love and with impartial justice.

A large company of ministers received their entire training in Waddel's school. Of these we may name Richard B. Cater, John H. Gray, David Humphreys, James Gamble, James C. Patterson and Thomas D. Baird. Some famous scholars and statesmen also were educated in this log college, among whom were William H. Crawford, Howell Cobb and A. B. Longstreet, of Georgia, and John C. Calhoun, Hugh S. Legaré, James L. Petigru, George McDuffie, and many others, of South Carolina.

The Willington school building was also a church. Waddel preached every Sunday to his students and to the people of the community. In 1809 these worshippers were regularly organized as a Presbyterian Church. A revival of religion took place there and many of the students became Christians.

During a period of about fifteen years Moses Waddel kept up at Willington the best school in all that part of our country. In 1819 he went to Athens, Georgia, to take charge of the University of Georgia as President. He was then the most famous teacher in the far South, and he at once placed this school upon a high plane of literary excellence. He preached the gospel every Sunday to the body of students assembled in the chapel. He conducted the university as a Christian

school throughout his presidency of ten years. At the
close of the year 1829 he gave up the heavy work at the
university and went back to Willington. The academy
was opened there again under the control of Waddel's
son. The old preacher himself spent nearly all of his
closing days in giving to the people of that region the
gospel of peace. He died in 1840.

CHAPTER XXX.

JOSEPH CALDWELL AND THE UNIVERSITY OF NORTH CAROLINA.

ONE day in November, 1796, at Chapel Hill, in North Carolina, a Presbyterian preacher, then in his twenty-fourth year, began to teach a class in mathematics. His name was Joseph Caldwell. He was a native of New Jersey, but was descended from Scotch-Irish and Huguenot ancestors. The course of study at Princeton College was completed by Caldwell in 1791. Then in 1796 he was licensed to preach, and in the autumn of that year, rode to the village of Chapel Hill, which is located twenty-eight miles from Raleigh, the capital of North Carolina. There he entered upon the double work involved in the professorship of mathematics and the presidency of the University of North Carolina.

Seven years before this time, that is, in December, 1789, the legislature appointed forty of the leading men of the state as trustees and authorized them to establish a state university. On the 12th of October, 1793, the cornerstone of the first university building was laid at Chapel Hill by William Richardson Davie, one of the trustees. Samuel E. McCorkle, pastor of the Presbyterian Church near Salisbury, also a trustee, spoke the solemn words of dedication: "May this hill be for religion as the ancient hill of Zion," he said; "and for literature and the muses may it surpass the ancient Parnassus." Some teaching was done at Chapel Hill under the guidance of David Ker, a minister and a teacher, during the months that followed the placing of the cornerstone. The real work of the school was begun when Joseph Caldwell called upon his class to recite in mathematics in November, 1796. From that time until his death in January, 1835, a period of nearly forty years he worked without ceasing to build up the institution. Great success crowned his labors, for Joseph Caldwell was the founder of the University of North Carolina.

Upper North Carolina was, at that time, filled with schools of high grade, all of them under the management of Presbyterian ministers. David Caldwell's academy in Guilford was still sending out well-trained preachers. Samuel McCorkle, in Thyatira congregation, near Salisbury; James Wallis, in the Providence congregation, near Charlotte; James Hall, in Bethany congregation, near Statesville; John Makemie Wilson, at Rocky River Church, whose school was opened a little later and sent out twenty-five preachers within a few years; John Robinson, in Poplar Tent congregation, and at Fayetteville; Samuel C. Caldwell, son of David Caldwell, whose school began later in Sugar Creek Congregation—all of these faithful ministers conducted academies as a part of their regular church work. In 1793, at Chatham, William Bingham, the preacher, established the famous Bingham School, which has continued to do its work until the present time, under a long line of Presbyterian elders of the Bingham family. There was also the public academy at Charlotte, the academy in Duplin County, Science Hall near Hillsboro, Warrenton Academy, Granville Hall, and academies in the towns of Edenton, Newbern and Onslow. These schools trained the people of North Carolina to believe that Christianity must fill the atmosphere even of a state school. For this reason, Joseph Caldwell preached the gospel every Sunday in the chapel at the university, had the Bible taught in the school itself and opened the work of each day with public prayer in presence of all the students.

Caldwell upheld the Christian religion as a necessary

element in the training given by a university. William
R. Davie, the soldier and statesman, had fallen away
from the belief in the Bible, which he learned in the
home of his uncle, William Richardson, of the Wax-
haw Church. As a trustee of the university, Davie
came in close touch with President Caldwell. The latter engaged Davie in discussion about the Bible,
pleaded with him and, probably, won him to a saving
faith in Christ.

In 1833, just before Caldwell's death, an academy
under Presbyterian church control was founded at
Greensboro; later it was removed to Hillsboro. It was
named Caldwell Institute, because Caldwell led the movement that resulted in the building of the school. "He
strongly urged upon his brethren a return to the old
fashioned discipline and studies of Presbyterian classical schools, the course somewhat enlarged. He declared it was not sectarian for denominations to have
denominational schools; that religion must be taught
by somebody and in classical academies, and that but
one denomination could be engaged in a single school
to advantage."

When Caldwell took charge of the North Carolina
University there were many men throughout our country
who refused to accept the teachings of the Bible as true.
Caldwell had to deal with some of these unbelievers. He
stood firm always in the defense of the religion of his
God. "He fought a great battle without noise and gained
a great victory without triumphing." Daily prayer and
worship and the study of the Bible were left in the
university as parts of its work, after Caldwell's life had
ended.

CHAPTER XXXI.

PRESBYTERIANS IN KENTUCKY AND THE REVIVAL OF 1800.

In the summer of 1783, a written invitation, to which three hundred names were signed, came from the land of Kentucky to David Rice. This minister was then the shepherd of the flock that lived near the foot of the Peaks of Otter, in Virginia. Rice obeyed the call and, in October, 1783, made the long journey westward through a gap in the Cumberland mountains. He founded churches at Danville and in the region near that place, and from that time was known as "Father Rice," the patriarch of the Presbyterian Church in Kentucky.

Nearly all of the company of three hundred people who urged David Rice to come into Kentucky, had moved into that fair western region from the Valley of Virginia. Just ten years before Rice accepted the call to service, that is in 1773, the first real homebuilders entered Kentucky. They left their former places of abode in the mountains of Virginia and started westward under the leadership of Capt. Thomas Bullitt and three brothers bearing the name of McAfee. Bullitt laid the foundation of the city of Louisville and the McAfees settled the Salt River country. In 1775, Daniel Boone and Henderson led a company of settlers from North Carolina through the Cumberland mountains. At the same time Benjamin Logan left his home on the Holston River, in the congregation of Charles Cummings, and built cabins for his family and his slaves near Harrodsburg. These pioneers were followed by a continuous stream of home builders, some of them from North Carolina, but the greater part from Virginia. Among these were the Todds, Floyds, Bowmans, Callaways, Pattersons, Mastersons, McConnels, Lindseys, Morrisons, Flemings, Barbours, Triggs, Thompsons, McDowells, McKees, Greens, Breckenridges, Browns, Youngs, and many others. In 1776 Kentucky was organized as a county of Virginia. In 1783 courts of justice were established and David Rice was called from Bedford County to establish Presbyterian churches. Many Baptists from Eastern Virginia entered Kentucky before the arrival of Rice. About one year after the journey of Rice—that is, on October 1, 1784, a number of families left their homes in Augusta County, Virginia, and started toward Kentucky. They met, according to agreement, in the town of Staunton. Jane Allen Trimble, wife of Captain James Trimble, was a member of the party, and wrote an account of the journey. She tells us that on the previous Sunday she attended James Waddell's church at the Tinkling Spring, and heard the blind preacher for the last time, as she then supposed. Waddell "spoke of the separation of parents and children, brothers and sisters, friends and neighbors, who had been united in sweetest bonds of fellowship, in such a pathetic strain as to make all eyes fill with tears."

All of the grown members of the party, says Mrs. Trimble, "rode upon horses, and upon other horses were placed the farming and cooking utensils, beds and bedding, wearing apparel, provisions, and last, but not least, the libraries, consisting of two Bibles, half a dozen Testaments, the Catechism, the Confession of Faith of the Presbyterian Church, and the Psalms of David. Each man and boy carried his rifle and ammunition, and each woman her pistol." Mrs. Trimble carried one young child in her lap, while another, a boy three years of age, was placed on the horse behind his mother. This boy, Allen

Trimble, was afterwards governor of Ohio. By the time the party reached the Holston River, in Southwest Virginia, they had increased to three hundred persons. A little farther on the way westward "they were joined by two hundred more from Carolina. Threefourths of these were women and children." In this and in later companies a great multitude of Allens, Trimbles, Bells, Montgomerys, Glasses, Moffetts, Robertsons, and other Scots from the western parts of Virginia passed into Kentucky. The year 1790 found 75,000 people in this region, and in 1792 Kentucky was admitted as a state of the Federal Union. Many of her leaders in establishing a permanent form of government were Presbyterians. The president of the convention which framed the first constitution of Kentucky was Samuel McDowell, grandson of Ephraim McDowell, of Rockbridge County, Virginia. John, Levi and Thomas Todd, kinsmen of the minister, John Todd, of Louisa County, Virginia, helped to start the new government in Kentucky. The first governor of the state was Isaac Shelby, the Presbyterian elder from the Tennessee country. Shelby's secretary of state was James Brown, son of Rev. John Brown, pastor of Timber Ridge and New Providence Churches, in Rockbridge County, Virginia. John Brown, brother of James, and eldest son of the preacher of Rockbridge, was elected one of Kentucky's first United States Senators. The first speaker of the State senate was Alexander Scott Bullitt, and the speaker of the house was Robert Breckinridge, who went to Kentucky from Botetourt County, Virginia. One of the three judges of the first supreme court of Kentucky was Caleb Wallace, from Virginia, who had given up the work of preaching to become a lawyer.

On November 10, 1783, a small company of men met at Crow's Station, now known as Danville. They were David Rice, Caleb Wallace, Isaac Shelby, James

Speed, Samuel McDowell, Robert Johnson, Christopher Greenup, Willis Green, Walker Daniel and John Craig. They formed the board of trustees of *The Transylvania Seminary*, to which the legislature of Virginia had given 20,000 acres of land. David Rice was elected chairman of the board, and two years later the work of the seminary began in the house of Rice, near Danville. This was the first school taught in Kentucky. It was removed to the town of Lexington, and in 1798 was organized as *The Transylvania University*. Since the Presbyterians had collected the sum of ten thousand dollars and a library for the school, it was provided in the charter that a majority of the twenty-one trustees of the university should be Presbyterians. The Presbyterian members of the board did not exercise due wisdom and foresight to retain this control, however, and twenty years later—that is, in 1818—there were only seven Presbyterian trustees on the board. "As vacancies occurred from time to time, they were filled not by devout persons of the same or like faith, but by prominent political characters whose popularity and influence would, it was hoped, reflect a sort of *éclat* upon the College." A crisis came and the Presbyterians were in a minority.

While the seven were struggling to regain their legal rights, the legislature of Kentucky deposed the entire old board and appointed new trustees. These placed a man of Unitarian beliefs at the head of the university, and thus it passed from the hands of those who had founded and built it up.

After losing their first school, the Presbyterians bent every energy toward the establishment of another. A charter was secured at once (1819) and a church college was planted at Danville, to which the name of Center College was afterwards given. With such ministers in charge of it as Jeremiah Chamberlain, Gideon Blackburn, John C. Young, Lewis W. Green and Wil-

liam L. Breckinridge, Center College entered upon a
great work in behalf of religion and good government
in the West and Southwest.

Near the close of the year 1796, James McGready
went from North Carolina to Kentucky and became
pastor of congregations in the southern part of that
state. He was then about thirty-three years of age;
his preaching was earnest and marked by passionate
appeals to his hearers on the subjects of regeneration,
faith and repentance. "If I were converted would I
feel it, and know it?" This question was often asked
by members of McGready's flocks. In 1799 there was
much excitement in his churches, but in July, 1800, a
great revival began at Red River. Camp-meetings
were held at the various churches on the Green and
Cumberland rivers and farther south, also, in Tennessee. Those who became spiritually aroused at first
manifested their emotions by loud cries and lamenta-
tions. Then, as if overcome by their feelings, some fell
to the ground. After lying there for a time, apparently insensible, they arose with great rejoicing. In
August, 1801, a great throng of about 20,000 people
was assembled in an encampment at Cane Ridge, near
the town of Paris. During the preaching and the singing, sudden spasms seized upon many and dashed them
to the ground. It was claimed by some that about
3,000 persons were thus overcome during this series
of services. As the revival movement spread, men and
women began to act in the strangest and wildest manner. Some of them ran, some danced, some rolled over
and over on the ground, and some of them barked like
dogs. A number of persons went through such strange
bodily motions that they were said to have the "*jerks.*"

In spite of these extravagant actions, a large number
of genuine conversions took place. The Spirit of God
was evidently touching the hearts of the people. The
revival continued throughout the years 1800-1804, and

hundreds were brought into the churches of Kentucky, Tennessee, North and South Carolina and Virginia.

This remarkable outburst of religious enthusiasm led to the formation of the Cumberland Presbyterian Church. In October, 1802, the Synod of Kentucky was organized at Lexington. Then the Cumberland Presbytery was organized in the southern part of Kentucky, where McGready's revival began. This presbytery licensed and ordained a number of men who were without education; nor did this presbytery require new ministers to subscribe the Westminster Confession, but openly rejected some of the fundamental doctrines of Calvinism. The Synod of Kentucky sent a large commission to deal with the presbytery (1805). The presbytery refused to submit to the authority of synod's commission, and the latter suspended the presbytery. Thus began the career of an independent body of Presbyterians who held, for the most part, Arminian doctrines.

CHAPTER XXXII.

JOHN HOLT RICE AND THE ORGANIZATION OF UNION
THEOLOGICAL SEMINARY IN VIRGINIA.

THE war of the Revolution was in progress when John Holt Rice was born (1777). His early years were spent upon a farm near the Peaks of Otter, in Virginia. During childhood a long and wasting sickness came upon him, and at one time it was supposed that he would die; his life was spared, however, as his relatives thought, in order that he might do some great and good work. His mind was so active that when he reached the age of four years he was a good reader, and often sat at his mother's knee and read aloud to her from the Bible and hymn book. His father was so greatly pleased at the child's skill in reading that he said: "That boy shall have a good education." The father was a nephew of David Rice, the apostle of Kentucky.

At the age of eight years, young Rice began the study of Latin. He did not receive much instruction from teachers, however, and his progress in systematic study was slow. But a great thirst for knowledge filled him, and he read all of the books that he could get into his hands. He often read a borrowed book or studied his regular Latin lesson by the light of a rich pine knot burning on the hearthstone of his father's home. He tells us that he would throw himself at full length upon the floor of the old farmhouse, drawing nearer as the flame of the pine knot wasted away, "and finally thrusting my head into the very ashes," he declares, "to catch the last gleam of light."

Rice was a student under William Graham at Lib-

212

erty Hall Academy for a little less than two years. Then he spent a year in the New London Academy under the guidance of its principal, George A. Baxter. After that more than a year was given to the work of teaching in a private family at Malvern Hill, on the James River, below Richmond. In December, 1796, he was appointed as tutor in Hampden Sidney College, and there came into close friendly relationship with President Archibald Alexander. During all of this period of academic study and teaching Rice was devouring every book that he could find. At the same time he was writing, writing constantly, setting forth in his own words and in his own style the substance of that which he had read. Thus he was training himself in the art of writing clear, strong English.

"The years these young men [Archibald Alexander and John Holt Rice] passed at Hampden Sidney were years of vast improvement," wrote William H. Foote. "The college gained in numbers and in reputation; the trustees gained confidence; the public gained in their educated sons; and the church gained gems, the value of which she could not know, and does not now, after more than half a century, fully estimate. In the spring of 1797 the college classes all commenced anew. The talents of the young men [Alexander and Rice] for instruction, discipline, arrangement of classes and the course of college studies, were fully exercised. The college began, went on enlarging, unfolding, improving, advancing. The salaries were small, the labors great, and the trials many. If the students were few, the salary of the teachers was, of course, small; if numerous, still it was limited to a very moderate amount. But their own mental improvement was incalculable. When they left the college, as both did in about nine years, they were worthy of the positions they occupied, and were prepared for any exertions the church might demand. From preparing boys for college studies, and arranging the upper classes, and educating youth for the various departments of life, both went to arrange theological seminaries [Princeton and Union] and prepare ministers of the gospel of Christ."

For a little more than a year Rice gave up his work as teacher and spent his time in reading books about the practice of medicine. He made up his mind that he would become a doctor. His friends persuaded him, however, to take up again the task of teaching at Hampden Sidney. He returned to that school in the fall of 1800, and soon afterwards decided to become a preacher. In July, 1802, John H. Rice and Ann Smith Morton, daughter of Major Morton, were united in marriage. In September, 1803, Rice was licensed to preach the gospel, and in the following April (1804) he became shepherd of the flock at Cub Creek, in Charlotte County.

In early life Rice drew a small circle of intimate friends close to his heart. In later years, his sympathies became strong and wide-reaching. "There was in him," said his friend, Conrad Speece, "a vein of dry, playful humor, which made his conversation very pleasant to all companies which he frequented." Archibald Alexander said that Rice had great moral courage. "He knew how to exercise that species of self-denial, so difficult to most young men, of suspending his judgment on any subject until he should have the opportunity of contemplating it in all its relations. 'He was swift to hear and slow to speak.'"

A small salary was paid by Rice's congregation. He worked a farm, therefore, and taught school five days in the week in order to gain a support. Many negro slaves were members of his congregation. To these he preached regularly, taught them to read and trained them in the study of the catechism. The preacher and pastor made for himself a place in the hearts of all of his people. Then in May, 1812, he went to Richmond to become the first pastor of the first Presbyterian congregation organized in the capital city of Virginia.

Before this time, John D. Blair had been preaching twice a month in the capitol building in Richmond. On the alternate Sundays Mr. Buchanan, an Episcopal clergyman, preached in the capitol. Mr. Blair sustained himself by teaching a classical school. When Rice came he preached at first in the Masons' Hall. Large crowds came to hear him. On June 12, a Presbyterian church was organized and steps were taken to build a house of worship. In May, 1813, Dr. Rice organized the *Virginia Bible Society*, which continues to this day the beneficent work of distributing Bibles among the poor.

Rice was poor himself. The church, at first, consisted of only sixty members, and the small salary promised to the pastor was not paid with promptness. On one occasion, the only article of food in the minister's house was a bag of black-eyed peas. There was no bacon to be used in giving the peas the proper flavor and Rice had not a cent of money. Mrs. Rice decided to sell their mahogany dining-table in order to supply the necessity of the hour. "I trust, my dear, the Lord will provide," said the husband with a smile, as he turned toward his study. Just then a knock was heard and a servant was found standing at the door with an ample supply of food sent by a friend who lived in the country near Richmond.

This straitened manner of living did not continue for a long period of time. The church was multiplied in numbers, and in 1816 people and pastor entered into their own house of worship. At a later time, the First Church of Richmond was built upon the spot where the handsome City Hall is now located; later still, the church was removed to its present position on Grace Street.

In July, 1815, Rice began to issue in Richmond an

eight-page magazine called *The Christian Monitor*. A year later it was doubled in size, and issued twice a month. Another change was made in January, 1818, when Rice began to publish a monthly named *The Virginia Evangelical and Literary Magazine*. This periodical was continued for a period of ten years, and through its pages Rice wrought a great work in moulding the religious sentiment of Virginia and the South. When it was proposed, in 1819, to elect Dr. Thomas Cooper, an Englishman, as teacher at the University of Virginia, Dr. Rice published an article in opposition to the plan. Cooper was an infidel, and Rice pointed out the danger of selecting him as a teacher of youth. Rice's opinion prevailed, and Cooper was not given the place. Afterwards Cooper became president of the South Carolina College, but after a few years the people of that state forced him to withdraw from the position. In 1820, as we have seen, Moses Hoge died and left vacant two fields of work—the presidency of Hampden Sidney College and the professorship of theology. Two years later (1822) Dr. Rice was called by the Hanover Presbytery to the work of giving regular instruction to young men who were preparing themselves to preach the gospel. A few words in review are now necessary in order that we may see how the Union Seminary was founded.

The first definite step toward the establishment of a Theological Seminary in the American Presbyterian Church was taken in 1789. This was the formation of a class of seven or eight young men who entered upon a systematic course of study in theology at Liberty Hall Academy, in Virginia, under the instruction of the Rector, William Graham. Two years later (1791) the Synod of Virginia determined to establish two seminaries for the training of preachers, one in Virginia and the other in Western Pennsylvania. The synod then entered into a written agreement with the trustees of

Liberty Hall Academy, as we have seen, whereby Graham was appointed to give regular, systematic instruction in theology. In accordance with this agreement two of the presbyteries of the synod—the Hanover and Lexington presbyteries—raised money to erect a stone building for the use of the Academy. At the same time the synod determined to raise a fund for the maintenance of a permanent system of theological training.

The second step in the development of the Seminary was the establishment of a special endowment fund by Hanover Presbytery. In 1795 this body determined to retain control of the money raised within its borders for this special purpose. Money was collected, and in October, 1797, the presbytery adopted a plan, drawn up by Archibald Alexander, for the education of ministers of the gospel. The chief part of this plan dealt with the collection of the necessary funds. In April, 1806, the presbytery appointed a committee to ask the people to give money for the purpose of establishing a *Theological Seminary and School at Hampden-Sidney College.* William Graham had passed away and the presbytery evidently wished to make Archibald Alexander, president of Hampden Sidney, their instructor in theology. John H. Rice was sent out among the churches of the presbytery to ask for contributions. A considerable sum was secured. Then in the fall of 1806 Alexander went to Philadelphia. Early in 1807 Hoge was made president of Hampden Sidney. Then, in 1808, Dr. Hoge was chosen as the presbytery's "teacher of theology in the theological school." A part of the interest received from the presbytery's fund was used for the support of the theological teacher. This appointment of president Hoge, in 1808, as the presbytery's instructor of gospel ministers may be regarded as a third and decisive step in the work of founding a Seminary. From this time onward there was, in fact, a permanent theological seminary in Virginia.

In 1812 the Presbyterian General Assembly established a Seminary at Princeton. Two months after the in-
auguration of Archibald Alexander at Princeton, the
Virginia Synod determined to have a Seminary under its
own control and patronage. The synod adopted the
school already founded by Hanover Presbytery. Lexington, in the Valley, was selected as "the permanent seat,
and Hampden-Sidney the temporary seat of the institution." This was intended to carry out the agreement,
made in 1791-93, with the trustees of Liberty Hall
Academy. Moses Hoge, already at work as the presbytery's teacher, was elected, also, as the synod's professor
of theology. Three years later (1815) the plan of re-
moving the Seminary to Lexington was given up, for
the reason that the friends of Hampden Sidney were
raising more money for theological instruction. In
1822 the synod transferred to Hanover Presbytery the
management of the Theological Seminary, together
with the sum of about ten thousand dollars, which
formed the endowment of the school. The presbytery
accepted the trust and called John H. Rice to undertake
the work laid down by Moses Hoge.

Two calls came to Dr. Rice in the fall of 1822; one
was the invitation of the presbytery to give all of his
time to the work of teaching theology. The other,
his election as president of Princeton College. "We
need your services to build up our failing institution;
to elevate Nassau Hall to that rank among sister colleges which it formerly sustained." This was the urgent
appeal from Princeton. Severe sickness seized Dr. Rice
and held him in its grasp for many weary weeks. He
was feverish and restless. A great burden was evidently
resting upon his heart. "Dear old Virginia! Richmond and the dear people there! Oh God! Oh God! for
life and health to labor and glorify thee! O for health
and strength to do something for old Virginia. A
theological school—we must have a theological school.

Where does duty call?" These broken prayers and exclamations gave some sign as to the direction in which his inclinations were tending. In the spring of 1823, when health had returned, he declined the call to Princeton. Then, "with deep anguish of spirit," he separated himself from his flock in Richmond and went to Hampden Sidney. He was inaugurated as professor of theology on January 1, 1824. Only three students were present to begin the course of study. Work was begun upon a seminary building, and in the fall of 1825 Dr. Rice moved into it. More money was secured and students came in increasing numbers. In June, 1825, Archibald Alexander came from Princeton and made his famous preaching tour among the churches of Virginia. He exerted all of his powers to persuade the Virginia people to endow their seminary. Money was secured from churches in North Carolina and some from friends north of the Potomac River. In the autumn of 1826 the money and property of the seminary were equal in value to the sum of fifty thousand dollars. The Hanover Presbytery then asked the synods of Virginia and North Carolina to take control of the school. They both consented (1826). The seminary was named Union Seminary, as a mark of the co-operation of the two synods in its management. In May, 1827, the General Assembly approved and ratified the plan of union.

In June, 1827, Dr. Rice wrote to a friend as follows: "During the last year, the pressure on me was so heavy that for five months I had a continual headache and my nerves became so irritable that the click of a penknife or the scratching of a stiff pen on paper, after an hour's confinement, was just like a strong shock of electricity through my brain. I may say that half of my time was spent in torture. I felt that I must either give up this great enterprise in which I am engaged for the South, or sink under the load which was pressing on me. The Lord, just at that time, put it into the hearts of a few of my beloved friends in New York to raise a fund to support a young man who should assist me."

More than this, Dr. Rice had used, for the maintenance of his printing press, all of the money received from the sale of his little farm in Charlotte County. Without money of his own and with less than half the necessary amount in the treasury to keep the Seminary in operation, he went out among the Presbyterians to ask for help. "The work I am in is painful. It is extremely laborious; it excites the feelings and exhausts them, of course, more than preaching or study." And, yet, onward he moved in the work. Friends in Philadelphia, New York and Boston were generous, and in 1829 the seminary buildings were made larger and the force of teachers was increased. A recent revival of religion had stirred the hearts of the Virginia people and a larger body of students came to sit at Rice's feet. The seminary was upon safe and permanent foundations, but the life of John Holt Rice was drawing near the end. Much of the strength of his life had been yielded up to the work of building the school of the prophets.

"Too much to do," he wrote concerning himself in March, 1830. He spoke, at the same time, about a slow fever that had begun to consume him, yet he went into the field for money to strengthen the school. In December, 1830, he betook himself to his chamber. His strength was slowly passing from him. As he lay upon his couch his mind and his pen were still busy. Letters were sent to friends; articles were made ready for publication. Plans were formed for the advancement of the work of the Presbyterians in education and in foreign missions. Months of suffering followed. On September 3, 1831, there was a look of great joy upon his face as he said slowly, "Mercy is triumphant." Then he entered into rest.

CHAPTER XXXIII.

GEORGE ADDISON BAXTER EXTENDS THE WORK OF WASH-
INGTON COLLEGE AMONG THE PEOPLE OF THE
SOUTH AND SOUTHWEST.

JUST before the war of the Revolution began, a land
surveyor named George Baxter made his home in the
lower Valley of Virginia. His father was an Englishman, and was connected, it is said, with the family of
the great English preacher, Richard Baxter. George
Baxter became the owner of large tracts of land and had
a number of indentured white servants in his country
home in Rockingham County. His wife was Mary Love,
a Scot from Ireland, whose religious faith was strong
and active. Their second son, George Addison Baxter,
was born in July, 1771.

When this child, George Addison, was about ten years
of age, he suffered a severe injury. One morning early
he climbed a tree to catch a squirrel. A limb of the
tree broke, the boy fell to the ground and an ankle was
fractured by the fall. When the wound healed this
leg was shorter than the other. He always wore a high
heel on the shoe, and used a cane, but a slight lame-
ness marked his manner of walking as long as he lived.
A white servant from Ireland, an intelligent young
man, gave instruction, in the Baxter home, in all of the
English branches of study. The boy, George, was possessed of a quick and active mind and he became eager
to gain more knowledge. His mother's teaching and
prayers led him to become a Christian, and at an early
age he was brought into the church now known as
Cook's Creek Church, which was then under the care
of that godly shepherd, Benjamin Erwin. Then George

decided that he would enter the gospel ministry, and at
the age of eighteen he placed himself under the instruction of William Graham at Liberty Hall Academy. There
he began the study of Latin. His work was carried on
with so much energy and persistence that within a few
weeks he completely mastered the elementary principles
of that language. The effort injured his health, however, and he was forced to return home and rest for a
whole year. Again he took up his studies, but his
manner of work was so close and persistent that his
bodily strength failed once more. A short rest made
him ready again for his tasks at school. He learned
from experience, no doubt, that it is wise to keep the
body in good condition by exercise, for he completed
his course of study in due time and then taught and
took charge of the Academy at New London in Bedford
County, Virginia. Then again he returned to Liberty
Hall to become a member of Graham's class in theology.
This work of ministerial study was completed in November, 1796, and in the following April (1797) he was
licensed to preach the gospel by the Lexington Presbytery.

Baxter took up again the work of teaching at New
London. Within a year he gathered a large body of
students around him. Now that Graham had departed,
Baxter was held to be the best teacher of young men
in the Valley of Virginia. In October, 1798, he was
appointed to teach at Liberty Hall, which had then
been given the name of Washington Academy. A year
later, that is in October, 1797, he was made President
of the Academy, and this post he held for a period of
thirty years. In 1813 the school was given the title
of Washington College. Along with the headship of
the college, Baxter held also the pastorate of the congregations at Monmouth and Lexington. A house of worship was erected in the latter place in 1802. As preacher
and teacher he exerted a mighty influence over those

who were committed to his care. His own great intellect expanded during these years and his heart was always filled with tender sympathy. In 1801 he went to Kentucky to see for himself the manner in which the great revival was making progress through the southern part of that state. In a letter to his friend, Archibald Alexander, Baxter said: "This revival operates as our Saviour promised the Holy Spirit should when sent into the world; it convinces of sin, of righteousness, and of judgment, a strong confirmation to my mind both that the promise is divine and that this is a remarkable fulfillment of it." Soon afterwards, however, when more violent bodily exercises were seen among those who were affected by the revival movement, Baxter expressed his disapproval.

The students of the college called Dr. Baxter "Old Rex." He was not stern and severe in his government. Like a wise father, he administered punishment when it was necessary; sometimes he gave advice and fatherly counsel and then sent the offending student back to his room and his books. "The students loved him through life; they loved to talk about him, and his absolute dominion and his inherent greatness."

Baxter's first work as Rector of the Academy was to make journeys among the church congregations to ask for money. He gave his own salary to the assistant teachers in order that they might receive as much as had been promised to them. He supported his own family upon the small amount of four hundred dollars a year, paid him for preaching, and upon the rental received for his lands.

The Virginia canal stock, donated by Washington, bore a face value of twenty thousand dollars. We have already seen that it was not until March, 1802, five years and six months after Washington's assignment of it, that the stock yielded a dividend. This amounted to three per cent. on the capital, or the sum of six hundred dollars. In

June, 1802, a second dividend of six hundred dollars
was paid, and some months later a third, of twelve
hundred dollars. In January, 1803, the Academy building caught fire and was soon destroyed. Only the stone
walls were left standing as a memorial of the Presbyterian faith that had erected them. New buildings were
erected within the limits of the town of Lexington, and
there Baxter continued his work. The canal stock furnished irregular dividends until 1820, when the State
of Virginia agreed to pay interest to the extent of 2,400
dollars annually for twelve years, and after 1832, an
annual dividend of three thousand dollars. John Robinson, a Scot of Rockbridge, gave his estate to the college and this furnished a considerable fund after the
year 1824. The Virginia branch of the Cincinnati
Society also donated its funds to the Academy, but
nothing at all was realized from this gift until the year
1848.

Baxter's wife, a daughter of Colonel William Fleming, of Botetourt, inherited large tracts of land from
her father, in addition to the land given to Baxter by
his own father. As many as eleven or twelve large bodies
of land in the mountains of Virginia were thus owned by
Baxter and his wife. He came to the conclusion, however, that it would require several of the best years of
his life to manage this property with any degree of
success. "He did not think," writes his daughter,
Louisa Baxter, "that he had any more right to take
this time to keep a fortune than to take it to make a
fortune." Some of it was sold, and some of it was lost,
through Dr. Baxter's inability to give it proper attention.

Thus, with a small amount of money at his command
each year, Baxter built up the school and extended its
power until it became the chief institution of learning
among the Southern Presbyterians. It was the privilege
of this man of God, this teacher of the Word, to estab-

lish Washington College upon a broad and liberal foundation and to extend her work by sending many well-
trained lawyers, physicians, statesmen and preachers
into the states of the South and Southwest. The first
teacher who came to assist Baxter was Daniel Blain, a
young preacher from Abbeville, South Carolina. Then
Henry Ruffner, another Presbyterian minister, became
his chief assistant, and was, at a later time, made president of the College.

William H. Ruffner, a son of Henry Ruffner, de-
scribes Baxter as "a man of extraordinary ability and
great influence." "My earliest recollections," he says,
"are associated with Dr. Baxter. He was pastor of the
Presbyterian Church [in Lexington] until I was seven
years of age; and he impressed me much more than
did the House Mountain. Remembering him as I do,
I can understand the feeling of the child who stood
before Dr. Plumer and asked him solemnly, 'Are you
God?' My mother's counsels as to reverencing Dr.
Baxter were not needed. By his ponderous frame, his
massive head, his dignity, his rich, tender voice, the
majestic march of his pulpit discourse, his swelling
emotions, his unconscious tears—he impressed my boyish mind as the very embodiment of all that was great,
good and loving. I watched him from our square pew
in front of the pulpit, and from beginning to end his
services fascinated as much as ordinary services afflicted me."

One Sunday afternoon in September, 1822, Dr.
Baxter preached to a large congregation of worshippers who were seated among a grove of trees and upon
the side of the mountain near the southern gateway of
the famous Goshen Pass, in Rockbridge County, Virginia. "The wicked are like the troubled sea" was the
preacher's theme. His voice rang out like the sound
of a trumpet, while he declared that peace never abides
in the heart of an evil man. To confirm this he recited

the confessions of Rousseau, Voltaire, Hume and many others. Then he made a searching appeal to those among his hearers who were still unreconciled to God, and as he made this appeal "his benignant face was bathed in tears." The whole congregation was deeply moved by the preacher's words. With great solemnity, Dr. Baxter pointed them to the hour of death and the day of judgment, "when such a sense of avenging justice shall seize upon you as will completely reverse the very instincts of nature itself." "Suppose, as you are seated here this moment," he said further, "that you should see the heavens above suddenly gathering blackness, and feel the earth, under some mysterious power, trembling beneath your feet; and you, who are seated upon the mountain, should feel it shaking to its foundation, and looking up to its top we should see it nodding to its fall. What would nature dictate? We should all flee in horror from the fatal spot. But how completely will all this feeling be reversed to the impenitent at the last day! O, you will then say to the mountains and to the rocks, 'Fall on us, and hide us from the wrath of the Lamb, for the great day of his wrath is come and who will be able to stand?' " The effect of these words was marvellous. The whole assembly seemed to sway back and forth as if moved by a mighty wind and many of those who were seated in the grove and on the mountain side arose and turned "to see if the mountain was not really about to fall."

A group of young men and boys, some of them college students, sat near Dr. Baxter while he was preaching. The words of the minister filled their hearts with a feeling of awe and reverence that remained with them through life. Two of these young listeners afterwards became influential as Presbyterian ministers. These were William S. Plumer and William Brown.

Dr. John Leyburn has written as follows about a communion service which he attended as a boy

at the old stone church called Monmouth, near
the town of Lexington: "Our minister [Dr. Baxter]
preached the morning sermon. He was always evangelical, solemn and impressive, and at times there
was a sublime and majestic roll in his utterances which
marked him the great man all acknowledged him to be.
But today there was a power, a vivid spreading out of
eternal things, a directness and earnestness altogether
peculiar. At times his voice would falter, as he almost
choked with the swelling emotion. A divine afflatus
had breathed upon his heart, and from its profound
depths he spoke as a dying man to dying men." This
sermon, says Dr. Leyburn, was held in memory for
years by many of those who heard it.

In 1829 Dr. Baxter gave up the presidency of Washington College. Through long labors and much self-
sacrifice he had established a strong church school with.a
regular patronage from various parts of the South and
Southwest. He wished more time for study and for
pastoral work among the people of his congregation.
Two years later, John H. Rice passed away and Baxter was chosen to be the teacher of theology in Union
Seminary. The call of the two synods of North Carolina and Virginia he could not refuse, and in December, 1831, Baxter began his work of training preachers.
"All the great topics he was called upon to handle," says
one of his pupils, Dr. John Leyburn, "had been themes
of reflection during almost all his life. They were im-
bedded, too, in his heart as well as in his understanding.
In the discussions of the lecture-room, even when others might have been taken up with the more intellectual
aspects of the subject, his tear-filled eyes would give
evidence that the truths he was examining had pene-
trated further than the regions of the understanding.
He was sometimes, however, full of humor. This was
particularly manifested when he could get a student into
a logical dilemma. In order to do this, he would begin

with questions remote from his ultimate purpose, and having elicited from the unsuspecting pupil one answer after another, would finally bring him, very much to his surprise, right up into a corner. This feat was always accompanied by our venerable professor's shaking his great sides with good-natured laughter."

Baxter's chief delight, says Dr. Leyburn, was in preaching the gospel. But "his sermons were never long. I think I have seldom, if ever, heard him exceed three-quarters of an hour." It is said that the people at Hampden Sidney asked him to give them longer sermons than those which he began to preach there each Sunday. We are told that he prepared each sermon in the following manner: On Saturday afternoon he sat down upon a bench in the front porch of his home. With his back against the wall "he would begin a low whistle, at the same time passing his forefinger back and forth in front of his lips as if to modulate the sound. There he would sit meditatively, murmuring a little at times, and occasionally breaking forth as if to a public audience. In such cases he would sometimes pause and repeat with changes of expression, and again relapse into his quiet whistle. The students who overheard him would listen next morning for the spoken and amended passages, and they always found that in due time the sentences came rolling out in the Doctor's grand style exactly as he had prepared them."

A difference in opinion about certain matters of theology was becoming widespread among Presbyterians in 1831. John H. Rice saw clearly, just before his death, the coming of a great storm in the church from the North and Northwest. Only thirty years before, that is in 1801, the Plan of Union was adopted, whereby a large number of Congregational churches in New York and in the regions north of the Ohio River were made a part of the Presbyterian body. Into these northern and western churches the modified Calvinism of New

England found its way. They neglected the Westminster Confession by not requiring young ministers
at their ordination to accept it; moreover, the office of
ruling elder was not always maintained among them.
Those who held the New England doctrines were called
the "New School," while those who maintained the Calvinistic system were termed the "Old School."

On May 11, 1837, a great convention met in the
Sixth Presbyterian Church of Philadelphia. It was
made up of delegates from the "Old School" Presbyterians of the entire country. Dr. Baxter was chosen
to preside over this important body. With great dignity and simplicity of manner he directed the work and
deliberations of the convention. This body prepared
a list of those errors in doctrine, in church order and
in discipline which were held by the New School. This
list was presented in the form of a memorial to the
General Assembly, which met in Philadelphia on May
18. The Assembly placed the memorial in the hands of
a special committee consisting of four Southern ministers, namely: George A. Baxter, Archibald Alexander,
W. S. Plumer, A. W. Leland, and one Northern minister, Ashbel Green. Two elders were also members.
The committee went into the Assembly with a report
that condemned the New School errors. A long debate
followed. The chief speakers in favor of the Old School
system were Plumer and Baxter, John and Robert
Breckinridge, of Kentucky, John Witherspoon, of
South Carolina, with Alexander, Miller and Green.
These men towered above all the rest and won the fight.
The Plan of Union of 1801 was abrogated. Then Plumer
moved that the synod of the Western Reserve, in Ohio
and Indiana, should be considered as no longer a part of
the Presbyterian Church. Baxter supported the motion
with a strong, forcible address and the synod was deposed. Then three other New School synods of western New York were cut apart from the Presbyterian

body. Thus was the church divided in 1837 into the
Old School and New School branches. In the following
year two separate assemblies were organized. A few
ministers and elders in the South joined the New School
Assembly. The great body of the Southern Presbyterians, however, remained in the Old School Assembly.

We have, already, followed Dr. Baxter from Washington College to his class-room at the Union Seminary.
There he continued his work without a break until the
close of the session in the spring of 1841. One morning,
a few days later, in his own home, he fell to the floor.
There were a few minutes of keen suffering. Then the
pain ceased, and he looked with great tenderness upon
the members of his family and then his expression
changed suddenly to one of rapture. He had seen the
Pilot face to face; with Him this teacher and leader of
men crossed the bar.

Baxter "had the meekness and simplicity of a little
child." This was the opinion of all of those who sat
at his feet in the teacher's classroom. "But yesterday,"
said Dr. Stuart Robinson, "and I was sitting at his
feet. His bland and noble countenance shone upon me
to cheer the hours of laborious investigation, and his
pure and peaceful wisdom directed my footsteps in the
way of knowledge. But now he belongs to a departed
race, and to the mighty men of old. His sun was
eclipsed when it shone with the greatest brightness. In
the full maturity of his transcendent talents, and while
exercising an incalculable influence for good, his mantle
fell from him and his spirit returned to Him who gave
it." According to Robinson, Baxter had "quick pene-
tration and comprehensive grasp of mind," and held all
the treasures of his reading and thinking at ready
command.

Dr. John H. Bocock, another student trained by
Baxter, wrote of him as follows: "There arises the
vision of another form, a brow in whose massy pro-

portions nature had carved nobility, a countenance in which with the native beamings of a giant intellect Divine Grace had blended a sacred tenderness, which adored and trembled and loved and wept like some holy and sweet-spirited infant. We remember him in the pulpit—how the blood flushed his face, and the tears suffused his eyes, when his own or another's tongue depicted the awful retributions which await unbelieving sinners. As some one passing Dr. Payson's Church, after his decease, pointed over to it and said, 'There Payson prayed;' so, as we pass the neighboring church, the words paraphrase themselves to our thoughts, and we feel, 'There Baxter wept.' " Dr. Bocock spoke also concerning the wondrous light that flashed from the many-sided mind of Baxter as he walked through the realms of reason and logic; and concerning the visions of the solemnities of eternity and of the glory of the exalted Saviour that were the creations of the might of Baxter's mind, "as mighty a mind as I can well conceive of in the possession of a mere mortal."

CHAPTER XXXIV.

LET us suppose that a traveller set forth in the summer of the year 1800, to make a journey through the congregations of the Virginia Synod. The Synod then contained eight Presbyteries, as follows: Hanover, Lexington, Redstone (covering a part of the present state of West Virginia), Ohio, Winchester, Transylvania, West Lexington, Washington. The three last named were in Kentucky and Ohio. Baltimore Presbytery formed a part of the Synod of Philadelphia. In the city of Baltimore, Patrick Allison was drawing near to the close of a Presbyterian pastorate that began there in 1763. He was succeeded in his work in the First Church by James Inglis (1802). The Second Church, Baltimore, was organized in 1803 with John Glendy as first pastor and John Breckinridge as his successor. In Georgetown, on the Potomac, our traveller found Stephen B. Balch preaching to a congregation which he had organized there in 1780. John B. Slemons and Samuel McMaster were then in charge of churches in eastern Maryland, then within the bounds of the Presbytery of Lewes. At Alexandria, Virginia, the gospel was preached with a strong Scotch accent by that minister of guileless heart, James Muir, of the Presbytery of Baltimore.

When the traveller rode across the Potomac River, in 1800, he found himself in the midst of Moses Hoge's congregation at Shepherdstown, in Virginia. Not far away, John Boyd was at work in the churches named

Tuscarora and Falling Waters. One of Boyd's places for preaching was Martinsburg, where a strong church was afterwards organized. In Winchester the people were just organizing their own separate church and William Hill came this same year to begin his long pastorate of thirty-four years. The aged soldier, General Daniel Morgan, was one of the members of Hill's church. In the previous year, 1799, the General Assembly met at Winchester and chose Samuel Stanhope Smith as Moderator. Nash Legrand was still looking after the flock in the Opecquon field and John Lyle was at Springfield and Romney on the upper Potomac. William Williamson, full of energy and boldness, was at that time riding across swift streams and over rough hills and mountains, to carry the message of peace to the people who lived in the region around Front Royal. His school was then located in that town, but was afterwards removed to Middleburg in Loudoun County. Thus went forward the work of a ministry that was to continue forty-eight years longer.

Our traveller next pursued his way up the Valley of Virginia. In the churches at Cook's Creek and Mossy Creek, near Harrisonburg, he heard sermons from that quiet, godly minister, Benjamin Erwin, who was, of course, far advanced in years. Not long afterward, Dr. John Hendren took up the work which Erwin laid down. At the Stone Church, among the oak trees upon the hill, in Augusta County, William Wilson was repeating, from memory, to his friends line after line from ancient Greek and Latin masters. Every Sunday Wilson gave to his people strong, earnest sermons.

After Wilson, the pastorate of the Augusta Church was undertaken by Conrad Speece, a man of German origin, who was born in Bedford County, Virginia. On October 20, 1796, Speece and Baxter stood together at Liberty Hall Academy to receive diplomas at the end of the course of study under William Graham.

The latter had just given up his work as Rector of
the Academy. Now, in the year 1800, Baxter was Rector of Washington Academy, the new name given to
Liberty Hall, and Speece was one of the teachers
in Hampden Sidney College. If our traveller could
have looked forward to the year 1813 he would have
seen the grove around the Augusta Church crowded
with worshippers, assembled to witness the installation of
Speece as pastor. John McCue, of the Tinkling Spring
Church, and William Calhoun, of Staunton, were the
ministers who took the chief parts in the ceremony.
The tall, awkward Speece himself preached with great
power, as he entered upon a ministry that was to continue until 1835.

Conrad Speece was a great reader of books, a clear-
minded scholar. He made no notes when preparing his
sermons, and, yet, we shall, in later years, find Dr.
Henry Ruffner writing this of him: "When he preached,
his thoughts were so lucid and so well arranged, his
diction so accurate, and the flow of his utterances so
easy, so full and so unbroken that all seemed to have
been elaborately prepared." Dr. Speece was one of the
first Southern ministers who made a place for himself
among the writers of hymns. His most beautiful lines
begin as follows :—

> "Blest Jesus, when thy cross I view,
> That mystery to the angelic host."

When the traveller arrived at Bethel, the people of
that congregation told him about the virtues and the
labors of their late pastor, Archibald Scott, who had
been recently called away from earth. Five years
afterwards, William McPheeters, a son of this congregation, took up the work of the pastorate among his
own people. Then in 1810 he became preacher and
teacher in Raleigh, North Carolina, where success

crowned the twofold ministry. This godly patriarch became, moreover, the head of a long line of worthy sons, who through many generations have rendered noble service as elders and preachers in our Southern Church.

At New Providence, in 1800, the pastor was Samuel Brown. He grew to maturity at his father's home near the Peaks of Otter and studied under William Graham at Liberty Hall Academy. In 1796, when the venerable John Brown closed his pastorate of 43 years and went to Kentucky, Samuel Brown became the preacher in the Stone Meeting-house. He established a school and began to teach some of the brightest boys of our land, among them Samuel B. Wilson, Samuel McDowell Moore and James McDowell, afterwards governor of Virginia. The visitor in 1800 was deeply impressed when he heard the preaching of Samuel Brown. A tall, thin man, having a thin face with small, deepset eyes, stood up in the pulpit. He caught the attention of his audience and held it to the close of the sermon. Sometimes the deepset eyes seemed to glow like fire. Sound, practical sense marked this leader of his people, who remained the pastor of New Providence until his death in 1818. The congregation grew in strength. The old stone house of worship gave place to a large brick church.

The wife of Samuel Brown was Mary Moore, to whom he was united in 1798. The people of the congregation never wearied in telling our traveller the wonderful story of her early life, for she was one of the famous "Captives of Abb's Valley," of Southwest Virginia. One morning, when Mary was about nine years of age, she saw a company of savage Indians surround her father's log cabin in the valley. They killed the father, burned the house, and led away the mother and some of her children beyond the Ohio River. There the mother and one of her daughters were put to death in the most cruel manner. The child Mary went bravely on through the long days of trial and suffering, holding fast always to a New Testament, which she had carried away from her father's house. After three years she was rescued and brought back to her friends. In later years, as the wife of Samuel Brown, she and her husband knelt in prayer every night and asked God to set apart their sons as preachers. Five of these sons became successful ministers of the gospel. The youngest of these was William Brown of blessed memory. When Samuel Brown passed away, his son-in-law, James Morrison, took up the work of the pastorate at New Providence.

The rider proceeded on his journey, and spent a day with Dr. Baxter in the Washington Academy, then the largest Presbyterian church school in the South. At Falling Spring Church and at the Natural Bridge the preacher was Samuel Houston, who laid aside the rifle, with which he fought in the Revolution, to become a pastor. Near the Peaks of Otter, James Mitchell, a small man of quiet, gentle manners, was the minister. Associated with him in the pastorate was a tall, strong man, James Turner. As the years passed, Mitchell became the white-haired patriarch, called Father Mitchell by all who knew him. His tender pleadings in the pulpit were kept up until the close of his long life of ninety-five years. Turner, the strong, gifted orator, had the power to move his audiences to smiles and to tears. Without envy or strife, these two men of God continued to work side by side until Turner heard God's call and left the venerable Mitchell as the only shepherd of the flock.

In September, 1800, the Hanover Presbytery held its regular session at the Cove Church in Albemarle County and licensed John Todd to preach. This John was the son of the elder John Todd, of Louisa County. The young man tried his gifts in the Virginia churches and afterwards (1809) went to Kentucky.

Our traveller next paid a visit to James Waddell, the blind preacher, who still lingered in his country home in Orange County. Then he rode to the town of Fredericksburg, on the Rappahannock. Only one or two Presbyterians dwelt there in 1800. Six years later, Samuel B. Wilson, a native of North Carolina, and a member of the Bethel Church, York County, South Carolina, came to Fredericksburg to assume the care of the little flock of three Presbyterians. The leader of these three was John Mark, a merchant, whose native land was Scotland. The godliness of Wilson's life and the instruction embodied in his sermons drew the best people of the community into his church, until it became one of the strongest Presbyterian congregations in the South. Many families that had grown up in the Episcopal fold sent their children to Wilson's classical school, and the heads of these families became members of Wilson's flock.

Another traveller, Dr. William H. Foote, at a later time (1816-18), spent several months here and attended the services at Wilson's church. Foote tells us about the solemnity of the members of the congregation as they entered the house of God. "What silence reigned within! A whisper, a rustle would nave been rude while these gentlemen and ladies worshipped God with their beloved pastor." Many forms and faces in that church attracted the attention of Foote. "Half way from the right hand door of entrance to the pulpit" was the regular pew of Daniel Grinnan, who felt himself under obligations, says Foote, for "an opportunity of showing kindness." "Near by Grinnan, when his profession permitted, sat [Robert] Wellford, the physician, of extensive reading, and wonderful memory, and great skill in the healing art; his amiable wife and his sons by his side." Foote saw, also, Seddon, "the widow's friend;" Philip Alexander, "always kind;" the devout Henderson, the manly Morson, and "that genuine

Scotch elder," Andrew Glassel, with short grey hair, long boots and knee buckles, "a full believer in his own creed." Foote marked also the erect bearing of James H. Fitzgerald, who was just then beginning his great work as ruling elder and man of business in church affairs, which was continued until 1852.

From Fredericksburg, our traveller rode to Richmond and there attended a service held in the Capitol building by John D. Blair. Near St. John's Church he saw the new-made grave of William Graham, who had died the year before (1799). Then our traveler made the long journey westward into the land of Kentucky, where Father Rice was keeping a careful watch over the whole field. McGready was holding there the first camp-meeting and was moving the multitudes with fiery sermons. Robert Marshall, another revivalist, was holding the attention of thousands by his bold denunciation of sinners. John Page Campbell, with voice and pen, was guiding the church of that region in the straight way of the orthodox belief. Archibald Cameron and James Blythe were also pillars in the Kentucky church. Two years later (1802) the Kentucky Synod was organized, with three separate Presbyteries, Transylvania, West Lexington and Washington. Thirty-seven ministers formed the synod when it thus began its independent life. Among the elders of the church were some of the sons of John Brown, Ephraim McDowell and John Breckinridge, of Virginia. The latter had four sons. The eldest was Joseph Cabell Breckinridge, a lawyer and an active ruling elder, who was in the habit of carrying his Bible with him into the law courts. In the year 1800 Robert Jefferson Breckinridge was born, third son of John Breckinridge. Afterwards, three of the latter's sons, bearing the names John, William L., and Robert J., as ministers of the gospel became great leaders in the Kentucky Presbyterian Church.

CHAPTER XXXV.

TOWARD the Holston and Watauga rivers our traveller next directed his course. There he found the Abingdon Presbytery already organized, while farther west in Tennessee was Union Presbytery. Both of these formed a part of the Synod of the Carolinas and Georgia. The other presbyteries of this synod were the following: Orange and Concord, in North Carolina; First Presbytery, Second Presbytery, and Greenville, in South Carolina, and Hopewell Presbytery, in Georgia. Besides these, the independent Presbytery of Charleston had been organized since 1790.

In 1800, Charles Cummings was still living in Tennessee, but no longer in active control of a congregation; Samuel Doak was engaged in the work of teaching at Salem. Edward Crawford was pastor of the churches at Rocky Spring and Glade Spring. The Presbytery of Union, in Tennessee, contained six ministers. Hezekiah Balch was in the midst of his successful labors as president of Greenville College. Samuel Carrick was the pastor of the Knoxville Church and president of Blount College. At Grassy Valley and in neighboring congregations the pastor was Samuel Graham Ramsey. Robert Henderson was in charge of Hopewell. The most active preacher of the gospel in Tennessee in the year 1800 was Gideon Blackburn, a native of Augusta County, Virginia. He was more than six feet in height and rode on horseback at a rapid pace across the country to visit his various congregations. In 1803 he began his great missionary work among the Cherokee Indians. Then in 1811 he became pastor at Franklin, Tennessee, and was there appointed principal of Harpeth Academy. From 1823 until 1833 Dr. Blackburn was in Kentucky; first, as minister in Louisville, then as president of Center College and afterwards as preacher at Versailles. His later years were spent in Illinois. Two of the sons of Dr. Doak, namely, John W. Doak and Samuel W. Doak, succeeded their father in the presidency of Washington College. Dr. Doak's grandson, A. A. Doak, also became president of this school which furnished to the church a large number of capable ministers of the gospel.

There were more than twenty-five Presbyterian congregations in Tennessee in 1800. A chain of them extended from Watauga to Nashville. In the year 1800, Charles Coffin became pastor at Greenville. He was a man of high character and liberal education and in 1810 was chosen president of Greenville College. In 1808, James W. Stephenson with a number of fellow-colonists bearing the names Frierson, Witherspoon, Mayes, Dobbin, Fleming and Blakely, from Williamsburg District, South Carolina, founded Mt. Zion in Maury County. In the same year Robert Henderson began to preach at the point now known as Murfreesboro. In 1829 the Presbytery of Western District was formed and in 1830 Samuel M. Williamson founded the first Presbyterian Church in the city of Memphis.

Our traveller next entered North Carolina and there found Pattillo, the patriarch of the people at Grassy Creek and Nutbush, in Orange Presbytery. David Caldwell continued until 1820 to minister to the congregations of Buffalo and Alamance. William Paisley came to Hawfields about the year 1800 and under his preaching the revival began there. Samuel Paisley and John Paisley afterwards preached well and lived godly lives among the people of the Eno congregation. For years the shepherd of the New Hanover congregations was Robert Tate. In 1801, John Robinson left Duplin County and went to Fayetteville. Samuel Stanford took up the work in Duplin and labored with success for more than a quarter of a century. In March, 1801, at Barbacue Church, Cumberland County, a group of David Caldwell's students was given authority to preach, as follows: Ezekiel B. Currie, John Matthews, Duncan Brown, Murdock McMillan, Malcolm McNair, Hugh Shaw and Murdock Murphy. These became strong upbuilders of the church in North Carolina. McMillan and McNair labored for many years in the Fayetteville region in that State. William Bingham began to preach at Wilmington in 1785. The classical school, which he founded in 1793, was conducted with great success. In the upper country, under the administration of a continuous line of Binghams, this school has continued to be a strong arm of the Presbyterian Church.

When our traveller rode southward he found Samuel E. McCorkle at Thyatira, James Hall at Bethany, James Wallis at Providence, and Lewis T. Wilson at Concord and Fourth Creek. Other pastors were Joseph D. Kilpatrick, Third Creek; John Carrigan, Ramah; John Andrews, Little Britain.

McCorkle died in 1811. Twenty years later (1831) the short ministry of another remarkable preacher, Thomas Espy, came to an end at Thyatira. Espy had a living faith. The godliness of his conduct won a large number of people for the Master. Even the manner of his dying, marked as it was by great confidence and joyful anticipations, caused many persons to announce their readiness to become Christians.

Lewis Feuilleteau Wilson, pastor of Concord and Fourth Creek Churches, was born in the West Indies and received his early training at a grammar school in London, England. In his eighteenth year young Wilson came across the Atlantic and entered Princeton College.   He there became a Christian and made up his mind to enter the ministry.   The war of the Revolution disturbed his plans, however, and he began the study of medicine.   Afterwards for a number of years he rendered service to the American colonies as a surgeon in the army.   When the war was ended James Hall, who had known Wilson at Princeton College, persuaded him to come to North Carolina.   For a period of about four years Wilson practiced medicine in Iredell and then he asked Orange Presbytery to grant him licensure as a minister of the gospel.   This was done in 1791.   Two years later he became shepherd of the flocks of Fourth Creek and Concord, as the successor of James Hall.   Many were led into the kingdom through the faithfulness of this man of God.   Through much physical suffering, but with triumphant spiritual hope, his life came to an end in December, 1804. One of his sons, Hugh Wilson, organized the first Presbyterian Church in the republic of Texas.

In 1792 Samuel C. Caldwell, son of David Caldwell, became shepherd of the flocks at Sugar Creek and Hopewell in Mecklenburg County.   In manner he was modest and winning and he persuaded many people to enter the church of God.   Behind the mildness of his demeanor there was hidden strong purpose and a firm will.   In 1793 the elders of Caldwell's two churches met together and adopted resolutions binding the two congregations to maintain the following principle:

"As a church judicature we will not intermeddle with what belongs to the civil magistrate, either as an officer of state, or a minister of justice among the citizens. The line between the church and state being so fine, we know not how to draw it, therefore we leave it to Christian prudence and longer experience to determine."

In 1805 Caldwell moved away from his home near the Hopewell Church and gave himself to the work at

Sugar Creek and Charlotte. He continued to preach the gospel of peace until 1826, and then he was laid to rest at the very spot where once stood the log church of Sugar Creek.

In the year 1800, Humphrey Hunter was pastor of Graham and Unity. About 1805 he became shepherd of the Steele Creek and New Hope Churches, and there kept up his earnest preaching until the end of his life in 1827. James McRae left the Steele Creek pastorate about 1798 and went to the Center congregation, where he preached with power and success for about thirty years.

In the year 1800, John Robinson became pastor of the Fayetteville Church. He established there a classical school. Then, in 1801, he removed to the Poplar Tent Church, which stands fourteen miles east of the present Davidson College. With the exception of a brief interval he spent the rest of his life in that congregation until death came in 1843. It was a long and fruitful ministry. Tall and slender, courteous in manner, and persuasive in his mode of speaking, Robinson led a great multitude of people into Christ's kingdom.

Throughout the long period of thirty years from 1801 until 1831, John Makemie Wilson held together in the bond of affection as one congregation the two churches of Rocky River and Philadelphia. Wilson was born in 1769 in Mecklenburg County. His father died before the close of the Revolution. In 1781, when the British were laying waste the region known as the Waxhaws, the Widow Jackson with her young son, Andrew Jackson, fled for refuge to the Sugar Creek congregation and lived there for a time in the home of the Widow Wilson. The two boys, John Makemie Wilson and Andrew Jackson, the latter afterwards President of the United States, worked and played together in the home of Wilson's mother.

Wilson became a student at Hampden Sidney College while John Blair Smith was president of this school. Moses Waddel was one of his classmates. Wilson studied theology under the instruction of James Hall and was ordained as pastor in Burke County, North Carolina, in 1795. Six years later he was called to Rocky River and Philadelphia. As a preacher, Wilson was filled with the eager desire to win the souls of men. His discourses were marked by intense earnestness. "It was amazing," said one who often heard him speak, "how he would hold the attention of his audience from the beginning to the end of his sermon, using so little gesture, often manifesting deep feeling, seldom any excitement." God gave him marvellous success. The Rocky River congregation grew so rapidly in numbers that it became probably the strongest country church in the South at that time. He opened a school and trained twenty-five men for the ministry. Wilson went among his people at regular periods and examined the children as to their knowledge of the catechism and all members with reference to Bible doctrines.

"No cases come to court from that part of Mecklenburg," was a remark often made about the district embraced in his two fields of labor. He worked always in behalf of peace and concord. "He believed," writes one who knew him, "that the members of the church are competent to settle their differences by friendly reference to each other, and that they are bound to do so by the laws of the Lord Jesus Christ." Through judicious and affectionate counsels he persuaded his people to adopt this course of procedure.

Wilson was only sixty-two years of age when the Master called him to his reward. It was due to his calm, quiet temperament, perhaps, that this man of God who maintained such intimate fellowship with the unseen Father, stated distinctly "that in facing death he had no transporting views or rapturous feelings, but a firm and sustaining hope of heaven, founded solely on the merits of Christ. He alluded to the labors of his life only to praise God for the tokens of His grace; expressed entire submission to the divine will in reference to his dissolution, and a joyful expectation of spending eternity in the presence and work of the Redeemer. Nothing could be more animating than the confidence he expressed in our Lord, Jesus Christ."

John Makemie Wilson furnished two sons for the work of the ministry. One of them, John Wilson, became the successor of James Hall, at Bethany. The other, Alexander E. Wilson, spent his strength as a missionary in western Africa and died among the wild tribes whom he sought to win.

Fayetteville's first preacher, David Kerr, was also a teacher in the classical school located in that town. In 1794, as we have seen, he became the first president-professor in the North Carolina University. Early in the year 1800 John Robinson assumed the double work of preacher and teacher at Fayetteville. Soon after his arrival he organized a church. The burden of two offices was too great, however, for Robinson's strength and he went away. In January, 1803, Andrew Flinn undertook the twofold work at Fayetteville. A successful ministry of three years followed, but in 1805, Flinn gave up the work. Some of the preachers, who came in later years to Fayetteville were the following: William Leftwich Turner, son of James Turner, of Bedford, Virginia; Jesse Turner, brother of William L.; William D. Snodgrass, who went afterward to the Independent Church, Savannah; Robert Hall Morrison, James E. Hamner, Josiah Kilpatrick and James W. Douglass.

Andrew Flinn was born in Maryland in 1773, but his parents took him to Mecklenburg, N. C., and he there grew to manhood. A period of training under James

Hall fitted him for the course of study at Chapel Hill. After graduation at the University of North Carolina, Flinn went to Fayetteville. In 1806 he was called to Camden, South Carolina, by a number of Presbyterians, who wished to give a new life to the Presbyterian Church which had been in existence at that place before the Revolution. Andrew Flinn became pastor of the restored church. In 1809, however, he was summoned to Charleston and there became first pastor of the Second Presbyterian Church, often called "Flinn's Church."

In October, 1802, the Synod of the Carolinas enjoined upon each of its presbyteries "to establish within its respective bounds, one or more grammar schools, except where such schools are already established; and that each member of the several presbyteries make it his business to select and encourage youths of promising piety and talents and such as may be expected to turn their attention to the ministry of the gospel." Our traveller found in the year 1800, many church schools already planted among the congregations in North Carolina, as we have seen. When he crossed the state line and entered South Carolina, he found Joseph Alexander still engaged in preaching and teaching at Bullock's Creek, York County, South Carolina. The following year (1801), however, marked the end of Alexander's great work in that field, and in 1809 his earthly life came to a close.

As early as July, 1785, Robert Hall was ordained as first pastor of the two churches of Upper Long Cane and Greenville (then called Saluda), in South Carolina. In 1794 Robert Gilliland Wilson became the shepherd of these two flocks. Soon afterwards Wilson made his home in Ohio and, in 1800, Hugh Dickson began to preach at Greenville and at Smyrna. The fruitful labors of this man of God were continued at Greenville through the space of seven and forty years. His ministry there came to an end January 1, 1847.

Union Church, organized in 1765, was served for a time by Dr. Joseph Alexander. From 1802 until 1805 William Williamson was pastor. In 1805 Daniel Gray became pastor of Union, Fairforest and Grassy Spring churches. The neighboring church of Bethesda, in York County, also sent a large number of her sons into the gospel ministry.

Bethel Congregation, in York County, had Francis Cummins as pastor and teacher of the church's school from 1784 until 1789. From 1796 until 1801 George G. McWhorter was pastor of Bethel and Beersheba. In 1811, James S. Adams, the beloved shepherd, took charge of the flock at Bethel and continued with great success until 1840. In that year he was succeeded by S. L. Watson. In 1842 the church of Yorkville was organized. The Bethel Academy was meanwhile training many ministers for the churches of the South.

Near the headwaters of Tyger River, in Spartanburg County, stands old Nazareth Church. The congregation was organized by Dr. Joseph Alexander about 1772, although a log house for worship was built before that time. From 1794 until 1801, James Templeton was shepherd of the flock. About the same time James Gilliland, Jr. conducted a classical school in Spartanburg, in which a number of preachers were trained for their work. Among the latter were Samuel B. Wilson and John McElhenney. In April, 1803, Gilliland, the teacher, was ordained as pastor of Nazareth and Fairview congregations. He was succeeded in 1821 by Michael Dickson. Soon after 1833 John Boggs assumed charge of these two congregations. In 1843 the Spartanburg congregation was organized and in the following year Z. L. Holmes became pastor of the two churches of Nazareth and Spartanburg.

The Fairforest congregation was organized in 1771 by Rev. Josiah Lewis. Among the founders were John Thomas and his wife. Thomas was one of the heroes of this region in the struggle for American independence, being the leader of the Spartanburg regiment. In 1794, William Williamson was ordained pastor. He was succeeded in 1805 by Daniel Gray, in 1817 by Joseph Hillhouse, in 1824 by Francis Porter and in 1828 by Daniel L. Gray.

About 1789 a congregation, called Hopewell, was organized near the town of Pendleton, in the present Pendleton County, South Carolina. The leading members of the congregation were General Andrew Pickens and Colonel Robert Anderson. A log house of worship was built in 1791, but this gave place in 1802 to a stone building. Thomas Reese was pastor from 1792 until 1796. This church is still standing and is known as the Old Stone Church. The Anderson family came to Pendleton County from the neighborhood of the old Stone Church, in Augusta County, Virginia. Most probably the idea of erecting a sanctuary made of stones was brought from Virginia to South Carolina by members of the Anderson family. Moreover, John McElhenney, pastor of the Stone Church at Lewisburg, West Virginia, was a brother of James McElhenney, who was, for a number of years, pastor of the Pendleton Stone Church.

Among all of these and many other congregations our traveller wandered in the year 1800. He found many faithful ministers engaged in the work of strengthening the walls of Zion—many whose names are worthy, but which cannot find a place in this record through lack of space. When the traveller rode into Columbia, the capital of South Carolina, he found David E. Dunlap established there as Presbyterian preacher. From 1795 until 1804, Dunlap continued his work as minister, and then, on the same day, he and his wife were called together into the presence of their Redeemer. The congregation at Columbia was not completely organized, however, until 1810. Early in that year, John

Brown, a Presbyterian minister, who was also a teacher in the South Carolina College, called the members of the Church together and superintended the business of choosing officers. Brown was elected President of the University of Georgia and, in 1812, Benjamin R. Montgomery, chaplain of the college, began to preach regularly to the Presbyterian congregation. After him, in order, came the following pastors: T. C. Henry, Robert Means, John Rennie, A. W. Leland, John Witherspoon and James H. Thornwell. The latter began his ministry in this church in the year 1839.

When our traveller entered Charleston in the year 1800, he found the workmen just bringing to completion the new Huguenot Church building. This was replaced in 1844 by the present edifice. The leading minister in the city at that time was George Buist, pastor of the First Church, known as the Scotch Church. He was born in Scotland, educated at Edinburgh and came to Charleston as pastor in 1793. Through the gentleness of his manner he won the hearts of all whom he met. His style of preaching was impressive in spite of the fact that in the pulpit he read his sermons. He read them admirably, we are told, and "the graces of his delivery won the attention and conciliated the favor of his hearers." Dr. Buist was a man of wide learning and, in 1805, he was made President of the College of Charleston. In 1808 a sudden illness brought his earthly labors to an end. In 1809 Dr. Buist was succeeded as pastor of the First Church by John Buchan, of Scotland. Then, in 1813, A. W. Leland assumed charge of the congregation, and in the following year (1814) the present house of worship was built. Arthur Buist, son of George Buist, preached for a number of years in the First Church. In 1832, John Forrest, a native of Edinburgh, Scotland, entered upon his long and useful ministry among the people of this congregation.

On April 3, 1811, the present house of worship
of the Second Church, Charleston, was dedicated by
the pastor, Dr. Andrew Flinn. The work of this
eminent man of God was brought to a close by his
death in 1820. He was succeeded in the pastorate
by T. C. Henry, William Ashmeade, and Thomas
Smyth. The latter began his long ministry here in
1832.

In 1800, there were about twenty-six Presbyterian
congregations in Georgia, located in the upper part of
the state. These were all embraced in the Presbytery
of Hopewell and were founded soon after the Revolution by various groups of people who moved into that
region from Virginia and the Carolinas. Some of the
early pastors were John Newton, John Springer, Robert M. Cunningham, William Montgomery and Moses
Waddel. Beneath the shade of a poplar tree, in the
town of Washington, Georgia, on July 21, 1790, John
Springer was ordained by the presbytery. He was
the first Presbyterian minister thus set apart in the
region south of the Savannah River. The Congregational Church of Midway, Liberty County, was under
the pastoral care of Cyrus Gildersleeve, from 1791
until 1811. He was succeeded by Murdoch Murphy,
Robert Quarterman and I. S. K. Axson. From this
congregation came a large number of consecrated, successful Presbyterian ministers. The Independent
Church, of Savannah, was founded, as we have seen,
some time before the year 1756. Thomas H. McCaule,
one time principal of Mt. Zion College, in Winnsboro,
South Carolina, founded a classical school in Savannah and preached in the Independent Church. Walter
Monteith was pastor in 1797-1799, and in 1800, Robert Smith took charge. Then came Samuel Clarkson
and Henry Kollock. The latter dwelt as shepherd
among the people of this flock from 1806 until 1819.

In the year 1804, the Presbyterian Church in the

city of Augusta, Georgia, was organized by Washington McKnight. The year 1807 marked the beginning
of the ministerial labors of John H. Thompson in this
congregation. In 1812, the present handsome church
building was dedicated. Four years later (1816) Dr.
Thompson died. The next pastors were Mr. Moder-
well and S. K. Talmage. The latter was called to
Oglethorpe University and was afterwards its president. In 1838, Alexander N. Cunningham was ordained pastor of the Augusta Church.

The Presbyterian congregation of Macon, Georgia,
was organized in 1826. The first pastor here was
Joseph C. Stiles, afterwards widely known as an effective preacher of the word.

In October, 1800, three horsemen rode from North
Carolina to Nashville, Tennessee. Thence they turned
southward over the "Natchez Trail" in obedience to
the command of the Synod of the Carolinas. These
three were Dr. James Hall, preacher and soldier of the
Revolutionary period; James H. Bowman and William
Montgomery, who were sent forth as evangelists to the
people of the Southwest. A pack-horse, bearing an
outfit for establishing a camp, was taken with them.
Swollen streams were crossed by swimming. Their
supply of food failed, and during a part of the journey they lived on corn meal moistened with water. A
preaching station was established on the Big Black
River, and at other places to the southward. The first
town reached by the evangelists was "Gibson's Port,"
now called Port Gibson. Headquarters were established at Natchez, Mississippi, and the gospel was
preached during the winter months in all of the neighboring territory. The people heard them gladly and
the foundations of many churches were laid. In April,
1801, the citizens of Natchez held a public meeting to
express their gratification at the presence of these ministers. The latter turned their faces homeward and at

the next meeting of Synod told about the success of
their work. In 1811, William Montgomery returned
to Mississippi, where he was made president of Jefferson College, located in the town of Washington. Afterwards, for a period of thirty-seven years he was pastor of Ebenezer and Union Churches. One of his sons,
Samuel Montgomery, was, in later years, pastor of
Union and Barsalem. John Matthews, Hugh Shaw,
Daniel Brown, Malcolm McNeil and James Smylie
were also sent as evangelists into the Southwest. Smylie
conducted a church school which became a fountain of
beneficence among the people of this entire region. He
also gave instruction to the negroes. In 1818, the
first presbytery of Mississippi was organized, embracing all of the territory lying west of the Perdido River.
In 1824, three ministers, bearing the names Sloss,
Alexander and White, preached in Montgomery, Alabama. A church was organized and in 1825, George
G. McWhorter was chosen pastor.

The First Presbyterian Church of New Orleans was
established in 1823, as the result, for the most part, of
the preaching of the consecrated young evangelist, Sylvester Larned. The principal pastors of this flock were
Doctors Joel Parker, John Breckinridge and W. A.
Scott, until Dr. Benjamin M. Palmer began his work
there in 1854. On Janury 25, 1828, James Wilson
Moore rode into the town of Little Rock, Arkansas, and
began to preach the gospel. Later in the same year a
Presbyterian Church was founded here, the beginning
of the work of evangelizing the vast region west of the
Mississippi River. The First Presbyterian congregation in the republic of Texas was organized by Hugh
Wilson, a son of Lewis Feuilleteau Wilson, of the Old
Concord Church, in North Carolina. Hugh Wilson was
at work delivering his message in the Lone Star State
when she entered the Federal Union in 1845.

CHAPTER XXXVI.

ONE Sunday morning in April, 1810, a young teacher, Thomas Goulding by name, twenty-four years of age, stood up in the old Congregational Church, at Midway, Liberty County, Georgia, and made a profession of his faith in Christ. He was born (1786) within the limits of the Midway congregation, but received his early education under private teachers in Connecticut. In 1806, he married Anne Holbrook, of Connecticut, and in 1807, began to study law and to teach school in his native state. About a year after his public acceptance of the Christian faith, Goulding gave up the plan of becoming a lawyer and was received under the care of Harmony Presbytery as a candidate for the ministry. In October, 1813, in the church at Augusta, Georgia, the Harmony Presbytery licensed him to preach the gospel. Goulding was the first native licentiate of the Presbyterian Church in Georgia, or, as he himself set it forth, "the first Presbyterian preacher born in the State of Georgia since the foundation of the world." His first pastoral charges were at White Bluff and Lexington, Georgia. At the latter point, Lexington, in 1828, he was set apart by the Synod of South Carolina and Georgia as first professor of theological instruction. In the same year (1828) his young son, Francis Robert Goulding, stood up in his father's church and acknowledged that he had become a Christian. His son, afterwards a minister,

253

became the author of the volume so widely read in this and other lands, "The Young Marooners."

Let us now return to the period when Thomas Goulding began his life as a Christian. On the first Wednesday in March, 1810, a small body of ministers and elders met in the First Presbyterian Church, Charleston, and organized the Presbytery of Harmony. Andrew Flinn, pastor of the Second Church, Charleston, was chosen moderator. One of the delegates present was John R. Thompson, pastor of the church of Augusta, Georgia. The Synod of the Carolinas was thus made to consist of the following presbyteries: Orange, Concord and Fayetteville, in North Carolina; South Carolina Presbytery in the upper part of the State of the same name; Hopewell Presbytery, in Upper Georgia, and Harmony Presbytery, on the seacoast of South Carolina and Georgia. In November, 1813, the three presbyteries last named were organized as the Synod of South Carolina and Georgia. The establishment of Harmony Presbytery was accompanied by the erection of three handsome houses of worship, which are still in constant use for the upbuilding of Christ's kingdom. In April, 1811, the present sanctuary of the Second Church, Charleston, was dedicated; in May, 1812, the present building of the First Church, Augusta, was set apart; on December 29, 1814, the present First Church, Charleston, was dedicated to the worship of God by the pastor, Aaron Whitney Leland. The Third Church, now the Westminster Church, of Charleston, was organized in 1823, and Doctor Leland preached also on that occasion. The latter was born in Massachusetts, in 1787, a lineal descendant of many illustrious English Puritans of the same name. He was graduated at Williams College in 1808; four years later he was ordained as a preacher by Harmony Presbytery and soon afterwards became pastor of the First Church, Charleston. From that work he was trans-

ferred to James Island, to become shepherd of the
flock in that place. He was summoned thence in 1833
to become professor of theology in the Columbia
Seminary.

George Howe, like A. W. Leland, was born in Massachusetts. He sprang from the Howes, Goulds and
Dwights, of New England. At the age of twelve years,
he came with his father and mother to live in Philadelphia. At the age of twenty, he was graduated from
Middleburg College, Vermont (1822); three years
later he completed the course of study at Andover Seminary. After his ordination to the ministry (1827) he
was elected to a professorship in Dartmouth College,
but ill health sent him southward, and in December,
1830, Howe landed from a vessel in Charleston Harbor.
A month later, in January, 1831, in response to the
call of the Synod of South Carolina and Georgia, he
began to teach Hebrew and Greek to the students of
the Theological Seminary, in Columbia.

As early as 1817, the Hopewell Presbytery, of Georgia, took the first step with reference to the erection
of a theological school in the cotton-planting States.
This body appointed a committee to draw up a plan
for such an institution and in 1819 it was decided to
locate it at Athens, Georgia. No further steps, however, were taken by the Presbytery, and in the following year (1820) the Synod of South Carolina and
Georgia united with the Synod of North Carolina in
an effort to endow a chair in Princeton Seminary. At
that time there had been established in our Presbyterian
Church only three theological seminaries. These were
Andover, Massachusetts, founded in 1806, New Brunswick, New Jersey, opened in 1810, and Princeton,
founded in 1812. At Hampden Sidney College, in 1812,
President Moses Hoge was appointed professor of theology by the Synod of Virginia. A few years later, the
Synod of South Carolina and Georgia collected and paid

into the treasury of Princeton Seminary the sum of more than $42,000.

In the year 1821, Auburn Seminary, in Western New York, opened its doors, and on January 1, 1824, Union Seminary, in Virginia, as a theological school set apart from Hampden Sidney College, began its work. Three months later, that is, on April 1, 1824, the Presbytery of South Carolina took steps to establish a classical and theological institution. The presbytery itself was to constitute the board of trustees, and the institution was to be located in Pendleton District, in the upper part of South Carolina. The presbytery agreed to allow the synod to assume control of the work. The synod, therefore, decided to make the school purely theological, and on December 15, 1828, it was determined to put the seminary into immediate operation. Thomas Goulding was appointed professor of theology and, during the year 1829, he taught a class of five students at his home in Lexington, Georgia. Early in January, 1830, the teacher and his students made the journey to Columbia, South Carolina, and the course of instruction was there continued. Colonel Abraham Blanding procured the present site in the heart of the city of Columbia, and on January 25, 1831, Dr. Goulding and his associate, Dr. Howe, entered the present central building and organized the first regular class, consisting of six members. About two weeks later the Society of Inquiry on Missions was formed. Two of the members of this first class, J. Leighton Wilson and James L. Merrick, afterwards became foreign missionaries.

The spiritual needs of the entire Southeastern part of our country were resting upon the hearts of the men who founded Columbia Seminary. The two states of South Carolina and Georgia were at that time sending large numbers of their people southward and westward, as colonists, to fill up the fertile regions within the borders of Alabama, Mississippi, Louisiana and

Florida. The vast territory embraced in these six commonwealths, occupied by a homogeneous people, was calling for ministers of the word. The other seminaries were not sending them. The leaders in the synod saw that a school for training preachers must be planted within their own bounds, and they established it at Columbia. At that time there were 10,000 members of the Presbyterian Church within this group of cotton-planting States. Eighty years later, there were nearly 70,000 Presbyterian Christians within the same territory, a fruitage that was due almost entirely to the work of Columbia Seminary and the labors of the seven hundred and fifty candidates for the ministry who passed through her halls during that period. Many of these men have labored, of course, and with success, in other parts of our country and in the lands across the sea.

After six years of service as teacher in the seminary, Dr. Goulding returned to the work of the pastorate at Columbus, Georgia. His remaining years were filled with abundant labors until the end came in 1848. His intellect was vigorous, his manners were marked by simplicity and a commanding dignity. He was a polished scholar, but above all else, he was the devout man of God. Great physical suffering marked his last moments. A beloved son, upon whose shoulder he was then leaning, heard his father say, "Come, Lord Jesus, come quickly." The prayer was heard and, in a moment, Dr. Goulding was at rest.

In the year 1833, Dr. Leland was summoned from his work as shepherd to become teacher of theology in the seminary. Throughout a period of thirty-one years this stalwart man of God continued his labors. He towered above most of his fellowmen in height and manly dignity. The courtliness of his bearing marked him as an ambassador from some great sovereign. And such he was,—for he represented the Lord, our Sovereign, and with fervid eloquence urged the heavenly message upon the hearts of all who had the good fortune to sit at his feet. A stroke of paralysis, in 1863, brought Dr. Leland's public labors to a close. Eight years later, after manifesting great patience in affliction, he passed away.

From time to time, after the beginning thus auspiciously made, other men of God, filled with the spirit of wisdom and of power, came to the seminary to take part in the work of training young ministers. Only their names can be set down at this point in our story of the work of the church: Charles Colcock Jones, Alexander T. McGill, Benjamin M. Palmer, James H. Thornwell, John B. Adger, James Woodrow, William S. Plumer, Joseph R. Wilson, John L. Girardeau, James D. Tadlock, Francis R. Beattie, W. T. Hall, and others who are still dwelling among us. In the matter of efficiency of service rendered to our entire church, what similar company of men may be preferred in honor above these worthies of Columbia Seminary?

The life and character of Dr. George Howe, like a golden cord, ran through the long period from 1831 to 1883 to bind together in one body the teachers and students connected with the Seminary. Dr. Howe's scholarship was accurate in quality and wide in range. The sacred Scriptures in the Hebrew and Greek languages constituted Dr. Howe's special field of labor. With unwearied zeal, he continued to lead young ministers into a deeper knowledge of the divine messages. Sound methods of Hebrew and Greek exegesis were disseminated by him throughout our Southern country. As much as any other man among us, he labored for the maintenance of a high standard of ministerial training.

In 1849, in response to the call of the Synod of South Carolina, Dr. Howe began to prepare a history of the Presbyterian Church within the borders of this synod. Twenty-one years afterwards (1870) the first volume of the work came from the press. With unfailing patience he continued the labor of love until the close of his life. The last pages of the manuscript of the second volume were sent to the printers only a brief space of time before the Lord called his servant hence. The two volumes form a great work, worthily wrought out,—a priceless treasure for the enrichment of our church and a fitting memorial to the writer, Dr. Howe.

Those who knew him best tell us that in personal characteristics he was first pure, then gentle and modest, and full of all charitableness. Strong convictions dwelt in his mind and heart, but over all the elements of his personality there rested that beautiful veil known as simplicity of character. The art of the politician was unknown to him. Truth was always his aim and truth was ever the pathway followed in attaining it.

On the evening of November 4, 1881, a great company of the alumni and friends of the Seminary met in the First Presbyterian Church, Columbia. Dr. Benjamin M. Palmer, as chairman, welcomed the members of the audience to the "fiftieth anniversary of our venerable mother," the Seminary, and to "this golden wedding of the Senior Professor who was married to her in his youth, and has given to her the affection and toil of his life." Then James H. Saye, veteran preacher of the gospel, a member of the class of 1837, came forward to offer words of congratulation to Dr. Howe. The latter arose to receive the message from the sons of the old school. He used a crutch, for an affection of the right knee had made that member weak. But Dr. Howe's frame was massive; his countenance was open, with features that spoke of intellectual strength. Heavy locks of hair and a long beard, now grown white, gave the venerable minister that personal appearance which is usually associated with the ancient

Hebrew patriarchs. His blue-gray eyes were filled with tears, as "with unaffected humility and grace," writes an eye-witness; in rich and melting tones, and in a manner simple, but sublime, he acknowledged the kindness of his brethren, and dwelt upon the wisdom and the goodness of that holy providence which first led him to cast in his lot with theirs, and had conducted him through all the vicissitudes of so protracted a term of labor to that auspicious hour.

Dr. Howe's bodily infirmities were multiplied during the last months of his life. In spite of great suffering, he continued steadfastly at work each day and far into the night in order that he might finish the tasks laid upon him. When the summons came he was ready. He read aloud the closing chapters of the Epistle to the Romans, clasped his hands upon his breast and in a fervent prayer commended his beloved wife and "the dear Seminary," as he called it, unto the fatherly care of God. A little while afterwards he fell asleep.

CHAPTER XXXVII.

JOHN FORREST AND THOMAS SMYTH, PASTORS IN CHARLESTON, SOUTH CAROLINA.

In the early part of the year 1832, the congregations of the First Church and of the Second Church, Charleston, prepared formal calls and placed them in the hands of John Forrest and of Thomas Smyth. The theological seminary, as we have just seen, was then entering upon its work at Columbia. These two men of God became shepherds in the Charleston field, therefore, at the opportune moment when they could help to nurture the growing theological institution. This work of nurture and aid they rendered most efficiently throughout a period of more than forty years.

John Forrest was a Scot, born in Edinburgh in 1799, and trained in the University that is located in his native city. In February, 1732, the First Church, Charleston, made out a call and sent it across the sea to the young preacher who was well spoken of by those who had heard him. The Presbytery of Edinburgh laid hands upon him in the regular ordination ceremonial. He came at once and began his work in Charleston in October, 1832, but retained his membership in the Church of Scotland. Faithfulness in the discharge of regular duties; devotion to the spiritual welfare of his people; these qualities marked his daily life. The church increased in numbers under his guardianship. Union services, in association with other denominations, were inaugurated by Dr. Forrest, and thus God's kingdom was made stronger. In

times of sorrow this pastor was more than an ordinary
messenger of comfort. His strong faith and his eager
sympathies enabled him to lead troubled souls into the
pathway of peace.

In 1852, the Charleston Union Presbytery was admitted into the Synod of South Carolina. Prior to
that time, this presbytery had been an independent
body, but thenceforth the churches of this region,
under the title of the Charleston Presbytery, formed
a part of our General Assembly. Dr. Forrest became
a member of the Charleston Presbytery and a solemn
communion service was held in his church to celebrate
the binding together of all the Presbyterian elements
of the tidewater region of South Carolina. Into this
bond of union the Central Church, of Charleston, entered. This, congregation was organized in 1823, and
William A. McDowell was the first shepherd of the
flock. William C. Dana, a minister from Massachusetts, began his long pastorate in 1836. Twelve years
later (1848) the present handsome house of worship
was erected. The name of the church has since been
changed to Westminster.

Dr. Forrest continued his labors in the First Church
until the summer of 1879. Then, after a ministry that
had been extended throughout a period of well-nigh
forty-seven years, "the silver cord was loosed," and he
was set free from all pain and infirmity of the flesh.
Dr. Dana, of the Westminster Church, delivered an address in commemoration of the work of Dr. Forrest.
A few months later (1880) Dr. Dana himself heard
the Master's call and went to join his friend and colleague in the church above.

The life-long associate of Forrest and Dana in the
work in Charleston was Thomas Smyth. As a
frail young man, twenty-four years of age, the latter
took charge of the Second Church in 1832, although he was not formally installed as pastor until

1834.   He was born in Belfast, Ireland (1808), of
Scotch and English parentage, and received his academic training in Belfast College.   An excessive love
of books marked his childhood and youth, and he won
prizes in every branch of study during his course in
the college.   Young Smyth's superior scholarship was
acknowledged by his entire class of nearly one hundred
students when they unanimously voted that he should
receive the highest academic honors.   Near the close
of his collegiate course he gave his heart to Christ and
decided to become a minister.   A beginning of theological studies was made at Highbury College, in London, and there his "appetite for books became rapa-
cious," as he tells us.   He often sold his food and fuel
in order to secure books.   In the year 1830, he came
with his parents across the Atlantic to New Jersey.
One year was spent at Princeton Seminary, and in the
autumn of 1831, he came to Charleston, South Carolina.

The spring of the following year found him in the
pulpit of the Second Church.   Nature had bestowed
splendid gifts with respect to both intellect and physical appearance, and these made their impression even
at that early stage in his career.   He had a vigorous
and brilliant imagination and his scholarship became
wide and accurate.   His piety was fervent and his
heart was full of sympathy for all who were in need.
We are not surprised, therefore, to learn that his messages from the pulpit were marked by great spiritual
power.

First of all, Dr. Smyth was an expounder.   He
sought to make clear to his people the fundamental
principles of the Christian faith.   The life and work
of Christ, the Psalms, and the Epistles of the New
Testament were set forth in a long series of expository
sermons.

Dr. Smyth was a Missionary Pastor.   That is to

say, he preached to his people and pleaded with them
continuously to maintain the cause of missions beyond
the seas. His enthusiasm touched the hearts of his own
people and the hearts of many others throughout our
church.

The training of a godly ministry enlisted the most
eager zeal of Dr. Smyth. To this end he gave loyal
support to the Columbia Seminary. With voice, pen
and purse he aided in upbuilding this school of the
prophets. Numerous gifts in money and books came
from himself and his people. The chief part of his
large, well-selected library has become the property of
the seminary.

The entire series of duties that belongs to the shepherd of a flock was met by Dr. Smyth with unwearied
fidelity. Upon the floor of the church court he was
always ready with wise counsel; he was an able debater
in all matters pertaining to the honor and efficiency of
the church.

As a standard-bearer, however, Dr. Smyth must have
a large place in the esteem and affection of all of the
people of our church. Evangelical Christianity was, at
that time, fiercely assailed and Dr. Smyth, as the strong
Christian warrior, delivered battle in behalf of the truth.
His pen was his chief weapon, and a large number of
books, sermons, tracts and pamphlets were put forth.
These have been reprinted in our own time in ten large
volumes, under the editorship of his son-in-law, Dr. J.
William Flinn.

The claims of prelatic and Romish churches to an
exclusive possession of the rights and privileges of the
church were advanced with great boldness and arro-
gance at the time when Dr. Smyth began his work in
Charleston. In 1841, therefore, he published a volume
in defense of the Protestant ministry against the prelatical doctrine of apostolic succession. In 1843,

his volume on "Eclesiastical Republicanism" appeared. "All the principles of republicanism," he said, "are found in our Presbyterian system. The framers of this system," said Dr. Smyth, "designed that it should be neither a monarchy nor a democracy, but a republic." Proceeding upon this basis with clear logic and great learning, he advanced to a demonstration of the true liberality and catholicity of the Presbyterian system of doctrine. That presbytery and not prelacy is the scriptural form of church government constitutes the subject of an important volume issued in 1844. "The character of the church and its ministry during our Lord's continuance with it was Presbyterian and not prelatical," wrote Dr. Smyth. Presbyters, or ordinary ministers, he claimed, are "divinely authorized" to preach the gospel, to conduct public worship, to celebrate the sacraments of baptism and the Lord's Supper and to ordain men to the work of the ministry.

With great courtesy and dignity, with rhetorical skill and with learning, Dr. Smyth presented these and other discussions. His books were widely read by members of various denominations; the final effect was of lasting benefit to evangelical Christianity.

This Christian warrior bore for years a heavy burden of physical pain. Twice he was stricken with paralysis, and his tall, commanding form became bent, and he was forced to go upon crutches. "I have lived from day to day," he wrote, "as a tenant at will, looking any moment for an ejectment and change of residence. I awake in the morning asking myself, 'Is it possible I am alive?' When worn and exhausted by pain and wakefulness, I have wondered with a great amazement what invisible power held together a body and spirit so willing to dissolve partnership."

His suffering seemed never to affect his mind and spirit. Cheerfulness marked his bearing always. His will was unconquerable. Sometimes he bade defiance to his own bodily pain and went forth to his work. "No act of his life," says his successor, Dr. Brackett, "was more positive than that of obeying the order of his Great Captain to put off his armor and go up to receive his crown."

CHAPTER XXXVIII.

On the first Monday in March, 1837, a company of young men came together near the present site of Davidson College, in the northern part of Mecklenburg County, North Carolina. Classical and mathematical text books were opened and a course of study was begun at once under the instruction given by Robert Hall Morrison, pastor of Sugar Creek Church, and Patrick Jones Sparrow, pastor of the church at Salisbury. M. D. Johnston took charge of the work in mathematics. Regular work upon the college farm constituted a part of the training imparted by the school.

After the spring session, in the year 1835, the Concord Presbytery, embracing the upper part of North Carolina, took the first step in the movement to establish the school. Bethel Presbytery, composed of the Presbyterian Churches of the upper part of South Carolina, joined hands with Concord. Morganton Presbytery, of Western North Carolina, likewise engaged in the work. The name Dividson was given to the school established by these North and South Carolina Presbyterians, in honor of General William L. Davidson, who was slain in battle against the British forces of Cornwallis at Cowan's Ford, on the Catawba River. The patriotic origin of the college is indicated in the motto which is incorporated in the college seal: *Alenda lux ubi orta libertas* (Let learning be cherished where liberty has arisen). On the 9th of November, 1836, a meeting was held in old Center Church, and the votes of the three presbyteries named above were cast for Robert Hall Morrison as first

president of Davidson College. A few months later the
president and his associates began the work of instruction which has continued with growing success until the
present time. This school was established near the center of a territory, in the upper portions of North and
South Carolina, which contained in 1837 some 9,000 or
10,000 Presbyterians. Davidson College was the culmination of their constructive efforts in behalf of the
cause of education under the control of the church.
Within a brief period they raised the sum of $30,000,
and upon this financial basis the school entered upon
its work. Robert Hall Morrison, a son of Rocky River
Church, received his early knowledge of Latin and
Greek in the school of John Makemie Wilson, his pastor. In the University of North Carolina, young Morrison was a classmate of James K. Polk, and at their
graduation (1818) shared first honor with the future
President of the United States. He held pastorates
at Fayetteville and Sugar Creek and preached often
in the town of Charlotte. His contributions to religious
magazines gave promise of scholarship and literary
skill. "His chaste and elegant diction," wrote Dr.
Arnold W. Miller, "his dignified mien, his impressive
delivery, his heart on fire with the love of Christ, capti-
vated his hearers and made his ministry a ministry of
power."

Dr. Morrison married Mary Graham, daughter of
General Joseph Graham, of the Revolution, and sister
of Hon. William A. Graham, who became governor of
North Carolina, United States Senator and Secretary
of the Navy, in President Fillmore's cabinet. A worthy
company of sons and daughters blessed the union of
Robert H. Morrison and Mary Graham. Four of their
sons entered the military service of the Southern Confederacy. Moreover, five Confederate officers married
daughters of the first president of Davidson College;
these were Judge A. C. Avery, General Rufus Barringer,

General D. H. Hill and Colonel John E. Brown, of
North Carolina, and General Stonewall Jackson, of
Virginia.

When Dr. Morrison was formally inaugurated he
made an address which contained the following announcement of principles:—

"Religious instruction is not only important, but
indispensable in education. Religious instruction
should be held where God has placed it as *paramount*
to everything else. The Bible must be supreme in seats
of learning, if their moral atmosphere is to be kept
pure. Learning should be imbued with the spirit of
heaven to give it moral power."

He said further: "Education without moral principle only gives men intelligence to do evil. Let any
system of education prevail which renounces God and
disowns the Bible and how long would magistrates be
honored, parents obeyed, truth spoken, property safe
or life secure?"

In concluding the address, he referred to the first
college building, then already erected, as "a goodly
temple to God, standing in the midst of this grove, a
just emblem that the gospel to be preached in it is
the main spring to the whole system."

It was a worthy beginning of a noble work. A multitude of young men has already received in the halls
of this school, within the limits of less than a century of
labor, the inspiration that comes from high Christian
ideals. An increasing number of these have been led
to devote their energies to the work of the gospel ministry. Thus, the temple of learning, dedicated to God,
by Robert Hall Morrison, continues to be an efficient
agency of the church and a fountain of blessing to the
people of the entire country.

In 1840 Dr. Morrison withdrew himself from the
work of teaching. On account of the weak state of his
health he retired to his farm, Cottage Home, in Lin-

coln County, North Carolina, and remained there until death came in 1889. His successor as president of Davidson was Dr. Samuel Williamson (1841-1854), a native of York County, South Carolina. He received his classical training at the College of South Carolina, studied theology under Rev. James Adams, and about 1822 became pastor of Providence Church, North Carolina.

In 1840 he was appointed professor of mathematics in Davidson College. The following year marked his promotion to the presidency, a position which he filled with credit and success. Through toil and self-denial and good, sound judgment he brought the college through a period of great difficulty, and ushered it into an era of wide success.

During the period 1855-1861 Dr. Drury Lacy was president of the college. He was born near Hampden-Sidney College, in Virginia (1802) and received his classical preparation in the school conducted by his father, Rev. Drury Lacy. The latter, as we have seen, was the friend and associate of Archibald Alexander and John Holt Rice. The son, Drury, completed the course of study at Hampden-Sidney College in 1822, taught school for a series of years, and finally went forth from Union Seminary in 1832. His principal pastorates were at New Berne and Raleigh, North Carolina. Fervent piety and deep sympathy were joined in beautiful harmony in his character. A nephew wrote of him as follows: "Uncle Drury is about the best hearer in the world. He leans forward and drinks in with his whole face and form and all his senses. He reflects every emotion, beaming on you if you are cheerful, and weeping if you are tender. Even then he does not hide his face with a handkerchief, but beams on, and lets the big honest tears roll and take care of themselves. If I had a whole audience of Uncle Drurys, I should think I was the greatest orator in the world. If every face were such a mirror of emotion, the speaker who stood in the focus would be consumed."

During his pastorate at New Berne, young Moses Drury Hoge, a nephew, dwelt for a time in Dr. Lacy's home, and was there prepared for college. Dr. Hoge in later years wrote the following about his Uncle Drury Lacy: "He is without doubt the best specimen of a *man* I ever saw; frank, generous, sincere, affectionate; but his finest quality is his perfect freedom from dissimulation or artifice of any sort. He is entirely transparent. He reminds me of some deep, pure river, through whose clear depths one may look and see pearls and gems sparkling."

The presence of such a man in the president's chair at Davidson College instinctively drew the confidence of all men toward the school. In the first year of Dr. Lacy's presidency, Maxwell Chambers, Esq., of Salisbury, North Carolina, made to the college a gift of a quarter of a million dollars. By means of this fund, the main college building, with its massive pillars, was erected, apparatus and cabinets were secured, and new members were added to the force of teachers.

Students came in increasing numbers to gain benefit from these educational agencies and to witness the beauty of holiness as it was manifested in the life and work of President Lacy. His manners were polished and his scholarship was of high grade. The college was recognized as a school of high rank because of the moral and intellectual power of the man who directed its work.

Dr. Lacy went to the field of war as a Confederate chaplain. Afterwards, throughout a long period of years, he taught school at Raleigh. One day in the year 1884 he returned from a walk, lay down to take a rest, went to sleep and awoke in the presence of his Lord.

During the period of warfare, 1861-1866, Dr. John

L. Kirkpatrick, a native of Mecklenburg County, North Carolina, was President of Davidson College. Dr. Kirkpatrick had a varied experience as pastor and editor before entering the Davidson field.

The students were few in number in this time of storm and stress, and at the close of it the finances of the school were almost exhausted. When Dr. Kirkpatrick was invited to assume the chair of Moral Philosophy at Washington College, in Virginia, Dr. George Wilson McPhail became President of Davidson (1867-'71). He was a native of Norfolk, Virginia, and for a short period served as president of Lafayette College, Pennsylvania.

Out of the labors and prayers of these founders sprang the modern Davidson College. Her efficient work in imparting a liberal education in immediate connection with wise religious training is known of all men. This work seems to show us that the Church, acting through the College, is still able to furnish her sons with that physical and intellectual and spiritual preparation that brings success in every field of human activity. In addition to this, as the crown of her own labors, Davidson College can point to a great multitude of her sons who have strengthened and extended the Church herself through their ministrations as preachers of the gospel.

CHAPTER XXXIX.

THE tenth day of August, 1830, marked a memorable
era in the life of Daniel Baker. At an early hour that
morning he went out of his house with Dr. Payson's
Memoirs in his hand. After walking through a stretch
of woods near the city in which he was then living,
namely, Savannah, Georgia, Dr. Baker found a lonely
burial ground. He entered the place and sat down
under the shade of a tree, near a brick tomb, for he had
decided to spend the day there in prayer and fasting
and meditation. His mind and heart were disturbed by
the fact that his ministerial labors were not receiving the
blessing of God. "I know not," he wrote in his journal
that day, "that a single individual has been awakened
under my preaching for six months past. It will not do
to live on at this poor dying rate. Lord, revive me!"

The cry of his heart found an answer. The lonely
burial ground became to him as the house of God. Payson's *Memoirs* furnished him with the idea of a prayer-
meeting held in behalf of "those for whom prayer might
be specially desired." Just one week later he held a
meeting of this kind. In response to invitations given a
day or two in advance, forty-six notes were sent to him.
These were all read to the congregation. Some of these
letters were from parents, "entreating that prayers
might be made for their dear unconverted children."
Some were from members "praying for the conversion
of their brothers and sisters." A husband desired the
conversion of his wife; a sinner longed for the conversion of his own soul; an unconverted wife asked the

people of God to pray for the salvation of herself and her husband. "I put in a note myself," writes Dr. Baker, "requesting the prayers of my people for me; that the Lord would give me a more intense love for souls, and signal success to my labors."

Through the agency of these prayers the hearts of many were melted. Early in the following year (1831) a series of services was held in Dr. Baker's church, with preaching three times a day. The work of grace ran throughout the city of Savannah, and as many as two hundred and fifty persons were led into Christ's kingdom.

At once Dr. Baker was invited to preach in various small towns along the Atlantic Coast near Savannah. A wondrous revival of religion swept throughout that region wherever he preached the word. "Never, surely, since the days of the Apostles," wrote one who heard Dr. Baker at that time, "has more fervid zeal, or ardent piety, or untiring labor, been devoted by a Christian minister to his cause. For ten unwearied days, from morning until nine at night, have we heard the strongest and most impassioned appeals to the heads and hearts of his hearers. All that is terrible or beautiful; all that is winning or appalling; all that could steal and charm and soothe the heart, or shake its careless security and command its attention to the truths of religion, we have seen pressed upon our community with an earnestness, energy and affectionate persuasiveness almost irresistible. Politics were forgotten; business stood still; the shops and stores were shut and the schools closed; one subject only appeared to occupy all minds and engross all hearts. The church was filled to overflowing. When the solemn stillness was broken by the voice of the preacher citing the impenitent to appear before the judgment-seat of heaven, reproving, persuading, imploring by the most thrilling appeals to every principle of his nature; when crowds moved forward and fell prostrate at the foot of the altar and the rich music of hundreds of voices and the solemn accents of prayer rose over the kneeling multitude, it was not in human hearts to resist the influence that awoke its sympathies and spoke its purest and most elevated policy."

" 'There stood the messenger of Truth; there stood the legate of the skies.' "

Multitudes were brought into the churches of South Carolina and Georgia as the result of Dr. Baker's preaching. Eight of these converts became ministers of the gospel. So manifest was the hand of God upon him that Dr. Baker at once gave up the pastoral care of the Independent Church, of Savannah, and entered the field as an evangelist.

The story of the early life of Daniel Baker is soon told. He was born in 1791, a son of Christian parents, in the old Midway congregation in Georgia. As a lad of about fourteen years he went to Savannah, mounted upon a bale of cotton in a cart. In that city he found work as a clerk in a store. Soon afterwards he became a Christian, and decided that he would attempt to preach the gospel. In the year 1811 he entered Hampden-Sidney College. Two years later he became a member of the Junior Class at Princeton. In that institution, among one hundred and forty-five students, he found only two who were willing to join him in the organization of a prayer-meeting. Out of this sprang a religious revival; fifty of the students were converted and twenty of these became ministers of the gospel.

In the year 1815 Mr. Baker took up his residence in Winchester, Virginia, expecting to study theology under the direction of Dr. William Hill. The only book placed in Baker's hand by his teacher was Butler's *Analogy*. In addition he studied the *Shorter Catechism* and the Bible, and in the autumn of 1816 he was licensed to preach. "But I must confess," writes Baker, "that I was by no means prepared."

In 1818 Daniel Baker became pastor of the churches
in Harrisonburg and New Erection. He also taught
school, and one of his pupils was Gessner Harrison, who
became afterwards a famous teacher in the University
of Virginia. In 1821 Dr. Baker entered a larger field
as pastor of the Second Church of Washington City.
President John Quincy Adams and General Andrew
Jackson were among the members of his congregation
in that place; they showed the young preacher many
marks of their respect. The year 1828 marked his settlement in Savannah as successor of Dr. Kollock in the
Independent Church, but in 1831, as we have seen, he
gave up this attractive pastorate, with its comfortable
salary, and became a home missionary. In this work
he received only a moderate income, barely sufficient for
the support of his family. The ingathering of souls,
however,—the abundance of that harvest,—brought
gladness to his spirit. Within the period of two years
after leaving his pastorate he led as many as two thousand five hundred persons to acknowledge Christ as
Saviour. This result was accomplished through the
preaching of the gospel regularly three times a day
during the revivals. His method of speaking was the
colloquial. The utmost simplicity and the highest degree of earnestness marked the manner of Dr. Baker in
the pulpit. His discourses were filled with stories and
illustrations. Intensity of conviction multiplied the
power with which he spake,—a power that proceeded
from the Spirit who dwelt within him.

"He acted as though he felt in the inmost recesses of
his heart that he was an evangelist, an apostle sent forth
with the commission of his Master."

On one occasion an irreligious man determined to go
to the door of the church in which Dr. Baker was conducting services. He wished to catch a glimpse of the
preacher about whom nearly everybody in that community was speaking. Taking some of his comrades

with him, he reached the door at the moment when Dr. Baker was leading the congregation in prayer. After listening a few moments, the man whispered to his associates: "That man prays as if he were really talking with God." He had come to scoff, but he remained to pray.

In the summer of 1834 Dr. Baker conducted revivals in the eastern part of Virginia. He then took his family into Ohio with the expectation of remaining in that state. A wide circuit was made and the gospel was preached in many towns and villages, but the full blessing from heaven seemed to be withheld. The following entry in Dr. Baker's journal throws some light upon the situation: "Finding myself in the midst of rabid abolitionists who poured almost unmeasured abuse upon my Southern friends, I felt myself, as it were, in a nest of hornets. Although I was myself no slaveholder, yet I was no abolitionist. I verily believed that the relation of master and slave was recognized in the Bible, and that ecclesiastical bodies have no right to legislate upon the subject. Pained by the harsh remarks which poured into my ear from day to day, I became very restless and wished to return to the South again. Providentially I received at this time an invitation to labor as a missionary in Kentucky. Accordingly, leaving Ohio, I went to Kentucky, my first point being Danville."

The church at Frankfort, Kentucky, called Dr. Baker to become pastor, and this office he filled for nearly three years. Another pastorate followed at Tuskaloosa, Alabama. Revival services, attended with manifold blessings, were conducted at Memphis, Mobile, New Orleans and other strategic points in the Mississippi Valley. Early in the year 1840 he embarked on a steamer at New Orleans, and after a brief journey caught his first glimpse of Galveston. He went ashore and began to lay foundations in behalf of the Master in the vast region known as Texas.

On April 3, 1840, a small body of presbyters, consisting of three ministers and an elder, met in Chrisman's schoolhouse, in the little town of Independence, near the Brazos River. The ministers were Hugh Wilson, a native of North Carolina, and member at that time of South Alabama Presbytery; John McCullough, of New Jersey, and W. Y. Allen, of Tennessee. The elder was John McFarland, of Independence, Texas. These four organized the Presbytery of Brazos, the first presbytery established in Texas. Dr. Baker, as a member of Tuskaloosa Presbytery, was invited to sit in conference with the members of the new organization. The subject under consideration was the building of a Presbyterian college in Texas. A commanding eminence near the home of Hugh Wilson was chosen as a site for the college, and Dr. Baker began at once to ask for subscriptions.

Dr. Baker came again, however, to the eastern bank of the Mississippi to establish a home for his family. For several years he was pastor at Holly Springs, Mississippi. At the same time he held revival services in Nashville, Vicksburg, St. Louis and at various other points in the great Valley. The call of the Southwest was ever in his ears, and one afternoon in June, 1848, he sailed into Matagorda Bay. Going ashore at Lavaca, Texas, he found the people eager to hear the word of life. That very night he spoke to a crowded house. Hungry souls were found everywhere, and Dr. Baker made his way westward, riding alone across vast plains, sleeping under the sky with wild beasts prowling all about him, entering small towns and gathering audiences by his own personal invitation. His voice was heard in Austin, the capital of Texas. He journeyed to the mouth of the Rio Grande and began there an evangelistic campaign which carried him into every hamlet along that stream. He even crossed the river and spent a brief period of time in Mexico. He spake as the prophet of God and men everywhere gave him heed. Hundreds were led to Christ, and this was sufficient satisfaction to Dr. Baker for days and nights of hunger, fatigue and sickness. His energy was marvelous. His faith never failed.

In 1849, the presbytery established their college in the town of Huntsville and Dr. Baker was appointed to the office of president. He made six journeys through the states to raise money for the school, which was named Austin College in honor of Stephen F. Austin, the Texas pioneer. Many thousands of acres of land were given and he collected the sum of one hundred thousand dollars in money. "The one idea of its founders, that for which they wept and prayed and toiled and gave of their means, was that it might be an institution wherein there might be raised up for Texas, generation after generation, a native ministry. Palsied be the hand which shall ever cast a ballot to alienate the school in any way from this the main purpose of its existence." The college was afterwards removed to the town of Sherman and there it has continued to furnish a godly ministry for the Texas field. Under the guiding hand of S. M. Luckett, the college was made larger and stronger. A little more than fifty years after the founding of Austin College there was a body of 25,000 Presbyterians in Texas, the strong theological seminary located at Austin, the Presbyterian College for girls at Milford and Daniel Baker College at Brownwood. These are some of the fruits that have grown in large measure out of the labors of Daniel Baker. When the news of the death of this man of God was announced to the legislature of the state, then in session at Austin (1857), both branches of that body adjourned at once as an expression of esteem for one whom they called a "public benefactor." The title which he asked his son to carve on his headstone was this: "Daniel Baker, Preacher of the Gospel."

CHAPTER XL.

IN the month of March, 1808, a tall, slender young man, with long, oval face, clear blue eyes and a nose like the eagle's beak, rode through the passes of the central Alleghany range and entered the wide upland region now called Monroe County, in Western Virginia. In the first house in which he sought shelter, the young man preached a sermon. The journey was again taken up and in the courthouse in the little town of Union the young preacher delivered his gospel message. He then pressed northward across the beautiful mountain stream known as Greenbrier River and his voice was next heard preaching the gospel in the town of Lewisburg, in the County of Greenbrier. The preacher continued his journey westward, delivering the gospel message at various points in the Kanawha Valley, even as far as the Ohio River. Turning eastward again, he rode through the mountains to the Valley of Virginia to sit with his brethren of the Lexington Presbytery in the old Timber Ridge Church. With their consent he came once more to the Greenbrier country and on the first Sunday in June, 1808, preached again in the stone church at Lewisburg. In this manner began the work of John McElhenney as shepherd of the two flocks at Lewisburg and Union.

John McElhenney was born in the Waxhaws community, South Carolina, in 1781. His father was a Scot from Ireland, who bore an honorable part in the war of the Revolution and died when John was an infant. An elder brother, James McElhenney, took charge of

John's education. The latter sat at the feet of James Hall of North Carolina, and of James Gilliland, pastor and teacher at Nazareth Church, South Carolina. In Gilliland's school Samuel B. Wilson, afterwards pastor at Fredericksburg, Virginia, was a fellow-student with John McElhenney. When McElhenney turned his steps towards Yale College he found that school closed by reason of an epidemic of yellow-fever. In 1802, therefore, he joined his schoolmate, Samuel B. Wilson, at Washington Academy in Virginia. For the space of six years he studied Greek and Latin under Daniel Blain and the Bible and theology under President George A. Baxter. In February, 1808, Lexington Presbytery laid hands upon the head of McElhenney and bade him cross the mountains into the valley of the Greenbrier. In that journey we have already followed him to the Stone Church of Lewisburg. There, in the summer of 1809, Dr. Baxter delivered one of his solemn discourses and formally installed McElhenney in the office of pastor.

About the same time, the elder brother, James McElhenney, became pastor of the Old Stone Church* near the present Clemson College in South Carolina, and there, in 1812, he passed away. His youngest daughter, Emily, became the mother of the Southern poet, Paul H. Hayne.

The region in which John McElhenney became pastor was at first a part of Augusta County, Virginia. About the year 1751, John Lewis and his son Andrew set forth from the Valley of Virginia to explore the country west of the mountains. On the bank of a clear stream, John Lewis became entangled in a thicket of vines. For this

---

*Some members of the Anderson family removed from the neighborhood of the Stone Church, Augusta County, Virginia, to the present Pendleton County, South Carolina. In the latter place about the year 1802 they helped to build the Stone Church of which James McElhenny was pastor. Perhaps they carried with them from Augusta the idea of a sanctuary built of stone. See page 248.

reason he named the stream Green-brier River. Soon afterwards a number of Scotch-Irish families removed from the Valley and built homes near this river. Among the early settlers were the families of McClanachan, Stuart, Arbuckle, Withrow, Gibson, Renick, McClure, Mathews, Irwin, Hunter, Anderson and others. For protection against the Indians a fort was built and named Camp Union. From this fort, as we have already seen, General Andrew Lewis set forth in the fall of 1774 to deliver battle against the Indians at Point Pleasant. In the army of Lewis there were two companies of riflemen from the settlements on the Greenbrier, led by Robert McClanachan and John Stuart. In 1777 a county was laid off and named Greenbrier, after the river. Scotch-Irish settlers from Augusta County continued to pour in, and Camp Union received the name Lewisburg in honor of Andrew Lewis. Colonel John Stuart built a house of stone on the main street of the town and assigned it to the county to be used as a court house. In 1796, Colonel Stuart and his wife, Agatha, a daughter of Thomas Lewis, erected in Lewisburg, at their own expense, the Stone Church, which is still standing in all of its original strength. It was a square structure of grey limestone, with a sounding-board hung above the pulpit. The gallery was reserved for the colored people.

John McElhenney's field of labor extended from the summit of the Alleghenies to the Ohio River, a region embracing the chief part of the present commonwealth of West Virginia. John McCue of Augusta County had founded the three churches of Lewisburg, Spring Creek and Union, and Benjamin Grigsby of Augusta was their next shepherd. McElhenney took charge of these three flocks, and after the space of more than sixty-two years under his pastorate the number of members had become a multitude.

At the morning hour on Sunday he would preach to

the flock at Lewisburg. After the sermon he would mount his faithful horse and ride at a steady pace to Union, twenty miles away. There he would preach at the close of the same day to the members of his second flock. Side journeys in great number were made by this apostle on horseback. Over great mountains and through deep, swift mountain streams he urged his horse in the work of planting new churches. Through his own preaching and through the work of men trained by him, congregations were organized at Parkersburg, Tygart's Valley, Point Pleasant, Charleston, the present capital of the state, and, also, near the headwaters of the Greenbrier. In this manner he claimed for Presbyterianism the entire region of Western Virginia.

In the autumn of 1808, six months after his first entrance into the Greenbrier Valley, the pastor of the church established a school under the shadow of the stone sanctuary at Lewisburg. For many years Dr. McElhenney himself was the principal teacher. Afterwards he committed the school unto faithful men who continued the good work. From this academy came forth many who have rendered great service among their countrymen. Lawyers, physicians, merchants and ministers were trained by McElhenney. Among the preachers who sat at his feet in the school room were Dr. Henry Ruffner, president of Washington College in Virginia, and Dr. William S. Plumer.

In 1838 the churches established by McElhenney and his helpers had grown so numerous that they were formed into the separate Presbytery of Greenbrier. His work widened with the passing of the years. His labors at home were abundant, for he owned a small tract of land and became the best farmer in that region. He was a fine judge of horses and also a good horseman, and seemed never to grow weary as he urged his steed across the breezy uplands. He was up "at six in the morning, riding or walking over the farm," writes his

granddaughter, Rose W. Fry; "in his study by nine
o'clock, writing or meditating; on horseback again after
an early dinner, visiting the sick or riding to fill an appointment." And in all the South in that day, no man
rode and preached more than John McElhenney.

"He appears to be ever in a hurry to do good," writes
one who knew him. "He has been in a hurry all his
life. He has no time for elegant circumlocutions. As
soon as his message is delivered, he is in motion again to
deliver his message somewhere else. He is the very per-
sonification of motion. He is a striking example of how
much a man can do who does it with all his might." He
preached with power and in great tenderness of spirit.
His voice was musical and his eye was piercing in its
look. The love of a great heart was ever ready to
respond to the call of any member of his flock. For
miles and miles in every direction throughout a wide
region all men knew that good, grey head, and all loved
him.

On the 5th of June, 1858, Dr. McElhenney stood up
in the old Stone Church to deliver a sermon in commemoration of fifty years of labor as minister in that field.
During that period he had preached sermons to the
number of nearly eight thousand, administered the rite
of baptism thirteen hundred times and united in the
marriage bond as many as one thousand five hundred
couples. "As to the number of times," he said, "that
I have administered the sacrament of the Lord's Supper,
and the addresses and exhortations I have delivered, I
can form no idea."

During the later years of his ministry, an associate
pastor labored by his side; at first, Dr. J. C. Barr, and
then Dr. Matthew L. Lacy. At last in the year 1871
the silver cord was loosed and the faithful man of God,
the patriarch among his people, having reached well
nigh the age of ninety years, was gathered unto his
fathers.

In a grove of oak trees by the side of the roadway that leads from Lewisburg to Union stands a small church called Salem. All that fair upland region of field and forest slopes gently to the southern bank of the Greenbrier. The soil is fertile, and every summer the ripening harvests seem to change the fields into meadows of gold. The sons and daughters of Scotland have entered this region in such great numbers that the district near the river has been called from the earliest days the Scotch-Irish "Corner." Under the shadow of Salem, the quiet house of God frequented by these Scots, the writer of this present volume spent the years of his childhood within that period when the apostolic McElhenney was nearing the end of his pilgrimage. Even now this writer recalls the fragrance of the memory that Dr. McElhenney left behind him among the Scots who with their children still worship at Salem. And not at Salem alone, but in every congregation like unto it, in all the region of Western Virginia, wherever the Scots continue to dwell among whom Dr. McElhenney labored as messenger of peace and salvation, his memory abides as an inspiration unto every good word and work. "Dr. McElhenney is the greatest man I ever knew in the ministry," wrote Dr. Stuart Robinson of Louisville; "great, I mean, with the greatness of action and faithfulness in the Master's work."

CHAPTER XLI.

A TOWN now called Darlington in Pennsylvania was
the birth-place of William Swan Plumer (1802). Scotch
courage and persistence carried him through many
strenuous days as youth and young man. When
Plumer was about nineteen years of age, he walked over
the mountains from Charleston, on the Kanawha River,
to Lewisburg in Greenbrier County, Virginia, to become
a pupil in Dr. McElhenney's Academy. Dr. Plumer
afterwards referred in the following terms to his first
glimpse of the beautiful town that nestles amid the hills
of Greenbrier: "Many years ago," he said, "when I
first came late on a Saturday afternoon to the brow of
the western hill overlooking the village, I thought from
the noise that reached my ear that Lewisburg must be a
busy manufacturing town; but when I came down into
its streets I found that it was only the servants in the
back yards chopping wood for Sunday."

Young Plumer was received with open arms by Dr.
McElhenney. Since he was one of the oldest students
in the academy, Plumer was called "Daddy." He was
even then tall and strong, had fine, black eyes, and was
dignified in manner. We are told that he made rapid
progress in the study of the ancient languages and that
he was in the habit of working at his tasks in the open
air, perched upon a woodpile near the academy building.
He entertained a great affection for his instructor whom
he called "Father McElhenney." This love was returned by the teacher who always addressed Plumer, the
most promising pupil in his school, as "Dear William."

From the academy Plumer passed on to Washington College to sit at the feet of that inspiring teacher, Dr. Baxter. Then in the autumn of 1824 he entered Princeton Seminary. Two years later (1826) he was licensed to preach. The church which he organized at Danville, Virginia, and another organized at Washington, North Carolina, were the first fruits of his ministry. A short pastorate at Briery Church, Prince Edward County, Virginia, was followed by a call to Petersburg. Three years later (1834) he became shepherd of the First Church, Richmond, and there he remained for more than twelve years.

William S. Plumer was pre-eminent as a preacher of the gospel. In height he stood a head and shoulders above his brethren. His step was slow and measured and his majestic presence in the pulpit impressed all beholders with the ideas of strength and dignity. Dr. Moses D. Hoge writes of him as follows: "His prayers were the tender pleadings of a soul in communion with God. There was a pathetic *tremolo* in his tone as he read the hymns for the day. He occasionally prefaced the announcement of his text with some striking remark, arresting the attention of his entire audience. His voice was one of great flexibility and power. Its cadences varied with the sentiments which filled his mind and heart. When the thought was tender, the expression of it came in accents soft and low. The words fell like the dropping of tears. In the utterance of some sublime and stirring thought, his voice rang out like the sound of a trumpet. These transitions at times were abrupt and startling as a bugle call to battle. Nervous persons were occasionally agitated by them; his audiences generally were aroused and impressed by them. In the fulness of his strength in middle life he could have filled a. great cathedral with the melodious thunder of his marvelous voice."

One Sunday in the summer of 1860, Dr. Plumer

preached to the guests at the While Sulphur Springs, in Virginia. It was a time of excitement and the band of music at that resort often played the patriotic melody of the French people, the Marseillaise hymn. The preacher, therefore, arose and said to his audience, in his deep, rich voice, "Let us begin the worship of God by singing the Marseillaise hymn of the Christian Church, 'All hail the power of Jesus' name.' " The reverential attention which was thus gained was held by the minister to the very close of the service.

The church of which he was pastor in Richmond was rapidly built up in numbers and in spiritual influence. Plumer's great heart was full of love for his fellowmen and with joy he called them into God's kingdom. Multitudes heard him and obeyed his call. Throughout our whole land, wherever he journeyed, crowds came to hear the Gospel of love and truth as it fell from his inspired lips. He was full of the highest courage in meeting his duties as pastor. Face to face he talked in all plainness and sincerity with wicked and profane persons. His heart bled for the poor and afflicted. Words of sympathy spoken by his lips seemed to find their way at once into the hearts of those afflicted with sorrow.

A minister so gifted soon made his way to the front as a leader in presbyteries and synods. In 1837, when Dr. Plumer was only thirty-five years of age, he shared with Dr. Baxter the chief part in the work of separating the church into the Old and New School assemblies. In the General Assembly of 1837 he was the leading speaker on the floor from the South. Dr. Beman was the principal Northern speaker and he made a strong plea in favor of remaining in union with the Congregationalists. When he sat down, the majority of the whole assembly was probably ready to vote with him against division. "In this state of the debate," says Dr. William H. Foote, "Mr. Plumer took the floor. Those who knew him well said that he was oppressed. His friends were moved,

lest his anxiety should destroy his composure. His first
few sentences were not particularly interesting; like
the skiff putting off into the eddies of the river, heading
one way and then another, till by a dexterous stroke of
the paddle it shoots to the main current and then sweeps
down the stream. The whole house was off its guard.
Suddenly he struck the current and was carrying us all
along with him before we could be aware; and the flow
of the stream went on broader and deeper. His great
effort was to do away with the effect of Dr. Beman's
speech upon that part of the house that was wavering.
He first sought out all the weak places in his adversary's
armor, and hurled his darts with appalling directness
into the open joints of his harness. His declamation was
powerful. His language was varied; sometimes terse,
sometimes flowing, sometimes quaint almost to obscurity
and sometimes florid almost to superfluity. Intermingled
all along were anecdotes and sarcasm, till the weaker
points of his opponent seemed to have swallowed up the
stronger. He then repeated the constitutional argument, and the causes of the action, and from the greatness
of the difficulties in the way showed the absolute necessity of a great reform. He produced a profound impression, that a great evil was to be boldly met, and
speedily met and no better means yet appeared than
citation. His speech changed the fate of the question."
At a later time during the same assembly, Dr. Plumer
had a large share in the final act of cutting off the four
western synods and thus of saving to our country the
system of Calvinism in doctrine and the Presbyterian
system in church government.

These principles had to be further defended at the
close of the summer of 1837; therefore, a new religious
paper made its appearance in Richmond, bearing the
name of *The Watchman of the South*. Plumer was
proprietor and editor. With a strong pen he upheld
the views of the Old School Presbyterians, and in the

following year (1838) he was chosen moderator of their assembly.

In the year 1846, a petition was presented to the legislature of Virginia asking the passage of a general law authorizing the incorporation of each congregation and religious society in the state. Dr. Plumer appeared before a committee of the legislature and spoke at length against the proposed law. Two of the most prominent lawyers of Richmond were his opponents, but Dr. Plumer showed himself so well equipped with arguments drawn from the history of the church, from the laws passed by various legislatures, and from the legal opinions expressed by eminent lawyers and judges, that he won his cause with ease. Dr. Plumer's breadth of liberality in sentiment and his genial, good humor won the favor of all who heard him engaged in this debate.

One of the lawyers who was somewhat pompous in manner charged Dr. Plumer with "imitating Don Quixote." To this charge Dr. Plumer replied as follows: "Concerning this Don, I am not very bright in my memory. But, if I remember rightly, the Don rode a sorrel horse. In this I do sometimes imitate him; but my horse is not, I think, so lean as Rosinante. I think, too, the Don was far from being a malignant man. If the gentleman intended to say the same of me, I thank him for his good opinion. I might admit also that the fates of the Don and of myself have been somewhat similar in at least one respect. If I am not mistaken he encountered a windmill or two. I am not sure but I have done the same."

In 1844 Moses D. Hoge was called to Richmond as Dr. Plumer's assistant. Three years later (1847) Dr. Plumer became pastor of the Franklin Street Church, Baltimore. There the pulpit was still his throne. With great power he continued to preach and to lead large numbers into the Kingdom.

The year 1854 marked Dr. Plumer's acceptance of the chair of theology in Alleghany Seminary, Pennsylvania. Afterwards, from 1862 to 1867, he was engaged in the work of preaching in Philadelphia and Pottsville, Pennsylvania. In 1867 he was made professor of theology in Columbia Seminary, in South Carolina. In that position he continued to labor with success until 1880. In the autumn of that year (October 22, 1880) he passed away.

Throughout his mature life Dr. Plumer was ever at work with his pen. Many books were written showing sound scholarship; among these were commentaries on the Psalms, the Epistle to the Romans and the Epistle to the Hebrews. A large number of tracts, practical and helpful, were prepared by him and sent out among all of the churches.

The touch of time changed Dr. Plumer's hair to the color of silver and then to the whiteness of the snow. It fell back in heavy masses from his forehead. His beard was also white during his later years, and fell down upon his breast like a beautiful vestment. To all who looked upon his tall, majestic figure, Dr. Plumer seemed like some ancient Hebrew prophet.

In May, 1877, Dr. Plumer made a visit to Chicago. The General Assembly of the Northern Presbyterian Church was then in session in that city and he accepted an invitation to address that body. When he moved quietly forward from the main entrance of the church building toward the platform, the scene that followed is thus described by a spectator: "As the grand vision dawned upon the upturned faces of the assembly, resistance to its charms was impossible; generous impulse overcame the heat of prejudice, and courtesy paid voluntary tribute to the highest type of manliness. The applause rose and swelled and waned again, then waxed higher and more fervent as the royal form went on down the aisle; and as the gallery caught the first glimpse of his advancing figure, ladies and gentlemen rose *en masse* and cheered and cheered again."

Later in the same year (1877) fourteen commissioners crossed the Atlantic to represent the Southern Presbyterians in the Presbyterian Council that assembled in Edinburgh, Scotland. Foremost among these were William S. Plumer, Stuart Robinson and Moses D. Hoge. Like princes among the great men of Israel stood these Southern delegates. Dr. Hoge tells us that Dr. Plumer "commanded the most marked attention" in Edinburgh, "and left an impression upon the thousands who saw and heard him, which will not be forgotten in this generation."

Marvelous Chapter!

CHAPTER XLII.

CHARLES COLCOCK JONES, JOHN B. ADGER AND JOHN L. GIRARDEAU.

On December 2, 1832, a minister of the gospel, then about twenty-eight years of age, began his special work as spiritual shepherd among the negroes of Liberty County, Georgia. This was Charles Colcock Jones, a son of old Midway congregation, born on his father's plantation near that famous church in 1804. He received his education at Sunbury Academy at the mouth of the Medway River under the guidance of the veteran teacher and preacher, Dr. William McWhir. The latter was a native of County Down, Ireland, and an alumnus of the University of Glasgow. Jones became a merchant's clerk in Savannah, but afterwards, upon arriving at the age of twenty years, he went to the academy located at Andover, Massachusetts, in order to fit himself for the gospel ministry. Two sessions at Princeton Seminary under Doctors Alexander and Miller made him ready for licensure. A period of nearly two years was spent as pastor of the First Church, Savannah, with Daniel Baker as his friend and neighbor at the Independent Church. Then, in 1832, as indicated above, he returned to his own plantation home near Midway Church and entered upon the work to which he gave the chief part of his life; namely, the evangelization of the negroes.

In the district of which old Midway Church was the center, there was a body of about 4500 negro slaves. To the work of instructing these negroes Dr. Jones gave himself by day and by night throughout a period of

about four years. Drawing his own support entirely
from his own plantation, he gave his money, his time and
his strength to the colored people. Three separate
houses of worship, located at convenient points, were
built for their exclusive use. Every Sunday, at an
early hour, Dr. Jones mounted his horse and rode to
one of these churches. From all of the neighboring
plantations the servants came in crowds, men, women
and children. First in order, a meeting for prayer
was held. During this service a number of the negroes,
known as "watchmen," one after another led the assembly in prayer. Then followed the sermon, preached by
Dr. Jones himself, with the usual accompaniment of
sacred hymns. In the afternoon the same congregation
was called together as a Sunday-school. The principal
part of the exercises in the school was a series of questions and answers drawn from a catechism specially prepared by the leader himself and widely known as Jones'
Catechism. Then followed an inquiry meeting for the
benefit of those who were concerned about their spiritual
condition. Afterwards the "watchmen" of the district,
that is, negroes appointed to that work, made reports
to the pastor with reference to the conduct of the church
members on the various plantations. Then Dr. Jones,
as chief shepherd, gave to these helpers some words of
counsel and encouragement and sent them away with
his blessing. The day was well nigh spent when the
servant of God was able to turn his face homeward.
Every hour of the Lord's Day was thus given to the
work of bringing light and knowledge and spiritual help
to the benighted Africans.

During the week Dr. Jones had a regular series of
appointments for preaching the gospel on the plantations. Sometimes in the planter's mansion, with white
and colored people together as his auditors, Dr. Jones
would deliver his sermon. Again, the service would be
held in a building called a "praise house," constructed

especially for that purpose. On his own plantation Dr. Jones erected a neat house of worship and provided it with a bell whose sweet tones rang out over the adjacent region to call the workmen to the place of prayer. With simplicity of speech and with spiritual power, this consecrated man of God persuaded many of the negro men and women to lead quiet and peaceable lives in godliness and honesty.

Dr. Jones did not fail to speak the truth as he was enabled to see it, not only to servants, but also to the masters. In 1833 the Synod of South Carolina and Georgia adopted and published the following exhortation written by Dr. Jones: "Religion will tell the master that his servants are his fellow-creatures, and that he has a Master in heaven to whom he shall account for his treatment of them. The master will be led to inquiries of this sort: In what kind of houses do I permit them to live? What clothes do I give them to wear? What food to eat? What privileges to enjoy? In what temper and manner and proportion to their crimes are they punished?"

In March, 1832, even before he began to devote his entire time to the work among the negroes, Dr. Jones organized "The Association for the Religious Instruction of the Negroes." Baptists, Methodists, Episcopalians and Presbyterians, all together, the leading citizens of Liberty County, Georgia, formed this association. Dr. Jones, as secretary, presented to this association from 1833 to 1848 an annual report which was printed and distributed throughout the South. The demand for these reports was so great that some of them ran through two and three editions. Dr. Jones' addresses before ecclesiastical bodies were also published, "stirring the churches of every name as with the blast of a trumpet." Moreover, his personal correspondence was conducted on a wide-reaching basis. With men of influence in every part of the South he exchanged views through the agency of private letters, and thus he taught masters in every section their duty to their servants.

For a period of two years, from November, 1836, to November, 1838, Dr. Jones occupied the chair of Ecclesiastical History and Church Polity in the Columbia Seminary. An accurate scholarship and a personal aptness in imparting instruction gave him good success in this field of labor. But the call of the colored people was ever in his ears, and he returned to his former work in Liberty County. Throughout an additional period of ten years he continued to preach the gospel to the negroes on the plantations. Long rides at night through the swamps near the Savannah River gave the fever an opportunity to begin its deadly work within him. In 1849 he resumed the task of teaching in Columbia Seminary, but in October, 1850, he removed to Philadelphia to take up a new work as secretary of the Assembly's Board of Home Missions. Just before this removal a disastrous fire consumed all of his household goods with his books and papers. His energy, however, was unchecked. Systematic business methods were introduced by him into the administration of Presbyterian missions throughout our entire country. The financial wisdom and practical sense of Dr. Jones soon established this work upon a sound basis. In the fall of 1853 his health failed and he had to seek rest in his old home near Midway, Georgia. The unceasing toil of years among the colored people wrought out its effect upon his physical nature. He became a martyr to his missionary zeal in behalf of the negroes.

For the space of ten years longer he continued to live, broken in health, but continuing the work of instruction among the Africans. When no longer able to stand he would take a seat in the pulpit and preach from his chair. Once again in this volume we shall have a glimpse of this consecrated servant of God before the first Southern

Assembly in 1861. Two years later, in 1863, the Master called the pure spirit of the missionary to leave the frail tabernacle of clay in order that it might find a new joy in the house above.

In the summer of 1846 John B. Adger began to preach to a separate congregation of negroes in Charleston, South Carolina. In Dr. Smyth's church there were at that time some three hundred colored members, and in Dr. Forrest's church a negro membership of some five hundred. The negro members of the Baptist and Methodist churches in Charleston carried the total number of professing African Christians into the thousands. A large company of these began to assemble at regular seasons in the basement of the lecture room of Dr. Smyth's church to listen to the instruction given by Dr. Adger. This zealous man of God organized also a separate Sunday-school among the negroes and held prayer-meetings at various points in the city.

On May 9, 1847, the congregation of the Second Church held a formal meeting and resolved to erect a building "for the express purpose of giving to the colored people sound and careful religious instruction. Those [colored people] who may become church members will be received into the Second Presbyterian Church by its session after careful examination."

The result of this resolution was the construction of a house of worship in simple Gothic style in the shape of the letter T. The transepts or wings of the building were assigned to the use of white persons, but the main body of the church was reserved for the negroes. The cost of the house of worship was seven thousand and seven hundred dollars, and this was paid by the congregation of the Second Church.

On Sunday, May 26, 1850, this church building was solemnly dedicated as a house of God for the benefit of the slaves. A large congregation of white persons, the masters of the slaves, assembled in the church to listen to a special sermon by Dr. James H. Thornwell. "Masters, give unto your servants that which is just and equal, knowing that ye also have a Master in heaven" (Colossians 4: 1). Upon these words as a basis, the preacher built up a system of duty which, he said, the slaveholder must adopt. "The slave has rights," said Dr. Thornwell, "all the rights which belong essentially to humanity, and without which his nature could not be human or his conduct susceptible of praise or blame. In the enjoyment of these rights, religion demands he should be protected. The right which the master has is a right not to the *man*, but to his *labor*."

"This building," said Dr. Thornwell, "is a public testimonial to our faith that the negro is of one blood with ourselves." "The ideas of personal rights and personal responsibility pervade the whole system of slavery," he continued. "It is a relation of man to man; Paul treats the services of slaves as duties. Slavery is a part of the curse which sin has introduced into the world and stands in the same general relation to Christianity as poverty, sickness, disease and death. That it is inconsistent with a perfect state—that it is not absolutely a good, a blessing—the most strenuous defender of slavery ought not to permit himself to deny.

"The meanest slave has in him a soul of priceless value," cried Dr. Thornwell in conclusion. "One of the highest and most solemn obligations which rest upon the masters of the South is to give their servants, to the utmost extent of their ability, free access to the instructions and institutions of the gospel."

John B. Adger, the organizer of this separate work among the negroes, was born in Charleston in 1810. His father came to America from North Ireland, but was probably of Huguenot descent. In his sixteenth year the son John was sent to Union College, located at Schenectady, New York, to become a member of the sophomore class. After completing the course of study there, he spent a year in his father's home, where the conviction was forced upon him that he should become a preacher of the gospel. From 1829 until 1833 he sat at the feet of Alexander, Miller and Hodge, the great triumvirate who then constituted Princeton Seminary. In the summer of 1834, in the Second Church, Charleston, John B. Adger was solemnly set apart to the work in the foreign field. The autumn of that year found his wife and himself at Smyrna in Asia Minor. An important part of the work of Dr. Adger during the succeeding years was the translation of the Greek New Testament into the modern Armenian tongue. He translated also the Westminster Shorter Catechism and Charles Colcock Jones' Catechism, prepared, as we have seen, for the use of the colored people of Georgia. We learn that years afterwards (1860) as many as fifteen hundred Armenians in a certain part of Asia Minor met regularly every Sunday to pursue together the study of the Bible and Jones' Catechism.

In 1846 Dr. Adger turned his face homeward for a brief period of rest. The twelve years of his labor among the Armenians had borne much fruit. Not only the books already named had been given by him to the Armenians in their own form of speech, but also many tracts and pamphlets and religious works. He had taken part also in the task of translating the Psalms into the Armenian language. He was ready and eager to return to Smyrna to continue this good work, but a dark cloud was rising above the horizon in Adger's homeland. The Abolitionists were already in 1846 making fierce attacks against the people of the South because of the institution of domestic slavery. Dr. Adger did not own a slave in his own right, but his wife had inherited some negro servants, and on this account a difficulty was raised with reference to his return to the mission field. The New England members of the American Board of Foreign Missions did not wish to send a slaveholder beyond the seas as a missionary. For this reason Dr. Adger gave up his great work in Smyrna and began to preach the gospel to the negroes in Charleston. After a period of five years spent in zealous work among the colored people, Dr. Adger's eyes began to grow weak and he withdrew to a plantation to regain his strength. In the year 1857 he entered upon the work connected with the chair of Church History and Church Polity in the Columbia Seminary. With growing success he continued for seventeen years in this school of prophets. The transparent honesty of Dr. Adger, combined with the simplicity of his religious faith, left deep impressions upon the hearts of all who sat at his feet. In 1874 he laid aside this work, and a few years later, in the fullness of years and prestige, he was gathered unto his fathers.

During the years 1852 and 1853 the colored congregation organized by Dr. Adger was under the pastoral care of Ferdinand Jacobs, a faithful shepherd and preacher. In December, 1853, John L. Girardeau, then pastor of the church at Wilton, came to Charleston to preach to the colored people. This gifted man was a native of that region in South Carolina which lies near the sea, where he was born in 1825.

Even as a young man he held prayer-meetings for the benefit of the colored people on his father's plantation. On another plantation a prayer-meeting which he attended became a widespread revival of religion, including many of the white masters of the slaves. While teaching school in another place he visited a number of plantations one after another on certain afternoons during the week and gave religious instruction to the negroes. In early life he came to Charleston, and in the Second Church, under Dr. Smyth's pastoral care, he found, as he said, "a new home, and received from the hand of this church, as from a tender mother, the bread and the water of another and a holier life."

Young Girardeau completed the course of study in Columbia Seminary, and in 1848 he was licensed to preach. He refused a call to a larger and important church because he considered it to be his duty to preach to the mass of slaves on the seaboard of South Carolina. He accepted an invitation to preach in a small church located in a region that was occupied by a large number of negroes. The black people came in crowds to hear him. Dr. Girardeau tells us that he often saw the negroes moving along the road at a trot, or "double-quick," in order to reach the church in time to take part in the opening hymn. After the first service, held for white and colored members together, another service was begun for the slaves alone. These would "pour in and throng the seats vacated by their masters—yes, crowding the building up to the pulpit. I have seen them," writes Dr. Girardeau, "rock to and fro under the influence of their feelings, like a wood in a storm. What singing! What hearty handshakings after the service. I have had my finger joints stripped of the skin in consequence of them."

Dr. Girardeau's next field of labor was Wilton Church. The work among the slaves in this region, he tells us, consisted in preaching to them each Sabbath at noon "in the church building in which their masters had just worshiped, preaching to them again in the afternoon on the plantations, and preaching at night to mixed congregations of whites and blacks. This in summer. In winter I preached at night on the plantations, often reaching home after midnight. Many a time I have seen the slaves gathered on their masters' piazzas for worship, and when it was very cold, in their dining-rooms and their sitting-rooms. The family and the servants would worship together." * * *

"My last service with the negroes at this church I will never forget. The final words had been spoken to the white congregation and they had retired. When a

tempest of emotion was shaking me the tramp of a great
multitude was heard as the negroes poured into the
building and occupied all available space up to the little
old wine-glass shaped pulpit.   When approaching the
conclusion of the sermon I turned to the unconverted
and called on them to come to Jesus.   The great mass
of the congregation simultaneously broke down, dropped
their heads to their knees and uttered a wail which seemed
to prelude the judgment."*

When Dr. Girardeau came to Charleston the earnestness that marked the delivery of his message drew so
many into his church that a larger building became necessary.   An immense home of worship was therefore
erected at a cost of twenty-five thousand dollars.   This
was paid for by the white people of Charleston as an
expression of their interest in the religious welfare of
their slaves.   Dr. Girardeau's church, the largest edifice
for worship then in Charleston, was named Zion Church.
The lower story was used as a Sunday-school room.
The preaching service was held on the second floor; the
galleries facing the pulpit were set apart for white
people.   Every Sunday afternoon a large company of
colored people, usually as many as one thousand in
number, sat on the main floor of this great auditorium
to hear the word of God from Dr. Girardeau's eloquent
lips.

"Besides Sabbath preaching," writes Dr. Girardeau,
"most of the nights in the week were spent at the church
in the discharge of various duties—holding prayer-
meetings, catechising classes, administering discipline,
settling difficulties and performing marriage ceremonies.
Often have I sat for over an hour in a cold room instructing individual inquirers and candidates for membership; often have I risen in the night to visit the sick
and dying and administer baptism to ill children.   I

*"Plantation Life Before Emancipation."   By Dr. R. Q. Mal-
lard.   Pp. 162-167.

made it a duty to attend all their funerals and conduct them. * * * The most glorious work of grace I ever felt or witnessed was one which occurred in 1858 in connection with this missionary work in Charleston. It began with a remarkable exhibition of the spirit's supernatural power. For eight weeks, night after night, save Saturday nights, I preached to dense and deeply-moved congregations."

"I have no doubt," writes Dr. Adger, "that the influence of his [Girardeau's] apostolic instructions to thousands and thousands of negroes who frequented his ministry during those nine years in Zion Church had much to do with the quiet, peaceable and submissive behavior of the colored people in Charleston while the war went on, just as I am sure the same effect was produced among the slave population all over the South by the sound religious instruction they had been receiving publicly and privately for many years before the war."

In 1862 Dr. Girardeau joined the Confederate forces in the field as a chaplain. He was captured and held for a time as a prisoner on Johnson's Island. Even there he preached the gospel to his fellow-prisoners and formed a class for regular biblical instruction. In the summer of 1865, after his release from prison, Dr. Girardeau returned to Charleston and gathered together in the Second Church "a great congregation from all the dismantled Presbyterian churches of the city." To these sorrow-stricken people he spoke of the rest that belongs to the people of God (Hebrews 4: 9). "He who did not think it beneath him to die for us," said the preacher, "will not think it beneath him to provide for us. He has assured us that he cares for the sparrow, and that we are of more value than many sparrows. Poor and insignificant we may be, but he has spread his garment over us and acknowledged us as his kinsmen." His former colored congregation, composed now of emancipated negroes, entreated him "to come back and preach to them as of old." This request he frequently complied with, but others were calling for his services. Dr. Girardeau's years of training as a preacher to the poor had developed his powers as a minister of the gospel of comfort. His most characteristic personal quality, we are told by those who knew him best, was deep and fervent piety. This quality marked his discourses, and now there were multitudes in South Carolina and other states who desired to hear the gospel of grace from his lips. Thus was he gradually led away providentially into that larger field of service as preacher and teacher which he occupied with signal success for many years.

"Dr. Girardeau possessed many qualities which appeared to advantage in the pulpit," writes Dr. W. T. Hall. "In person and voice, in intellectual vigor, in sweep of fancy, in depth of feeling and in dramatic power he was richly endowed. * * * For many years he was regarded as 'the great preacher of this [South Atlantic Seaboard] section of the church." From 1876 until 1895 he occupied, with distinguished success, the chair of Systematic Theology in Columbia Seminary as the successor of William S. Plumer and James H. Thornwell. In 1898 he was called to receive the reward that God bestows upon those who keep the faith.

Three choice and capable men, Jones, Adger and Girardeau, were thus given by the Presbyterians of the South to the work among the colored people. Others less conspicuous gave their entire time to the same field of labor. Among these may be mentioned Rev. James Smylie of Mississippi, who in his later years "devoted his time exclusively to the religion of the negroes." He organized large classes for study and trained them to recite the whole of the Westminster Shorter Catechism. Even before the publication of Dr. Jones' Catechism, Mr. Smylie prepared a catechism for the benefit of the colored people, and this book was adopted for colored members by the Synod of Mississippi.

Moreover, every minister of the Southern church preached regularly to negroes as a part of his congregation. The large galleries in the churches were always crowded with colored people. Special sermons were preached to them, and colored members were received into every church. Prayer-meetings and Sunday-schools were organized for their benefit. The infant children of colored church members were baptized. The white minister officiated at their marriage ceremonies and in the burial of their dead. In some of the Presbyterian churches, as, for example, in the Old Stone Church, now near Clemson College, South Carolina, the colored members were allowed to elect from their own ranks negro elders "to superintend the conduct" of these same negro members and make report to the session of the church. In the lists of church members these chosen negroes were reported as "Elders."

A great multitude of godly men and women, masters of the colored people, gave religious instruction to their own wards in their own homes. The personal relationship between master and servant was, in most cases, based upon mutual sympathy and affection. In thousands of homes in the South there were servants in whom masters reposed that high degree of trust and confidence which Abraham, the master, manifested toward his servant, Eliezer. These faithful Southern patriarchs gathered together every Sunday all the members of their households, both white and black, and taught them the fundamental truths of the Christian religion. They nursed these servants during sickness, cared for them in old age and gave them comfort when death was near. As far as possible masters enforced faithfulness to the marriage bond and taught their servants to walk in godliness and honesty.

The fruit of all these evangelistic labors was not

small. At the end of eleven years of toil among the colored people, Dr. Charles C. Jones wrote as follows: "The religious instruction of the negroes has made remarkable and rapid advances throughout the Southern and Southwestern States during the past year (1845)." He made reference to a widespread religious revival, and then declared that "those congregations in which the religious instruction of servants received most attention shared most signally in the blessing of God." Many negroes, he declared, were entering the church side by side with white members of the same households. "The Lord has made no distinctions," wrote Dr. Jones, "but has poured out His Spirit as well upon servants as upon masters. We must identify the progress of the religious instruction of negroes with the progress of true religion in the South." Dr. Jones then quoted at length from the reports sent in by Baptist, Methodist, Episcopal and Presbyterian workers, and closed with this comment: "The religious instruction of the negroes has advanced in our churches in a remarkable degree throughout the Southern States. We behold the subject appearing in the acts of ecclesiastical meetings of all denominations. We behold individuals of the highest standing both in Church and State the most efficient laborers in the work."

The closeness of the personal relationship between the races in the South may be measured by the fact that the average number of negro servants was less than ten to each master. The teaching and example of the master had great weight with the African retainer. We are not surprised, therefore, to learn from trustworthy records that in 1860, as the result of all the public and private evangelistic agencies in operation, nearly 500,000 negroes were members of the various churches. This represents a proportion of about one in every eight of the colored population. How many of these were sincere Christians it is impossible to say. These church members, however, formed a strong conservative element among the negroes. Most probably this large body of professing Christians constituted the principal factor that held the vast majority of the Southern slaves in a purely voluntary servitude upon the plantations during the period of the war. What a spectacle was that, when millions of black slaves not only refrained from pillage and acts of violence, but actually by the labor of their own hands produced the crops that gave food to the white men of the South who were absent from home in the field of war. Such devotion on the part of the negroes could have had no other source than the faithfulness and uprightness of the Southern masters.

CHAPTER XLIII.

JAMES HENLEY THORNWELL AS PREACHER AND TEACHER.

In Marlborough District, South Carolina, December 9, 1812, James Henley Thornwell was born. His father, James Thornwell, who was of English descent, made a slender support for his family by acting as manager of a plantation. In 1820 the father died and left wife and children to a struggle with poverty. This wife, whose maiden name was Martha Terrell, was descended from some of the worthy Welsh settlers who came at an early date to the upper Pee Dee River. She was endowed with a strong mind and a yet stronger will, and by unceasing toil, after her husband's death, kept the wolf from the door.

Young Thornwell was about eleven years of age when he entered the country school taught by Peter Mc-Intyre, a Scot. The schoolhouse, built of unhewn logs, stood not far from his mother's home. Eagerness to learn seemed to burn like a fire within the lad's heart. A large part of every night, while others were asleep, he spent at work upon the lessons assigned for the following day, and in reading the volumes of history and literature that were furnished by kind neighbors. While other boys were at play, this lad of small stature and pale brow was bending over his books. He made a rapid study of Hume's History of England, and when men heard him talk about the historian's work they were astonished at young Thornwell's understanding.

Friends were speedily raised up for a boy so richly endowed with mental gifts. Mr. W. H. Robbins, a young lawyer, brought Thornwell to the town of Cheraw

.and gave him a place of honor in his own home.   As if he were an elder brother to the lad, Robbins took personal charge of Thornwell in his studies for the space of three years.   The latter attended the Cheraw Academy, and, during a part of the time, also, read law in the office of his patron.   General James Gillespie, a wealthy planter of Marlborough District, also came forward with generous help for the orphan.   Acting jointly, Gillespie and Robbins furnished the money that enabled Thornwell to complete the course of study offered by the South Carolina College.   Moreover, these two friends were always ready with advice and encouragement to assist the young scholar in his upward course.

Thornwell was just entering his eighteenth year when he began work in January, 1830, as a member of the Junior Class of the South Carolina College.   In stature he was shorter by a head than most of his comrades; he was, also, very lean, his skin had the color of old parchment, and his face and hands were covered with black freckles.   In spite of these physical disadvantages, Thornwell was regarded from the beginning by his classmates as foremost among them all.   A strong, keen mind, associated with relentless toil, enabled the lad from the country district to make remarkable progress. Fourteen hours a day he gave to severe study.   The classics of the Greek and Latin tongues engaged his chief attention.   Besides these, however, he read many volumes in mental philosophy.   "He used the library," we are told, "as no student before him had ever done." In order to improve his style in speaking and writing he filled his mind with the choicest treasures of the English form of speech.   "Language," said Thornwell, "was my great difficulty in early life.   I had no natural command of words.   I undertook to remedy the defect by committing to memory large portions of the New Testament, the Psalms, and much of the Prophets, also whole dramas of Shakespeare, and a great part of

Milton's Paradise Lost; so that you might start me at
any line in any drama or book, and I would go through
to the end." This practice was begun before entering
college, for we are told that while he was a boy at the
Cheraw Academy he could recite entire pages of Stewart's Philosophy. In later years he astonished his con-
temporaries by repeating in conversation or in debate
long passages from such writers as Jonathan Edwards,
John Owen, Robert Hall and Edmund Burke.

Thornwell was soon recognized as the best debater in
the College Literary Society of which he was a member.
Sometimes, in speaking, he indulged in sarcasm. His
words seemed to flow like a stream, rapid and strong.
Moreover, he won the admiration of his comrades by
the frequent quotation of both ancient and modern
writers. The highest distinctions which the college and
his classmates could confer were bestowed upon him at
his graduation in December, 1831, when he was only
nineteen years of age.

Teaching a few private pupils was the work that first
engaged the attention of the young graduate. At the
same time he continued his strenuous mode of studying
Greek, Latin and German. "I have commenced regularly with Xenophon's works," he writes, "and intend
to read them carefully. I shall then take up Thucydides,
Herodotus and Demosthenes. After mastering these I
shall pass on to the philosophers and poets. In Latin
I am going regularly through Cicero's writings. I read
them by double translations; that is, I first translate
them into English and then retranslate them into Latin.
In German I am pursuing Goethe's works. My life,
you can plainly see, is not a life of idleness."

A private school in the town of Sumter was secured
for Thornwell. About the time when he began work in
that place (May, 1832), he made an announcement
of his Christian faith by uniting with Concord Presbyterian Church of which John McEwen was then pastor.

Prior to this confession, a fierce conflict took place in his mind with reference to the Bible doctrines of sin and salvation.   With this issue adjusted, and the principles of the gospel firmly established in his understanding, the Spirit entered and assumed control, but in a manner so quiet that Thornwell was unable to point out the exact time when he became a Christian.   In connection with his public profession as a Christian, he told his friends of his purpose to become a minister of the gospel.

During the period of about two years, from 1832 to 1834, Thornwell was engaged as teacher in the Cheraw Academy, the school in which he had received his own preparatory training.   The work of acquiring knowledge had now become the ruling passion of his life.   His days and nights were given up to mental toil that knew no rest.   At the same time, the imparting of knowledge to others called into play the highest powers of mind and heart.   He began to show enthusiasm as a teacher. His intellect seemed to expand, and, strange to say, his diminutive body began again to grow.   He became a head taller, thus reaching the ordinary height of men, and his complexion threw off its sallow hue.   Transformed in physical appearance he stood before his friends as a man of vigor and power.   He felt that he was ready to enter upon the special field of work that he had chosen.   In the summer of 1834, therefore, Thornwell entered the theological seminary located at Andover, Massachusetts.   He had been persuaded by a friend that he could find superior advantages in this school. Within a few weeks he left the seminary, announcing to his friends that he was not at all pleased with the character of the instruction given at Andover.   Moreover, the courses of study were limited, he wrote, since he was not able to secure any instruction in German, Syriac, Chaldean and Arabic.   The early days of August, therefore, found him established as a student in Harvard University.   He devoted himself chiefly to the study of

Hebrew and German, at the same time attending lectures in the Divinity School in Cambridge. Moreover, the libraries gave him intense satisfaction. He wrote to his friends that he was giving fifteen hours a day to study and that he was collecting material for an elaborate book which he proposed to write "on the philosophy of the Greek language." He did not complete the book, but, no doubt, he enjoyed many a strenuous conflict in debate with his fellow-students. "I room in Divinity Hall," he wrote, "among the Unitarian students of theology, for there are no others here. I shall expect to meet and give blows in defense of my own peculiar doctrines, and God forbid that I should falter in maintaining the faith once delivered to the saints. I look upon the tenets of modern Unitarianism as little better than downright infidelity."

When the autumn of the year came upon Thornwell in Cambridge, the severity of the weather gave warning that so delicate a frame as his could not endure the northern climate. He came southward again, and in November, 1834, was licensed by Harmony Presbytery to preach the gospel. For more than a year prior to this time he had been devoting all of his energies to the mastery of theological subjects and the presbytery found him well prepared. Early in 1835 he became pastor of the church in the small town of Lancaster, South Carolina. Two other congregations, the old mother church of Waxhaws and the church of Six-Mile Creek, were also placed under his care. From one of these charges to another he was in the habit of driving through the country at a very high rate of speed behind a mettlesome horse named "Red Rover." His style of preaching caught the attention of the people and held them fast. He manifested great earnestness in the pulpit; his eye kindled with excitement and his whole frame quivered. His theme, at that early day in his career, was a practical appeal to sinners to accept now the salvation which is offered. So many came to hear him that each one of his small churches was crowded with eager listeners. The ordinary length of his sermons was, at that time, about thirty minutes. One Sunday morning, however, after he had been preaching for an hour and a half, he stopped suddenly, looked at his watch and made an apology by saying that he had not been conscious of taking so much time. "Go on! Go on!" This was the exclamation heard from every part of the house. He continued to preach, therefore, an hour longer. After hearing the sermon, an old father said to his boy: "My son, if you ever had a doubt about the truth and perfection of the plan of salvation, you surely can have none now. I have been studying that subject all my life, but I never saw it before as I do now. Now I am ready to die, that I may enter upon its full enjoyment."

On December 3, 1835, James H. Thornwell and Nancy White Witherspoon were joined together in holy wedlock. Graciousness of spirit and practical wisdom were the ruling qualities of the woman who became henceforth his chief counsellor. Through her influence his character became more nearly complete. A certain sensitiveness that marked his early years passed away, and the spirit of sympathy took possession of him. A native buoyancy of spirit asserted itself and his friends were delighted with the play of his wit. As in a flash he could pass from the severe to the gay and exchange abstract reasoning for the exuberant pleasantry of good fellowship. His religious experience, also, assumed a more devout character. The careful searching of the Scriptures, day after day, drew him into closer communion with his God. He was strengthened, moreover, through association with a fellow-minister of the gospel, Pierpont E. Bishop, whom Thornwell called "a precious and a godly man." Bishop's piety was so gentle and pervasive in its quality that it shed sweet fragrance upon the heart and life of Thornwell. The latter soon became one of the most lovable among men. The charm of his personality, combined with the power of his eloquence, led many souls into the kingdom of God. A ministry so fruitful could not be limited to a narrow field, and at the close of a pastorate of a little more than two years he was offered a chair in the South Carolina College.

On January 1, 1838, he began to teach logic and mental philosophy. The latter was a favorite subject of study with him, and the charm of his lectures upon this theme soon drew a large company of pupils to his feet. Two years later, however (1840), he gave up the teacher's chair and became pastor of the Presbyterian Church in the town of Columbia. Dr. B. M. Palmer, who first met Thornwell about that time, tells us that the latter had "a thin, spare form, with a slight stoop in the shoulders;" that his soft black hair fell obliquely over his forehead, and his small eye had "a wonderful gleam when it was lighted by the inspiration of his theme." The opening exercises of the service, writes Palmer, were conducted with simplicity and quietness, "but from the opening of the discourse there was a strange fascination" exercised by the speaker upon his congregation. "As link after link was added to the chain of a consistent argument expressed with that agonistic fervor which belongs to the forum, the effect at the close was to overwhelm and subdue." Thus, even at the early age of twenty-eight years, Thornwell was showing forth from the pulpit that matchless power of speech which never failed to enchant every audience that he addressed.

In January, 1841, Thornwell resigned his pastorate and again accepted a chair in the South Carolina College. The pressure upon him from friends of the college in every part of the state was so strong that he could not refuse their appeals. Moreover, the chaplaincy of the college, now assigned to him, gave an opportunity to preach directly to the body of students. His work as teacher was confined chiefly to the evidences of Christianity. However, that marvelous voice as preacher of the word was not silenced, and regularly each Lord's Day he delivered the message of salvation.

In the spring of the year 1841 sudden attacks of physical weakness warned him that rest was necessary. He set sail at once, therefore, for a journey across the Atlantic. Several weeks in England, Scotland and upon the Continent opened his mind to a consideration of the art treasures of the old world. His strength was soon built up, and in September, 1841, he returned home. As he drove across the border-line separating North Carolina from South Carolina, Thornwell sprang out of the carriage and, falling down upon the soil of his native state, kissed it reverently with his lips. This act was only a sign of this great man's sincere devotion to his own people.

During the years that followed, Thornwell was gradually led into controversial speaking and writing with reference to ecclesiastical issues until he became recognized as the most powerful debater in the Presbyterian Church at that time in our entire country. Some of the issues discussed were the functions of church boards, the jurisdiction of elders in church courts and the relationship of church courts to temperance societies. In connection with these discussions, Thornwell entered into an intimate friendship with Robert J. Breckinridge, then pastor of the Second Church, Baltimore. Thornwell's articles began to appear in the church periodicals, and in 1845 he published a volume in refutation of the teachings of the Church of Rome. In 1847 he was chosen moderator of the General Assembly in session at Richmond, Virginia. Before that body he delivered a discourse on popery, with reference to which Dr. James W. Alexander wrote as follows: "Dr. Thornwell is the great man of the South, and I do not think his learning or powers of mind overrated. His speech on taking the [moderator's] chair was a masterpiece. His sermon was ill-delivered, but, nevertheless, a model of what is rare, viz: burning, hot argument, logic in ignition, and glowing more and more to the end."

With reference to a system of education, Dr. Thornwell at that time held the view that the state is competent to establish and conduct *religious* schools and that the churches, therefore, need not undertake to build colleges. The security for the maintenance of religion in state colleges, he asserted, "lies in the public opinion of the whole community." Later in his life, however, he declared that if the state schools should fail to give a religious education that the churches must undertake that work. His letters show that he was not satisfied with holding a teacher's position, but longed continually to take up again the work of the pastorate. In the spring of 1851 he resigned his chair and became pastor of the Glebe Street Church in Charleston. Once more large audiences flocked to hear him in his own pulpit. The friends of the college, however, would not release their hold upon him, and in December, 1851, he was chosen president of the South Carolina College. Throughout a period of four years, therefore, from the beginning of 1852 to the close of the year 1855, he occupied with increasing success that important position. Through the force of his own character Dr. Thornwell moulded the opinions and shaped the conduct of virtually all of the students who attended the college during his presidency. The church, however, was in sore need of his services, and in December, 1855, he began the work of teaching theology in the Columbia Seminary. At the same time Dr. B. M. Palmer was made professor of church history in the same institution. The presence of these two men of genius and spiritual power in the faculty of the seminary placed the latter among the very foremost divinity schools in our country. Thornwell became at the same time editor of the *Southern Quarterly Review,* and for the most part, also, served the church in Columbia as pastor.

In the classroom Thornwell's pupils regarded him as without an equal. The accuracy of his knowledge, together with its wide range, made him without doubt the most illuminating instructor of his time in theological and philosophical subjects. His writings upon these themes, moreover, have come down to us to bear witness to the depth of his understanding. As a preacher of the gospel, however, more than in any other respect, Thornwell stood supreme in his own generation. One of his sermons was pronounced by Dr. J. Addison Alexander "as fine a specimen of Demosthenian eloquence" as he had ever heard from the pulpit, and that it "realized his idea of what preaching should be." At Indianapolis, Indiana, during the sessions of the Presbyterian Assembly in 1859, he delivered a sermon which, we are told, melted his entire audience into tears. Dr. Hewitt of Connecticut said of one of Thornwell's discourses that "no sermon has been produced in our country, in my day, in any pulpit, equal to it." "The feature most remarkable in this prince of pulpit orators," writes Dr. B. M. Palmer, "was the rare union of vigorous logic with strong emotion. Dr. Thornwell wove his argument in fire, and the speaker was borne along in what seemed to others a chariot of flame. Kindling with a secret inspiration, his manner lost its slight constraint, his slender form dilated; his deep black eye lost its drooping expression, until his fiery eloquence, rising with the greatness of his conceptions, burst upon the hearer in some grand climax overwhelming in its majesty and resistless in its effect. In all this there was no declamation, no straining for effect. All was natural, the simple product of thought and feeling wonderfully combined." "In the most rapid flow of his speech," writes Palmer again, "his diction was beyond impeachment.

It was always the right word for the thought.   To pre-
cision and copiousness was added a certain richness of
expression, a courtliness of style which can only be
explained by the majesty of the thought.   This generation will never look upon his like again; a single century
cannot afford to produce his equal.   It may listen to
much lucid exposition, much close and powerful reasoning, much tender and earnest appeal, much beautiful
and varied imagery; but never from the lips of one man
can it be stirred by vigor of argument fused by a
seraph's glow and pouring itself forth in strains which
linger in the memory like the chant of angels."

Thornwell was a delegate to the General Assembly on
ten separate occasions.   Each time, at least during his
later years, he exercised an influence greater, perhaps,
than that of any other member.   The clearness of his
thinking made him a natural leader in every debate.
"But the moral quality," writes Palmer, "which more
than all contributed to his vast influence, was the transparent honesty of his heart.   He was no intriguer;
had no by-ends to accomplish; never worked by indirec-
tion.   His heart was in his hand and every man could
read it.   Straightforward himself, he dealt honestly
with his colleagues, and if he could not carry his point
by fair argument, he was content to fail."

Dr. Thornwell's last appearance in the General Assembly of the undivided church was at Rochester, New
York, in May, 1860.   A great debate took place in that
assembly between Dr. Thornwell and Dr. Charles Hodge
with reference to church boards.   Thornwell opposed
them on the ground that they were not organs of the
church, but separate organisms, appointed to take the
place of the assembly.   He did not secure a majority vote
for his view, but the close of his address had a marked
effect.

We are told that the whole of the vast audience

sat in breathless attention while Thornwell, in a thrilling
appeal, summoned the entire host of God's elect to come
up to the work of giving the Gospel to a lost world.
The summer of 1860 found Dr. Thornwell in a weakened
physical state. A few months spent in Europe, however, restored him to health. In the closing months of
the year the Southern people began the formation of
the Southern Confederacy, and in this work Dr. Thornwell enlisted himself, mind and soul. He had clung
to the old Federal Union throughout the crisis of 1850,
using voice and pen at that time to persuade his people
not to withdraw from the Union. But in December,
1860, after the secession of South Carolina, he wrote:
"I believe that we have done right. I do not see any
other course that was left to us. I am heart and hand
with the state in her movement."

Early in 1861 he published in the *Southern Presbyterian Review* a defense of the secession of the Southern
states, which Chancellor Job Johnston pronounced "a
model state paper." When the great struggle began
Thornwell's physical infirmities forced him to remain
at home, but he sent his son, a mere lad, to enter the
lists as a soldier. "A noble boy; he is all pluck; his
heart is in the cause." Such was the father's proud
boast concerning the gallant young hero who afterwards sealed with his life's blood his devotion to his
country. Dr. Thornwell's pen was a mighty power in
urging on his countrymen to struggle in behalf of their
rights. "Our Danger and Our Duty" is the title of
the principal pamphlet which he issued as an appeal to
the South to keep up the fight against the invasion of
her territory.

In May, 1861, the General Assembly of the Presbyterian Church, in session in the city of Philadelphia,
adopted the resolution offered by Dr. Gardiner Spring
of New York to the effect that the Presbyterian Church

must "strengthen, uphold and encourage the Federal government in the exercise of all its functions." Since the Federal government was at that time preparing to wage war against the Southern people, and since the great body of the Presbyterians of the South, ministers, elders, deacons, private members, including both men and women and even children and negro slaves, was entering the lists to meet the hostile forces levied by the Federal government, in the light of these facts it is clear that the Spring resolution meant that Southern Presbyterians could no longer regard themselves as members of the church of their fathers. Dr. Charles Hodge of Princeton as leader of the minority in the assembly made an earnest protest against the action of the majority on the ground that Southern members were thereby driven "to choose between allegiance to their state and allegiance to the church."

The Spring resolution was, of course, a political utterance given forth by an ecclesiastical body. During the summer and autumn of 1861, therefore, forty-seven presbyteries, each acting for itself, dissolved connection with the existing General Assembly. The reason assigned in each case was "the unconstitutional, Erastian, tyrannical and virtually exscinding act" of the Philadelphia Assembly. The ten Southern synods gave their sanction to the acts of withdrawal adopted by the presbyteries.

A convention, made up of delegates from the Southern presbyteries, was held at Atlanta, Georgia, in August, 1861, to formulate plans for the organization of a separate assembly. In the management of all of these separate and varied movements on the part of the presbyteries, Thornwell bore a leading part. In the next chapter in this book we shall see him once more as principal leader in an association of godly men, ministers and elders, at Augusta, Georgia, in December, 1861, using all of his great powers of heart and mind in formulating the principles of the Southern Presbyterian Church as a separate organization. Soon after that event a wasting malady seized upon his frame and he gradually faded away. On August 1, 1862, at Charlotte, North Carolina, with a smile of peace playing about his lips, Dr. Thornwell ceased to breathe and his pure spirit passed into the presence of God.

PART IV.—SOUTHERN PRESBYTERIAN LEADERS SINCE
1861.

CHAPTER XLIV.

JAMES H. THORNWELL SETS FORTH THE PRINCIPLES OF THE SOUTHERN PRESBYTERIANS.

ON the morning of December 4, 1861, a body of ministers and ruling elders, ninety-three in number, came together at the First Presbyterian Church in Augusta, Georgia. They presented their credentials and were enrolled as the representatives of the forty-seven presbyteries that composed the ten synods of the Southern states and territories. Fifty-nine of the delegates were of Scotch-Irish and Scotch descent, twenty-seven were English and five were of Huguenot origin. They were all men of experience, for the average age of the commissioners was more than fifty years. Among the ministers were John H. Bocock of Baltimore, William Henry Foote, James B. Ramsay, Theodorick Pryor, Peyton Harrison, William T. Richardson and Francis McFarland of Virginia; Robert H. Morrison, R. Hett. Chapman and Drury Lacy of North Carolina; James H. Thornwell, A. W. Leland, John B. Adger and J. Leighton Wilson of South Carolina; John S. Wilson, Charles Colcock Jones and Joseph R. Wilson of Georgia; John N. Waddel of Tennessee, Benjamin M. Palmer of New Orleans, and James A. Lyon of Mississippi. Among the ruling elders were Chancellor Job Johnston, one of the Supreme Judges of the State of South Carolina, Judge William A. Forward of Florida, Judge J. G. Shepherd and Dr. J. H. Dickson of North Carolina,

Judge J. T. Swayne of Tennessee, Hons. W. S. Mitchell of Georgia, William P. Webb of Alabama, Thomas C. Perrin and William P. Finley of South Carolina.   Dr. Francis McFarland, an aged minister from the Synod of Virginia, was called to the chair.   His first act as temporary moderator was to make the suggestion that Dr. Benjamin M. Palmer should deliver the opening sermon.   This suggestion received the cordial support of the commissioners, and Dr. Palmer came forward and began to preach upon the theme, "Christ, the Head of the Church" (Eph. 1: 22, 23).   As he brought his solemn discourse to a close, Dr. Palmer said: "Do we understand, fathers and brethren, the mission of the church given us here to execute?   It is to lift up throughout the world our testimony for this Headship of Christ.   The convocation of this assembly is in part that testimony.   But a little while since it was attempted in the most august court of our church to place the crown of our Lord upon the head of Cæsar—to bind that body which is Christ's fullness to the chariot in which that Cæsar rides.   The intervening months have sufficiently discovered the character of that state under whose yoke this church was summoned to bow her neck in meek obedience.   But in advance of these disclosures, the voice went up, throughout our land, of indignant remonstrance against the usurpation, of solemn protest against the sacrilege.   And now this parliament of the Lord's freemen solemnly declares that, by the terms of her great charter, none but Jesus may be the king in Zion.   Once more in this distant age and in these ends of the earth the church must declare for the supremacy of her head, and fling out the consecrated ensign with the old inscription, 'For Christ and His crown.'"

The assembly was formally organized by the election of Dr. Palmer as moderator, and, then, upon the motion of Dr. Thornwell, it was resolved that the name of the church should be *The Presbyterian Church in the Con-*

federate States of America. The Westminster Confession of Faith, Catechisms, Form of Government, Book of Discipline and Directory for Worship were adopted as the Constitution of the church. It was determined, also, that the work of the church should be conducted through the direct agency of executive committees, chosen by the assembly and immediately responsible to the assembly.

It must be remembered that, at the time when this Southern Church was organized, the fires of deadly warfare had been already kindled, and the great body of the men of the congregations were in the field with rifles in their hands. The members of this General Assembly were in full sympathy with the men in the armies of the South, and yet there was not heard in the church in which the assembly held its sessions even an echo from the field of war nor from the forum of political debate. The court of the church did not sound a call to arms, nor unfurl a flag, nor make an announcement of political principles. The assembly began its work with quiet dignity by declaring that the work of preaching the gospel in "all the world" is the chief work of the Southern Presbyterian Church and "the great end of her organization." The assembly determined to send at once six new missionaries to the Indian tribes of the Southwest, and the churches were called upon to give money for the support of those Southern ministers who were already laboring as missionaries in foreign fields. That stalwart man of God, Dr. J. Leighton Wilson, was appointed by the assembly to manage the foreign work.

On the evening of the sixth day the members of the assembly listened to an address upon the subject of evangelistic work among the negroes. The speaker was Dr. Charles Colcock Jones, the Apostle to the Africans in the South. By reason of long sickness, Dr. Jones was unable to stand throughout the delivery of the address. He, therefore, seated himself in a chair for an

hour and a half and held the unbroken attention of the
assembly and the great company of people who filled
the church. "These sons of Ham," said Dr. Jones with
reference to the negroes, "are black in the first pages of
history, and they continue black." "But," said he, "they
share our physical nature, our intellectual and spiritual
nature; each body among them covers an immortal soul.
They are men created in the image of God, to be acknowledged and cared for spiritually by us, as we
acknowledge and care for the other varieties of the
race."

"They are not foreigners," continued the speaker,
"but our nearest neighbors; they are not hired servants,
but servants belonging to us in law and gospel. They
are constant and inseparable associates; whither we go,
they go; where we dwell, they dwell; where we die and are
buried, there they die and are buried; and, more than all,
our God is their God."

With moving eloquence the devoted evangelist urged
the members of the assembly to devise enlarged measures
for giving the gospel of Christ to the black race. The
assembly manifested full sympathy with the views of
Dr. Jones and made a cordial response to his appeal.
The Executive Committee of Domestic Missions, with
Dr. John Leyburn appointed as secretary, was directed
to give serious and constant attention to "the great field
of missionary operations among our colored population."

On the morning of the fourth day of the session of
the assembly the slender form of Dr. Thornwell appeared
near the moderator's chair. As leading member of a
committee previously appointed, he asked leave to read a
paper which proposed to set forth the reasons for the
separate organization of the Southern Assembly. The
hush of a deep solemnity filled the sacred building as
Thornwell presented the "Address to all the churches
of Jesus Christ throughout the earth."

"We have separated from our brethren of the North," ran the address, "as Abraham separated from Lot, because we are persuaded that the interests of true religion will be more effectually subserved by two independent churches." Reasons for this course were assigned as follows:

1. Because the Presbyterian Assembly which met at Philadelphia, in May, 1861, virtually transformed itself into a political convention. "As a court of Jesus Christ," the address declared, "the Philadelphia Assembly undertook to determine the true interpretation of the Constitution of the United States as to the kind of government it intended to form. A political theory was, to all intents and purposes, propounded, which made secession a crime. * * * The assembly, driven from its ancient moorings, was tossed to and fro by the waves of popular passion. Like Pilate, it obeyed the clamor of the multitude, and though acting in the name of Jesus, it kissed the scepter and bowed the knee to the mandates of Northern phrensy. The church was converted into the forum, and the assembly was henceforward to become the arena of sectional divisions and national animosities."

"The provinces of church and state," said Thornwell, "are perfectly distinct, and one has no right to usurp the jurisdiction of the other. The state is a natural institute. * * * The church is a supernatural institute. * * * The power of the church is exclusively spiritual; that of the state includes the exercise of force. The church has no right to construct or modify a government for the state, and the state has no right to frame a creed or polity for the church."

"It is the consequence of these proceedings, at Philadelphia," continued Thornwell in the address, "which make them so offensive; it is the door which they open for the introduction of the worst passions of human nature into the deliberations of church courts. * * *

For the sake of peace, therefore, for Christian charity, for the honor of the church and for the glory of God * * * we have quietly separated; and we are grateful to God that while leaving for the sake of peace, we leave it with the humble consciousness that we ourselves have never given occasion to break the peace."

2. Because the Southern presbyteries would be able, in a separate, independent organization, to give free and full development to the spiritual principles of the church of their fathers.

"It is precisely," continued the address, "because we love that church [of our fathers] as it was, and that church as it should be, that we have resolved, as far as in us lies, to realize its grand idea in the country and under the government where God has cast our lot."

With reference to the black race, the address contained the following:

"In our ecclesiastical capacity we are neither the friends nor the foes of slavery; that is to say, we have no commission either to propagate or abolish it. The policy of its existence or non-existence is a question which exclusively belongs to the state. We have no right, as a church, to enjoin it as a duty or to condemn it as a sin. Our business is with the duties which spring from the relation; the duties of the masters, on the one hand, and of their slaves on the other. These duties we are to proclaim and to enforce with spiritual sanctions. The social, civil, political problems connected with this great subject transcend our sphere, as God has not entrusted to His church the organization of society, the construction of governments, nor the allotment of individuals to their various stations."

But, is slaveholding a sin? The Word of God must furnish the answer. Neither directly nor indirectly, declares the address, do the Scriptures condemn slaveholding as a sin.

"Slavery is no new thing. It has not only existed

for ages in the world, but it has existed, under every
dispensation of the covenant of grace, in the church of
God. Indeed, the first organization of the church as a
visible society, separate and distinct from the unbelieving
world, was inaugurated in the family of a slaveholder.
Among the very first persons to whom the seal of cir-
cumcision was affixed were the slaves of the father of the
faithful, some born in his house and others bought with
his money. Slavery again reappears under the law.
God sanctions it in the first table of the decalogue, and
Moses treats it as an institution to be regulated, not
abolished; legitimated and not condemned. We come
down to the age of the New Testament, and we find it
again in the churches founded by the Apostles under
the plenary inspiration of the Holy Ghost. These
facts are utterly amazing if slavery is the enormous
sin which its enemies represent it to be. It will not do
to say that the Scriptures have treated it only in a
general, incidental way, without any clear implication
as to its moral character. Moses surely made it the
subject of express and positive legislation, and the
Apostles are equally explicit in inculcating the duties
which spring from both sides of the relation. They
treat slaves as bound to obey and inculcate obedience
as an office of religion."

With reference to the condition of the negroes in the
South, the address declared that "we cannot but accept
it as a gracious Providence that they have been brought
in such numbers to our shores and redeemed from the
bondage of barbarism and sin. Slavery to them has
certainly been overruled for the greatest good. It has
been a link in the wondrous chain of Providence through
which many sons and daughters have been made heirs
of the heavenly inheritance. The providential result is,
of course, no justification if the thing is intrinsically
wrong; but it is certainly a matter of devout thanksgiving and no obscure intimation of the will and pur-

pose of God, and of the consequent duty of the church. We cannot forbear to say, however, that the general operation of the system is kindly and benevolent; it is a real and effective discipline, and, without it, we are profoundly persuaded that the African race in the midst of us can never be elevated in the scale of being."

The address was brought to a conclusion with a statement of the special ends which the Southern presbyteries proposed to accomplish as a church. "We wish to develop the idea," wrote Thornwell, "that the congregation of believers as visibly organized is the very society or corporation which is divinely called to do the work of the Lord. We shall, therefore, endeavor to do what has never yet been adequately done—bring out the energies of our Presbyterian system of government. * * * Our own scheme of government we humbly believe to be according to the pattern shown in the mount, and, by God's grace, we propose to put its efficiency to the test."

On the morning of the tenth day this address was read again and laid upon the moderator's table. Then, one by one, the members of the assembly went forward in silence and signed their names to the instrument. Dr. Palmer, who took part in this solemn ceremonial, writes of it as follows: "We were carried back to those stirring times in Scottish story, when the Solemn League and Covenant was spread upon the gravestone in the Greyfriar's churchyard, and Christian heroes pricked their veins that, with the red blood, they might sign their allegiance to the kingdom and crown of Jesus Christ, their Lord and Head."

CHAPTER XLV.

EIGHT hundred ministers of the gospel and a great company of ruling elders and deacons—these were the leaders of the Southern Presbyterian Church when it was organized in 1861. This number of leaders was increased, however, by the addition of other ecclesiastical bodies that sought union with the Southern Assembly. These bodies set forth in brief outline, with date of reception, were the following:

The Independent Presbyterian Church, consisting of eleven congregations located in South Carolina and North Carolina (1863.)

The United Synod of the South, consisting of one hundred and ninety-nine congregations of New School Presbyterians, located in Virginia, Tennessee and Mississippi (1864.)

The Presbytery of Patapsco, located in Maryland (1867.)

The Alabama Presbytery of the Associate Reformed Church (1867.)

The Synod of Kentucky, consisting of six presbyteries in Kentucky (1869.)

The Associate Reformed Presbytery of Kentucky (1870.)

The Synod of Missouri, consisting of six presbyteries in Missouri (1874.)

Since all of these bodies of Christians were in full sympathy with the Southern Presbyterians long before formal union was effected, their members may be estimated as forming a part of the larger body during the entire period of the war. The whole body of Presbyterians in the South was, therefore, in number, about one hundred thousand. They had about fourteen hundred churches and were under the guidance and instruction of more than one thousand ministers of the gospel.

It is not possible in this volume to tell the story of the lives of these fifty score men of God. And what shall be said concerning the elders, the deacons, the godly women of the Southern Church? Not even a list of the names of all of these worthies can be here placed on record. But their works do follow them, and the names of many still linger in memory among us as a sweet fragrance. Let us, therefore, suppose that a traveler sets forth at the beginning of the period of strife to make a journey throughout the region that lies between the Rio Grande and the Potomac. Through his eyes we may look upon the work of some of the Presbyterian preachers and elders of the South in the days when she was tried in the furnace of fire.

Our traveler begins his journey on horseback at the western limit of the State of Texas. At Brownsville, near the Mexican border, he hears the gospel message from the lips of Hiram Chamberlain. J. H. Frost is the minister at Corpus Christi, James Wallis at Concrete, and William C. Blair at Goliad. R. F. Bunting of the church of San Antonio has been sent by his brethren to serve as chaplain in the Confederate Army of Tennessee. More than seventy Presbyterian churches have been established in Texas when our traveler sets forth, and more than forty well-trained Presbyterians are preaching the word in that wide region. Among these are Hugh Wilson, the pioneer preacher; William M. Baker at Austin, Daniel McNair at Galveston, R. W. Bailey at Huntsville, Levi Tenney at Salado, W. K. Marshall at Henderson, and J. H. Hutchison at Houston. Samuel A. King and S. F. Tenney have just

entered upon long terms of worthy service in the Lone
Star State. Among the active elders we find D. Mc-
Gregor, R. H. Orr, James Sorley, W. T. Hill and
Joseph C. Wilson.

From Texas the traveler seeks the northward route
and enters Arkansas. He there finds a devoted company
of about forty Presbyterian ministers. James Wilson
Moore, founder of the Presbyterian Church in this
region, is still in active service. In like manner, Daniel
L. Gray and A. R. Banks continue their good work.
The saintly Aaron Williams and Cephas Washburn pass
to their heavenly reward just as the war begins. In
1863 James Martin, the ripe scholar and impressive
preacher, dies from exposure and severe treatment received in a Federal prison. His son, Judge Joseph W.
Martin, is ready and able as a ruling elder to continue
the Christian activity begun by his honored father. As
worthy, also, of most honorable mention in the work
of the eldership in Arkansas, these names must be placed
in this record: Roderick L. Dodge, John F. Allen and
James A. Dibrell, godly physicians; John R. Hampton,
Alexander W. Dinsmore, Samuel Wright Williams,
Isaac Lawrence, William A. Carrigan and John B.
Speers. In the First Church at Little Rock our traveler
finds Thomas Rice Welch as pastor. The latter, a native
of Kentucky and a graduate of Center College, is just
entering upon a long term of successful work in the
capital city of Arkansas. S. W. Davies is the minister
at Augusta, W. A. Sample at Fort Smith, W. S. Lacy
at Eldorado, and S. Williamson at Washington. Among
the Creek and Choctaw Indians, within the bounds of
Arkansas Synod, a number of faithful missionaries continue their labors during the Confederate war and afterwards. Writing in 1870, Dr. J. Leighton Wilson
speaks thus: "Hotchkin, Byington and Copeland have
followed each other in successive years to the better
world, leaving the venerable Dr. Kingsbury, the oldest

of them all, to toil on.   The world has seldom known
such men.   Scores and hundreds of Choctaws will
ascribe their salvation to the instrumentality of these
holy men."

The traveler and his horse now take passage on a
river steamer and make an easy journey southward to
New Orleans.   There he finds, in the pulpits, Benjamin
M. Palmer, Thomas R. Markham, S. Woodbridge and
Henry M. Smith.   A little later he will hear of William
Flinn, Robert Q. Mallard and A. F. Dickson as workers
in this great city.   Some of the elders of New Orleans we
shall meet in connection with our study of the work of Dr.
Palmer.   Time presses, and the traveler takes his rapid
way through Louisiana and Mississippi, paying visits
only to C. S. Hendrick at Baton Rouge, Joseph B.
Stratton, Benjamin Chase and James Purviance at
Natchez, S. R. Bertron at Port Gibson, E. H. Rutherford at Vicksburg, J. S. Montgomery at Yazoo City,
and John Hunter at Jackson.   James A. Lyon, pastor
at Columbus, is known throughout the Mississippi Valley; William T. Hall at Canton, and T. D. Witherspoon at Oxford, have just entered upon long and honorable careers as pastors, army chaplains and, at a later
day, teachers of theology.   Active men in the eldership
are the following: T. L. Dunlap, Thomas L. Carothers,
R. S. Stewart, James Patrick, A. R. Hutchison and
Israel Spencer.   More than seventy-five Presbyterian
ministers are engaged in the work in Mississippi, but
our traveler hastens into Alabama to catch a glimpse
of the work of the seventy preachers in that commonwealth.   George H. W. Petrie is pastor at Montgomery,
and the young George L. Petrie has entered upon work
at Union Springs.   James K. Hazen, afterwards the
efficient manager of our publication work, is shepherd
at Prattville; James H. Nall is at Tuskegee, A. B. Mc-
Corkle at Talladega, A. J. Witherspoon at Linden, G.
W. Boggs at Camden, H. R. Raymond at Marion, J.

R. Burgett and J. C. Mitchell at Mobile, A. M. Small, soon to be succeeded by W. J. Lowry, at Selma; W. H. Mitchell at Florence, and R. B. White at Tuscaloosa. Besides these, John M. P. Otts is a young licentiate at Greensboro, John W. Pratt as teacher at Tuskaloosa is preparing himself for later efficient work as preacher, while C. A. Stillman at Gainesville is in training for the later work of founding our excellent school for colored men at Tuskaloosa. Among the elders of Alabama we may note here the names of George J. S. Walker, J. M. McGowan, N. S. Graham, G. H. Dunlap, E. A. Archibald, James Montgomery and W. P. Webb.

Making a circuit near the waters of the Gulf of Mexico the traveler hears clear, strong preaching of the word by James Little at Quincy, Florida; by John E. Du Bose (Tallahassee), Donald Fraser (Madison and Monticello), T. L. De Veaux (Jacksonville), and Archibald Baker (Fernandina). Some of the elders of marked activity in Florida are Judge W. A. Forward, J. C. McGehee, J. M. W. Davidson, Joseph M. Hull, B. F. Whitner and Judge James Baker. David H. Porter shepherds the flock of the First Church, Savannah, Georgia, and I. S. K. Axson is in charge of Savannah's strong congregation of Independents. Richard Q. Way looks after the congregation at Riceboro, Georgia; Joseph R. Wilson at Augusta, J. B. Dunwody at Washington, Nathan Hoyt at Athens, and Francis R. Goulding at Macon. John S. Wilson and R. K. Porter are pastors in Atlanta. Wilson, as historian of the synod, tells our traveler about the worthies who have been called away in recent years from the scenes of their labor in Georgia. Among these ministers of the past were Robert Quarterman of Midway, and his son, Joseph M. Quarterman; William McWhir and Alonzo Church, who in 1859 completed a term of thirty years as president of the University of Georgia at Athens; Samuel J. Cassels, Donald J. Auld, Joseph Y. Alexander, Peter Winn and

Edwin T. Williams. Ripe scholars were most of these, and all were consecrated Christian ministers who bore faithful witness. Special mention must here be made of the work of Samuel K. Talmage, a native of New Jersey, who from 1841 until 1865 was president of Oglethorpe University. This school was under the control of the synods of Georgia, South Carolina and Alabama. The first president was Rev. Carlisle P. Beman (1836-1841). Through a period of more than a quarter of a century the institution was a most efficient agency in bringing young men into the ministry. The war swept away its endowment fund and its activities were soon afterwards brought to an end. The work of this school is a worthy memorial of its founders, the members of the Georgia Educational Society. The latter was organized in 1823 as follows:

Major Abraham Walker, president.

Rev. Moses Waddel, first vice-president.

Rev. Francis Cummins, second vice-president.

Rev. John Brown, third vice-president.

Rev. William McWhir, fourth vice-president.

Rev. William T. Brantly, fifth vice-president.

Rev. Peter Gautier, sixth vice-president.

Rev. Abiel Carter, seventh vice-president.

Secretaries, Rev. Thomas Goulding and Rev. Moses W. Dobbins.

Treasurer, Rev. James Nisbet.

The names of M. D. Wood (Decatur), James Stacy (Newnan), N. A. Pratt (Roswell), E. P. Palmer (Marietta), James A. Wallace (Dalton), H. F. Hoyt (Albany), complete the list of ministers whom our traveler visits within the State of Georgia. There are many other preachers within this region of equal worth with those named above, but with the mention of a few elders among a great multitude, we must allow the traveler to hasten northward across the Savannah River. The elders whom we shall name are: E. A. Nesbit of the

church at Macon, a prominent leader in the Georgia
Secession Convention; Thomas R. R. Cobb, elder and
Sunday-school teacher in the church at Athens, who
gave his life for the South on the battlefield of Fred-
ericksburg (1862); W. L. Mitchell, Samuel Barnett,
T. T. Windsor, J. A. Ansley and J. C. Whitner.

Almost six score is the number of Presbyterian ministers in South Carolina during the period of the war.
John Forrest, Thomas Smyth, John L. Girardeau and
W. C. Dana are the ministers in Charleston. Near this
city our traveler finds W. States Lee, John Douglas,
John R. Dow and Charles S. Vedder. Donald McQueen
has the oversight of the flock at Sumter, Samuel H. Hay
at Camden, James Douglass at Winnsboro, E. O. Frier-
son at Kingstree, T. R. English at Mayesville, R. H.
Reid at Nazareth Church, A. A. Morse at Anderson,
John McLees at Greenwood, M. D. Wood at Yorkville,
J. G. Richards at Liberty Hill, John C. Williams at
Greenville, and D. M. Turner at Upper Long Cane.
William Banks keeps the records for years as stated
clerk of the Synod of South Carolina. William Plumer
Jacobs and Gilbert R. Brackett have already entered
upon those labors, which will extend into much later
times.

Within the Theological Seminary at Columbia, South
Carolina, the traveler finds a special group of church
leaders, remarkable for learning and practical wisdom.
These are James H. Thornwell, teacher of systematic
theology; George Howe, Greek and Hebrew; A. W. Leland, pastoral theology; John B. Adger, church history
and polity, and James Woodrow, natural science in connection with revelation. But when the trumpet of war
calls the sons of the South to defend their homes against
the invader, the ministerial students seize their muskets
and go to the front. Our traveler, therefore, finds that
the work of teaching has been laid aside for a season.
Occasionally, during the war, some instruction is given,

but in the later years of the struggle sick and wounded soldiers find a place of rest in the seminary. Moreover, Dr. Woodrow changes some of the seminary rooms into laboratories, in which he prepares medicines for the suffering Confederates. Soon after the close of the struggle three other strong men are made members of the seminary faculty, namely, William S. Plumer, Joseph R. Wilson and John L. Girardeau.

Among the army chaplains from South Carolina the following names may be placed in this record: J. L. Girardeau, A. A. James, J. G. Richards, Samuel E. Axson, John N. Craig, James McDowell, H. M. Brantly and R. E. Cooper. Fragrant in the memory of the people of Charleston from the outbreak of the war and afterwards are the names of ruling elders, William Yeadon and James Adger. Judge John A. Inglis of the church at Cheraw, member of the South Carolina Secession Convention; Chancellor Job Johnston of Newberry, Col. F. W. McMaster of Columbia, and Col. W. P. Finley of Aiken, may stand as representatives of those South Carolina elders of this period who play a part in public affairs. Andrew Crawford, Henry S. Muller and R. L. Bryan of the Columbia Church, the two first named serving as treasurers of Columbia Seminary, and T. C. Perrin of Abbeville, president of the seminary board of trustees, are types of Presbyterians considered as judicious business administrators.

And what shall the traveler tell us of the shepherds and bishops in North Carolina, nearly seven score in number? Some are chaplains in the army, such as E. H. Harding, H. B. Pratt, James M. Sprunt, James H. Colton and Drury Lacy. Martin McQueen preaches the pure word at Wilmington. In and around Fayetteville, the home of the Highlanders, we find John M. Sherwood, Neill McDonald, Hector McLean, Hector McNeill and other Scots. Charles Phillips and A. D. Hepburn occupy chairs in the State University at Chapel Hill.

Joseph M. Atkinson is the chief shepherd at Raleigh, Jacob Henry Smith at Greensboro, H. G. Hill at Hillsboro, Jethro Rumple at Salisbury, Arnold W. Miller at Charlotte. Among the active elders we learn of the zeal and wisdom of William Bingham, James G. Shepherd, Thomas M. Holt, Joseph H. Wilson, E. Nye Hutchison, Jesse H. Lindsay, F. M. Wooten, W. M. Cocke.

A rapid journey across the mountains brings our traveler quickly into Tennessee. Knoxville is under the care of W. A. Harrison and T. R. Bradshaw, and Columbia's shepherd is A. L. Kline. J. Bardwell, R. H. Allen, J. W. Hoyt and R. F. Bunting are pastors at Nashville, T. D. Wardlaw at Clarksville, William Eagleton at Murfreesboro, I. Morey at Franklin, Thomas H. McCallie at Chattanooga, J. O. Stedman and P. H. Thompson at Memphis, D. H. Cummins and S. B. O. Wilson at Covington, E. C. Trimble at Jackson, E. S. Campbell at New Shiloh Church, A. H. Kerr at Delta, J. D. Tadlock at Jonesboro, J. W. Bachman at Rogersville, and John H. Bryson at Laurel Hill Church. Three ministers of the Doak family we find in service in Tennessee— Samuel W. Doak and J. W. K. Doak at Greenville, and Alexander Doak at Knoxville. Their contemporary, Daniel G. Doak, preaches at Oxford, Mississippi. We find also six representatives of the Frierson family engaged in ministerial labors—J. Simpson Frierson and J. Stephenson Frierson in Tennessee, D. E. Frierson and Edward O. Frierson in South Carolina, S. R. Frierson in Mississippi, and M. W. Frierson among the Mississippi soldiers in the army. J. H. McNeily and R. K. Smoot are young ministers in Tennessee during the early years of the war. Among the elders we find J. T. Swayne, S. B. McAdams, Joseph A. Brooks, A. W. Putnam, G. S. Cecil, Charles Lynn, B. M. Estes, E. B. McClanahan, George Thompson, R. P. Rhea, John P. Long, Samuel M. Neel, R. F. Patterson and D. N. Kennedy.

A ride up the Holston River brings our traveler from Tennessee into Southwestern Virginia. The valleys of this region are filled with Presbyterian flocks, and we meet in succession among a large company these shepherds, still young in years: Henry M. White, D. W. Shanks, Thomas L. Preston, George W. White, William T. Richardson and E. D. Junkin. The Greenbrier country is occupied by John McElhenny, J. C. Barr, S. R. Houston, J. H. Leps, M. H. Bittinger and R. R. Houston. William S. White is pastor at Lexington, W. E. Baker at Staunton, D. C. Irwin at Harrisonburg, William H. Foote at Romney, Charles White at Berryville (later at College Church, Hampden-Sidney), James R. Graham and J. W. Lupton at Winchester, Edgar Woods, William Dinwiddie and B. M. Wailes in and near Charlottesville, J. B. Ramsey and W. V. Wilson in Lynchburg, Theodorick Pryor and A. W. Miller (afterwards at Charlotte, N. C.) in Petersburg, T. V. Moore, M. D. Hoge and C. H. Read in Richmond, George D. Armstrong in Norfolk, and Peyton Harrison in Baltimore. In Southside Virginia the flocks are under the oversight of Henry C. Alexander, Thomas Wharey, Richard McIlwaine, William A. Campbell, C. R. Vaughan, John H. Bocock, S. W. Watkins, Alexander Martin and many other worthy bishops. As chaplains among the Confederate soldiers many ministers have been sent out by the Virginia churches. Among these preachers in camp are Abner C. Hopkins, James H. Leps, J. H. Gilmore, Samuel D. Stuart, William S. Lacy, L. C. Vass and George H. Gilmer.

At the beginning of the war Virginia holds within her borders a worthy company of Presbyterian teachers and scholars. At the Union Seminary in Prince Edward County our traveler finds the following: Samuel B. Wilson, successor of George A. Baxter, teacher of theology; Robert L. Dabney, teacher of theology; Benjamin M. Smith, Oriental languages; Thomas E. Peck, church history and polity. The traveler is told that a few years prior to the war Samuel L. Graham and Francis L. Sampson, members of the seminary faculty, completed their earthly labors, and that William J. Hoge withdrew from the work of teaching to become pastor of a flock in the city of New York.

The traveler is told the story of the eager zeal of the boys at Hampden-Sidney College. At the first call to arms they organized themselves into a military company and chose as their captain the president of the college, Dr. J. M. Atkinson, a Presbyterian minister. Captain Atkinson preached the gospel to his young soldiers on Sunday, and during the week drilled them in the manual of arms. At Rich Mountain, Virginia, in July, 1861, the college boys showed their bravery in battle. The fortune of war was against them, however, and the entire company was captured. On account of youth they were all paroled and allowed to return to their studies.

The president of Washington College in the Valley of Virginia was at that time a Presbyterian minister, Dr. George Junkin. As a native of Pennsylvania he did not sympathize with the secession movement, and he, therefore, returned to his Northern home in 1861. The students of Washington College, however, formed a company and selected James J. White of the chair of Greek as their captain. The latter was a Presbyterian elder. He led them to Manassas, Virginia, and in the first great battle on that field, July 21, 1861, this college company, known as the Liberty Hall Volunteers, stood bravely in the place of danger as a part of Stonewall Jackson's line of battle. Under the eye of Jackson himself, they helped that day to make an immortal name for the Stonewall Brigade.

At the University of Virginia our traveler finds the great scholar and teacher, Dr. William H. McGuffey, a Presbyterian minister who preaches the word with power. From him the traveler learns of the series of lectures delivered at the university in the years 1850-1851 on the general theme of the Evidences of Christianity by some of the leaders in the ministry of the Presbyterian Church of that day. The list of lecturers is as follows:

William S. Plumer, pastor in Baltimore.

Alexander T. McGill, Alleghany Seminary, Pennsylvania.

James W. Alexander, pastor in New York City; a native of Virginia.

Robert J. Breckinridge, pastor in Lexington, Ky.

Stuart Robinson, pastor in Frankfort, Ky.

Nathan L. Rice, pastor in Cincinnati; a native of Kentucky.

Francis L. Sampson, Union Seminary, Virginia.

Benjamin M. Smith, pastor in Staunton, Virginia.

Lewis W. Green, president of Hampden-Sidney College, Virginia.

Henry Ruffner, former president of Washington College, Virginia.

A. B. Van Zandt, pastor in Petersburg, Virginia.

Thomas V. Moore, pastor in Richmond.

Moses Drury Hoge, pastor in Richmond.

The names thus far given as recorded in our traveler's notebook may stand as representatives of the entire body of members in the ten synods that organized the Southern Assembly in 1861. Many of these ministers and elders were possessed of sound scholarship. Virtually all of them were judicious men, honorable in every respect, and living in the fear of God. As highminded servants of Jehovah, they gave their undivided attention to their tasks throughout the period of the war.

The work of preaching the gospel among the Confederate soldiers was assumed by the Southern Assembly itself through the appointment of commissioners to the main divisions of the army. Benjamin M. Palmer was sent as commissioner to preach to the Army of Tennessee; at a later time the work in the same field was assigned to William Flinn. The commissioners sent to the Army of Northern Virginia were Beverly T. Lacy and Theodorick Pryor. John N. Waddel was commissioner to the Army of Mississippi, Drury Lacy to the Army of Eastern North Carolina, John Douglas to the Army of South Carolina, Rufus K. Porter to the Army of Georgia and Florida, Henry M. Smith to the army west of the Mississippi. These ministers, as directors of the work, were aided by about one hundred and thirty other preachers of the gospel. The routine of their labors was as follows: To preach to the soldiers twice and sometimes thrice each Sunday; to hold prayer-meetings each night in the week; to teach Bible classes almost every day; to distribute Bibles, parts of the Bible, hymn books, tracts and religious newspapers; to visit the sick and talk daily to soldiers about the welfare of their souls. In the winter-camps, chapels were built by the soldiers themselves; as many as thirty-seven of these houses of worship were erected within a few months by the men of the Army of Northern Virginia. We are not surprised, therefore, to read this report concerning such earnest Christian work that "in many portions of the army our soldiers have received as much religious instruction as they ever enjoyed in the most favored part of their lives." This report is made, moreover, with reference to men who have grown up beneath the shadow of some of the strongest churches in our country. Special seasons of revival mark the preaching in the army. During the winter of 1862-1863 hundreds of men are led into Christ's kingdom. During the following winter, 1863-1864, the converts are numbered by thousands. The Southern ranks, in fact, are filled with Christian men in a proportion so large and so unusual, and so many of the Confederate officers are godly men, that we may here write it down without fear of contradiction that the Confederate forces, to a greater extent than has ever been known in so large a body of fighting men, constitute a great Christian army.

"Whatever disappointment may have been experienced by us as a people," writes Dr. J. Leighton Wilson in 1865, "in relation to the establishment of our independence as a church, we should ever be grateful to Almighty God for the repeated and abundant outpouring of his Holy Spirit upon our armies during the progress of the bloody conflict. That our camps should have been made nurseries of piety is something not only new and unprecedented in warfare, but may be regarded as an encouraging token of God's purpose to favor and bless our future Zion."

Our traveler, in prosecuting his journey far and wide throughout every part of the South, learns that the duty of teaching the colored people is not neglected by the church during the period of the war. Throughout this time, moreover, the slaves as a body remain in a remarkable degree faithful to their masters. At the close of the struggle they are gradually led away from the guardianship of the Southern churches. In view of this state of affairs the General Assembly of 1865 sends out a pastoral letter to the churches, written by Dr. William Brown of Richmond, editor of the *Central Presbyterian*. With reference to the former system of slavery, the letter declares that its overthrow has been sudden and violent, "whether justly or unjustly, in wrath or in mercy, for weal or for woe, let history and the Judge of all the earth decide." The modern theory that slaveholding is in itself a sin, says the letter, is a fanatical and unscriptural theory. "We are not called, now that it has been abolished, to bow the head in humiliation before men, nor to admit that the memory of many of our dear kindred is to be covered with shame, because, like Abraham, Isaac and Jacob, they had bondservants born in their house or bought with their money."

With the present wretchedness of the emancipated
negroes, "with their prospects, to human view dismal
as the grave, our church is not chargeable." She may
"hold up her hands before heaven and earth," continues
Dr. Brown's letter, "washed of the tremendous responsibility involved in this change in the condition of nearly
four million bond-servants, a change for which they were
unprepared." And yet, concludes the letter to the congregations of the South, these former servants are still
living near your own doors—"many of them are your
fellow-heirs of salvation. We are persuaded, therefore,
that you [the Southern Presbyterians] will not turn
away from them in this day of their imagined mil-
lennium—we fear of terrible calamity. Let it be shown
to all men that nothing shall withdraw the sympathy of
your heart or the labor of your hand from a work which
must of necessity ever rest chiefly upon those who dwell
in the land, not upon the strangers who visit it."

And what shall be said with reference to the official
attitude maintained by the Southern Presbyterian
Church toward the government of the Southern Confederacy? In setting down here the reply, let us remember that Southern Presbyterians, practically to a
man, are heart and soul in sympathy with the Confederacy. The members and officers of the church,
almost all of them, are in the field of war, contending
valiantly for the cause of the South against the North.
Some of the Southern ministers preach in their pulpits
about the Southern cause as a righteous cause. This
they do upon their individual authority as pastors.
When ministers and elders assemble in church courts,
in presbyteries, synods and as a General Assembly,
many of the delegates leaving the military camps to take
part for a time in discussing the affairs of the church,
the calmness of temper and the self-restraint manifested
are truly remarkable. Political measures are not formulated, nor even discussed in the sessions of the General

Assembly. The only apparent exceptions to this statement are certain expressions contained in the "narrative" adopted by each assembly during the war. The narrative is merely a survey of the state of religion within the limits of the assembly, and there are, of necessity, references to the Confederacy as the existing government. In the survey of the field, written by Dr. A. W. Leland and adopted by the assembly of 1861, we find the following: "Our first emotions are those of sadness and grief excited by the calamities and desolations caused by that cruel, fratricidal war which has been forced upon us. But, while some of our pastors are required to leave their homes and labor in the tented field and in the hospitals, and while large numbers are called to leave their seats in our sanctuaries and put on their armor in defense of their country, it is gratifying to learn that the ordinances of public worship are generally attended and Christian privileges enjoyed as usual. * * * In several places within our bounds there have been blessed revivals of religion, adding to our churches hundreds of hopeful converts among the colored people. Many of our pastors, evangelists and licentiates devote their ministry to servants as well as masters."

When the Assembly of 1862 meets there are armies all around it. Some of the ministers of the church have suffered persecution at the hands of Federal officers. For example, Dr. George D. Armstrong, pastor of the Norfolk Church, Virginia, a man of learning and a man of God, has been thrust into prison and subjected to severe personal indignities by General B. F. Butler, commander of the Federal garrison at Norfolk. Some of the ministers have been slain. From a burdened heart, therefore, Dr. John L. Girardeau includes in the survey of the state of religion adopted by the Assembly in 1862 the following tribute of respect: "Rev. Dabney Carr Harrison, a member of the presbytery of East Hanover,

a chaplain and an officer, fell mortally wounded while
leading his men in one of the bloodiest battles fought in
this war.   His name will be embalmed in the hearts of
his countrymen and will be held in veneration by the
church of which he was an ornament." In connection
with this, in the narrative, we find the following:

"Deeply convinced that this struggle is not alone for
civil rights and property and home, but also for religion,
for the church, for the gospel and for existence itself,
the churches in our connection have freely contributed
to its prosecution of their substance, their prayers, and
above all, of their members and the beloved youth of
their congregations.   They have parted without a murmur with those who constitute the hope of the church,
and have bidden them go forth to the support of this
great and sacred cause with their benedictions."

The survey of religion written, in May, 1863, by that
devout and judicious man of God, Dr. Joseph M. Atkinson of Raleigh, North Carolina, contains the following
expressions: "The blood of our brethren, our fathers
and our children, unjustly and untimely slain, cries to
Heaven.   *   *   *   It is to us matter of devout gratitude to Almighty God that He has so often and so signally baffled the efforts of our enemies to effect our
subjugation and that He has vouchsafed to our arms
victories so repeated and so wonderful."   The narrative of 1864, prepared by David M. Wills of Macon,
Georgia, speaks thus: The presbyterial narratives
"tell us of the terrible persecutions of our people in
those parts of the country which have been visited by the
invading foe.   They speak in tones of sadness of many
of our beautiful sanctuaries [about one hundred of these
having been injured or destroyed]; of the exile of pastors and their flocks for conscience's sake; of the loss
of large numbers of our noblest young men who have
been slain in battle; and of the numerous households
which are weeping over their martyred dead."

These and other like expressions of sympathy with the Confederate cause are found in the General Assembly's annual surveys of the religious state of the country. At no time during the struggle, however, does the assembly declare that it is the religious duty of its members to fight for the Confederacy, nor does the assembly adopt any rule whatsoever to require an examination of a man's political sentiments as a preliminary to his admission as church member. Moreover, the Southern Assembly makes no unfriendly reference whatever to the Northern Assembly. In this most vital sense the Southern Presbyterian Church does not mingle political sentiments with religious faith. When the circumstances are considered, perhaps no church on earth has ever kept herself so free from alliances with political parties and from intermeddling with governmental affairs, as the Southern Presbyterian Church. When the end of the struggle comes, Dr. William Brown, in the Assembly's Narrative of 1865, utters this final exhortation to the Southern congregations: "You have been called to pass through deep waters; you have had sorrow upon sorrow. It was the path your Saviour trod and He will grant you in it the comfort of His love and the fellowship of His Spirit. Some of our dear brethren in Christ, and some of them in the ministry, have had cruel mockings and scourgings, have suffered stripes and imprisonments and the loss of all things. Our prayer has been with you in your calamity. Remember, that the church of God has often passed through the heated furnace, but the form of the Son of God has been seen with her and she is still unconsumed."

CHAPTER XLVI.

AFTER the close of the war between North and South,
our traveler prepared himself for a journey among the
churches of Kentucky and Missouri, two border commonwealths whose people were divided in political sentiment during the great struggle. As a preliminary to
his journey, the traveler refreshed his memory concerning the action of the Presbyterian Assembly of the year
1845 with reference to the holding of slaves. This
action, be it remembered, set forth the views held by
Presbyterians at the very time when the Southern
Methodists (1844) and the Southern Baptists (1846)
were withdrawing themselves completely from association with their Northern brethren because the latter
were denouncing as a sin and crime the practice of holding slaves. The great Baptist and Methodist bodies
were thus rent asunder early in the course of the abolitionist movement. The Presbyterians of North and
South remained together, at that time, as one body, and
their General Assembly (1845) announced the following propositions, written by Dr. Nathan L. Rice, concerning slavery:

"The church of Christ is a spiritual body whose jurisdiction extends to the religious faith and moral conduct
of her members. She cannot legislate when Christ has
not legislated, nor make terms of membership which He
has not made. * * * Since Christ and His inspired Apostles did not make the holding of slaves a
bar to communion, we, as a court of Christ, have no

authority to do so; since they did not attempt to remove it from the church by legislation, we have no authority to legislate on the subject."

Our traveler found that the official utterance of the Assembly of 1845, thus quoted above, was in entire harmony with the attitude toward slavery maintained by the Southern Assembly throughout the period of the Confederate war. The declaration made by Dr. Charles Hodge of Princeton, in 1860, rests upon the same view. As a further preparation for the experiences through which he was about to pass, the traveler now read those passages in the minutes of the Northern Assembly that set forth the attitude of that body toward slavery, toward the war itself and toward the Southern Presbyterians. In these minutes he found that the Northern Assembly placed itself in a position of direct and total contradiction to the views expressed by the Assembly of 1845. The acts of the Northern Assembly during the progress of the war, stated in brief form, are as follows:

1. In 1861, the assembly, in session at Philadelphia, adopted the Spring Resolutions, to the effect that it is the solemn duty of all Presbyterians to "strengthen, uphold and encourage" the administration of President Lincoln in the prosecution of the war against the South. Our traveler read also the protest made by Dr. Charles Hodge and others that this adoption of the Spring resolutions by the assembly was an effort made to decide a great political issue, in direct violation of the constitution of the Presbyterian Church.

2. The Northern Assembly of 1862, through the agency of a paper prepared by Robert J. Breckinridge, declared that the people of the South by reason of taking part in the war, placed themselves outside the pale of "natural religion and morality"—that they were heathen and enemies of God. It was, therefore, the bounden duty of all people in the land "To crush force by force." In

addition to these assertions, the judgment of God was invoked upon all those officers and members of the Presbyterian Church who showed sympathy with the South, since these persons, it was claimed by the assembly, were "faithless to all authority, human and divine."

3. With the knowledge and consent of the Northern Assembly of 1863, the flag of the Federal Government was unfurled over the church building in which the assembly was holding its sessions as a sign to all men that the Northern Church was placing herself in open active allegiance with a political party in the North.

4. The Northern Assembly of May, 1864 (a) announced that the operations of Grant's army in the Wilderness formed the basis for gratitude to God and the assembly, therefore, spent an entire afternoon in *Thanksgiving* services; (b) the assembly enumerated six Republican party measures as proposed by President Lincoln, and urged all Presbyterians to labor honestly, earnestly and unweariedly for the success of the president's policy; since this utterance of the assembly was made upon the eve of the presidential campaign between Lincoln and McClellan, both of whom announced themselves as in favor of maintaining the Federal Union, the assembly's action was thus merely an appeal in behalf of the Republican candidate, and during the summer of 1864 it was actually circulated as a Republican campaign document.

Through these resolutions the assembly set forth the view that the qualities essential to membership in the Presbyterian Church were loyalty to President Lincoln's administration and the acceptance of the theory that slaveholding is a crime.

5. The Northern Assembly of 1865 again made the fundamental law of the church to consist in these same dogmas; namely, loyalty to the Federal administration, and denunciation of slavery as a crime:

(a) The assembly censured the Synod of Kentucky

for protesting against the utterances of the Assembly of 1864, and also for the synod's failure to adopt political resolutions in support of the war against the South.

(b) The assembly denounced the formation of the Southern Confederacy as a "great crime," and the formation of the Southern Presbyterian Church as "the schism."

(c) The assembly, assuming that there were few real Christians in the South, directed its Board of Domestic Missions to build up Presbyterian congregations in the South by recognizing as members only those who accepted the Northern dogmas about loyalty and slavery.

(d) The assembly ordered all of the Northern presbyteries to refuse to receive as a member any Southern preacher unless the latter should swear loyalty to the Federal administration and declare that he believed slaveholding to be a crime.

(e) The assembly ordered church sessions to refuse membership in the church to any former Confederate soldier or to any person from the South who denied that slaveholding is a crime, unless such applicants repented of their errors and adopted the Northern Assembly's views about the Confederacy and about slavery.

Against the acts of this assembly and of previous assemblies a protest was formulated. In the summer of 1865, Dr. Samuel R. Wilson of Kentucky, a man born and bred in the North and who was never at any time in sympathy with the Southern Confederacy, wrote a paper known as the "Declaration and Testimony." This paper was signed by a large number of ministers and elders in Kentucky and Missouri, and thus became their solemn protest against the course followed by the Northern Assembly.

"We do solemnly testify," ran Dr. Wilson's paper, "(1) Against the assumption on the part of the courts of the church of the right to decide questions of state

policy. This right has been assumed by all the courts
of the church." In proof of the assembly's share in
such a policy, citation was made of the acts of the five
assemblies from 1861 to 1865.

"(2) We testify against the doctrine that the church,
as such, owes allegiance to human rulers or governments.
Allegiance or loyalty, in respect to human governments,
is alone predicable of *persons* as citizens. The church
owes her allegiance alone to Jesus Christ, who is sole
King in Zion   *   *   *"

(3) The third part of the testimony is against "the
perversion of the teachings of Christ and His Apostles"
in such manner as to claim that Christians, *as citizens*,
must uphold "a particular form of government, or a
present administration of that government."

"(4) We testify against the action of the assembly
on the subject of slavery and emancipation in 1864, and
as confirmed in 1865. In that action the assembly
*   *   *   does not quote fairly from former utterances
upon the same subject. It omits altogether all reference to the uniform and most important declaration contained in its previous expressions of opinion, that *immediate, indiscriminate emancipation* of the negro slaves
amongst us would be *unjust and injurious to both master
and slave.* And then it leaves entirely unnoticed the
act of 1845 and treats it as a nullity   *   *   *   and
then, upon this basis of suppression and perversion,
there is laid down a new doctrine upon this subject of
slavery unknown to the apostolic and primitive church;
a doctrine which has its origin in infidelity and fanaticism; a doctrine which the Presbyterian Church had
before uniformly treated as a dangerous error, and
which the General Assembly of 1845 declared they could
not sanction 'without contradicting some of the plainest
declarations of the Word of God.'   *   *   *"

"We testify (5) against the *unjust*" declaration of
the assembly that the Southern people made no effort

to Christianize the negroes; (6) against the doctrine,
countenanced by the assembly, that the acts of church
courts may be shaped in accordance with the ordinances
of legislatures and the orders of military officers; (7)
that the will of God and the teachings of the Scriptures
are to be interpreted from particular providential events,
such as the emancipation proclamation and the enlist-
ment of slaves in the Northern armies; (8) against the
sanction given by the assembly to the Federal army's
usurpation of authority over the affairs of the church;
(9) against the alliance formed by the church with the
state, whereby "political dogmas" are made tests of
membership in the church; (10) against the acts of the
Assembly of 1865, which "virtually excommunicated the
whole Southern Presbyterian Church and in effect ordained that they should be treated as heathen and out-
casts;" (11) against the widespread perversion of the
commission of the ministry in such manner that political
topics are "ordinary and favorite themes of the pulpit,"
that ministers have become "the fiercest of political
partisans," and that church courts spend their time in
passing resolutions "to strengthen the government;"
(12) against the ordinance of the assembly of 1865 in
demanding that Southern members and ministers shall
repudiate opinions about slavery and state rights, while
members and ministers living in the North are allowed
to hold unquestioned those same opinions; (13) against
"all and every movement in the church, however cau-
tiously or plausibly veiled, which looks to a union of
the state with the church."

All of these parts of the protest were drawn out at
length and supported by references to the acts of the
Northern assemblies during the period 1861-1865. In
conclusion, the paper declared that the Northern Assembly had become "the prime leader in promoting a great
and distinctive schism" in the church, and that the
signers of this Declaration and Testimony refused

most positively to obey every order concerning political affairs issued by the assemblies of 1864 and 1865. On September 2, 1865, the Declaration and Testimony was adopted by the Presbytery of Louisville, Kentucky. Soon afterwards the Synod of Kentucky met, and in that body the proposition was made that the members of the Louisville Presbytery, and other ministers and elders who had signed the Declaration and Testimony, should not be allowed to sit as members of the synod. This was upon the alleged basis that the mere signing of the protest was an act of defiance offered to the assembly and, therefore, rendered the signers unfit to hold seats in any church court. The synod rejected the proposition by the vote of 107 to 22.

In May, 1866, our traveler made the journey to St. Louis to visit the Northern Assembly, called to meet in regular annual session in that city. He there heard the story of the efforts made by Federal commanders during the war to assume control over ministers, and church officers, and church courts in the State of Missouri. For example, in March, 1862, Samuel S. Laws, a Presbyterian minister and former president of Westminster College at Fulton, Missouri, was required by a Federal officer to take an oath binding himself to render active help in prosecuting the war against the South. At the same time a bond was demanded of him as security that he would keep the oath. Upon his refusal, Dr. Laws was cast into the Gratiot Street Prison in St. Louis. No charges were ever preferred against him. After months of confinement he was released upon parole on condition that he would live in the Northern States or go to Europe.

On March 8, 1864, General Rosecrans, Federal commander of the Military Department of Missouri, issued Order No. 62, that no person be allowed to sit as a member of a church court unless he took a solemn oath pledging himself to oppose and denounce the Southern

Confederacy. In May, 1864, Samuel B. McPheeters, pastor of the Pine Street Presbyterian Church, St. Louis, stood up in his place as a member of the Northern Assembly and protested against the making of political deliverances by the assembly. Upon his return to St. Louis Dr. McPheeters was ordered by the provost-marshal, a military official, not to preach at all within the state of Missouri, and to remove himself with his family beyond the borders of the commonwealth. The provost-marshal not only banished the pastor against the protests of the great body of the members of the Pine Street Church, but he placed the church building under the absolute control of three members who claimed that Dr. McPheeters was not making active resistance to the Southern Confederacy.

In October, 1864, when the delegates to the Synod of Missouri entered the place of meeting, a church in St. Louis, they found there a lieutenant of the Federal army, who proceeded to carry out Order No. 62. He stood in the church in his uniform and assumed authority over the organization of the synod. Only those delegates who took the special Rosecrans oath were permitted to sit as members of the church court. Two delegates, Dr. R. P. Farris, a minister, and Judge Watson, an elder, refused to recognize the soldier's right to organize the court. For that reason they were both debarred from taking their seats as members of the synod. The Northern Assembly of 1865 *sanctioned* these assumptions of power on the part of military officials by refusing to take any steps looking toward a reversal of the injustice visited upon Judge Watson, Dr. Farris and Dr. McPheeters. In October, 1865, however, the Synod of Missouri declared null and void all of the acts of the Synod of 1864, for the reason that the latter was "under military supervision and control," and was, therefore, "not a free court of our church."

The Northern Assembly of 1866 gave about threefourths of the entire time of its sessions to the consideration of the issues that had arisen in Missouri and Kentucky. Four delegates, appointed as representatives by the Presbytery of Louisville, presented themselves; namely, Dr. Samuel R. Wilson, Dr. Stuart Robinson, and elders Charles A. Wickliffe and Mark Hardin. The first act of the assembly, immediately after the organization of that body, was to exclude these four commissioners from the right to sit as members of the assembly until an inquiry should be made concerning the conduct of the Presbytery of Louisville. Then, after long debate, the assembly adopted an order, known as the "Gurley *ipso facto* resolution" from its author, Dr. Gurley of Washington, to the effect that the Declaration and Testimony was slanderous and schismatical in character and that its adoption was an act of rebellion.

Further discussion of the matter was postponed to the next assembly before whose bar were summoned all the signers of the protest, together with the Presbytery of Louisville. All of these ministers and elders were meanwhile suspended from the exercise of their functions in any church court higher than a church session. The order provided, finally, that if any presbytery should disregard this action of the assembly of 1866, and at any meeting enroll as a member any of the Declaration and Testimony men, then that presbytery would *ipso facto* be dissolved. Synods also were directed to follow the order issued by the assembly.

In October, 1866, the synods of Kentucky and Missouri both bade defiance to the Northern Assembly by giving seats to the signers of the Declaration and Testimony. When the stated clerk of the Kentucky Synod refused to call the names of these signers, Dr. Robert L. Breck proceeded upon his authority as moderator to call the complete roll of the members of the synod, in-

cluding the signers of the protest and the members of
Louisville Presbytery. Synod declared that the assembly in adopting the Gurley order had assumed an
authority over presbyteries not granted by the constitution of the church. The Missouri Synod by a formal
vote gave permission to the Declaration and Testimony
men to hold seats in the synod; at the same time synod
declared that these signers "are not rebels against
ecclesiastical authority, but have simply exercised a
great Protestant right and discharged a solemn duty."

When the Northern Assembly met again, in May,
1867, a reply was made to the two synods by the adoption of a resolution declaring that the Synod of Missouri and the Synod of Kentucky, and the twelve presbyteries in the synods, were all dissolved. Thus, sum-
marily, without trial, by an act of the assembly, the two
Old School synods and their presbyteries were removed
from their former place of membership in the Northern
Assembly. The Kentucky Synod held a called meeting,
June, 1867, and made reply that the Northern Assembly
was itself "a schismatical and revolutionary body, no
longer governed by the constitution." Steps were taken,
therefore, to effect organic union with the Southern Presbyterian Church. As the result of an agreement with the
Southern Assembly, commissioners appointed by the six
Kentucky presbyteries were, in 1869, received as members of the General Assembly of the Southern Church. In
like manner commissioners appointed by the six Missouri presbyteries were in 1874 admitted to seats in the
Southern Assembly. The Southern Church was in this
manner made stronger by the addition of two entire
synods with their twelve presbyteries, covering the states
of Kentucky and Missouri, and embracing about one
hundred and fifty ministers of the Gospel, two hundred
and fifty churches, five hundred ruling elders and fifteen
thousand church members. Among these we may here

set down the names of Stuart Robinson, Samuel B. Mc-
Pheeters, John S. Grasty, H. M. Scudder, R. K. Smoot,
L. G. Barbour, R. L. Breck, J. V. Logan, J. D. Matthews and others, ministers of the gospel in Kentucky;
and the names of A. P. Forman, J. M. Travis, J. L.
Yantis, J. M. Chaney, R. P. Farris and others, ministers
of the gospel in Missouri.

CHAPTER XLVII.

BENJAMIN MORGAN PALMER.

The birthplace of Benjamin M. Palmer was the city of Charleston, South Carolina. Through his father's line of descent, however, and also through his mother, he drew his life-blood from the heart of New England. The early home of Sarah Bunce, Dr. Palmer's mother, was near Hartford, Connecticut. The colony of Plymouth, Massachusetts, was the place in which the emigrant, William Palmer, established himself. He came thither from England in 1621. During the rest of his life and throughout four generations after him, the Palmers remained in Massachusetts, worthy citizens of the province. Samuel Palmer, fourth in descent from the emigrant William, was the successful pastor of the Congregational Church at Falmouth for a period of forty-five years. Samuel Palmer's son, Job Palmer, left Massachusetts and came to Charleston in the year 1771, where he lived as an honored citizen until his death in 1845. Job Palmer's fourth son, Benjamin M. Palmer, Sr., became a Congregational minister and was for many years pastor of the Circular Church in Charleston.

The seventh son of Job Palmer, who was given the name Edward, was the father of Dr. B. M. Palmer, the subject of this sketch. This Edward gave himself to the work of teaching until he reached the age of thirty-two years. Then the call of the Lord moved him to become a minister of the gospel. This was in the year 1820. At once he made the journey to Andover, Massachusetts, to take up the courses of study necessary

for his equipment as a preacher. His wife, Sarah
Bunce, of sturdy Connecticut lineage, opened a boarding-
school in Charleston and thus made a support for herself and her children. Among the latter was Benjamin
M. Palmer, a frail child of two years. During one year
of Edward Palmer's sojourn at Andover, his wife and
children lived there with him. Then, in 1824, he was
licensed as a Congregational minister and began active
work as pastor of the flock at Dorchester, near Charleston, South Carolina.

For a period of three years (1824-1827) Edward
Palmer remained in the pastorate at Dorchester. During that time the mother was the principal teacher of
the child, Benjamin. It was not an easy task to hold
him under control, but this mother was possessed of
unusual qualities of heart and intellect. She filled the
boy's mind, first of all, with Bible stories and Bible
teachings. She taught him also to read Shakespeare,
Milton and Scott. This course of instruction was continued during Edward Palmer's pastorate at Walterboro (1827-1832), near the seacoast, a few miles south
of Charleston. Within the same period young Benjamin was the brightest scholar in the Walterboro
Academy, making rapid progress in the study of Greek
and Latin and becoming an effective speaker in the local
debating society.

In the late summer of 1832, when Benjamin M. Palmer was yet in his fifteenth year, he entered Amherst
College, in Massachusetts. He was short in stature
and of slender frame, but the light that flashed from his
eyes revealed a courageous spirit within. "It was an
uncanny time," writes Dr. Palmer himself, "for Southern
men to trim their sails for Northern seas. The nullifica-
tion storm had just burst over the country and was not
yet appeased. The abolition fanaticism was rising to
the height of its frenzy. The elements of conflict were
gathering in the theological world, which a little later

[1837] resulted in the schism rending the Presbyterian Church asunder. The sky was full of portents."

Among the students at Amherst with whom young Palmer had close association was Henry Ward Beecher. They met often in friendly rivalry in the college debating society and in playing the game of chess. In both exercises Palmer showed himself a worthy foeman. In the work of the classroom, also, he maintained a high standing. This good progress toward a collegiate degree was suddenly interrupted in the spring of 1834 after he had spent somewhat more than a year at Amherst. The literary society of which he was a member was a secret fraternity, whose members were bound by a pledge not to reveal anything that took place in their meetings. On one occasion, however, the college faculty demanded that each member of this society should make a statement with reference to a certain incident. Palmer at once appeared as the leader of a number of high-spirited youths who declared that they were in honor bound not to disclose what had taken place at one of the sessions of the secret society. The faculty threatened him with expulsion, but Palmer replied: "I will take expulsion at your hands rather than trample upon my sense of honor." It is said that the faculty would not have proceeded to the point of expelling him, but his spirit was so filled with resentment concerning the entire affair that he determined to return home. One morning, therefore, just as the stage was about to leave Amherst, young Palmer took his place on top, waving farewell to his friends. The entire body of students was present and "gave him a great ovation, sending him off with ringing cheers." Stuart Robinson, one of his fellow-students at Amherst, declares that throughout this affair Benjamin M. Palmer displayed "the high qualities of honor and courage which marked his life."

Edward Palmer, the father, was not pleased to see his son returning from college. The high-spirited youth, however, was determined to make his own way. The work of teaching, upon which he now entered, occupied his attention for more than two years. In the summer of 1836, in response to the persuasions of his cousin, Dr. I. S. K. Axson, he gave his heart to Christ and became a member of Stony Creek Church, in South Carolina, of which his father was then pastor. In January, 1837, young Palmer entered the State University at Athens, Georgia, which was at that time under the presidency of Dr. Alonzo Church, a Presbyterian minister. He was especially proficient in classical studies and manifested wonderful fluency of speech in the debating society. In August, 1838, he was graduated with first honors.

Having now decided to become a minister of the gospel, Benjamin M. Palmer entered Columbia Seminary in January, 1839. Drs. Howe and Leland were then the only teachers in that school. A year later (1840) Dr. Thornwell became pastor of the church in Columbia, and from the hour of the first meeting between these two gifted men, Thornwell exerted a strong influence in moulding the mental and spiritual life of Palmer. In October, 1841, at the close of his seminary course, young Palmer was called to the First Presbyterian Church, Savannah. He took with him from Columbia, as his bride, Mary Augusta McConnell. Together these two entered with joy into their work as shepherds of the flock. Benjamin M. Palmer immediately found in the pulpit his own special place of successful labor. He was endowed with a full measure of tact and sympathy, and whenever he went among his people he won their love and confidence. His zeal, moreover, kept him constantly in motion from house to house. Wherever sorrow had entered into a home, there was this pastor with words of comfort. But when the morning of the Lord's Day marked the assembling of the people in the sanctuary for praise and worship, Palmer stood in the

pulpit as a royal ambassador, bringing a message from
the King of kings. His splendid powers were working
at their highest degree of efficiency. The people were
instructed and their emotions were stirred. The church
was built up in membership and in spiritual power.

The work in Savannah made Palmer ready for a wider
field. In January, 1843, therefore, he became pastor
of the church in Columbia, South Carolina. The duty
of the minister, he declared in his opening sermon there,
"is to study God's Book, to expound its doctrines, to
enforce its precepts, to urge its motives, to present its
promises, to recite its warnings, to declare its judg-
ments." This high ideal he followed with zeal and success throughout his life. So steady was the growth of
the Columbia Church under his instruction and leadership that in 1853 a new house of worship, the present
edifice, was opened for service. Dr. Palmer himself
preached the dedicatory sermon.

In June, 1847, the first issue of the *Southern Presbyterian Review* appeared in Columbia. The editors of
this periodical were Drs. Thornwell, Howe and Palmer.
Work was thus multiplied for the pastor, but his zeal
never wavered. Three times each Sunday he delivered
elaborate discourses to his people. These sermons were
full of Biblical exposition, knowledge gathered from an
extended course of reading, and keen insight into the
nature of men. Public addresses on college platforms
called also for a portion of his time. He was ready for
every occasion that demanded his presence. His intellect was aglow with life and power, and he stirred the
hearts of men and convinced their understanding by the
work of both pen and tongue. Invitations to become a
pastor in Charleston, Baltimore, Cincinnati and Philadelphia came to him, but in 1854 he was elected to the
chair of Church History in Columbia Seminary and
accepted the position, thus becoming the colleague of
his friend, Dr. Thornwell. Until the end of the year

1855, however, Dr. Palmer continued to fill the pulpit of the Columbia Church. Growing success marked his work as teacher in the seminary, but his own conviction was that his proper sphere of labor was the pastorate. An earnest call came from the congregation of the First Church, New Orleans, and after a lengthened opposition on the part of Dr. Palmer's brethren at home he was given permission to accept it. "It is our parting testimony," declared the Synod of South Carolina, "that he has nobly filled every department of duty and labor in which he has been engaged with us. Long and affectionately shall we remember the energy and efficiency with which he has accomplished his full orbed ministry among ourselves."

Dr. Palmer was just thirty-eight years of age in December, 1856, when he began his long term of service as pastor in New Orleans. He was of about medium stature and slender in frame, but the piercing eye and the firm jaw indicated the man of power. The congregation whereof he became shepherd had been first organized in 1823 as we have seen as the result of the preaching of Sylvester Larned. The three early pastors of the First Church were Dr. Joel Parker, Dr. John Breckinridge and Dr. William A. Scott. The roll of members had become large, and at this time these were actively engaged in erecting a new house of worship. In 1857, therefore, Dr. Palmer and his people formally set apart unto God's service the present handsome structure on Lafayette Square. The dedicatory sermon was the same that he had delivered four years before in setting apart the church in Columbia, South Carolina.

When Dr. Palmer thus entered New Orleans as a spiritual shepherd, that city had already become the business center of the lower Mississippi Valley. She was, moreover, one of the great exporting ports of the world. His voice, therefore, reached the ears of a vast

multitude that was constantly moving through this place
of traffic. His own flock grew in numbers and in activity, and thus his influence was spread abroad throughout
the city. By reason, therefore, of his position in a great
business center, his matchless powers as a preacher
were used of God in moulding the character of a large
part of the people of the southwestern part of our
country. Throughout a long period his church was
crowded every Sunday with as many as two thousand
listeners. These always sat with the attention fixed
upon the speaker, drinking in every word that fell from
his lips, and in many cases going forth from the sanctuary to put into practice the duties that this prince of
preachers had laid upon their hearts. When yellow
fever came to the city in the summer of 1858, and nearly
five thousand people were swept away by the pestilence,
Dr. Palmer went in and out among those that were
afflicted. Wherever he saw a sign displayed, showing
that the fever was within the house, he entered, offered
prayer, spoke a word of good cheer to the sick and then
continued on his way. "It was thus," said a Jewish
rabbi, "that Palmer got the heart as well as the ear of
New Orleans. Men could not resist one who gave himself to such ministry as this."

Dr. Palmer identified himself with his people in every
relationship of life. Their welfare was his chief concern. He strove to set before them their duty both
with respect to man and with reference to God. First
of all, however, he sought to practice the precepts which
he preached. When pestilence came in the form of
fever, Dr. Palmer held it to be his duty to enter every
home that was threatened with death. His leadership
thus became a part of their lives to such extent that in
the presence of any crisis it seemed natural to him and
to them that he should point out the way. When,
therefore, the discussion about slavery between the
Northern and Southern sections of our country finally

reached the stage of angry contention, the people of
New Orleans instinctively turned to Dr. Palmer for help
and guidance. It was characteristic of this prince
among men that he was always ready to help and to lead.
He was ready now in the autumn of 1860 to set forth
his views concerning the vital issue of the hour. He
had made a careful study of all the facts and all the
moral and legal principles involved in the great sectional debate and he did not fail to respond to the
expectation of the people of the Southwest. On Thursday, November 29, 1860, therefore, a great multitude
of people came together in Dr. Palmer's church, crowding it from floor to gallery, to hear what counsel he
might be prepared to offer to New Orleans and Louisiana. It was Thanksgiving Day, and a solemn stillness
reigned in the vast auditorium when the speaker arose
to face the audience. His discourse was written and,
contrary to his usual custom, he read it—read it calmly
and slowly, without the use of a gesture during the hour
of its delivery.

"At a juncture so solemn as the present," said Dr.
Palmer, "with the destiny of a great people waiting
upon the decision of an hour, it is not lawful to be still.
Whoever may have influence to shape public opinion, at
such a time must lend it, or prove faithless to a trust.
The question, too, which now places us upon the brink
of revolution was in its origin a question of morals and
religion. It was debated in ecclesiastical councils before it entered legislative halls. It has riven asunder
the two largest religious communions [Methodists and
Baptists] in the land, and the right determination of
this primary question will go far toward fixing the attitude we must assume in the coming struggle. It is my
purpose, not as your organ, but on my sole responsibility, to state the duty which, as I believe, patriotism and
religion require of us all." Having thus asserted his
right to speak upon a subject that had been for years

a topic of discussion in church courts, Dr. Palmer proceeded to elaborate his theme, which was that the promotion of the welfare of the negro slaves was the solemn trust that had been "providentially committed" to the people of the South. This could be done, he claimed, only through the maintenance, for the present, of the existing relationship of master and servant. He did not consider it necessary to deal with the question whether this relationship is "precisely the best," nor was he prepared to "affirm that it will subsist through all time." Emancipation might come in the future and the burden of training the negro thus lifted from the white race. A burden it is, he asserts, an "intricate social problem" which none but the white people of the South are competent to solve. The latter, moreover, are the only true friends of the negro. In their present state of development the best interests of the colored man will be most successfully maintained only through the conservation of the existing relationship between the races in the South. "All that we claim for them, for ourselves," said Dr. Palmer, "is liberty to work out this problem, guided by nature and God, without obtrusive interference from abroad."

To sustain his claim that the African slave and his proper training and development constituted a solemn trust committed to the South, Dr. Palmer presented a series of arguments to the following effect:

That the greatest need of the African is the discipline to which he is subjected by his white master. "By nature the most affectionate and loyal of all races beneath the sun," said Dr. Palmer, "they are also the most helpless; and no calamity can befall them greater than the loss of that protection they enjoy under this patriarchal system." "My servant," he continued, "whether born in my house or bought with my money, stands to me in the relation of a child. Though providentially owing me service, which, providentially, I am bound to exact,

he is, nevertheless, my brother and my friend, and I am
to him a guardian and a father.   He leans upon me for
protection, for counsel and for blessing; and so long as
the relation continues, no power but the power of
Almighty God shall come between him and me.   Were
there no argument but this, it binds upon us the providential duty of preserving the relation that we may save
him from a doom worse than death."

Dr. Palmer argued further that if the slaves were at
once set free, "the wisdom of the entire world, united in
solemn council, could not solve the question of their
disposal."   It would be "refined cruelty," he said, to
attempt to transport them to Africa, for in that land
they would starve; nor would they be able to hold their
own in our own American land if they should try to live
here as free men in the presence of the Anglo-Saxon.
From this fundamental viewpoint that the welfare of
the negro himself could be promoted only by maintaining the existing patriarchal system, Dr. Palmer proceeded further to argue that the interests of the white
people of the South, both material and religious, were
also vitally connected with the continuance for the
present of the same institution.   To render the negro's
condition worse than that of sheep without a shepherd, and then to bring the Southern shepherds into a
state of vassalage under control of the North, this would
mean the utter ruin of the South.   The movement that
demanded this unwise course of immediate emancipation,
the abolitionist crusade, was due, said Dr. Palmer, to
ignorance and fanaticism, and ought to be resisted.   This
movement had already, he said, broken "the union of
our forefathers."   The organization of a new and
homogeneous Confederacy of States in the South was
the only method open, he declared, for preserving the
principles that formed the original basis of that old
union.   The formation of such a Southern Confederacy
had become the duty of the hour, since only in this way

could the Southern people maintain the solemn trust laid upon them. "This trust," he said, "we will discharge in the face of the worst possible peril."

It must be remembered that Dr. Palmer held in mind the origin of the great body of the Southern people as descendants of worthy ancestors; that for the most part the Southerners were Bible readers—men and women who feared God and had a keen sense of right and justice; that their social and political fabric was organized in the best possible way to promote the present welfare of both the negro and the white man. The overthrow of that existing fabric he regarded as a fearful calamity, not only for the South, but for the entire country. Therefore it was clear to his mind that religion and patriotism demanded resistance to the wild fanaticism of the abolitionists who were seeking to make a wreck of the best civilization on the earth—that of the Southern States.

Dr. Palmer's address was circulated widely throughout the country and was accepted as giving expression to the practically universal sentiment of the people of the South that force must be met with force. In May, 1861, Dr. Palmer preached a special sermon to a company of Confederate riflemen who were then setting forth for the battlefield. He told them that the war forced upon them by Northern aggression was for the South a war of defense. To the Washington Artillery organized in New Orleans he declared that the war was "for your homes and your firesides—for your wives and children—for the land which the Lord has given us as a heritage."

After the adoption of the Spring resolutions by the Presbyterian Assembly at Philadelphia in May, 1861, Dr. Palmer bore a leading part in withdrawing the Southern presbyteries from their former connection with the Northern presbyteries. On December 4, 1861, he was present in Augusta, Georgia, as a delegate, and there delivered the sermon that constituted the beginning of the work of the Southern Presbyterian Assembly. Early in the year 1862 he left New Orleans for a time and joined the Confederate army under Albert Sidney Johnston. We are told that he made a stirring address to a portion of the Confederate forces as they were on the point of entering the battle of Shiloh. Soon after this battle, Dr. Palmer spoke to a large assemblage of citizens in the State House at Jackson, Mississippi. "It was a most profound, philosophical and exhaustive exposition of the grounds of our defense in the great struggle. It was designed to present the argument upon which the Christian moralist and patriot may rely and upon which we may justify the position assumed by the seceded states. As his vast audience hung entranced, they knew not which most to admire, the charm of classic imagery, the rich and glowing eloquence, the grand and massive proportions of the argument, which challenged conviction and defied criticism, or the catholic spirit of the Christian patriot who confides in the justice of his cause and the justice of his God."

On September 17, 1862, in Columbia, South Carolina, Dr. Palmer delivered an address in commemoration of the life and work of Dr. Thornwell. To this revered friend, who had recently died, Dr. Palmer referred as "Our Chrysostom," he of the "Golden Mouth," who was moreover "so brave, so generous and true that admiration of his genius was lost in affection for the man, and the breath of envy never withered a single leaf of all the honors with which a single generation crowned him." On December 20, 1862, Dr. Palmer also delivered a sympathetic address over the body of General Maxcy Gregg, leader of a South Carolina brigade, who had fallen in the hour of victory on the battlefield of Fredericksburg, in Virginia.

During the winter of 1862-1863, Dr. Palmer occupied the chair of Systematic Theology in Columbia Seminary, left vacant by the death of Dr. Thornwell. In May, 1863, Palmer wrote in honor of the memory of Stonewall Jackson the tribute adopted by the Southern Assembly. Then, under authority given by the assembly, he went as commissioner to the Army of Tennessee and for several months he was in camp preaching the gospel to Confederate soldiers. To soothe with words of hope and comfort the last hours of one of his daughters, Dr. Palmer came again to Columbia in the late summer. Again during the two succeeding sessions he taught theology in the seminary, and the early days of 1865 found him in Columbia preaching and teaching. When Sherman's army drew near, Dr. Palmer marched away with the Confederate soldiers. A month later he returned to find the once fair city in ashes and his books and household effects all destroyed. Then the work of Dr. Palmer's life was at once revealed to him in its fullness. This was to heal the sorrow of his people by pouring out the balm of his sympathy; by describing with matchless power the blessings that form the eternal inheritance of God's children.

On Sunday, July 16, 1865, Dr. Palmer stood once more in his own pulpit in New Orleans. He had come at the earliest possible moment to share with his flock the trials through which they were now to pass. He was full of hope. His voice rang out as of old to encourage the members of his congregation to meet their duties with faith and courage. In 1867, when the yellow fever came again to New Orleans, Dr. Palmer forgot the danger that threatened himself and went everywhere to comfort those who were dying of the dread disease. As to his own land, the South, he said: "How dear she is to us now that she sits a desolate widow upon the ashes of what was once her home. All scarred and battered as she is, with the cruel furrows of war traced all over her broad bosom, I would not exchange her for the brightest and wealthiest land upon which the sun shines.

Affliction makes her surprisingly beautiful, and I cling to her in her tears as I never did in the days of her laughter and pride." With reference to the Confederate soldiers, he declared that they had "stood for truth, for honor and for right, till truth and right were trampled together in the dust."

The entire South seemed now to become, in a measure, Dr. Palmer's field of labor. Urgent invitations called him to many different cities to deliver sermons and addresses. Men seemed to be held fast under some strange spell when he spoke. In New York City, in Dr. Van Dyke's church, his message was accompanied with such power that an old Federal soldier who heard him said, "The arch rebel! He preaches like an archangel!" In Charleston, the congregation that listened to him was eager to hear more even after he had preached for the space of one hour and twenty minutes.

On public occasions of great moment, men instinctively turned to him to give expression to the sentiments that filled their hearts. Soon after the death of General Robert E. Lee, in October, 1870, a great throng came together in the St. Charles Theater, New Orleans, and there Dr. Palmer delivered a striking eulogium upon the character of the Confederate leader. In June, 1872, he delivered at Washington and Lee University, Virginia, an address upon the duty of the Southern people in the "present crisis" after the overthrow of the Confederacy. The peril which he dreaded, said the speaker, was, that in the struggle for wealth, "the fine sense of honor which formed the beautiful enamel of Southern character may be rubbed away." "The patriotism which these days demand must suffer as well as act," he continued. "Strong in the consciousness of rectitude, it must nerve itself to endure contradiction and scorn. If need be, it must weep at the burial of civil liberty, and wait with the heroism of hope for its certain resurrection."

On Thursday evening, June 25, 1891, a large body of men and women met together in the Grand Opera House in New Orleans to protest against the continuance of the system known as the Louisiana lottery. Dr. Palmer, the principal speaker of the occasion, was introduced to the audience as "the first citizen of New Orleans." For a long period before this time he had been using his pen in the work of setting forth the iniquities of the lottery, an institution that had been chartered by the negro legislature of 1868, and thus for more than twenty years had been a source of great evil throughout the country. He was ready, therefore, to lay bare the nature of the scheme. With fiery words he denounced the lottery as a menace to the very life of the commonwealth. "There is but one issue before this people," he declared, "and I announce it without hesitation upon this platform: Either the lottery must go or Louisiana is lost." As he proceeded to point out the crimes of the lottery system, the applause of the audience gave clear indication of the state of public opinion in New Orleans and in the state. Through the persuasions of Dr. Palmer and other leaders the people did very speedily destroy the iniquitous institution.

On May 30, 1900, Dr. Palmer made an address to the Confederate Veterans on the occasion of their annual reunion at Louisville, Kentucky. "Accustomed through sixty years to address public assemblies," he began, "I am nevertheless subdued with awe in your presence today; for we stand together under the shadow of the past. It is the solemn reverence one might feel in the gloom of Westminster Abbey, surrounded by England's illustrious dead. Indeed, we are here the living representatives of countless comrades who sleep in cemeteries throughout the land * * * martyrs who fell in the defense of country and of truth. * * *

"Fellow citizens, it is simply folly to suppose that such a spontaneous uprising as that of our people in

1860 and 1861 could be effected through the machina-
tions of politicians alone. A movement so sudden and
so vast, instantly swallowing up all minor contentions,
would only spring from great faith deeply planted in
the human heart and for which men are willing to die."

Examples drawn out of the history of the past came
into Dr. Palmer's mind, and he spoke of many of them—
spoke of peoples who had struggled to maintain the
right and had been defeated. And, yet, those who had
boldly fought to uphold truth and honor and had failed
in the struggle had not been in later times called crimi-
nals. The story of the ancient Athenians and their
vain struggle against the invader, Philip of Macedon,
was portrayed by Dr. Palmer as perhaps the most
striking parallel in connection with the failure of the
Southern Confederacy. The men of Athens fought for
home and country, but the invader overthrew them in
battle. Was it worth while to make the fight? Were
the men of Athens wise in offering resistance to Philip?
Yes, replied Demosthenes, speaking in that voice that
stirred men as if it were a trumpet that called them.
They were wise. The disasters that had come upon
Greece, said Demosthenes, in no manner affected the
question of the wisdom and righteousness of the policy
of resistance against Philip. The men of Athens had
at least performed their duty; they had acted like men
who placed a right value upon the freedom inherited
from their fathers. Their policy of daring everything
in behalf of liberty had left behind it no sting of
humiliation to be added to the pain of defeat. Quoting
Demosthenes to this effect, Dr. Palmer placed by the
side of the patriotic Athenians the people of his own land
of the South. The latter had been overthrown, it was
true, he said, but only in the attempt to do their duty.
With the suffering involved in defeat no disgrace could
be mingled. They ought to have entered into the war
to defend their liberties, even if they had known in ad-

vance that the struggle would end in failure. "We of
the South," declared Dr. Palmer, "convinced of the
rightfulness of our cause, can accept defeat without the
blush of shame mantling the cheek of a single Confederate of us all; and while accepting the issue of the
war as the decree of destiny openly appeal to the
verdict of posterity for the final vindication of our
career."

With both voice and pen, Dr. Palmer made vigorous
opposition to the reunion of the Northern and Southern
Presbyterian Churches. This issue was brought forward in May, 1870, when the Southern Assembly met
in Louisville, Kentucky. Dr. R. L. Dabney as moderator appointed Dr. Palmer chairman of the Committee
on Foreign Correspondence, and to the latter was referred the overture from the Northern Church asking
that the difficulties in the way of closer relations be
considered by committees from the two bodies. The
attitude of the Southern Church toward this proposition
is set forth in the pastoral letter sent out to the various
congregations by the assembly in session at Louisville.
This letter, written by Dr. Palmer, was to the effect that
the Southern Assembly in response to the request of the
Northern Assembly had appointed a conference committee. But, continued the pastoral letter, "the overture from the Northern Assembly was based upon the
fatal assumption that mutual grievances existed, in
reference to which it became necessary to arbitrate.
This presumption is precisely what we cannot truthfully
concede. Our records may be searched in vain for a
single act of aggression, or a single unfriendly declaration against the Northern Church. We have assumed
no attitude of hostility toward it. In not a single case has
there been an attempt to wrest from them their church
property. In not a single case has there been hesitation in receiving their members into our communion
upon the face of their credentials among the hundreds

who have come to make their home with us since the war. In not one instance has there been exhibited a spirit of retaliation in regard to any of those very measures instituted against ourselves by the Assembly of 1865 and by subsequent assemblies.

"Whatever obstructions may be in the way of ecclesiastical fellowship were not created by us, and we could not allow ourselves to be placed in the false position before the world of parties who had been guilty of wrong to the Northern Church. Having placed nothing in the way of Christian fraternity, there was nothing for us to remove. Whilst, therefore, in Christian courtesy we were willing to appoint a committee of conference, it was necessary to guard against all misconstruction and misrepresentation by instructing our commissioners. * * * Inasmuch as we had never been aggressors against the peace, security and prosperity of the Northern Church, Christian candor required us as the party approached to state exactly the difficulties which did embarrass this question of correspondence."

The difficulties thus referred to, said Dr. Palmer, were four in number as follows:

(1) That in 1861 the Northern majority changed the Presbyterian Church into a political organization and that this policy had since been continued. On the other hand, the Southern Assembly, thus forced out, had been organized upon the principle that the church is nonpolitical.

(2) That the method pursued in uniting Old School and New School Presbyterians of the North (1869) had made the Northern Church "a broad church, giving shelter to every creed."

(3) That the action of the Northern Assembly with reference to the Synods of Kentucky and Missouri was revolutionary, overthrowing the Presbyterian system of church government, since the assembly had practically

obliterated the lower church courts and had assumed for itself an authority never before assigned to it.

(4) That the Northern Church, through formal resolutions of its assembly, had made "judicial accusations" extending even to charges of heresy and blasphemy against the Southern Church and that these had never been withdrawn.

The views thus elaborated by Dr. Palmer and adopted by the Assembly of 1870 were put forward by him as long as he lived as representing his matured convictions.

But was Dr. Palmer broad and liberal in his views? According to the testimony of some who did not agree with all of the opinions that he held, he was most liberal. "He was a man who had outspoken convictions which he never concealed, knowing neither policy nor advantage in warring against what he considered wrong. Yet this outspoken man was revered and loved by all sects, for his heart was rich with a love that swept away every barrier; his genial smile knew no sectarian bounds. * * * He was across all religious barriers, the minister of all of us." These words about Dr. Palmer were written by a leading Jewish rabbi of the city of New Orleans. He won the affection of the Jewish people, not only by his ministrations among them when yellow fever was doing its deadly work, but by his open sympathy at a time when their racial troubles were grievous. In 1882 a great assembly of citizens in New Orleans gave voice to their protest against the persecution of Jews by the Russians. Dr. Palmer, one of the speakers at the public meeting, won the hearts of the Jews by pouring out his feeling of indignation upon their enemies. "Whenever persecution bursts upon the Jew," he said, "there would I be at his side, an Hebrew of the Hebrews, to suffer and to do."

In this brief sketch little more than the titles of some of Dr. Palmer's publications can be given. The Life and Letters of Dr. Thornwell kept him busy throughout a long period; the volume appeared in 1876. "In this case my heart held the pen," said Dr. Palmer with reference to this biography. The book itself reveals his own masterly skill in drawing the portrait of the man whom he admired and loved. "The Theology of Prayer," "The Threefold Fellowship," "The Family in Its Civil and Churchly Aspects," "The Formation of Character," —these four volumes represent Dr. Palmer's formal treatment of certain practical themes. It is all work well done. His insight into the meaning of the Scriptures, and the wide range of his experience, fitted him to deal with these subjects in the most illuminating way. "The Broken Home" is a book whose story is drawn out of Dr. Palmer's own heart and life. Four of his daughters, one after another, were called away from the home on earth; his only son, also, was taken away in early childhood; their mother, the wife of his bosom, followed them. During the time when these severe blows were falling upon him, Dr. Palmer was also called to mourn the death of his own mother. A nature so full of affection as Dr. Palmer's was moved to its uttermost depths by these bereavements. He sought to put into words his own tender love for those whom God had summoned by writing a sketch of each. He told how suffering was borne with quiet fortitude and how the heavenly messenger was met in each case with no shadow of doubt resting upon the hope in Christ. And then he told in this same book the story of the merging of his own agony into that enlarged hope which God bestows upon believers through the agency of discipline. "The earthly lights are put out," he declares, "that no earthly love may come in between Him and us." Then, changing the figure, he tells us that God strings the harp to a greater tension here, "that the praise may hereafter rise to its higher and sweeter notes before the throne when we shall carry the memories of earth to heaven and pour them into songs forever." With this tone of lofty assurance maintained throughout, "The Broken Home" takes its place among the foremost books in all that literature whose purpose is to bring the message of comfort unto hearts acquainted with grief.

The ministry of consolation was the work for which Dr. Palmer seemed to have a special commission from his Lord. In public discourses he often led his hearers into the very heavens and then, with words of matchless power, seemed to place them in full possession of the glories of that inheritance which is held in reserve for God's people. In his personal work as shepherd of his own flock, he was continually pouring the oil of rejoicing upon souls that had been wounded. And, then, through the agency of written messages, the personal letters that were continually forged by his pen, he communicated to a multitude of friends some share of his own steadfast hope. Dr. Palmer's letters reveal to us the great heart of the man himself. Many of these epistles are given in the biography of Dr. Palmer prepared by Dr. Thomas Cary Johnson. To one friend Dr. Palmer wrote about his own sorrow as "the discipline of love, having its fruit in what is to be;" then he called that sorrow a cloud which a gracious Father was filling "with Himself—and covering me in it takes me into His pavilion; in this dark cloud I know better what it is to be alone with Him. It is the old experience of love breaking through the darkness as it did long ago through the terrors of Sinai and the more appalling gloom of Calvary." To another friend he wrote concerning the last hours of one of his own daughters that the "thin, wan face was radiant like that of Stephen." He wrote again, "It teaches me whole volumes of theology—these tender, timid girls treading upon the fears of death and the solemnities of the tomb as if they were roses strewn upon their bridal path. I never knew before how strong

grace is, nor how easy it is for faith to walk upon the
sea. My dead children have been my teachers, and I
bow with awe before them."

To his own father, on the latter's ninetieth birthday,
Dr. Palmer wrote, "How near you are to immortal
youth! And what a clear, bright day has your life
been on the earth, a whole burnt-offering of service and
of sacrifice to God and to man. * * * Death will
touch you with its gentle sleep and its terrors be lost in
the translation to the home of the redeemed." After
passing his own seventy-first birthday a serious infirmity kept Dr. Palmer for several weeks in severe
physical pain. "I recognize the first blow of the batter-
ing-ram which is to demolish the earthly tabernacle.
So be it; I shall soon be at rest, and bow with my beloved one before the throne."

In spite of infirmities, however, he moved steadily
onward to the completion of his work. Throughout his
entire career in New Orleans calls were coming from
churches and theological seminaries and universities,
asking him to take up elsewhere the work of preaching
and of teaching; but he remained to the end with his
own beloved people on the lower Mississippi. To the
last his voice continued to ring out like a trumpet, speaking his Master's message.

On May 5, 1902, he received the injury from the
street car. Then followed the days of suffering, borne
as became a child of God until the afternoon of May 25,
when he was permitted to pass beyond the veil to bow
there before the throne in company with his beloved.

"He is the last of the great philosophic preachers
who justified the ways of God to men," writes Dr. W.
McF. Alexander, fellow-pastor with Dr. Palmer in New
Orleans. "He never spoke without laying deep as a
foundation of his discourse some great principle of
eternal truth. He belonged to the Henry Clay and
Webster class of orators, that class which seems to be

passing away. There was never but one Dr. Palmer and the mould is broken. There will be no other."

"His eloquence was not a mere outpouring of well-chosen words arranged in pleasing phrases. It was in the flood of ideas, always expressed in the most fitting words, moving the heart at one moment, or convincing the understanding at another, that his wonderful oratory excelled." Thus wrote the editor of the New Orleans *Picayune.*

Dr. Eugene Daniel, himself a leader among Southern Presbyterians, knew well the mind and heart of Dr. Palmer. Speaking of the latter's marvelous power as a preacher of the gospel, Dr. Daniel says, "By nature, by God's grace, by his own experience, he was made with a soul to feel another's woe. His power of pathos—for that is what it was, power—was plainly never sought by him nor cultivated by him; it was just naturally and simply within him, and the ease with which he wielded it was nothing less than majestic."

CHAPTER XLVIII.

ROBERT LEWIS DABNEY.

ROBERT L. DABNEY was born in the year 1820 on
the South Anna River, in Louisa County, Virginia.
His lines of family descent were English, Huguenot and
Scotch. His father was a planter and a member of the
county court, and in the modest country home the child,
Robert, received his first lessons in piety and in industry.
Soon after attaining the age of seven years he began
the study of Latin in a school-house built of logs near
his father's house. The teacher was his oldest brother,
Charles William Dabney. The study of Greek was
begun in another log building soon after he entered the
twelfth year of his age. These studies were continued
until the end of the year 1835; then a few months of
special training in algebra and geometry, under the care
of Rev. James Wharey, a Presbyterian minister, made
young Robert ready for the sophomore class in Hampden-Sidney College. Three years before this time his
father died, leaving the son the heritage of an honest
name and a godly example.

From June, 1836, until September, 1837, he was pursuing the course of study at Hampden-Sidney. Rapid
progress marked his career in the college, but the lack of
money held him back from completing the course. The
regular session ended there in the month of September,
and he carried home at the close of his collegiate work
the affection of his classmates and also a deep religious
impression. This had come to him in connection with
a spiritual revival that visited the school. One Sunday,
therefore, in the autumn of 1837, young Robert was

received into Providence Presbyterian Church in Louisa County.

Young Dabney now went to work on the plantation, for his widowed mother needed help. Some negro slaves belonged to the estate left by his father, but these were unable to carry all the burdens connected with farming operations. Moreover, the old mill that made flour and meal for the people of the community, forming a part of his mother's property, must be rebuilt. The tall, slender lad, not yet eighteen years of age, went into the rock quarry and with his own hands helped to give shape to the stones that were needed for the walls of the mill. A few months in the winter were given to the work of teaching school near his mother's home. Then the fields called him again and he set out to follow the plow. Through the long summer days of 1838 and 1839 he was in the cornfields and wheatfields, toiling steadily with his own hands. Another term of school teaching in the autumn of 1839 brought him to the day when he left his mother's home once more and entered the University of Virginia. His course of study in the languages embraced French and Italian as well as Latin and Greek. Three sessions of close application brought him to the happy hour when he received the university degree of Master of Arts (1842.)

From midsummer in the year 1842 until the autumn of 1844 young Dabney was engaged at home, managing his mother's farm, teaching school and writing articles for the Richmond papers. So high an estimate was placed upon his capacity as a writer that an editorial position of considerable importance was offered him. But in November, 1844, he entered Union Seminary at Hampden-Sidney and began his theological studies as a candidate for the ministry. Systematic theology was at that time taught in the seminary by Dr. Samuel B. Wilson, church history by Dr. S. L. Graham, and Oriental languages by Dr. Francis S. Sampson. The latter was

possessed of an exceedingly accurate scholarship and he
made a lasting impression upon young Dabney's mind.
Among the students then at the seminary, with whom
Robert Dabney was associated also in his later years,
were William T. Richardson, Jacob Henry Smith and
Clement R. Vaughan. Dabney completed the course of
study in May, 1846. Then bearing with him a preacher's
license issued by West Hanover Presbytery, he went
back to Louisa County and began to preach the gospel
in his old home church, Providence. Long continued
toil in study, with only brief periods of recreation, had
impaired his health, but with strong determination he
kept up the work of preaching and pastoral visitation.
About one year later he was invited to become shepherd
of the flock at Tinkling Spring Church in Augusta
County, Virginia. He was pastor there from July,
1847, until August, 1853. Under his leadership the
present house of worship was built by that congregation.
In the pulpit he sought to instruct the people by setting
forth in order the teachings of the Word. He built a
home near the church and brought into it as his wife
the daughter of James Morrison, pastor of New Providence. The house was of stone and the young preacher
helped to build it with his own hands. During a part of
the period of his pastorate at Tinkling Spring he conducted a classical school near the church. In August,
1853, however, he accepted the call of the Union Seminary trustees and returned to Hampden-Sidney to take
the chair left vacant by the death of Dr. Graham. For a
period of six years with growing success he taught the
subjects of church history and church government. In
addition to this he was active in securing an endowment
and an increased number of students for the seminary.
His pen was now increasingly busy. Articles for the
church papers and for the secular papers, prepared with
great care, drew attention to him as a man of marked
capacity.

In 1859 Dr. Dabney began his long career as teacher of systematic theology. Dr. Wilson, former occupant of that chair, was now so far advanced in years that he was assigned a lighter task. A year later Thomas E. Peck, that prince among teachers, became a member of the seminary faculty and was placed in charge of the department of history. Benjamin M. Smith had been previously appointed successor to Dr. Sampson in the department of ancient languages. Dr. Dabney now entered with enthusiasm into that field of work for which he was most admirably fitted. The native vigor of his intellect had been reinforced by the severe mental discipline through which years of study had led him. His scholarship was full and accurate. Clearness in thought enabled him to manifest an unrivalled clearness of expression. He was soon to become one of the most efficient expounders of the Calvinistic system of theology that our country has ever known.

In addition to the work of teaching he assumed also the duty of regular preaching. Nearly every Sunday in the College Church at Hampden-Sidney he occupied the pulpit. Pastoral labors also engaged him, and his pen was turning out strong, timely articles for the church periodicals. A new house of worship was built at Hampden-Sidney, and he was in personal superintendence of the work. In 1860 the chair of church history in Princeton Seminary was offered him, but he saw his place of duty in Virginia. A great variety of tasks in connection with the promotion of the seminary's interests were set before him, and he labored zealously to complete all of them.

When the skies of his country began to grow dark with war clouds, Dr. Dabney sought to maintain peace. "A Pacific Appeal to Christians" was issued by him in January, 1861. Again and again he preached in favor of preserving a state of peace. His efforts did not check the aggressions of the abolitionists, and when

President Lincoln called for volunteers to aid in an invasion of the cotton-growing states, Dr. Dabney, like virtually all other Virginians, was at once ready to oppose the Federal administration with arms.

In the early summer of 1861, Dr. Dabney went to Manassas, Virginia, and began his labors as chaplain of a Confederate regiment, the Eighteenth Virginia. His first pulpit in the camp was a wooden box upon which he stood to speak to the soldiers. Some of these were seated on logs, some on camp-stools, some upon the ground, while others stood up throughout the service. When the minister stretched forth his hands in prayer, "instantly every head is reverently uncovered," wrote Dr. Dabney. "Then follows an old, familiar Psalm. There are no strains of woman's sweeter melody to mingle with the stern melody of the men, but the wind sighing through the pine trees around us is the accompaniment, not unfitting, to the hundreds of manly voices which roll the hymn to the heavens. Then follows the sermon, short and informal, but swallowed with solemn and eager faces."

"It has been customary," he wrote further, "to speak of camps as schools of temptation and evil. And there is too much in them to pain the Christian's heart and to try the graces. But our camps are places of much prayer and afford many shining examples of Christian consistency. * * * Let Christians arise and conquer in this war by the power of prayer."

Dr. Dabney remained in camp with the Confederate army during the weeks that followed the first battle of Manassas. He preached regularly and with gratifying effect. Many were persuaded by his sermons to become Christians. A frequent attendant at the services conducted by him at this time was General Jackson, already known to the army and the country as "Stonewall" Jackson. A friendship began here between these two men that became more intimate a few months later.

A fever seized upon Dr. Dabney in the military camp
and he returned to his home at Hampden-Sidney. The
wrestle with the fever continued through the principal
part of the winter. Moreover, the death of a beloved
sister was a most severe blow to him. As often as possible he attended the class-room and taught the small
body of students that remained at the seminary during
this period. Mrs. Jackson came to Hampden-Sidney
to become a guest in Dr. Dabney's home, and through
her agency a close relationship was established between
the preacher and the great soldier. On April 8, 1862,
General Jackson wrote to Dr. Dabney, offering him the
position of adjutant, or chief of his staff. "Your rank
will be that of major. Your duties will require early
rising and industry," wrote Jackson. To this he added,
"Your duties would be such that you would not have an
opportunity of preaching, except on the Sabbath."

Dr. Dabney had doubts about his own fitness for the
position. He rode to the Valley of Virginia to ask
Jackson to assign to him the work of a chaplain. But the
Confederate leader knew Dabney's qualities; he had
learned about his energy, his experience in managing
plantations and in directing the work of laborers in the
fields. He, therefore, made him chief staff-officer and at
once began to cummunicate all military orders through
Major Dabney. The latter's quickness of perception
and his retentive memory enabled him both to comprehend in a moment the meaning of the General's orders
and to deliver them in the exact form in which he had received them. He, therefore, played a worthy part in
Jackson's great Valley Campaign of April, May and
June, 1862. When each Sunday came, if the army was
not marching nor fighting, the chief of staff preached at
headquarters to a large assembly of soldiers, eager to
hear the words of comfort from the minister's lips.
Thus Dr. Dabney had a share in the work leading and
teaching Stonewall Jackson's army of Christians.

It was a hard service. There were periods of keen hunger from the lack of food. There was weariness from long marches, but Major Dabney was always by the side of his great leader as long as the Major's health was sufficient for the task. At the battle of Gaines' Mill, near Richmond, in June, 1862, although Major Dabney was suffering from an attack of sickness, his efficiency as staff-officer in carrying out Jackson's orders had much to do with winning the victory for the Confederates. Severe illness came upon him, however, and after July, 1862, he was never again able to serve with Jackson. "The most efficient officer" that he knew, was Jackson's expression of praise for the adjutant whom he gave up with great reluctance.

After Jackson's death, May 10, 1863, Dr. Dabney was requested by Mrs. Jackson to prepare a biography of her husband. He began at once the work of gathering together the literary material, and early in 1865 the book was published. The entire volume is a fine example of the author's clear, vigorous style of writing, and is a worthy tribute to the great Christian hero with whose life it deals. With clear insight the biographer lays bare the qualities of Jackson's heart and mind. He read the character of the Confederate leader far better than any other man was ever able to understand him, and he presents in bold outline every feature of that strong, lofty character. It may be questioned if any other officer in either army, Federal or Confederate, had so competent a biographer among fellow-officers or associates as Stonewall Jackson had in Dr. Dabney. The latter rendered his countrymen a great service in thus setting forth their hero's life and character. The biography itself seems likely to become one of the most enduring parts of Dr. Dabney's literary work.

In 1864 Dr. Dabney's strength was sufficiently restored to enable him to pay two or three visits to the Army of Northern Virginia as a preacher. The Confederate veterans who were making their last gallant stand against invasion listened eagerly to the minister's exhortations. In the same year he took a prominent part in bringing the New School Presbyterians of the South into organic union with his own Old School Assembly. Then, when the surrender of the Confederate army took place at Appomattox, and Federal bayonets became dominant in the South, the iron entered Dr. Dabney's soul. The elevation of the negro to the position of authority and control for which he had no fitness brought evil days to the South, and Dr. Dabney felt the keen agony of that period along with the rest of the white people. He did not, however, cease to work. During the summer of 1865 he toiled, day after day, as a laborer in the cornfield. The crop which he gathered in the autumn removed from him for the time the apprehension that his family would be without bread. Throughout the succeeding winter he taught a group of girls in his own home in connection with his regular work in the theological seminary. In 1866 some of the friends of the seminary, living in Baltimore, furnished the money necessary to continue the work of the school upon a more satisfactory basis.

Dr. Dabney's activities as teacher and writer became now more varied. His principal work was in the classroom, where the intensity of his convictions and the vigor and clearness with which he set forth the principles of the Reformed faith, made lasting impressions upon the young men who sat at his feet. A rare combination of scholarship, philosophical insight and the power of continuous thought gave Dr. Dabney a worthy place among the foremost theologians of our country.

Dr. Dabney continued to occupy until 1874 the position of pastor of the church at Hampden-Sidney. "There may have been others," writes Dr. P. P. Flournoy, "with oratorical gifts which he lacked, who were, for the average audience, more popular preachers; but as a preacher for preachers and educated thinkers of all professions, I think there can be no question that he stood without an equal."

In the church courts, Dr. Dabney played a leading part. He contended strenuously throughout his life against any approach toward an organic union of the Northern and Southern Churches. As moderator of the Southern Assembly at Louisville in 1870 he made a powerful plea in favor of the maintenance of the independent position of the Southern Presbyterians.

During these years, also, Dr. Dabney was busy with the pen. His *Life of Jackson* was followed by the *Defense of Virginia and the South*, which was given to the public immediately after the close of the war. In 1870 his lectures on the preparation and delivery of sermons were published under the title, *Sacred Rhetoric.* In 1871 the *Syllabus* of his class-room lectures on theology was issued in the form of a book. During subsequent years, however, these lectures were rewritten with many amplifications, and in 1878 were published again, constituting the only formal treatise on *Theology* that he ever gave to the public. This volume, filled as it is with the strong, clear presentation of lofty themes, is sufficient to give its author a place of honor among the foremost theological writers of our country.

Dr. Dabney's volume on *The Sensualistic Philosophy of the Nineteenth Century* (published in 1875) reveals him to us as a man of wide learning in the field of philosophy, of keen insight and strong reasoning powers. Articles in various periodicals upon similar themes, forming a great body of philosophical doctrine, give evidence of unwearied industry and of great intellectual ability. Many of these papers were afterwards gathered into a set of volumes entitled *Collected Discussions,* under the editorship of Dr. Dabney's lifelong friend, Dr. Clement R. Vaughan. In his later years (1896), Dr. Dabney published *Practical Philosophy,* a series of lectures concerned with the feelings, the will, ethical theories and applied ethics. We are told that he himself considered this volume the best book that he ever wrote.

In his written essays and in the addresses delivered in church synods and assemblies, Dr. Dabney sometimes used such vehemence that he seemed like a warrior fighting against principalities and powers. First of all, with marvelous clearness of statement, he would lay bare the weakness of theories that he held to be erroneous. Then, with all the energy of his strong nature, he would pour out the living fire of his wrath upon falsehood and wrong-doing. Men sometimes thought, therefore, that he was unduly stern and severe. Those who knew him well, however, tell us that his nature was filled with the spirit of kindness; that he extended a warm, personal sympathy toward all who sought help or instruction from him.

Dr. Dabney's labors were incessant. In order to make the burdens lighter, he resigned in 1874 the pastorate of the College Church at Hampden-Sidney. In 1880 he made a brief visit to Europe. His strength was now declining, however, and in 1883 his physician advised a warmer climate. For this reason he resigned the chair of theology at Union Seminary and took up the work connected with the chair of mental and moral philosophy and political economy in the new University of Texas, at Austin. For eleven years (1883-1894) Dr. Dabney taught in this school with signal ability and success. During this period his great name and fame were among the chief assets of the Texas University. In the year 1884, in connection with Dr. R. K. Smoot, pastor of the Presbyterian Church in that place, Dr. Dabney founded the Austin Theological Seminary. Teachers and pupils were alike few in number, but Dabney's *Systematic Theology*, taught by the great master himself, constituted an admirable training for

ministerial work. Serious illness, accompanied by a
total failure of eyesight, came upon Dr. Dabney, and
in 1894 he withdrew from the work of teaching in the
university.

In May, 1897, when the Southern Presbyterian
Assembly began its sessions at Charlotte, North Carolina, Dr. Dabney took his place among the members as
a delegate from Texas. The utmost deference was
shown to the great leader on the part of the other commissioners. Many of his former pupils were present
to express their personal affection and gratitude. A
series of addresses was delivered before the assembly in
commemoration of the work of the Westminster Assembly, and Dr. Dabney was led to the platform to inaugurate these special services with prayer. The activities
of former days seemed to fill the patriarch's memory,
for as he sat, apparently lost in meditation, he repeated
to himself the words of Isaiah, "We all do fade as a
leaf!" Then he stood up to plead for God's blessing
upon the assembly and upon the church. Who that
looked upon him there can forget the majestic figure,
the flowing locks? His mental force seemed unabated
when he took part afterwards in some of the debates of
the assembly. One of the series of Westminster addresses was prepared by him upon the subject of the
doctrinal contents of the Confession of Faith. As men
listened to the reading of the clear exposition, they were
convinced that Dr. Dabney's powers of analysis were as
strong as in the former days when he reigned supreme
in the class-room at Hampden-Sidney.

But the course was now almost finished. The months
that followed the Charlotte Assembly were marked by
the delivery of a number of sermons and a series of
lectures at Davidson College and Columbia Seminary.
During the autumn he made his way slowly homeward
to the town of Victoria, Texas. There, on January 3,
1898, after a few hours of acute suffering, the Master's

summons came and he answered the call with joy. "The blessed rest is here!" These were among his last words. Then, in accordance with his own wishes, his body was laid to rest beneath the shadow of the old church at Hampden-Sidney, in Virginia, within the same plot of ground that holds the ashes of John Holt Rice, George Addison Baxter, Samuel L. Graham, Samuel B. Wilson, Benjamin M. Smith, James F. Latimer and Thomas E. Peck.

"No church on this continent," said Moses Drury Hoge, speaking of the Southern Presbyterians, "has been more favored of heaven than our own, in having at its very organization three such men as Thornwell, Palmer and Dabney, each fitted by splendid genius and profound scholarship—alike consecrated to the noblest uses—to give direction to its future life, and to enrich it for all time by their published contributions to theological science."

Dr. B. M. Palmer wrote of Dr. Dabney as "a pillar of strength in the house of our God. How we shall miss him, who leaned upon him for defense in the great battle for truth! He was mentally and morally constituted a great polemic, with a massive intellect capable of searching into the foundations of truth, and with an intellectual as well as moral indignation against every form of falsehood."

CHAPTER XLIX.

WITHIN a country home, in the eastern part of South Carolina, on March 25, 1809, John Leighton Wilson was born. His father, William Wilson, a planter, dwelt with his wife, Jane James, in a simple frame house beneath the shadow of long-leaf pine trees, near the headwaters of the Black River. Just seventy-five years before the birth of this child, the great-grandfather, Robert Wilson, in company with John Witherspoon and other Scots from North Ireland, entered the mouth of the Black River, and passing upstream (1734) built their log houses near the King's Tree in Williamsburg District. Another member of that group of early settlers was William James, a native of Wales, great-grandfather of Jane James, who was the mother of the subject of this sketch. The emigrant, William James, one of the original elders of the Williamsburg Church, married Elizabeth Witherspoon. The son of this couple, Major John James, an elder of the church at Indiantown, was that stalwart hero whom we have already seen as he rode by the side of General Francis Marion during the American Revolution. One of the sons of Major James was Captain John James, the gallant soldier, who also won for himself a share in the glory of Marion's victories. From these courageous men of war of the James family line, John Leighton Wilson inherited, through his mother, a stalwart physical frame, sound judgment and strenuous energy. "He was a Wilson in humility of soul, simplicity of life, loveliness of character, and consecration to the church,"

writes his biographer, Dr. Hampden C. DuBose; "but
it was the James blood coursing through his veins that
made him a Joshua to the Southern Church in her days
of poverty and desolation."

William Wilson, J. Leighton Wilson's father, was an
elder in Mount Zion Church, in the present Lee County,
South Carolina. Every Sunday, therefore, throughout
the period of childhood and youth, the subject of this
story took part, in association with the other members
of his family, in the solemn religious service held in the
old sanctuary that stood upon the site of the present
handsome brick church, still called Mount Zion. In the
home the child was trained in the knowledge of the
Bible and the catechisms, and in due time he took upon
himself the vows of church membership. He began his
studies in a log schoolhouse near his father's home and
continued them at the famous Zion School, in the town
of Winnsboro. In 1827 J. Leighton Wilson entered
the junior class at Union College, Schenectady, New
York. One of his fellow-students there was John B.
Adger of Charleston, South Carolina. In 1829 young
Wilson completed the course of study in the college and
returned home to spend the following winter under the
personal instruction of his mother's eldest brother,
Robert Wilson James. The latter was a preacher of
wide learning and great spiritual power, at that time
pastor of Salem Church, on Black River. The closing
months of the year 1830 were given by young Wilson
to the work of teaching at Mount Pleasant, near Charleston. During that period the preaching of the Presbyterian evangelist, Osborne, aroused within his heart a
sense of his obligation to render full service to the Lord.
Laying aside, therefore, the tasks of the schoolmaster,
he entered Columbia Seminary in January, 1831, as a
candidate for the ministry. A year later, as the result
of a spiritual awakening among the Columbia students
with reference to the needs of the heathen, young Wilson

made up his mind to become a worker in the foreign
field.   When a letter came to him from the American
Board of Foreign Missions announcing the probability
that an opportunity would be given to labor in Africa,
Wilson expressed his willingness to go.   "The people
are degraded enough," he wrote; "still they are our
brethren   *   *   *   and I am willing to labor, live and
die for them."

The desire to give the gospel to the people of Africa
was implanted in J. Leighton Wilson's heart during
his earlier years.   As a child he lived in daily association with the colored men and women on his father's
plantation.   Every Sunday morning he saw virtually
all of the negroes of the community assemble for worship in the grove of pine trees near Mount Zion Church.
He heard their hymns of praise, and often listened to
the words of the pastor of the church as he preached
the first sermon of the day to the slaves who lived within
the limits of the congregation.   When this service was
ended, then the negroes entered the seats reserved for
them in the deep galleries of the church and took part
in worship there in association with the white members
of the congregation.   Moreover, many of these negro
slaves were members in good standing, with their names
enrolled in the list of the regular membership of the
church.   On two Sundays in each year, therefore, all
of these colored members were brought into the body of
the church and given seats at the long communion tables,
and there the elements of the Lord's Supper were administered to them.   Besides all this, every Sunday
afternoon throughout the year the heads of the household called together all of their slaves, young and old,
and taught them portions of the Bible.   Sometimes,
also, the pastor of the church would preach to the colored
people every evening for an entire week.   One of the
ministers whose preaching to negroes was followed by
many of the signs of God's presence was Robert Wilson

James, the uncle of J. Leighton Wilson. We are told that the slaves often came in large numbers from the plantations on Black River to hear the pastor of Salem Church deliver the "simple, lucid, earnest" sermons which he prepared with great care for the benefit of the colored people. The zeal of this consecrated man of God, most probably, first kindled in young J. Leighton Wilson's soul the desire to give his life in behalf of the spiritual welfare of the colored race.

In the spring of 1833 young Wilson completed the course of study in Columbia Seminary. On Sunday, September 8, in that same year, Harmony Presbytery assembled in old Mount Zion Church to ordain the missionary. Robert W. James preached the sermon and Dr. George Howe delivered the charge in connection with the laying on of the hands of the presbytery. On that same afternoon Wilson preached in the grove near the church to the negroes of the congregation. After the sermon an old negro slave came up to the preacher and said that it was "in answer to his prayers" that this white missionary was going to Africa. Then the entire company of colored people present, "an immense number," pressed forward to shake hands with Mr. Wilson, showing their affection for him by much weeping and lamentation.

During the winter of 1833, J. Leighton Wilson made a preliminary voyage in a sail vessel to the western coast of Africa. Upon his return home, in May, 1834, he was united in marriage with Jane Elizabeth Bayard of Savannah, Georgia. The month of November found husband and wife upon the sea in full sail for Africa. Soon afterwards they were established in a house at Cape Palmas, near the southern border of the negro republic of Liberia, on the African coast, the first American missionaries sent to the Dark Continent. Within full view of their residence, near the seashore, were three towns occupied by savage tribes; near these dwelt a few emancipated negroes sent out from America as colonists.   In the dense jungles near the house of the missionaries lurked the germs of the African fever, and these at once assailed the Wilsons.   The wife was the first to recover her strength, and then for weeks she watched alone by the bedside of her husband as he raved in delirium, expecting that each hour would be his last.

A period of about eight years, from the beginning of 1834 until 1842, was spent by these two messengers of peace at Cape Palmas.   The language spoken on that coast, the Grebo dialect, had never been brought into written form.   Mr. Wilson, therefore, prepared a dictionary and a grammar of this rude tongue.   He also translated portions of the Bible.   Within a short space of time he was able to deliver his message with the spoken word, and then his personal work was multiplied.   A church building was erected and schools for boys and girls were established.   With his staff in his hand and accompanied only by colored helpers, Wilson made long journeys into the interior of Africa.   He also made voyages in sailing vessels for hundreds of miles along the coast to study the customs and characteristics of the native tribes.   Thus through perils by sea and in the jungles, perils from serpents and wild beasts and man-eating savages, he continued his work and organized a small congregation of believers.   There was lack of harmony, however, between the native negroes and the free negroes from America, and Mr. Wilson, who was looked upon by the natives "as a king," had to spend much of his time in maintaining peace between the two classes.   Moreover, the free negroes looked with great jealousy upon the influence exercised by Mr. Wilson over the natives, for the latter regarded the missionary as their chief friend and counsellor.   For these reasons it was not possible to make the Republic of Liberia, composed of emancipated negroes from America, the central station in a great missionary movement among the savages of Africa. In 1842, therefore, Wilson transferred his headquarters to a point farther south along the African coast, near the mouth of the Gaboon River. Here he was within a few miles of the equatorial line, and within the territory, north of the Congo River, claimed by France.

From 1842 until the early part of the year 1852, a period of ten years, the Wilsons prosecuted their work in the region near the Gaboon. The dialect of that coast, the Mpongwe, was reduced to writing; a dictionary and grammar were prepared; printing-presses were set up, and the natives were taught to read their own language. After a residence of only nine months on the Gaboon, Mr. Wilson began to preach to the people there in their own tongue. At six different stations along that coast he continued to deliver the gospel message and to train the children in schools. In addition to this regular work, he was making those observations which afterwards formed the basis of his History of Western Africa, a volume which still holds high rank as an authoritative account of the natural resources and the people of that part of the Southern Continent. He made valuable contributions to the annals of science concerning the birds, animals and serpents that dwell in the African forests. The culmination of his work as a man of science consisted in his discovery of the skeleton of a new species of ape hitherto unknown to civilized men. This skeleton, to which the missionary gave the name *gorilla*, was sent by him in 1846 to the Natural History Museum of Boston. Some years after Wilson's discovery of the skeleton, Paul du Chaillu, the famous African traveler, who had been a pupil of J. Leighton Wilson in the latter's home in the Gaboon country, met a living *gorilla* face to face in the jungle and published a description of the appearance of the man-like ape.

A notable service was rendered to mankind by J. Leighton Wilson during the period of his sojourn in

the country north of the Congo in connection with the
final suppression of the African slave traffic. During
his journeys along this coast he marked the coming and
the going of swift vessels bearing the flag of Portugal
or Spain. From the natives themselves he heard story
after story concerning the visits made by these ships to
the coast under cover of the darkness of the night, followed by the spreading of broad sails in the early morning, with cargoes of slaves borne away as freight to
Brazil. In the year 1850, therefore, Mr. Wilson wrote
in detail an account of what he had seen and heard, and
sent it to a friend in England. Lord Palmerston, Prime
Minister of England at that time, secured a copy of
Wilson's letter and had ten thousand copies printed and
spread broadcast in pamphlet form. The effect of J.
Leighton Wilson's disclosures was the sending of additional English war vessels of the fleetest type to the
western coast of Africa. A few months afterwards the
slave traders were forced to give up their business in
that part of the world.

In the summer of 1852, after a service of more than
eighteen years in Africa, the strength of the tropical
sun forced the Wilsons to seek to regain their health by
making a visit to the homeland. The following spring
(1853) found Dr. Wilson at the General Assembly in
Philadelphia. There the Presbyterian Board of Foreign Missions invited him to become one of their secretaries. He accepted the position, and in September
began the task of superintending the mission work of
his own church in foreign lands. The city of New
York became his place of residence, and there, with wisdom and energy, he labored successfully until his
departure to the South in 1861. During the time of
this sojourn in a Northern city, although the cloud of
war was lowering over the entire country, Dr. Wilson
won the friendship, we are told, of "the entire body of
the Presbyterian Church of New York."

In the autumn of the year, 1860, Dr. Wilson was in attendance at some of the synods in the South and Southwest. Throughout the regions which he visited he found among the people a "spirit of determined resistance" against the policy of the Republican party, and with this spirit he said that he was in warm sympathy. With reference to the conflict that had been in progress many years between the North and the South, his heart, he declared, had "always been with the South as the injured party." To Dr. Charles Hodge of Princeton, in December, 1860, Dr. Wilson wrote thus: "I desire and pray most earnestly for the preservation of the whole Union. If the North will concede what is just, and what the South imperatively needs, the Union may be saved. Otherwise, we go to pieces."

This attitude of sympathy with the South did not mean that he had no interest in the welfare of the negro. In the year 1833, he expressed his conviction that "every human being, who is capable of self-government and would be happier in a state of freedom, ought to be free. I am not, however, a friend of immediate and universal emancipation, for the simple reason that all negroes are not ready for freedom and would be worse off in that than in their present condition."

Dr. Wilson's wife inherited about thirty negro slaves. These were given their freedom, and, at the expense of several thousand dollars, drawn from Mrs. Wilson's estate, were sent as colonists to Liberia. In that negro republic they soon disappeared from Dr. Wilson's view and he was never able to trace them. It became, therefore, a lasting regret with him that these worthy colored people were sent to Africa to drift back again, no doubt, into the savage state. Two young negroes whom Dr. Wilson himself inherited were given their freedom and told to go whither they pleased. The freedom thus offered was refused and the two Africans remained in voluntary servitude on the plantation, asking for no other treatment than that which fell to the lot of the entire company of slaves at the home of Dr. Wilson's father.

In addition to the offering of freedom to his slaves, Dr. Wilson had spent his entire life, thus far, in striving to befriend the African in his native jungle, both in the work of checking the slave traffic and in that of giving the gospel to the tribes of the western coast. But when the issue was joined between the North and the South over the question of the immediate emancipation of the Southern serfs, Dr. Wilson entertained no shadow of doubt in his own mind as to the complete justice of the Southern cause. In spite of his years of association with the people of the North, he was heart and soul with the South. In January, 1861, when the news reached New York city that a South Carolina battery had fired upon the Federal vessel, *Star of the West*, as she was attempting to enter Charleston Harbor to strengthen Fort Sumter, and had forced the ship to withdraw from this act of hostility against the state of South Carolina, Dr. Wilson manifested the liveliest satisfaction to learn that the people of his native commonwealth were ready to fight for their inherited rights. His heart was filled with grief to see the tenacious purpose of a party in the North to urge on the war movement against the South. Nevertheless, he hesitated not a single moment with reference to his own course. "You see the great power and the tremendous forces of the North, their intense hatred of secession, and their fixed determination to crush the South if they do not yield to the Federal Government. I pray God to avert the storm and save us from the hands of civil war; but if it comes, my mind is made up; I will go and suffer with my people." There were tears in his eyes and a tremor in his voice as he spoke these words to Dr. J. J. Bullock in February, 1861. He sold his home in the city of New York at a financial loss, settled his accounts with the Foreign Mission Board with the most scrupulous exactness, and then in May, 1861, at Philadelphia, bade farewell to his brethren of the Northern Assembly. He came southward across the Potomac to identify himself with his own people, without a home and without the means of subsistence. He rented a small farm-house near the home of his youth in South Carolina, and then stood ready to give the remainder of his days to the Southern Church. "Our wisest man is gone out from us," said Dr. Charles Hodge of Princeton when Dr. Wilson returned from New York to South Carolina. It was this same great Princeton leader who said further that Dr. J. Leighton Wilson "was the wisest man in the Presbyterian Church and had more of the apostolic spirit than any one I ever knew."

Dr. Wilson was a man of sleepless activity with reference to the work entrusted to the church. In the early summer of 1861, almost immediately after his arrival in South Carolina, with the aid and sanction of some of the Presbyterian ministers and elders of his native state, he began to collect money for the support of our missionaries in the Indian Territory. Within a few weeks the sum of about four thousand dollars was secured and expended for the benefit of the red men·in the Southwest. When delegates from a number of the Southern presbyteries came together in the Atlanta Convention, in August, 1861, this body advised Dr. Wilson to continue the work which he had already begun. He secured at once, therefore, by personal appeal to the people of the churches, a large additional sum of money for the support of the missionary work among the Indians. In October, 1861, he made a journey to the Indian Territory and set the work forward through his own wise supervision. When, therefore, the first Southern Assembly met at Augusta, Georgia, on December 4, 1861, Dr. Wilson was present to tell about missionary tasks already accomplished. After its organization the first

regular order of business arranged by the Augusta
Assemby was "the hearing of a report by Dr. J. Leighton Wilson on the subject of Foreign Missions."

When Dr. Wilson arose in the presence of the assembly to read the report of his own activities during the
preceding months, he was the impersonation of physical
and moral manhood. His height was about six feet two
inches, and he was then in the fifty-third year of his age.
The story of the years of service spent in Africa and
in making journeys among the churches in his own
country was written in the lines that furrowed his brow.
His outward manner was marked by a quiet dignity, but
his heart was filled with the fire of missionary enthusiasm. In spite of the fact that the South was at that
time surrounded by hostile armies and navies, the
Augusta Assembly, under the leadership of Wilson,
determined to send six new missionaries to the Indians
of the Southwest, to raise the sum of $20,000 each year
for the support of evangelistic work in that region, and
made plans, also, to send gospel messengers to Japan,
China, Africa and South America "as fields where we
are soon to be called to win glorious victories for our
King."

The work of Foreign Missions was placed under the
care of Dr. Wilson as secretary. In 1863, when Dr.
John Leyburn, secretary of Home Missions, was forced
by the Federal authorities to leave New Orleans, the
work connected with that cause was assigned also to Dr.
Wilson. As Home Secretary he was charged with the
task of arranging a large part of the chaplain service in
the Confederate armies. His call was sent out at once
among the Presbyterian ministers of the South, and, as
we have seen, there were many who left their regular
pastoral charges and joined the preachers who were
already in the Confederate camps. Dr. Wilson himself
made visits to the various synods to secure funds and to
arrange for the preaching of the gospel in all of the

churches and in all of the armies of the South. One
day he would be formulating plans in his offices in the
buildings of the Theological Seminary at Columbia,
South Carolina; another day he would be making an
address before a synod, laying the necessities of the
work upon the hearts of the members; on yet another
day, while acting as chaplain, he would preach the word
to Confederate soldiers. Near the close of the war he
was moving about among the Confederate regiments
near Petersburg, Virginia, supplying chaplains to the
army. Dr. R. L. Dabney tells us that, in front of
Petersburg, one windy Sunday in March, Dr. Wilson
"preached to a South Carolina regiment in the trenches,
and even administered the Lord's Supper under a dropping picket fire." The day following this service in the
trenches, Dr. Wilson held a personal conference with
General R. E. Lee "concerning the spiritual wants of
the army." In May, 1865, it was Dr. Wilson who, in
his report on Home Missions, made the declaration
already quoted in this volume, to the effect that the outpouring of God's Spirit upon the Confederate armies
"may be regarded as an encouraging token of God's
purpose to favor and bless our future Zion."

To build up again a broken country and a broken
church—that was the task resting upon the people of
the South in 1865. For such work J. Leighton Wilson
had been made ready through a life of discipline.
Thenceforward, for twenty years, he pointed out the
way through the wilderness as one of the most efficient
leaders that God ever sent to any people.

> "Strong, simple, silent,   *   *   *   such was he
> Who helped us in our need."

Not altogether silent, indeed, was Dr. Wilson, for he
knew how to prepare admirable reports concerning work
done, and he could make stirring appeals for men and

money to carry out his plans. The plans for restoring the walls of Zion were well laid, and he went about among the people of the entire Southland, breathing into them the spirit of his own marvelous courage. "A dark cloud hangs upon our horizon," he wrote in one of his official reports after the war, "but the great mediatorial King reigns and the church is safe. He who has hitherto defended us from every enemy, upheld us under every trial, and from time to time has bestowed so many precious tokens of His favor upon us as a church, surely will be faithful to the end. Let us then go forward in the path of duty with a firm step and a courageous heart."

The *firm step* and the *courageous heart* in a pre-eminent degree marked this great leader. The principal activities of the entire Southern Church, apart from her educational and publishing agencies, were entrusted to the care of Dr. Wilson. Work of a twofold character was laid upon him through his appointment as secretary of Foreign Missions and secretary of the work of sustentation. The latter was established to take the place of the cause previously designated as Domestic Missions. To sustain congregations that had been weakened by the ravages of warfare, to repair shattered churches and erect new buildings, to send evangelists from field to field throughout the wasted land—such was the burden laid upon this stalwart man. In addition, he must encourage the church to remain steadfast in her purpose to continue to send missionaries beyond the seas. From 1866 until 1872 Dr. Wilson walked alone beneath this double burden. In 1872 the Home Mission department was assigned to Dr. Richard McIlwaine, and, in 1883, to Dr. John Newton Craig. The activities of our church in foreign lands were thus left to the sole management of Dr. Wilson. In 1866 he began to plant mission stations in China and Colombia. This was followed by missions in Italy (1867), Brazil

(1868), Mexico and Greece (1874). At a later time our church has entered Japan (1886), Cuba and the Congo region (1890), and Korea (1892).

Let us here repeat the statement already made that, during the period following the close of the war our country was passing through the various stages of a revolution, the only real revolution that has ever affected the administration of the internal affairs of the American commonwealths. During that time the dominant political party holding full control of every department of the Federal Government, and using the legislative department as its most aggressive agency, was engaged in a persistent attempt to Africanize the Southern states. The lives and the property of the white people of the South were placed under the control of the negroes. While the latter, to their credit be it said, did not thirst for blood, yet they destroyed property, wasted public revenues, checked and even paralyzed every industry, brought humiliation upon the white people and laid upon them the terrible burden of debts that must be borne for generations yet to come. Changes so radical and afflictions so grievous have seldom been imposed upon any people, not even upon France as the result of the movement known as the French Revolution of the eighteenth century. Throughout those years of bitter trial and sorrow, J. Leighton Wilson moved among his people as a tower of strength. He met his countrymen always with a smile and bade them trust God and cease not to work. He must be assigned, therefore, a worthy position, not merely among Presbyterian leaders, but also in that company of noble guides in every sphere of life who brought the South through the period of her greatest need into the peace of these later years. Dr. Wilson "wielded more real power in the Southern Presbyterian Church than any other man in it," writes Dr. Robert L. Dabney. "Every one was certain of the purity of his aims. Always modest and conciliatory, yet he was perfectly candid and manly. He practiced no arts nor policies, but relied solely upon the appeals of facts and reasoning to the consciences of his brethren." "The law of kindness was in his lips," writes Dr. M. Hale Houston; "his spirit of love and the clearness of his convictions made him stand firm as an oak."

From 1875 until 1884 Dr. Wilson's office as secretary of Foreign Missions was in Baltimore. In this large business center his ability as a manager of financial affairs was demonstrated more and more as the church became more able to contribute funds for the support of mission work. In Baltimore he was in close personal association with Dr. J. J. Bullock, Dr. J. A. Lefevre and Dr. W. U. Murkland, preachers of great efficiency and attractiveness. "One of the best and noblest men" was the form in which Murkland set forth his estimate of Wilson. On May 21, 1884, the faithful messenger of peace celebrated with his wife their golden wedding. The General Assembly, then in session, sent words of affectionate greeting. A few months later the weary leader laid down the pen in the office, spoke some words of good cheer to Dr. M. H. Houston and Dr. J. N. Craig, who had been appointed to carry forward the work, and quietly went back from Baltimore to Salem, the Wilson home on Black River, in South Carolina. There in July, 1885, the beloved wife was called away from his side. For a few months longer he continued to walk beneath the great trees near his dwelling-place, saying, "I look to the end with much comfort, having learned from my dear wife how to die." Within less than a year after her departure the heavenly messenger called for him. Side by side they are sleeping today near the door of the house of God in which his fathers offered worship, the sanctuary among the pine trees known as Mount Zion.

CHAPTER L.

THE subject of this sketch was born in the town of Lexington, Virginia, in August, 1820. His mother's family was of Scotch descent; his father was a German, whose ancestors for several generations had dwelt among the Scotch-Irish people of the Valley of Virginia. Jacob Henry Smith was received at an early age as a member of the Presbyterian Church in Lexington, whose pastor at that time was Dr. George A. Baxter. In the summer of 1843 he completed the course of study at Washington College, the Presbyterian church school located in his native town, of which Rev. Henry Ruffner, D. D., was then president. The autumn of 1843 found him in Union Seminary, Virginia, seeking to prepare himself for the gospel ministry. One of his fellow-students in the seminary was Robert Lewis Dabney, who has written these words about Jacob H. Smith: "It was difficult for me to avoid envying his gifts and habits as a student. He was compact in build, with perfect vigor and health, of a cordial and joyous temperament, with methodical habits and the greatest capacity for labor. His classmates said that he studied fourteen solid hours out of the twenty-four."

From the seminary, in 1846, he entered a pastorate at Pittsylvania Courthouse, Virginia. From 1850 until 1854 he was the headmaster of an academy in Halifax County, Virginia. Marked success rested upon his management of this school, and also upon his work here as teacher of both Latin and Greek. Then in 1854 he became shepherd of the Presbyterian flock in the city

of Charlottesville, Virginia. His preaching already had
that flavor that comes from the reading of many books,
and for this reason some of the scholarly men connected
with the University of Virginia often came to hear him.
At the same time his words were so filled with earnest
pleading that many souls were persuaded to enter
Christ's kingdom.

In April, 1859, Dr. Smith began his career as pastor
of the Presbyterian Church in Greensboro, North Carolina. This work was continued with increasing success
throughout a period of well nigh forty years until his
death in 1897. Knowledge of the Scriptures and of the
ancient languages in which they are written, knowledge
of men, knowledge acquired by reading books of many
kinds—knowledge that was both accurate and of wide
range formed an important part of the equipment of
this great preacher as he entered upon his life-work at
Greensboro. His heart, moreover, was as a fountain
of sympathy. Wherefore, when he appeared among
the people as a man sent from God to point out the way
of salvation, the clear, strong message found a place in
the hearts of many. As a pastor he knew the infirmities and the virtues of every member of his flock, and he
knew how to offer help and good counsel and good cheer.

When the war began between North and South he
showed his qualities as a leader in a field wider than that
of his own congregation. On June 16, 1861, only a
short space of time after the adoption of the Spring
Resolution by the assembly in Philadelphia, Dr. Smith
arose during one of the sessions of Orange Presbytery,
of which he was a member, and proposed that steps
should be taken to organize the Southern presbyteries
as an independent assembly in the South. Thus, among
the earliest proposals in behalf of the complete separation of the Southern Church from the Northern Church,
was the measure advocated by this wise, conservative
shepherd of the flock at Greensboro, North Carolina.

The blessings poured out upon the labors of Dr. Smith during his long pastorate constitute one of the memorials of the fact that God's presence has been with the church in the South. The years of the pilgrimage of the Southern Presbyterian Church throughout the period of the war and the Reconstruction have been marked by the pillar of fire and the pillar of cloud. By day and by night, in the home, in the house of God, and in the military encampment, God was speaking through His heralds unto His people. And the people heard the message and gave heed. The church increased in numbers and in good works. Among the congregations, therefore, that multiplied exceedingly in strength and in service, Dr. Smith's church must hold a worthy place, and Dr. Smith himself, as the quiet, tireless husbandman at home, must be called one of the great and worthy leaders of the people of the South. Two churches as colonies have been sent out from the Greensboro congregation. Ten ministers of the gospel, including three sons from Dr. Smith's own fireside, have been brought into the service of the church from the Greensboro field during this single pastorate. Elders and deacons, and Christians who held not any office in the church were trained through the agency of Dr. Smith to manifest wisdom and honesty and godliness in discharging their trust as officers of the civil government. And thus this strenuous laborer continued to enlarge his work to the very end.

"Such success," writes Robert L. Dabney, "represents a huge aggregate of diligent toils; yet Dr. Smith was behind few of those who devoted themselves exclusively to study and teaching. In theological learning he was an accurate scholar; in the Biblical languages an accomplished exegete. He was not only a profound theologian, but abreast with the general literature of the day."

When one sought out Dr. Smith in his study, says Bishop Edward Rondthaler, one "found a true and enthusiastic scholar in the midst of his books. At the time when I first visited him he was rereading Thucydides in Greek with all the ardor of a young student. His readings were wide and appreciative. This was, doubtless, part of the secret of his wonderful freshness of thought in old age."

"More than any other person I have known," writes James M. Rawlings, "he rejoiced in the sweetness and light of the Christian life and escaped life's bitterness and gloom." Others speak of Dr. Smith's keen sense of humor, his rare skill in telling a story, and how he rejoiced with those who rejoiced, and wept with those who wept.

His chief work, however, was that of preaching the Word of God. "He made all his study and reading flow through his sermons," says Dr. E. H. Harding. "This kept him fresh and thoughtful. There was no letting down in his work; the average was always high. His people were instructed, built up, developed. No man was more at home in the pulpit; he belonged there; it was his throne and he reigned there as one born to the purple."

"It was as a preacher of the truth that Dr. Smith excelled," writes Dr. William S. Lacy. "All his powers of mind, all his rich stores of knowledge, all his spiritual gifts and graces, all his intellectual and physical ability were made to contribute to this one great end. His sentences were finished with skill and grace. He used with exquisite art apt citations of poetry and appropriate illustrations. He took the utmost pains in all the details of preparation, writing in full his discourse. Yet the sermon, work of art and thought as it was, was in his hands but a weapon, the sword of the Spirit, which he used with masterly skill. He was one of the most solemn and convincing preachers to the conscience I ever heard. * * * He had a strong, rich, full voice; his articulation was admirable, his pronunciation fault-

less. He was a type and a model of a great preacher
of the Word." Many public positions of trust and
honor were bestowed upon Dr. Smith by his brethren in
the church. As member of two separate boards of
directors, he gave wise help in the work of building up
Davidson College, in North Carolina, and Union Seminary, in Virginia. Through the mercy of God he was
permitted to continue his marvelous activities until the
very end of a long life. Then, in November, 1897, the
strenuous laborer was called to receive his reward.

CHAPTER LI.

Among the Scots of North Ireland, in the month of November, 1814, Stuart Robinson was born. Soon after this event, his father, a linen merchant, brought the family across the Atlantic and established a home in the lower part of the Valley of Virginia. There, not far from the Potomac River, Stuart's boyhood was spent. Every Sunday for several years he walked six miles to Falling Water Church to receive instruction in the Sunday-school which his own mother organized and there to listen to the words of grace that fell from the lips of the pastor, one of the most effective preachers of that day, John Blair Hoge. During the week, under the mother's guidance, he stored up in his memory the words of the catechism and various selections from the Bible. When the lad was about thirteen years of age the faithful mother died. Then the father, on account of his own physical infirmities, was forced to break up the home and his six sons became members of other households. Stuart was received into the home of Rev. James Moore Brown, who had become pastor of the church. This minister was one of the sons of Samuel Brown and Mary Moore. The latter, as we remember, endured many hardships during a period of captivity among the Indians. Her son, inheriting her sound judgment and her piety, sought to develop these qualities in young Stuart Robinson. The latter was a diligent student, eager to learn, and under the instruction of James M. Brown he laid the foundations of an accurate scholarship. In these days of early youth he became a

Christian and, while he was yet living under Mr. Brown's roof, decided to become a preacher of the gospel. He sought special instruction from William Henry Foote, who was then in charge of the Presbyterian church and the academy at Romney, Virginia. Then, in October, 1832, young Robinson entered Amherst College, Massachusetts, and remained there until he completed the entire course of study in 1836. One of his fellow-students in that school for a brief period was Benjamin M. Palmer. A year in Union Seminary, Virginia, followed by two years of teaching, and then by a session at Princeton Seminary, brought him to the time of licensure as a minister in 1841. He began preaching at Malden, on the Kanawha River, as a close neighbor of his friend, James M. Brown, who had become shepherd of the flock at Charleston on the Kanawha, the present capital of West Virginia.

In 1847 Dr. Robinson entered the ministerial field at Frankfort, the capital of Kentucky. He was then thirty years of age, and gave the impression that he was a man of great physical vigor. And so he was. The people soon learned that he was filled with tremendous energy. In order to guide his flock aright, he accepted the office of city councilman, and also that of director in a new bank. These positions were used, however, only to win the friendship and confidence of the people of the city. His expositions of the Word of God began to attract an increasing number of hearers into his church. He began to deliver a series of lectures on the Old Testament at the Sunday night services, and these soon drew large congregations. A spiritual revival among the members of his flock in the summer of 1849 gave evidence that the divine approval was resting upon his work.

In September, 1852, he became pastor of the Associate Reformed Church, located on Fayette street in Baltimore. "Overflowing and delighted houses" greeted

him, not only when he preached his regular morning
sermons, but every Sunday night when he gave lectures
on Old Testament history. A mission chapel was organized, but differences of opinion arose between Dr.
Robinson and some of his people about the administration of church affairs and he resigned the pastorate.
A large number of the members of the flock persuaded
him to organize a new church. This he did, and a new
building was erected, called "Central Presbyterian
Church." With this congregation he remained from the
spring of 1853 until the autumn of 1856. During a
part of this time he was associated with Dr. Thomas E.
Peck, another pastor in Baltimore, and afterwards a
well-known theological teacher, in managing a monthly
review entitled the *Presbyterial Critic*. With reference
to the period of his labors in Baltimore, it was said by
one who knew well the facts, that "hundreds of souls
will bless him forever as the means of their salvation,
or of the revival of their faith and love."

For two sessions, from the fall of 1856 until the
spring of 1858, Dr. Robinson was engaged in teaching
the subjects of church government and pastoral
theology in the Danville Theological Seminary in Kentucky. In 1858 he became pastor of the Second Presbyterian Church in Louisville, thus resuming the work
for which his great powers of mind and heart fitted him,
that of preaching the gospel in a large city. A new
church building was erected for him and its pews were
crowded at every service to hear his expositions of the
Bible. At the same time, as the editor of a religious
journal called the *True Presbyterian*, he was appealing
to a larger constituency by way of uttering a solemn protest against the practice of bringing political issues into
church pulpits and church courts. When the General
Assembly at Philadelphia, in 1861, virtually adopted the
platform of the dominant political party and thus cut
off Southern Presbyterians from membership, Dr. Rob-

inson assailed the position of the Northern majority.
The statements made in his editorial columns were marked by such bold frankness that the Federal military authorities in control of the city of Louisville, early in
1862, suppressed the *True Presbyterian*. In July of
that same year he went to Canada to visit an invalid
brother. By reason of urgent warnings that the Federal authorities would cast him into prison if he should
return to Louisville, Dr. Robinson remained in Canada
until the close of the war. The years of his enforced
exile were filled with the work of preaching and with the
writing of that admirable volume of Biblical expositions,
entitled *Discourses of Redemption*. In the month of February, 1865, just as the armies of the South were beginning to taste the final bitterness of defeat, Dr. Robinson
delivered before his Canadian congregation a discourse
bearing the following title: "Slavery as recognized in
the Mosaic Civil Law, and as recognized, also, and allowed in the Abrahamic, Mosaic and Christian Church."
The opinion of most of the people in his audience was
not in harmony with his own view; nevertheless, he felt
impelled to declare his testimony concerning the principles set forth in the Bible. Having thus spoken in
defense of the South, he soon afterwards came again
to Louisville to help his own people in the hour of trial.
From April, 1866, through many years, his voice continued to ring out from the pulpit of the Second Church.
With reference to the quality of his utterances, Dr.
Thomas E. Peck, who knew Dr. Robinson well, declares
that he stood before the people "with the conviction
that he is the anointed ambassador of the King of kings.
* * * Wonderfully gifted indeed, and capable of
interesting men in anything, yet, as a preacher and
ambassador, confining himself to his written instructions,
he has demonstrated that the people need no other
attraction to draw them to the house of God than a
simple, rational and practical exposition of the Bible.

*   *   *   The secret of his popularity is his aiming to
make the Bible a living message from God to men, by
translating it into the current forms of thought and
speech."

In addition to the messages sent forth from the pulpit,
Dr. Robinson was in these same years speaking to his
countrymen through the pages of his book, *Discourses
of Redemption.* This volume, the product of his sojourn
in Canada, deals with "the whole work of Christ and the
doctrine of the church." "It is a matter of wonder to
many," writes Dr. Thomas E. Peck, "that a man of war
like Mr. Robinson, incessantly battling for the truth
against overwhelming odds, an exile from his country
and the object of a venomous and unrelenting persecution, should be able to write a book like this. To us
there is no wonder in the case, any more than there is in
Bunyan's writing the *Pilgrim's Progress* in Bedford
jail, in Luther's translating the Bible in the Wartburg,
or in Rutherford's dictating his letters in prison-bonds
at Aberdeen. The fragrance of the *Saints' Rest* is due
to the bruising of Baxter. Persecution and exile have
been 'Christ's palace' to our friend. While we could
not but be burdened with his afflictions, we now thank
his Master and ours for this precious fruit."

Dr. Robinson continued in Louisville the publication
of his paper under the title, *The Free Christian Commonwealth.* The complete independence of the church as
a spiritual organization was, of course, the principle for
whose maintenance he contended in the editorial columns
of this periodical. Thus, in the days of storm and stress
in Kentucky, after the war, with pen and voice he sought
to help his brethren. He was a signer of the paper
known as the *Declaration and Testimony,* and in company with those who were in sympathy with the principles set forth therein he was thrust out of the Northern
Presbyterian fold by the summary act of the Assembly
of 1866. In 1867 Dr. Robinson was the **principal**

writer of the declaration of principles, upon which as a basis of mutual understanding the Synod of Kentucky entered into organic union with the Southern Presbyterians. Among the principles thus elaborated by Dr. Robinson was the following: That the Church has no commission either to discharge any functions of the State, or to direct, advise or assist the State; nor has the Church any light in regard to the affairs of the State which the State has not already. * * * Neither can the State have any commission from God to discharge the functions of the Church. * * * Hence this synod and its presbyteries have steadfastly protested against and resisted the assumption of authority by the church courts to advise, direct and assist the civil government in its policy by the exercise of their spiritual authority, or to interpose the power of the spiritual sword for enforcing any theories of social organization, or theories of labor, or political theories, or to direct men as citizens in the choice of their civil policy."

In 1869, when delegates from the Kentucky presbyteries took seats for the first time in the Southern Assembly in session at Mobile, Dr. Robinson was by acclamation called to the moderator's chair. In 1877, as a representative from the South, in company with Moses D. Hoge and others, he held a conspicuous place in the Council of the Presbyterian Alliance at Edinburgh, Scotland. Soon afterwards his unceasing labors wore away his strength, and in October, 1881, he entered into rest. Dr. Benjamin M. Palmer, a life-long friend, came from New Orleans to Louisville to take part in the funeral service and to pay this tribute to Dr. Robinson:

"He had a great heart," said Dr. Palmer; "a heart that throbbed in generous response to every cry of distress, from whatever quarter it should come. His broad sympathy took hold of human life at every point and identified him with all the great movements for the

amelioration of society at large. It overflowed into a
thousand tender fellowships, which knit him to the hearts
of his fellow-men. * * *

"God also gave to him a massive intellect. His was a
mind comprehensive in its grasp of ultimate principles
which he could co-ordinate and arrange into great
systems of science, philosophy and religion. * * *
He was a man pre-eminent for his loyalty to the truth.
What he believed was wrought into the very texture of
his being and became part of the bone and sinew of his
entire intellectual and moral nature. * * * This
man, with a heart as tender as a woman's, was ever
found in the thickest of the fight, brave and sturdy as a
lion, contending for the faith once delivered to the
saints."

Largely through his efforts the Southern Presbyterians of Kentucky nurtured the cause of education
until a separate institution under their ownership and
control was established in 1883, two years after the
death of Dr. Robinson. This church school was located
at Richmond, Kentucky, and was given the name Central University. A few years later a school of theology
was organized as a part of this university with Dr. T.
Dwight Witherspoon as the first teacher of theological
subjects. The university was afterwards transferred to
Danville in the same state and there combined with Center
College under the title, The Central University of Kentucky. Thus in promoting the work of church education as well as in the labor connected with religious
journalism and in the writing of books, Dr. Stuart
Robinson, the impressive preacher of the Word, enlarged
the field of his service in our Southern Church.

CHAPTER LII.

THE subject of this sketch spent the first seven years of his life (1812-1819) in the home of his father, Dr. Moses Waddel, at the Willington Academy in Abbeville County, South Carolina. In 1819 he went with the other members of his father's family to Athens, Georgia, where Dr. Waddel entered into service as president of the University of Georgia. Young John N. Waddel made such rapid progress in his studies that just as he was passing into the eighteenth year of his age he completed the entire course of work then offered in the university. He was especially proficient in the knowledge of the Latin and Greek languages. For a number of years after graduation he was engaged in the task of teaching in various academies. Nearly thirty years of his life passed away before he professed faith as a Christian. Then, after spending a few months of private study in theological subjects, he appeared before the Presbytery of Mississippi in September, 1841, and was given authority to preach the gospel. In connection with the work of preaching, however, he continued also to teach. Near the home which he established at Montrose, in the midst of the pine forests in Eastern Mississippi, about sixty miles from the capital city, Jackson, Waddel built a log school-house. In this he organized the Montrose Academy for the instruction of boys after the model of his father's academy at Willington in upper South Carolina. The Montrose school was located among tall pine trees on the summit of a ridge-like elevation. At the foot of this hill a bold spring furnished an ample

supply of water. During the week the principal of the
school trained the school-lads in their regular studies.
Then, every Sunday morning, he used the school building as a church and preached a sermon to his pupils and
to the people of the community. So many boys came
from distant localities that a much larger log house was
built to serve as school-room and house of worship. A
number of small log cabins were erected under the pine
trees as dwelling-places for some of the students. In
that college in the forest there was a regular prayer
service every morning and evening, public worship with
a sermon every Sunday, and systematic training in
Latin, Greek, mathematics and the higher English
branches throughout the week. For seven years (1841-
1848) Waddel continued thus to labor with great
success in Montrose Academy, preparing a large company of young men for efficient service as elders and as
preachers in the Presbyterian churches of the Mississippi Valley.

During this same period, Oakland College, in Western Mississippi, was rising to the height of her success
in training young men. This school was founded in
1830 as the property of the Presbyterians of Mississippi,
and was directed by Dr. Jeremiah Chamberlain, a Presbyterian minister, as president. Many preachers of the
gospel were sent forth from Oakland. The rude hand
of war left the college a wreck, however, and in 1876
the fragments of the property were transferred to the
Chamberlain-Hunt Academy, under Presbyterial ownership and control, located at Port Gibson, Mississippi.

In the autumn of 1848 the University of Mississippi
was founded at Oxford, in that State. The first president was George Frederick Holmes, and the chair of
mathematics was occupied by Albert Taylor Bledsoe.
Both of these scholars afterwards held positions in the
faculty of the University of Virginia. Dr. John N.
Waddel was appointed to the chair of the Greek and

Latin languages, and he at once, therefore, removed his home from Montrose Academy to the State University at Oxford. For a term of nine years he continued to teach the classics in that school with uniform success, at the same time preaching the gospel in various pulpits. In 1857 Dr. Waddel accepted the same chair of ancient languages in the Synodical College at La Grange, Tennessee. The president of the institution was Dr. John H. Gray, a son of Hopewell Church, Abbeville District, South Carolina. In 1860, at the urgent request of Dr. Gray, the office of the presidency was transferred to Dr. Waddel.

The cloud of war was hanging dark over the land when Dr. Waddel assumed the duties of the presidency at La Grange College in the autumn of 1860. He stood at his post, however, like a patriot and a Christian and breathed into the students a part of his own courageous spirit. In April, 1861, the older members of the body of students were allowed to leave the academic halls in order to take up arms at the call of their country. Dr. Waddel and Dr. Gray, with two assistants, kept the class-rooms open until they heard the thunder of heavy guns almost at their doors. This took place in the early part of 1862. Very soon the Federal soldiers were encamped in the town of La Grange, with Federal officers holding quarters in the homes of the people. The soldiers tore down the walls of the college, brick by brick, and used them in the construction of huts for their own comfort. Thus ended the life of a noble institution.

On December 4, 1861, Dr. Waddel was present as a delegate in the Presbyterian Church in Augusta, Georgia. As commissioner appointed by the convention of presbyteries held at Atlanta in the previous August, he called the meeting to order and thus took the first formal step in organizing the Southern Assembly. He was chosen stated clerk of the assembly and retained that position until the latter part of the war. After the closing of the college in the beginning of the year 1862, he made a number of journeys to various encampments of the Confederate forces, offering aid and comfort to the wounded men and preaching sermons to those who were still ready for battle.

One morning in December, 1862, at his home in La Grange, Tennessee, Dr. Waddel received a written order, signed by the Federal officer in control of the town, commanding him to "discontinue his labors as a minister of the gospel" in that place. This penalty was laid upon him because he had been preaching to Conferedate soldiers. His own home having thus become a place of imprisonment, he determined to escape from La Grange. Passing, therefore, through the Federal military lines under cover of night, he rode rapidly southward until he found himself among friends. Thereafter, for many months, he was engaged as a commissioner under authority of the Presbyterian Assembly directing the work of the chaplains among the Confederate forces in Tennessee and Mississippi. In 1864 he was placed in charge of the chaplains connected with Joseph E. Johnston's army in Georgia. Throughout that desperate campaign in defense of the lower tier of Southern states he was at his post, sustaining his brethren and preaching the word to the soldiers. In September, 1864, in a battle below Atlanta, Dr. Waddel's son, John Gray Waddel, a Confederate volunteer, just seventeen years old, was slain by the fragment of a shell. It was not a time for the expression of grief, however, and the stricken father went steadily forward with his work. When the struggle was over, in 1865, he went back to La Grange to wander for a little while amid the ruins of the Synodical College.

Dr. Waddel was always ready for work, and in the autumn of 1865 he was placed at the head of the University of Mississippi, at Oxford. As chancellor of this important institution from 1865 until 1874, he rendered great service to the people of the Mississippi Valley. This was the period, of course, of the direful revolution forced upon the South, and Dr. Waddel's soundness of judgment in discharging the duties of his position brought the school through her difficulties in safety. He must be assigned an honorable place among the leaders of the entire South during the days of reconstruction.

In 1874 he laid down the burden of executive duties and sought to give his services more exclusively to his church. For a time, therefore, he was secretary of the cause of ministerial education, but in 1879 he was called once more into collegiate work. In that year he was appointed chancellor of the Southwestern Presbyterian University, located at Clarkville, Tennessee, and formed upon the basis of Stewart College, an institution already established in that city. Five years later (1884) a school of theology was organized as a component part of the university, with a faculty made up of Drs. John N. Waddel, John B. Shearer, Robert Price, Joseph R. Wilson and J. W. Lupton. When Dr. Waddel's health failed in 1888 he laid aside his active collegiate duties, and Dr. Charles C. Hersman was appointed chancellor of the university. When Dr. Hersman was transferred to Columbia Seminary, in South Carolina, the chancellorship was assigned to Dr. John B. Shearer, who at a later time became president of Davidson College. Dr. Waddel, who had summoned the members of the first Southern Assembly to be in order as a body of representatives ready for work, was himself called, a short time in advance of the meeting of this same Southern Assembly, in the year 1895, to enter "the general assembly and church of the first born who are enrolled in heaven."

CHAPTER LIII.

At Hampden-Sidney College, Virginia, on September 17, 1818, a child was born, the eldest son of Samuel Davies Hoge and of his wife, Elizabeth Rice Lacy. The name given to the child was Moses Drury, in honor of his grandfathers; one of these was Dr. Moses Hoge, then president of Hampden-Sidney College; the other was Drury Lacy, who had succeeded John Blair Smith as acting president of the college. In the autumn of 1820 Samuel Davies Hoge became pastor of the Presbyterian Church at Hillsborough, Ohio. In 1823 he was appointed to the chair of mathematics in the University of Ohio, at Athens, but his health rapidly failed and he died there near the close of the year 1826. As a pulpit speaker, we are told that he lacked only voice and physical strength to have become one of the first preachers of his day.

Until he reached the age of fifteen years the subject of this sketch lived in his mother's home at Athens, Ohio. Other members of the family circle were two sisters of young Moses Hoge and his brother, William James Hoge. Their mother received boarders in the home and was thus enabled to keep the little group of children by her side. An important element in their training was the mother's unusual talent as a conversationalist.

In the year 1834 the young Moses Hoge made the journey on horseback from Ohio through Kentucky and Tennessee into North Carolina. At Newbern, on the seacoast, he entered the home of his mother's brother, Dr. Drury Lacy, who was afterwards president of

Davidson College. In Newbern he attended a preparatory school. A considerable part of his time was spent, however, in reading the books that he found in his uncle's library. A strong memory enabled him to retain for immediate use, as long as he lived, lengthy passages taken from these volumes. A controlling influence that hedged about the life of the growing lad during the period of his sojourn in his uncle's home was the personal character of Dr. Lacy himself. The transparent honesty and sincerity that marked the life of that man of God had much to do in keeping steady the nephew's purpose to spend all of his days in rendering service to his fellow-men.

In the fall of 1836, soon after passing his eighteenth birthday, Moses D. Hoge entered the junior class at Hampden-Sidney College. He had received a thorough preparation in the languages; in general literature he had already devoured many volumes. The habit of ceaseless work was continued when he took up his tasks as a college student. At five o'clock regularly every morning he arose, lit a candle and opened his books. From this early hour until ten at night he was engaged in strenuous labors. At the close of his first session, however, he realized his own lack of proficiency in elementary English studies. He determined, therefore, to perfect himself in these branches by teaching them. To this end he spent the entire winter of 1837-1838 in North Carolina in a log schoolhouse sixteen feet square. With tireless fidelity he taught there a group of children, and at the same time drilled himself in the knowledge and use of his native form of speech. During the following winter and spring he was engaged in the studies of the senior year at college and was graduated at the head of his class. The commencement then took place in the early autumn. On September 25, 1839, in the old church at Hampden-Sidney, just a week after passing his twenty-first birthday, Moses D. Hoge de-

livered an oration in behalf of his classmates as their
valedictorian.

In the month of May, 1838, young Hoge made a
public profession of his Christian faith; he was enrolled
as a member of Shiloh Church in Granville County,
North Carolina. After completing the senior year and
securing his degree, he spent one session as tutor in
Hampden-Sidney College. Then, in the autumn of
1840, he began the course of study in Union Seminary
as a candidate for the gospel ministry. The death of
his mother about this time led him to make the following
entry in his journal: "Were I to *say* that my mother
was the most perfect being I ever knew, the remark
would be ascribed to filial partiality, but the thought
may be cherished in my inner sanctuary of the bosom
which no eye but that of God can penetrate."

During young Hoge's first year in the seminary, Dr.
George A. Baxter was giving his last lectures in theology. The transcendent powers of that great teacher
left a deep impression upon Moses D. Hoge, who, long
afterwards, wrote about Baxter's "pulpit effectiveness"
and the "dignity and impressiveness" of his discourses.
"He had one unique peculiarity," writes Hoge. "Often
in the midst of a logical passage his cheek would flush,
his face quiver and great tears would flow down his
manly face. He was thinking of some tender scene in
the life of our Lord which he intended to depict. Before
he got to the place he was trembling with emotion at
the sight of the dear, sad cross, standing full in his
view, in its mournful, unutterable glory, and then flowed
the irrepressible tears—tears that touched all hearts and
prepared them for what was coming."

Baxter was succeeded by Samuel B. Wilson; Samuel
L. Graham and Francis S. Sampson were just then, also,
beginning their work as theological instructors. It
seems clear, however, that the art of "pulpit effectiveness" which Moses D. Hoge afterwards so efficiently

illustrated was acquired by him as he sat at the feet of
Dr. Baxter. Early in the year 1844, after licensure
as a preacher, Moses D. Hoge became the assistant of
Dr. W. S. Plumer, pastor of the First Presbyterian
Church, Richmond, Virginia. Young Hoge, then in his
twenty-sixth year, brought with him to Richmond as
wife and helpmate, Susan Wood, the daughter of James
D. Wood, whose country home was known as Poplar
Hill, in Prince Edward County, Virginia. The people
of Dr. Plumer's Church in Richmond built a chapel on
Fifth street, then in the western part of the city, and
there the assistant preached the Word. So many people
came regularly to hear him that a separate congregation
was soon organized in the chapel, and in February,
1845, Moses D. Hoge was installed there as pastor of
the Second Church. From the beginning of the work
in this field the second service each Sunday was held in
the afternoon, and thus for more than fifty years, as
the Lord's Day was drawing toward the twilight hour,
a large company of worshipers of every name and denomination was given the opportunity to hear the up-
lifting utterances of the pastor of the Second Church.

In 1847 Dr. Plumer entered upon another field of
work, in Baltimore, and Dr. Thomas V. Moore became
pastor of the First Church, Richmond. The two Christian shepherds, Moore and Hoge, wrought together in
full sympathy and fellowship. In 1851 each of them
delivered one of the lectures in the series given at the
University of Virginia on the general subject of the
Evidences of Christianity. In 1855 they purchased
The Watchman, a Presbyterian paper published in
Richmond. The name of the weekly periodical was
changed to *Central Presbyterian*, and under the joint
editorial control of Moore and Hoge it obtained at once
a wide influence among Southern Presbyterians. In
1859 the paper passed under the control of Dr. William
Brown; later still, it became the property of Dr. W. T.

Richardson, and then of Dr. James P. Smith, until the title was changed to that of *The Presbyterian of the South*.

Early in the year 1848 Moses D. Hoge's new church building was dedicated. At the same time, in order to help his people to meet the heavy financial obligations thus laid upon them, he opened in Richmond a Presbyterian school for boys. The double work imposed upon the young pastor by the church and the school seemed only to call forth new strength each day. He developed a remarkable capacity for continuous labor. The congregation was built up in strength and efficiency, and the pastor's influence was widely extended. The management of the school was at length transferred to others, and Dr. Hoge gave himself entirely to the duties of the pastorate. A summer in Europe (1854) broadened his vision and enabled him to do more effective work in the pulpit. Thus he grew in power, and when the shadow of war fell upon the city of Richmond, Dr. Hoge had become the leading figure among the churches in the capital of the Southern Confederacy.

One of the reasons that had led Moses D. Hoge's father to seek a field of labor in the State of Ohio was his opposition to the system of slavery in the South. Moses D. Hoge, also, after his marriage, offered freedom to the slaves that came under his control as a portion of his wife's estate; only one of these slaves, however, was willing to accept the gift of liberty. During the discussions of the year 1860, with reference to secession, Dr. Hoge was not in favor of the immediate withdrawal of the Southern States. Soon after the secession of Virginia, however, in April, 1861, he wrote the following:

"With my whole mind and heart I go into the secession movement. I think Providence has devolved on us the preservation of constitutional liberty, which has already been trampled under the foot of a military despotism at the North. And now that we are menaced

with subjugation for daring to assert the right of self-
government, I consider our contest as one which involves
principles more important than those for which our
fathers of the Revolution contended."

With the opening of active hostilities Confederate
soldiers began to assemble in large numbers at Richmond for the defense of the Southern capital. The
religious welfare of these men engaged at once the active
interest of Dr. Hoge. He began his work among them
by preaching in some of the military encampments every
Sunday afternoon and at least twice during the week.
At certain periods of special activity he delivered the
gospel message to the soldiers day after day in succession for many weeks. The preaching services in his
own church, twice on Sunday, with the mid-week service
for prayer, were regularly maintained. Dr. T. V.
Moore of the First Church frequently preached on Sunday afternoon from the pulpit of Dr. Hoge while the
latter was speaking to the fighting men at their place of
bivouac; then Dr. Hoge would occupy Dr. Moore's pulpit in the evening. This plan of strenuous work in
preaching to multitudes of soldiers was kept up throughout the four years of warfare, with the exception of the
period of ten months spent in England. During the
same long period, with few exceptions, he offered prayer
at the opening of the daily sessions of the Confederate
Congress in Richmond.

The work of preaching to soldiers upon a scale so
extensive most probably did not fall to the lot of any
other minister of the gospel of that period. Thousands
and thousands of the men from the South heard him
as they paused in Richmond for a little while on their
way to the front. As many as one hundred thousand
men heard the gospel from his lips in the camp of instruction maintained near Richmond during the early
years of the war. It was solemn work. Those who
listened to the preacher's words one Sunday would most

likely be on the march or in the line of battle on the
following Sunday. Within one brief hour, in many
cases, the minister must lay his message upon the hearts
of men who were soon to stand face to face with death.
Most of these Southern soldiers, however, had come
from Christian homes and from church-going communities. Their hearts were ready, therefore, as good soil
to receive the preacher's words of instruction and of
encouragement. Dr. Hoge had full knowledge of these
facts about the training and early association of the
men to whom he spoke, and he knew well how to present
the solemn appeal, urging the soldiers as they entered
the field of battle to put their trust in the God of their
fathers. They always listened with open minds and
melting hearts to the message which he delivered. Many
of them were persuaded by his preaching to accept the
Christian faith; many, very many, who were believers
already were strengthened by his exhortations to stand
like men in the hour of danger. The soldiers who passed
thus in solemn review before the preacher left upon him
the deep impression that they were of worthy character.
Earnestness and quiet dignity marked the Confederate
soldiers as they sat before Dr. Hoge during the hour of
worship; these qualities, together with their conduct on
the march and upon the field of war, led him to speak
of them afterwards as "not professional soldiers," but
"men who came from the sanctities of home, from the
peaceful vocations of business or professional life;
many of them merchants or mechanics; most of them
farmers; some of them students in schools, colleges and
theological seminaries; yet, all of them, every man of
them, every boy of them, at the sacred call of duty,
periled all and for principle sacrificed all, committing
their souls to God and their memories to us who might
survive them."

As time passed on Dr. Hoge's labors were rapidly
multiplied. Six sermons a week, the daily prayer in the

Confederate Congress, funerals in great number, pastoral visiting and the writing of articles for the press—these, he said, formed only the beginning of his duties. Work of every sort was laid upon him, whereof he wrote as follows: "Many people seeking office or employment come to me; many write, asking me to get them passports or do something for them in some of the departments. * * * A discharged soldier, knowing no one else in the city, writes to me to get his pay; a wife, separated from her husband, writes, begging me to get her a permit to pass through the lines and go to him; an exile, driven by the enemy from his home, writes, asking if I can assist him in getting a position where he can make bread for his destitute family; and as sure as I shut myself up in my study and resolutely refuse to open, no matter who knocks, then some one calls who *ought* to have been admitted."

In addition to these activities, there was the work of general teaching carried on among the soldiers at the camp of instruction. With reference to the help rendered him in that camp by Rev. Dabney Carr Harrison, a young Presbyterian minister, Dr. Hoge wrote as follows: "I saw him almost daily [in the camp] for three months or more. It was owing to his [Harrison's] agency that a Christian Association was formed in the regiment and completely organized for every species of usefulness. There was a Bible class, a Sabbath-school, and arrangements made even for teaching those who were unable to read. He rendered me most efficient aid in my work as chaplain during his stay in camp. He held prayers every evening in my large tent for several weeks. He interested himself in getting the men together on Sabbath afternoons, and this increased the attendance on my regular services. The influence of his presence and example in the camp during these months will never be fully appreciated until the day of final revelation."

On Saturday, May 31, 1862, Dr. Hoge mounted his horse and, in company with Colonel Benjamin S. Ewell, a brother of General R. H. Ewell, rode toward the battle-field of Seven Pines. The booming of cannon told them that the fighting was already in progress. As they drew near the field of action they met wounded Confederates making their way to the rear; they saw other wounded men, stretched on the ground, with the surgeons rendering every possible attention; then they met groups of prisoners, under guard, hurrying toward Richmond. Very soon the two horsemen were in the midst of the smoke of the battle, where the shells were screaming through the air and the musket balls were making that peculiar sound which, says Dr. Hoge, "renders their music more memorable than agreeable." A spent bullet struck Dr. Hoge's horse and "made him jump around in a very lively style." Soon afterwards he dismounted and yielded his horse to a Confederate soldier, about sixteen years of age, who had received a severe wound. Then Dr. Hoge took the young man's musket and, walking by his side, waded through the mud and water for about a mile until an ambulance was found; in this the wounded soldier was tenderly placed.

Near the close of the day fierce firing broke out near that part of the field where Dr. Hoge was moving about among the wounded and dying soldiers. The Confederates were driving back the enemy along that part of the line. A number of Confederate regiments, rushing to the aid of their comrades, passed Dr. Hoge as the latter was seated on his horse by the roadside. "I was astonished," he writes, "at the number of the men who recognized me with salutations and exclamations: 'What, Mr. Hoge, you here!' Many asked me how the battle was going. At my answer, 'successful all along the line,' they would cheer and press on with a quicker step." Dr. Hoge followed these soldiers until he entered the entrenchments from which the Federal forces had been driven. There he found his personal friend, General D. H. Hill, who was in command on that part of the field. Turning again homeward, Dr. Hoge saw a hospital near the roadside. When he entered the building and looked about in the dim light, for it was now late at night, he saw the wounded men lying upon the floor in such numbers that "it was difficult to walk without stepping on them." Having asked permission from one of the surgeons present, the minister knelt down in the center of the room "and prayed God to comfort them, give them patience under their sufferings, spare their lives, bless those dear to them and sanctify to them their present trials. To these petitions some of them audibly responded, and it was affecting to observe that even their groans were to a great degree suppressed." A few hours later, at the regular hour for worship on Sunday morning, Dr. Hoge was again in his pulpit preaching the gospel of comfort to his people.

Three weeks later, another Sunday morning found Dr. Hoge riding eastward from Richmond to the Confederate fortifications. There, in full view of the pickets of the Federal army, he preached to the Georgia troops forming the commands of Generals Howell Cobb and Thomas R. R. Cobb. "After service," he writes, "we dined in camp. The day was very hot; the ride to and from town was over twelve miles, and I got back just in time to get to Camp Lee for my afternoon discourse. There I had a larger congregation, for two regiments had just come in." Two days later, in spite of fatigue, he was again among the men in the lines of defense at the headquarters of General D. H. Hill and General Garland. After the battles of the Seven Days, Dr. Hoge entered into a close personal friendship with Stonewall Jackson and preached frequently among the men under Jackson's command. In brief it may be said that few of the brigades of General Lee's entire army failed to hear the preaching of the Richmond minister. With

Lee himself and with most of the officers of his military family, and with President Davis and the members of his cabinet, Dr. Hoge lived on terms of cordial friendship.

One dark, stormy night near the end of the month of December, 1862, Dr. Hoge stood upon the deck of a steamship known as a "blockade-runner" that was moving out of the harbor of Charleston, South Carolina, toward the open sea. Thirteen Federal warships, with guns ready to fire, were stationed near the outer edge of the harbor to keep any Confederate vessel from passing out into the Atlantic. The captain of the Confederate steamer had orders to sink or to burn his ship rather than surrender her. Dr. Hoge, however, was ready to face every danger, for he was on his way to England to secure Bibles and religious tracts for the soldiers in the Confederate service. "Our run through the blockading squadron was glorious," he wrote afterwards. "I was in one of the severest and bloodiest battles [Seven Pines] fought near Richmond, but it was not more exciting than that midnight adventure, when amid lowering clouds and dashes of rain, and just wind enough to get up sufficient commotion in the sea to drown the noise of our paddle-wheels, we darted along with lights all extinguished, and not even a cigar burning on the deck, until we got safely out and free from the Federal fleet." Sailing by the way of Nassau to Havana, Cuba, he embarked upon an English steamer for Southampton, England. Soon after arriving in London Dr. Hoge made an effective address before the Board of Managers of the British and Foreign Bible Society, with Lord Shaftesbury in the chair. These Englishmen listened with sympathetic ears while he told of the inability of the Southern people to print an adequate number of volumes of religious literature "because all the industrial energies of the Confederacy were devoted to the great work of self-defense." He gave an account of "the heroic manner in which our people had borne all the hardships and bereavements of the war; of their inflexible determination to succeed; of the religious character of our leading generals; of the eagerness of the soldiers to obtain copies of the Holy Scriptures." All that Dr. Hoge asked was permission to buy a supply of books on credit, but the Bible Society, after hearing his address, immediately made him a gift of their publications to the value of about twenty thousand dollars. This meant ten thousand Bibles, fifty thousand Testaments and two hundred and fifty thousand small volumes containing the Psalms and the Gospels. The latter had glazed covers, with rounded corners, "just the thing to put in the pocket of a soldier." Other societies in London listened to Dr. Hoge's story of the struggles of the Confederates, and these societies with a large number of individual friends made additional contributions of Bibles and tracts, "for the use of my countrymen," he writes, "so nobly battling in the sacred cause of liberty and independence." A special series of tracts with the Confederate battle flag on the cover was issued in London for the use of the Southern soldiers. All of these Bibles and smaller books were shipped in blockade-runners, and while some were captured by Federal vessels, the principal part of them made the voyage in safety and were distributed throughout the armies of the South.

Dr. Hoge won the permanent friendship of many influential people in London, among whom were Lord Shaftesbury and Thomas Carlyle. He was invited to visit a number of English homes, but even in the midst of the hospitalities there bestowed upon him, he never forgot the privations of his own people in the Confederate States. "I feel the war here," he wrote, "more than I did at home, for there I could at least share in the privations of my own people, and could do something to cheer and encourage those whose circumstances were

inferior to my own. On this account I am impatient to
get back, though were not our country invaded I would
remain here three months longer." The news of the
death of Stonewall Jackson was a heavy blow to Dr.
Hoge. This was followed by the intelligence that his
own first-born son had died in the home in Richmond.
Severe as was such discipline, his faith failed not, but
was the rather made stronger. "I pray to be prepared
by it," he wrote, "to be a comfort to my suffering people
when I return home; prepared to strengthen them, and
to be strong myself for all the trials we may yet undergo
before our independence is won."

On Sunday morning, October 11, 1863, Dr. Hoge
again stood upon the deck of a blockade-runner, the
swift steamer *Advance*. The vessel was making her way
from Bermuda toward one of the mouths of the Cape
Fear River, near Wilmington, North Carolina. A fleet
of Federal warships was lying at anchor just outside
the bar, guarding the entrance to the stream. Through
this fleet the *Advance* must pass if she would find safety
in the shallow waters of the Cape Fear. The runner
sailed in with such boldness that she had nearly passed
the blockading line before the Federal captains recognized her as the *Advance*. Anchors were raised at once
and the Federal vessels started in pursuit, at the same
time opening fire with their heavy guns. The big shells
flew all about the steamer, but she held her way at full
speed until the fire of the Confederate cannon in Fort
Fisher compelled the Federal warships to give up the
pursuit. Then the seamen and the passengers all met
together on deck and stood with bowed heads beneath
the sky, while Dr. Hoge returned thanks to God for their
deliverance from capture.

In the summer of 1864 another burden of sorrow was
laid upon him by the death of his brother, Dr. William
J. Hoge. Soon after the war began the latter had given
up his pastorate in New York city and had entered upon

ministerial work in the South, at the first in Charlottesville and then in the Tabb Street Church in Petersburg,
Virginia. From his successful labors among the people of
the latter city and among the Confederate soldiers, a fatal
malady suddenly removed, him. The Federal army was
then throwing heavy shells into every part of the city of
Petersburg and the funeral services could not be held
there. Setting forth, therefore, in an ambulance at the
close of the day, Dr. Hoge transferred his brother's
body by night through the country from Petersburg to
Richmond. "It was a lonely ride," he writes, "through
the dim woods and along the intricate roads as I lay
stretched on the straw alongside the body of my dead
brother; and I had full leisure to contemplate the greatness of my loss. We reached Richmond as day was
breaking." There the last tender rites were solemnized
by Dr. T. V. Moore and Dr. John Leyburn.

To the very end of the great conflict Dr. Hoge continued with increasing power to preach the gospel to
the Confederate soldiers. To the very end he was full
of hope that success would crown Southern arms in the
war which he called the South's "struggle for civil and
religious freedom." When defeat came he was overwhelmed with grief. He left Richmond in company with
President Davis and his cabinet and did not return to
his home until the last hope of the Confederacy had
failed. "I forgot my humiliation for a while in sleep,"
he wrote in May, 1865, "but the memory of every be-
reavement comes back heavily like a sullen sea surge, on
awakening, flooding and submerging my soul with
anguish. The idolized expectation of a separate nation-
ality, of a social life and literature and civilization of
our own, together with a gospel guarded against the
contamination of New England infidelity, all this has
perished, and I feel like a shipwrecked mariner. * * *
"I hope my grief is manly. I have no disposition, to
indulge in querulous complaints. God's dark providence

enwraps me like a pall; I cannot comprehend, but I will not charge him foolishly; I cannot explain, but I will not murmur.

"To me it seems that our overthrow is the worst thing that could have happened for the South—the worst thing that could have happened for the North, and for the cause of constitutional freedom and of religion on this continent. But the Lord hath prepared His throne in the heavens and his kingdom ruleth over all. I await the development of his providence, and I am thankful that I can implicitly believe that the end will show that all has been ordered in wisdom and love. Though He slay me, yet will I trust Him." A few weeks later he wrote to a friend that "other seas will give up their dead, but my hopes went down into one from which there is no resurrection."

In the pulpit, however, he never faltered in the work of unfolding the hope of life eternal as that hope is written in the pages of the divine Book. Multitudes, stricken with the same sorrow that filled his soul, came to his church to find peace in listening to the words of hope and consolation that fell from his lips. "I have been working hard," he wrote in February, 1866; "I am stimulated to make more careful preparation than usual for my Sunday services because of the crowds which throng my church. In the afternoon, especially, the people come long before the hour and many have to go away because they cannot find standing or sitting room. * * * The most animated and cheerful day we have is Sunday, when people seem to forget their troubles for a while and crowd the churches, seeking for solace there." Thus gradually he became the spiritual guide and counsellor of a large proportion of the people of the South, leading them out of the shadows into the light and speaking words of encouragement to the men and women who were busy with the task of building up again their church and their country.

Near the close of the year 1868 Dr. Hoge's beloved wife was called away from the earthly home. Thus were his earlier sorrows multiplied and, thenceforth, throughout a period of thirty years, he was to continue his pilgrimage alone. Sorrow and discipline, however, in his behalf wrought out their perfect work and gave him strength and serenity of spirit. Unto great multitudes at home and abroad he became as one sent from God to bring the message of heavenly comfort. His principal work during these years was the preaching of the gospel from his own pulpit in Richmond, and this preaching was always marked by simplicity and power. The church building was enlarged to its present proportions to accommodate the growing number of people that came to hear him. Other pulpits in every part of our country were opened to him, and in this manner his gracious ministry was extended. He delivered addresses of various kinds on both sides of the Atlantic, and he was personally identified with many public movements of a religious and benevolent character. The marvelous activities of this man of God throughout the period from 1869 to 1899 cannot be touched upon here except in the form of brief suggestion.

When a group of Englishmen gave to the State of Virginia a bronze statue of Stonewall Jackson, Dr. Hoge was selected to deliver the oration at the time of the unveiling of the monument. "Here on this Capitoline Hill," he said, in part, "on this 26th day of October, 1875, and in the one hundredth year of the Commonwealth of Virginia, in sight of that historic river that more than two centuries and a half ago bore on its bosom the bark freighted with the civilization of the North American Continent, under the shadow of that capitol whose foundations were laid before the present Federal Constitution was framed * * we have met to inaugurate a new pantheon to the glory of our common mother. * * * We come to honor the memory of one who was the impersonation of our Confederate cause, and whose genius illuminated the great contest which has recently ended." Beginning thus he proceeded to speak of the character of Jackson; of "the admirable commingling of strength and tenderness in his nature;" of his "supreme devotion to duty;" of his sincerity and purity "as a servant of the Most High God." It was Jackson's piety, said the speaker, that gave "consecration to the sacrifice when he laid down his life on the altar of his country's liberties." In this vein of loyalty to the cause of the Confederacy Dr. Hoge continued throughout his discourse, impressing all who heard him on that occasion, said General D. H. Hill, as "the most eloquent orator on this continent."

In May, 1875, Dr. Hoge was made moderator of the Southern Assembly in session at St. Louis. At that time and afterwards he advocated the establishment of closer "fraternal relations" with the Northern Presbyterians, although he was not in favor of organic union with them. He also urged the appointment of delegates to represent the Southern Church in the Council of the Presbyterian Alliance. Our church, he declared, ought to "come into line and take her legitimate place in the great family gathering of the Presbyterian churches of the world." In 1877, therefore, delegates were sent to Edinburgh to take part in the Council that met there in the month of June. Among the delegates was Dr. Hoge, with Drs. William Brown, William S. Plumer, Stuart Robinson and others. Dr. Hoge made an address in the evening of the first day's session in Edinburgh. An observer wrote that as the Virginia preacher stepped upon the platform, "a tall, spare, muscular man, of a military type of physique, his manner was almost painfully deliberate. Commencing with a graceful compliment to the chairman, admirable in its spirit and perfect in its manner, he dallied for a while with his subject in a lively and almost gay humor, and then mingling pathos

with humor with the happiest ease, he set forth with
dignity and breadth not inconsistent with great intensity
and emotional excitement the leading points of his many-
sided subject—the simplicity and scriptural character
of Presbyterianism."

In the spring of 1880 he made a journey through
Palestine. In 1881 he made an address in Dr. John
Hall's church, New York City, in connection with a
memorial service in honor of President Garfield. His
words on that occasion constituted "a remarkable discourse," said one of the city papers, "which for ability,
eloquence and pathos has seldom been equaled in New
York." In 1884, while traveling in Europe, Dr. Hoge
went to Copenhagen to hear the discussion in the Evangelical Alliance which was holding its sessions in that
city. He was not a delegate, but one evening he was
pressed into service to fill a vacancy in the list of speakers. With only fifteen minutes to collect his thoughts,
he spoke on the subject of *Family Religion*. The address thrilled the hearts of the audience; he spoke with
marvelous power, telling of the memories of his own life
and home. The month of July, 1888, found him once
more in London, this time as a delegate to the Council
of the Presbyterian Alliance. During the sessions of
that body he preached in a number of London pulpits.
In December, 1889, he was in Boston, making a great
address in Tremont Temple in connection with the sessions of the Evangelical Alliance. On May 30, 1893,
at the reinterment of President Davis in the city of Richmond, he offered a prayer wherein God's blessing was
invoked in behalf of the people of the South, "too brave
ever to murmur and too loyal to the memories of the
past ever to forget." The month of June, 1896, marked
his presence in Glasgow in attendance at the sessions of
the Presbyterian Alliance. Although he was now in his
seventy-eighth year, Dr. Hoge made an address at the
Council marked by strength and animation. A few

weeks later, in London, he was receiving social attentions on every hand from many of the great and worthy men of England. Then in May, 1897, he appeared in Charlotte, North Carolina, as a member of the Southern Assembly, at the same time delivering one of the addresses in connection with the 250th anniversary of the Westminster Assembly. Dr. Robert L. Dabney, as we have already seen, likewise made one of the Westminster addresses and was present in this assembly as a delegate. Thus these two great leaders, a few months before their translation, appeared together for the last time on earth in the highest court of our church.

Hundreds of addresses and sermons, besides those mentioned above, were delivered in every part of our country by Dr. Hoge. He went about everywhere preaching the Word of God with power. "It was a glorious, soul-lifting sermon," wrote one who heard him in London; "the power, pathos, pleading and spirituality of that address I have never heard surpassed. No notes, too! All free, direct, natural. He is our Spurgeon, Parker and Liddon in one."

Two anniversary celebrations were held in Dr. Hoge's church in Richmond, wherein those who loved and honored him spoke words of just commendation concerning his work. One night, early in 1890, upon the completion of his forty-fifth year as pastor of the Second Church, a great company of Richmond people assembled in the largest hall in the city to express their appreciation of him. Speakers representing various denominations told the story of his successful labors. "Few men in the country, few men in the world," said Bishop Wilson of the Methodist Church, "have been able to affect personally such multitudes as the pastor of this church."

The fiftieth anniversary was celebrated in February, 1895. An entire evening was taken up with the ceremonies of a public reception, when nearly every organ-

ization in the city of Richmond, religious, social and
military, and thousands of individuals, offered personal
congratulations to him whom they called "the first citizen
of Virginia." Then, on the next evening, a great multitude assembled in the church, and there from his own
pulpit Dr. Hoge delivered a notable discourse filled with
the memories of fifty years. Thus was celebrated that
which Dr. Hoge termed his "golden wedding." Three
more anniversaries were granted to him. Then, near the
close of the year 1898, there was an accident in connection with a street car. A few weeks of suffering followed; throughout this period his faith shone with increasing radiance. Early on the morning of January
6, 1899, he entered into the heavenly home to be numbered with the saints in glory everlasting.

CHAPTER LIV.

"AND what shall I more say? for the time will fail me
if I tell" the full story of Stonewall Jackson, Daniel
Harvey Hill, Thomas R. R. Cobb and other members of that great company of deacons and elders
of our own time who through faith wrought with might
in behalf of the upbuilding of our Southern Church.
And yet, there must be placed in this record a few brief
words concerning some of those men of God who walked
in advance with Thornwell, Dabney, Palmer, Hoge and
the other leaders during the period of the war and the
Reconstruction in the South.

Thomas J. Jackson, born in 1824, was of Scotch-
Irish descent and spent his early years in the midst of a
Scotch-Irish community, near Clarksburg, in the present
State of West Virginia. It was not, however, until he
had passed through the Military Academy at West Point
and had won distinction as the commander of a battery
of heavy guns upon several of the fields of battle in
Mexico that he announced his acceptance of the Christian
faith. In 1849, when he had entered his twenty-sixth
year, he received the rite of Christian baptism. Two
years later, in November, 1851, he became a member of
the Presbyterian Church in Lexington, Virginia, and
two years later still, in 1853, he married Eleanor Junkin, daughter of Dr. George Junkin, president of Washington College. Although Major Jackson's work as
professor of natural philosophy was in connection with

the Virginia Military Institute in Lexington, yet his
home life for a number of years was spent as a member
of the family of his wife's father, Dr. Junkin, within the
same town. This minister of the gospel, of Scotch-Irish
descent, was then presiding over the foremost Presbyterian church college in the South, the school founded before the American Revolution by the Hanover Presbytery, as we have already seen, and guided in its development by those wise, strong preachers, William Graham,
George Addison Baxter and Henry Ruffner. As was
most fitting, therefore, in the case of a leader connected
with the Presbyterian system of education, President
Junkin's household was regulated after the manner of
the typical Presbyterian homes of that time, with the
Word of God in daily use as the guide of faith and practice. The atmosphere of that godly home became one
of the most important factors in the development of the
character of Major Jackson. The earnest Christian
faith of his wife was the model in harmony with which
his own religious convictions were gradually moulded.
At the time of his marriage, his regard for the sanctity
of the Lord's Day was somewhat careless. Within a
brief period, however, his wife led him to accept her own
strict Biblical rules of conduct with reference to Sunday
observance, and these he continued to put into practice
as long as he lived. Her early death broke up, in a
measure, the habit of silence that had marked his conduct, and thenceforth his conversation was more frequently concerned with spiritual affairs.

In 1857, Major Jackson won as his second wife, Mary
Anna Morrison, daughter of Dr. Robert H. Morrison,
first president of Davidson College. The marriage
ceremony was performed by Dr. Drury Lacy, who was
at that time president of Davidson College. A few
months after this marriage, Major Jackson committed
to memory the Shorter Catechism, and his wife filled the
position of teacher while he recited it. Thus was his

training in spiritual affairs carried forward by a godly woman whose early life had been spent in connection with one of the most important Presbyterian schools of the South. The gracious influence of that childlike Christian faith in which she had been trained within her father's home helped to form the moral and spiritual nature of her husband. These two together, Major Jackson and his wife, conducted a Sunday-school every Sunday afternoon for many years for the benefit of the negro children of the community. Moreover, Major Jackson became a deacon in the church, and under the wise instruction and encouragement of Dr. William S. White, pastor in Lexington, gradually learned how to discharge the duties belonging to that office. When Major Jackson was afterwards revealed to the world as the great military genius, Stonewall Jackson, it was at the same time made clear to all who knew him that he was a man of faith and of prayer. His nature was saturated with the Biblical idea of life. He had an intense sense of God's presence with him. In every incident of life he saw the visible finger of God, and every victory that he won was ascribed to Providence. He maintained during his campaigns in the field, as far as possible, the personal habits of the head of a Christian household. Every morning and evening with strict regularity he held a brief prayer service in his tent, which the members of his staff were invited to attend. On Sunday, whenever possible, public worship was held at his headquarters and a sermon was preached by some minister of the gospel. There were frequent prayer-meetings during the week among the regiments under his command. From time to time, also, the sacrament of the Lord's Supper was celebrated and all of the Christians in his army were invited to participate. On such occasions he always took his place among the rank and file of the soldiers, in the most quiet way, presenting himself as a worshiper upon the same plane with the rest

of his Christian brethren. In addition to all this, we have
seen how he aided his chaplain, Rev. Beverley T. Lacy,
in conducting an evangelistic campaign throughout the
Confederate army in Virginia in the winter of 1862-63.
It was his chief desire, he often said, to command a
"converted army," a body made up entirely of Christian
soldiers.

Christian leadership in a form so admirable as that
of Stonewall Jackson was due in a measure, of course,
to the native vigor of the man, and it was rendered conspicuous by the position which he held as commander
of a large military force and by the brilliant victories
which he won in the field. But when he wrote to his
wife that "Our Lord has again thrown His shield over
me," or when he invited his entire army to render
"thanks to the Most High for the victories with which
He has crowned our arms," he was only giving expression to religious sentiments that filled the minds and
hearts of a great multitude of officers and private soldiers in the Southern armies. He stands, moreover, as a
worthy representative of that type of training in the
study of the Word of God, in prayer and in vital godliness that marked the home life of the Presbyterian people of the South. Thousands of men, with a Christian
faith as sincere and strong as that of Stonewall Jackson,
entered the armies of the South in 1861; many of them
yielded up their lives upon the field of battle; many of
them came through the strenuous period of war to show
their qualities as leaders in these later days. Let Jackson's life as a man and a soldier, therefore, stand before
the world as an example of that simple piety and god-like
faith that were brought to maturity in the great majority of the homes among the people of the South.

Christian faith as strong and clear as that of Stonewall Jackson dwelt also in the heart of another soldier
of the South, General Daniel Harvey Hill. His parents
were both of Scotch-Irish descent and he spent his early

years within the limits of Bethel Presbyterian congregation in York District, South Carolina. We have already seen the grandfather, Colonel William Hill, as he rode by the side of General Thomas Sumter in the desperate campaigns of the upper part of South Carolina during the American Revolution. After the close of that struggle Colonel Hill became an influential leader among the body of lawmakers chosen by the people of South Carolina. Colonel Hill's grandson, young Daniel Harvey Hill, was trained by his mother "who was noted for her piety, culture and common sense." The strict habits of life that were maintained in every Presbyterian household in the South were followed in that simple home in which the Widow Hill moulded the character of her children, for her husband died when the son, Harvey, was only four years of age. She drilled them in the knowledge of the Bible and the Catechism and exacted from each member of her household the most rigid observance of the Lord's Day. Daniel Harvey Hill passed through the course of study in the Military Academy at West Point, and afterwards won many promotions for gallant conduct during the Mexican war. General Joseph E. Johnston tells us that some of the officers of the regular service were in the habit of saying that D. H. Hill was "the bravest man in the army" in Mexico. His native State gave him a sword as a testimonial of honorable service in that conflict.

After the Mexican war Major D. H. Hill became the teacher of mathematics in the Presbyterian school at Lexington, Virginia, that is, Washington College, which was at that time, as we have just seen, under the presidency of Dr. George Junkin. A word of advice and suggestion offered by Major Hill led to the establishment of Major Thomas J. Jackson in a teacher's chair in the same town. Afterwards, Hill accepted the chair of mathematics in Davidson College, North Carolina. Major Hill's marriage with Isabella Morrison, eldest daughter of President Robert H. Morrison, made stronger the bonds of friendship with Major Jackson, for the latter, as we know already, also found a wife among the worthy daughters of the Morrison home.

As a representative, therefore, of two Southern Presbyterian colleges and of the Presbyterian homes of his mother and his wife, Daniel Harvey Hill entered the field of war in 1861. He was then just forty years of age and was in command of the First Regiment of North Carolina Volunteers, many of whose officers and private soldiers possessed a religious faith equal to his own. In June, 1861, he gained the first battle of the war at Bethel Church, near Yorktown, in Virginia. Hill's calm courage as he moved about in the midst of the hail of rifle balls inspired his men to rush forward and win the victory. When the battle was over Hill wrote to his wife as follows: "I have to thank God for a great and decided victory and that I escaped with a slight contusion on the knee. * * * It is a little singular that my first battle in this war should be at Bethel [the name of the church] where I was baptized and worshiped till I was sixteen years old, the church of my mother. Was she not a guardian spirit in the battle, averting ball and shell? Oh, God, give me gratitude to Thee, and may we never dishonor Thee by weak faith!" At a later time he wrote to his wife, "Pray for me that I may be well. * * * We are in the hands of God and as safe on the battlefield as anywhere else. We will be exposed to a heavy fire, but the arm of God is mightier than the artillery of the enemy."

Some of the fiercest fighting known in the annals of warfare took place again and again along that part of the line of battle of which General D. H. Hill was in command. Upon many a field of carnage men looked in amazement to see the iron nerve that marked him as he stood in the place of danger. When he rode forward in the midst of the rush and roar of battle, it was marvelous

to witness the calm, quiet courage of the man. Many of
those who knew him often said that no other soldier as
courageous as D. H. Hill had thus far been seen among
men. His courage, of course, formed an important part
of that skill in leadership which won high rank for him
as a commander. But the courage itself came to him
in part through inheritance and through contact with
the sublime faith of his Presbyterian mother in the
humble home among the fields of South Carolina. But it
was strengthened by the habit of constant prayer, for,
day and night, he was pleading with the Father to save
the souls of his men and to spare their lives in the hour
of conflict. For this was the faith of General D. H. Hill
that in battle Almighty God "directs the course of every
deadly missile with the same unerring certainty" that
marks His guidance of the planets in their orbits.

After the war General Hill gave himself to the work
of teaching and to journalism. As a member of the
body of elders of the First Church, Charlotte, North
Carolina, he was one of the bulwarks of our Southern
Presbyterianism. As a man of lofty ideals, of wide
sympathies and tenderness of manner, possessed of
humor and great patience and supreme trust in the
wisdom and mercy of God—as thus endowed he continued
to be a worthy leader among his people in the dark days
of the period of reconstruction.

Another hero of the faith was Thomas R. R. Cobb, a
ruling elder of the church in Athens, Georgia. The regular prayer-meeting service in that congregation was
maintained with success for many years through the efficient help of this consecrated leader. When the war between North and South called him into the field he made
rapid advancement as an officer by reason of his courage
and his ability. At the same time he won the love and respect of the men of his command, for they knew General
Cobb as a true soldier and a true Christian. During the
campaigns he spent much time in secret prayer. On

December 13, 1862, at Fredericksburg, Virginia, he fell at the head of his brigade of Georgia riflemen in the hour of victory near the foot of Marye's Heights. To his brother the following message was sent by the Confederate commander-in-chief, General R. E. Lee. "Your noble and gallant brother," wrote Lee, "has met a soldier's death, and God grant that this army and our country may never be called upon again to mourn so great a sacrifice. Of his merits, his lofty intellect, his genius, his accomplishments, his professional fame, and, above all, his true Christian character, I need not speak to you, who knew him so intimately and well. But as a patriot and soldier his death has left a gap in the army which his military aptitude and skill render it hard to fill. In the battle of Fredericksburg he won an immortal name for himself and his brigade. Hour after hour he held his position in front of our batteries, while division after division of the enemy was hurled against him. He announced the determination of himself and his men never to leave their post until the enemy was beaten back, and with unshaken courage and fortitude he kept his promise. May God give consolation to his afflicted family, and may the statesman and soldier be cherished as a bright example and holy remembrance."

CHAPTER LV.

SOME PRESBYTERIAN LEADERS OF OUR OWN TIME.

In the same sacred remembrance with the heroes of the faith of the earlier days, our Southern people should hold the names of many of the elders and ministers who have played well their part as leaders in our own time. First among these let us name a beloved instructor, that godly teaching elder, Thomas E. Peck. "He was so strong in his convictions, so unswerving in fidelity to truth, so powerful in his humility before God to prevail in prayer, so wise and considerate in counsel, that he always seemed a strong staff on which to lean in a time of trouble and of peril to the church." These words were sent by Benjamin M. Palmer as a message of comfort to Dr. Peck's mother. "It was a glory to you to be the mother of such a son," continued Dr. Palmer; "your grateful heart must often have burst into song as through the years you traced his noble career. * * * He has gone a little before you into the presence of the King where it will be his glory to introduce the mother whose earlier piety had so much to do with moulding his own."

This moulding of the character of Thomas E. Peck was the work that marked the earlier years which were spent in the home of his widowed mother in the city of his birth, Columbia, South Carolina. At her feet he was drilled in the principles of the Calvinistic system of religion. This course of training was continued by that prince among teachers, Dr. James H. Thornwell. Under the latter's personal guidance young Peck received instruction in the doctrines .of the Bible. As

Thornwell's theological disciple he began to preach the gospel. His chief work in the pulpit was carried on for a number of years in the city of Baltimore. In 1860, when he was in his thirty-ninth year, Dr. Peck began his career as a teacher, at first in the chair of church history, and afterward as Dr. Dabney's successor in the chair of theology in Union Seminary, Virginia. Thirty-three years was the length of the period of service granted to him in the exalted work of training young men for the gospel ministry. "As an expositor of truth," writes Dr. C. R. Vaughan, "as an exegete of Scripture, as a philosophic student of history, he [Dr. Peck] was probably without a rival in his day." "The power of analysis," continues Dr. Vaughan, "was the leading quality of his mind; inflexible integrity was the principal mark of his character. He would do what he thought was right, no matter if he stood alone against overwhelming odds."

Within the same theological school, Union Seminary, during the period under consideration, other men of God bore faithful testimony as teachers and preachers of the Word. Dr. Benjamin M. Smith added to his skill as an instructor, the administrative faculties of the financier. Dr. James Fair Latimer, who, in the period of youth carried a rifle as a private in a South Carolina regiment and afterwards won the honors bestowed upon scholarship in a German university, rendered worthy service as a learned teacher in the department of church history in Union Seminary. Dr. Henry C. Alexander spent here among an entire generation of ministerial students the years that had become rich with the fruits of study. He was able to claim as a personal possession wide tracts in the domain of human learning. From a heart that was a very fountain of sympathy he taught men how to enrich their lives by adding courtesy to brotherly kindness, and he wore always without reproach the double title of Christian and gentleman.

At Columbia Seminary the previous high standards in Biblical scholarship, skill in the art of teaching and power in preaching the Word, were maintained during these years by such ministers as William Swan Plumer, James Woodrow, Joseph R. Wilson, John B. Adger, James D. Tadlock, Francis R. Beattie and John L. Girardeau.

In like manner the work in the Southwestern Presbyterian University at Clarksville, Tennessee, was maintained by such consecrated scholars as John N. Waddel, Robert A. Price and William A. Alexander, the latter known to all Presbyterians in recent years as the keeper of the records of the Southern General Assembly.

T. Dwight Witherspoon, who carried a musket as a private soldier in a Confederate regiment and, whenever the opportunity presented itself, preached the gospel to his fellow-soldiers during the campaigns of the war, gave the later years of his career to the work of founding the theological department of the Central University in Kentucky. William G. Neville, of the younger generation of faithful witnesses, wrought with power and success during the brief years wherein he was president of the Presbyterian College of South Carolina.

Dr. C. A. Stillman, true and faithful witness, was placed in control of the institute for the training of colored ministers within our territory. This school was located at Tuscaloosa, Alabama, by our General Assembly in 1876, and afterwards called Stillman Institute in honor of its founder. God's blessing has been poured out upon the work of this school. Worthy preachers of the negro race have been made ready here for successful work. Not the least worthy among these colored ministers is William H. Sheppard, missionary in the Congo region in Africa.

Dr. John N. Craig as secretary labored with great zeal in behalf of Home Missions for a period of seventeen years (1883-1900), and then fell, like a soldier, upon the field. He suddenly breathed his last in the church at Newport News during the delivery of an address to the Synod of Virginia. The prostrate form of the man of God seemed even in death, writes Dr. P. H. Gwinn, to be "appealing for a more hearty, united and harmonious support of the greatest cause of the church."

Many worthy ministers from our Southern Church have gone across the seas to bear testimony among heathen people in many lands. Among those who were marked for wisdom and courage, these names may be set down in this record: John Dabney, John Boyle and Edward Lane, in Brazil; J. G. Hall, in Mexico and Cuba; Samuel Lapsley, in Africa; William M. Junkin, in Korea; D. C. Rankin, wise manager of our missionary enterprises, who died during a toilsome journey in behalf of foreign missions and was laid to rest in Korea; James E. Bear and Hampden C. DuBose, in China. Dr. DuBose was a native of the eastern part of South Carolina and began his early life by serving as a soldier throughout the Confederate war. In 1872 he went from Columbia Seminary to Soochow, China, and in that city he continued to proclaim the good news of salvation until his death in 1910. He wrought also with his pen in furnishing religious literature to the Chinese. Moreover, he became president of the Chinese Anti-Opium League and wrought with such marked success that when his life closed the effort to suppress the opium habit and the opium traffic "is the strongest movement in China." A traveler who has made close observations in the East tells us that "this daring and chivalrous soldier [DuBose] of a great ideal lived to see the approach of the consummation of the noblest ministry a white man ever rendered China."

Within the limits of the period of fifty years since the organization of the independent Southern Assembly, many shepherds have served as guardians of the flocks,

and the work of these shepherds lives after them. Among
the wise leaders in the Synod of Texas were Robert L.
Dabney and R. K. Smoot, who laid the foundations of
the Austin Theological Seminary; Angus Johnson and
Josephus Johnson were among the ministers who ren-
dered efficient help. In Arkansas lived and labored T.
R. Welch and Isaac Jasper Long; in Missouri, R. G.
Brank and R. P. Farris; in Louisiana, as coworkers
with Benjamin M. Palmer, were Thomas R. Markham, J.
H. Nall and R. Q. Mallard; in Mississippi, James A.
Lyon; in Alabama, J. H. Bryson, J. M. P. Otts, John W.
Pratt and Neander M. Woods; in Georgia, John S. Wil-
son, Donald Fraser, I. S. K. Axson, Groves H. Cartledge,
James Turner Leftwich, grandson of the godly James
Turner of Bedford, Virginia, George T. Goetchius,
Nathan Hoyt, "valiant for Gospel truth," for thirty-
six years pastor of the church in the city of Athens,
Georgia, and E. H. Barnett, third sergeant in the mili-
tary company of students from Hampden-Sidney Col-
lege in 1861, and in Atlanta after the war the faithful
messenger of the gospel of peace; in South Carolina, J.
H. Thornwell, worthy son of the illustrious leader of that
name; Donald McQueen, James B. Dunwody, Robert A.
Fair, James Douglass, J. H. Douglass, N. W. Edmunds,
R. H. Reid, William States Lee, Albert A. Morse, J. Wil-
liam Flinn and G. R. Brackett; in Tennessee, James D.
Tadlock and Ferdinand Jacobs; in Kentucky, W. F. V.
Bartlett, L. G. Barbour, F. B. Converse, S. B. Mc-
Pheeters, John S. Grasty and J. V. Logan; in North
Carolina, Joseph M. Atkinson, John Douglas, John A.
Preston, Jethro Rumple, Robert E. Caldwell and Arnold
W. Miller, whom Benjamin M. Palmer described as "a
mighty champion for the truth of God," and Charles
Phillips of Davidson College and the University of
North Carolina; in Maryland, W. U. Murkland, J. A.
Lefevre and J. J. Bullock; in Virginia, Thomas Verner
Moore, William Henry Foote, W. T. Richardson, Her-

bert H. Hawes, D. K. McFarland, J. K. Hazen, E. D.
Washburn, Edward P. Palmer, Jere Witherspoon, John
Leyburn, George W. Finley, D. C. Irwin, Charles H.
Read, William S. Lacy, J. A. Waddell, A. R. Cocke,
William S. White, George W. White, Daniel Blain,
Charles White, Theodorick Pryor, W. V. Wilson, I. W.
K. Handy, S. Taylor Martin, Alexander Martin, Samuel
J. Baird, John L. Kirkpatrick, William Brown, William
A. Campbell, William Dinwiddie, Joseph Stiles, J. G.
Shepperson, D. W. Shanks, John M. P. Atkinson,
Thomas L. Preston, George D. Armstrong, and George
W. Finley.

And what was the measure of spiritual power among
these witnesses of our own time? If the inquiry be concerned with the matter of personal faith, let the testimony
of Dr. Thomas L. Preston and Dr. G. R. Brackett make
reply on behalf of all. These servants of God were
made to walk in the pathway of physical suffering, and
then before their years had been far advanced, both
were removed from the field of labor. By a godly walk
they taught their people how the Christian ought to
live; in like manner, through a ready obedience to the
Master's summons, they taught us how the servant of
God should die. The cross in each case was borne with
marvelous patience, and each said at the close of life
that to die means only that "the child of God passes
from one room to another in the Father's house." If
the question be raised with reference to human learning
as the hand-maiden of religion, let Dr. George D. Armstrong and Dr. Charles Phillips stand in this respect
as types of our Southern ministers. If success in adding
strength to the church through efficiency in the pulpit
be considered, let Dr. W. U. Murkland, Dr. A. W.
Miller and Dr. E. H. Barnett represent their brethren
in the pastorate. If administrative powers in church
affairs be sought, let Dr. William A. Campbell and Dr.
Jethro Rumple teach all ministers everywhere how to

show practical wisdom in the management of educational and evangelistic work. If inquiry be pressed whether the pulpit in these later days is declining in power and efficiency, let the answer be found in the life and the work of Dr. Samuel Macon Smith. The first teacher of this prince among the men of the pulpit was his own father, Dr. Jacob Henry Smith. Years of close study fitted him for the principal work of his career, the pastorate of the church in Columbia, South Carolina, from the autumn of 1899 until the early days of the year 1910. Here was a man of strength, true and genuine in every part of his nature. "In him were mingled," writes Dr. W. M. McPheeters, "insight, understanding, the salt of wit, the grace of humor, sympathy and genuine humility." Rare skill in the reading of the Scripture lesson, and prayers that sought out the hidden secrets of the heart and pleaded for mercy upon human infirmities—these made his hearers ready to pay heed to the sermon. The latter was always based upon some passage of Scripture as it appeared in the original Hebrew or Greek, for the Hebrew Bible and the Greek New Testament were Dr. Smith's constant companions and he knew how to use them with telling effect as few ministers have ever been able to use them in pulpit work. And then from rich storehouses, made ready through theological study and through wide ranging in literary fields, he drew material for the discourse, adding thereto matters of personal experience, a touch of humor, a passage of graphic description and a word of passionate appeal. He spoke with authority, for the reason that his scholarship was genuine and that it was used merely as an agency in bringing God's message of rebuke or comfort to the hearts of the people.

"And these all," ministers of the Word, together with many deacons and elders and a great multitude of godly women, the worthies of our Southern Church, "having

had witness borne to them through their faith," received
the promises. From their character and from their
labors, as types of the people of whom they formed a
part, all men everywhere may learn to understand the
piety and the integrity and the intelligence that have
through many generations found a home among the
people of the South.

PRINCIPAL SOURCES

A list of the principal sources of information, both printed and in manuscript form, used in the preparation of *Southern Presbyterian Leaders* is herewith presented. This is not given, however, as an exhaustive bibliography, nor even as a complete list of all the sources consulted in the preparation of this volume.

BIOGRAPHIES.

ALEXANDER, ARCHIBALD, *Sketches of the Founder and the Principal Alumni of the Log College.* Princeton, 1845.

ALEXANDER, HENRY C., *Life of J. Addison Alexander.* 2 vols. New York, 1870.

ALEXANDER, JAMES W., *Life of Archibald Alexander.* New York, 1854.

BAKER, WILLIAM M., *Life and Labors of Daniel Baker.* Philadelphia, 1859.

BARNES, ALBERT, *Essay on the Life and Times of President Davies.* New York, 1851.

BAXTER, LOUISA, *A Brief Biographical Sketch of George Addison Baxter*, by his daughter. Unprinted manuscript.

BOWEN, L. P., *The Days of Makemie.* Philadelphia, 1885.

CARRUTHERS, E. W., *The Life and Character of David Caldwell*, Greensborough, N. C., 1842.

DABNEY, ROBERT L., *The Life and Campaigns of Lieutenant-General Thomas J. Jackson.* New York, 1866.

FOOTE, WILLIAM HENRY, *Sketches of North Carolina, Historical and Biographical.* New York, 1846.

FOOTE, WILLIAM HENRY, *Sketches of Virginia, Historical and Biographical.* Philadelphia, 1849.
——Second series. Philadelphia, 1855.

FORD, H. P., *Chronological Outline of the Life of Francis Makemie.* Philadelphia, 1910.

GILMORE, JAMES ROBERTS, *John Sevier as a Commonwealth-Builder.* New York, 1887.

GRAHAM, JAMES, *The Life of General Daniel Morgan.* New York, 1856.

GURLEY, R. R., *Life and Eloquence of Sylvester Larned.* New York, 1844.

HARLAND, MARION, *Autobiography.* New York, 1910.

HEADLEY, J. T., *The Chaplains and Clergy of the American Revolution.* New York, 1864.

HENRY, WILLIAM WIRT, *Life, Correspondence and Speeches of Patrick Henry.* 3 vols. New York, 1891.

HOGE, PEYTON H., *Life and Letters of Moses Drury Hoge.* Richmond, 1899.

JACKSON, MRS. M. A., *Life and Letters of Stonewall Jackson,* by his wife. New York, 1894.

JAMES, W. D., *Life of Francis Marion.* Charleston, 1821.

JOHNSON, THOMAS CARY, *Life and Letters of Robert L. Dabney.* Richmond, 1903.

————, *Life and Letters of Benjamin Morgan Palmer.* Richmond, 1906.

KOLLOCK, S. K., *Biography of the Rev. Henry Kollock.* Savannah, 1822.

MOORE, M. A., *Life of General Edward Lacey.* 1854.

PALMER, BENJAMIN M., *Life and Letters of James Henley Thornwell.* Richmond, 1875.

PARTON, JAMES, *Life of Andrew Jackson.* 3 vols. New York, 1860.

RANDALL, HENRY S., *Life of Thomas Jefferson.* 3 vols. New York, 1888.

RIVES, WILLIAM C., JR., *Life and Times of James Madison.* 3 vols. Boston, 1859.

SPRAGUE, W. B., *Annals of the American Pulpit; or Commemoration Notices of Distinguished American Clergymen.* Vols. III. and IV., *The Presbyterian Pulpit.* New York, 1859 and 1869.

WHITE, HENRY ALEXANDER, *Robert E. Lee and the Southern Confederacy.* New York, 1897.

————, *Life of Stonewall Jackson.* Philadelphia, 1909.

WHITE, HENRY M., *Life and Times of William S. White.* Richmond, 1891.

CHURCH HISTORIES.

BRIGGS, CHARLES AUGUSTUS, *American Presbyterianism.* With an Appendix of Letters and Documents. New York, 1885.

CALDERWOOD, DAVID, *A History of the Church of Scotland* (to 1625). 8 vols. Edinburgh, 1842-1849.

DAVIDSON, ROBERT, *History of the Presbyterian Church in the State of Kentucky.* New York, 1847.

GILLETT, EZRA HALL, *History of the Presbyterian Church in the United States of America.* Revised. Philadelphia, 1873.

GLASGOW, W. M., *History of the Reformed Presbyterian Church in America.* Baltimore, 1888.

HAYS, GEORGE P., *Presbyterians: A Popular Narrative of Their Origin, Progress, Doctrines and Achievements.* New York, 1892.

HILL, WILLIAM, *A History of the Rise, Progress and Character of American Presbyterianism.* Washington, 1839.

HODGE, CHARLES, *The Constitutional History of the Presbyterian Church in the United States of America.* Parts I. and II. Philadelphia, 1839-1840.

HOWE, GEORGE, *History of the Presbyterian Church in South Carolina.* 2 vols. Columbia, 1870 and 1883.

JOHNSON, THOMAS CARY, *History of the Southern Presbyterian Church.* Part of Vol. XI., in American Church Series. New York, 1894.

KILLEN, WILLIAM D., *Ecclesiastical History of Ireland.* 2 vols. London, 1875.

LATHAM, ROBERT, *History of the Associate Reformed Synod of the South.* Harrisburg, 1882.

REED, RICHARD C., *History of the Presbyterian Churches of the World.* Philadelphia, 1906.

REID, JAMES S., *A History of the Presbyterian Church in Ireland.* New (third) edition, with notes by W. D. Killen. 3 vols. Belfast, 1867.

NEVIN, ALFRED, *Encyclopedia of the Presbyterian Church in the United States of America, Including the Northern and Southern Assemblies.* Philadelphia, 1884.

SMITH, JOSEPH, *Old Redstone; or, Historical Sketches of Western Presbyterianism.* Philadelphia, 1854.

THOMPSON, ROBERT E., *A History of the Presbyterian Churches in the United States.* Vol. VI. in the American Church History Series. New York, 1895.

WEBSTER, RICHARD, *A History of the Presbyterian Church in America from Its Origin Until the Year 1760.* Philadelphia, 1858.

WODROW, ROBERT, *The History of the Sufferings of the Church of Scotland from the Restoration to the Revolution.* 4 vols. Glasgow, 1841.

COLLECTED WORKS.

DABNEY, ROBERT L., *Theology.* Third edition. Asbury Park, 1885.

————, *Discussions.* Edited by C. R. Vaughan. 3 vols. Richmond, 1890-1892.

PECK, THOMAS E., *Ecclesiology.* Edited by T. C. Johnson. Richmond, 1882.

————, *Miscellanies.* Edited by T. C. Johnson. 3 vols. Richmond, 1895.

SMYTH, THOMAS, *Collected Works.* 10 vols. Columbia, 1910.

THORNWELL, JAMES H., *Collected Writings.* Edited by John B. Adger. 4 vols. Richmond, 1871-1873.

GENERAL HISTORIES.

Various Standard Histories of the United States, including the works of Bancroft, Fiske, McMaster, Rhodes and others.

HISTORICAL COLLECTIONS.

Colonial Records of North Carolina. Edited by W. L. Saunders. 10 vols. Raleigh, 1886-1890.

GEORGIA HISTORICAL SOCIETY, *Collections.* Savannah, 1840.

SCOTCH-IRISH SOCIETY OF AMERICA, *Annual Proceedings, with Addresses, etc.* Cincinnati and Nashville, 1889-1901.

SOUTH CAROLINA HISTORICAL SOCIETY, *Collections.* 5 vols. Charleston, 1857-1897.

VIRGINIA HISTORICAL SOCIETY, *Collections.* 11 vols. Richmond, 1882-1892.

Washington and Lee University Historical Papers. Edited by William McLaughlin, W. A. Glasgow and Henry Alexander White. 5 vols. Baltimore, 1890-1895.

LOCAL HISTORIES.

ASHE, SAMUEL A., *History of North Carolina.* Vol. I. Goldsboro, 1909.

BREWER, W., *Alabama.* Montgomery, 1872.

CAMPBELL, CHARLES, *History of Virginia.* Philadelphia, 1860.

CRAIG, D. I., *Presbyterian Church in North Carolina.* Richmond, 1908.

GAYARRÉ, CHARLES, *History of Louisiana.* 4 vols. New Orleans, 1885.

GILMORE, JAMES ROBERTS, *The Rear-Guard of the Revolution.* New York, 1886.

HUNTER, C. L., *Sketches of Western North Carolina.* Raleigh, 1877.

JONES, CHARLES COLCOCK, *The History of Georgia.* 2 vols. Boston, 1883.

LEWIS, VIRGIL A., *History of West Virginia.* Philadelphia, 1887.

McCRADY, EDWARD, *History of South Carolina.* 4 vols. New York, 1894-1902.

MOORE, JOHN W., *History of North Carolina.* 2 vols. Raleigh, 1880.

PEYTON, JOHN HOWE, *History of Augusta County, Virginia.* Staunton, 1882.

PHELAN, JAMES, *History of Tennessee.* Boston, 1888.

RAMSAY, DAVID, *History of South Carolina.* 2 vols. Charleston, 1809.

ROOSEVELT, THEODORE, *The Winning of the West.* 3 vols. New York, 1889.

RUMPLE, JETHRO, *A History of Rowan County, North Carolina.* Salisbury, 1881.

SALLEY, ALEXANDER S., JR., *History of Orangeburg County, South Carolina.* Columbia, 1898.

TOMPKINS, D. A., *History of Mecklenburg County, North Carolina.* 2 vols. Charlotte, 1903.

WADDELL, JOSEPH ADDISON, *Annals of Augusta County, Virginia.* With Supplement. Richmond, 1888.

WHEELER, JOHN H., *Historical Sketches of North Carolina.* 2 vols. (in one). Philadelphia, 1851.

WHITE, HENRY ALEXANDER, *The Making of South Carolina.* New York, 1906.

MEMOIRS.

BEASLEY, FR., *A Brief Memoir of Samuel Stanhope Smith.* Philadelphia, 1821.

DABNEY, ROBERT L., *Memoir of Francis S. Sampson.* Richmond, 1854.

DUBOSE, HAMPDEN C., *Memoirs of John Leighton Wilson.* Richmond, 1895.

FLEMING, WILLIAM S., *Genealogical Account of the Frierson Family.* Columbia (Tenn.), 1907.

GRASTY, JOHN S., *Memoir of Samuel B. McPheeters.* Louisville, 1871.

MAXWELL, WILLIAM, *A Memoir of John H. Rice.* Philadelphia, 1835.

McELHENNEY, JOHN, *Recollections of,* by his granddaughter, Rose W. Fry. Richmond, 1893.

McILWAINE, RICHARD, *Recollections.* New York, 1909.

WADDEL, JOHN N., *Memorials of Academic Life: An Historical Sketch of the Waddel Family.* Richmond, 1891.

WARDLAW, JOSEPH G., *Genealogical Account of the Witherspoon Family.* Yorkville, S. C., 1910.

WOODROW, JAMES, *Memoir of, by his daughter.* Columbia, 1910.

NEWSPAPERS.

Central Presbyterian. Richmond, Va.

Christian Observer. Louisville, Ky.

Dispatch. Richmond, Va.

News and Courier. Charleston, S. C.

North Carolina Presbyterian. Wilmington, N. C.

Picayune. New Orleans, La.

Presbyterian of the South. Richmond, Va.

Southern Presbyterian. Columbia and Clinton, S. C.
Southwestern Presbyterian. New Orleans, La.
St. Louis Presbyterian. St. Louis, Mo.
The State. Columbia, S. C.
Times. Richmond, Va.
Times-Democrat. New Orleans, La.
Times-Dispatch. Richmond, Va.

PERIODICALS.

South Carolina Historical and Genealogical Magazine. Charleston, 1900-1911.
Southern Presbyterian Quarterly. Richmond, Va., 1887-1899.
Southern Literary Messenger. Richmond, 1834-1859.
Southern Presbyterian Review. Columbia, 1847-1885.
Southern Quarterly Review. Charleston, 1842-1856.
Virginia Magazine of History and Biography. Richmond, 1893-1911.

RECORDS OF CHURCH COURTS.

ALEXANDER, W. A., *A Digest of the Acts of the General Assembly of the Presbyterian Church in the United States*, 1861-1867. With Historical Notes. Richmond, 1888.
BAIRD, SAMUEL J., *A Collection of the Acts of the Supreme Judicatory of the Presbyterian Church.* Philadelphia, 1855.
MOORE, WILLIAM E., *New Digest of the Acts of the Presbyterian Church.* Philadelphia, 1861.
————, *The Presbyterian Digest. A Compend of the Acts of the General Assembly of the Presbyterian Church in the United States of America.* Philadelphia, 1873.

MINUTES.

Minutes of the General Assembly of the Presbyterian Church from 1789 until 1861. Philadelphia.
Minutes of the General Assembly (South). Augusta, Columbia and Richmond, 1861-1911.
Minutes of the General Assembly (North). Philadelphia, 1861-1911.
Minutes of Various Presbyteries and Synods.

SPECIAL ACCOUNTS.

BAIRD, C. W., *History of the Huguenot Emigration to America.* 2 vols. 1st and 2nd editions. New York, 1885.
BAIRD, H. M., *History of the Rise of the Huguenots of France.* 2 vols. 2nd edition. New York, 1883.

BAIRD, H. M., *The Huguenots and Henry of Navarre*. 2 vols. New York, 1886.

BAIRD, SAMUEL J., *History of the New School*. Philadelphia, 1868.

BERNHEIM, G. D., *German Settlements in North and South Carolina*.

BOARDMAN, HENRY A., *The General Assembly of 1866*. Philadelphia, 1867.

BRACKETT, R. N., *The Old Stone Church (South Carolina)*. Columbia, 1905.

BROCK, R. A., *Huguenot Emigration to Virginia*. Virginia Historical Collections, vol. V.

COBB, T. R. R., *Law of Negro Slavery in the Various States*. Philadelphia, 1856.

DABNEY, ROBERT L., *Defense of Virginia*. New York, 1867.

DRAPER, LYMAN, *King's Mountain and Its Heroes*. Cincinnati, 1887.

ECKENRODE, H. J., *Separation of Church and State in Virginia*. Richmond, 1910.

GREGG, ALEXANDER, *History of the Old Cheraws*. Columbia, 1867 and 1905.

HANNA, CHARLES A., *The Scotch-Irish; or, The Scot in North Britain, North Ireland and North America*. 2 vols. New York, 1902.

INGLE, EDWARD, *Southern Side-Lights*. New York, 1896.

JAMES, C. F., *Documentary History of the Struggle for Religious Liberty in Virginia*. Richmond, 1900.

JONES, CHARLES COLCOCK, *Religious Instruction of the Negroes in the United States*. Savannah, 1842.

KIRKLAND, THOMAS J., and R. M. KENNEDY, *Historic Camden*. Columbia, 1905.

LAWS, S. S., *Letter to the Synod of Missouri*. New York, 1873.

MALLARD, R. Q., *Plantation Life Before Emancipation*. Richmond, 1892.

MAURY, R. L., *Huguenots in Virginia*. Richmond.

MCILWAINE, H. R., *Struggle of Protestant Dissenters for Religious Toleration in Virginia*. J. H. U. Studies, 12th series. Baltimore.

WILSON, SAMUEL R., *Defense of the Declaration and Testimony*. Louisville, 1865.

INDEX